VICTORIANS READING THE ROMANTICS

VICTORIANS READING THE ROMANTICS

Essays by U. C. Knoepflmacher

U. C. KNOEPFLMACHER
EDITED BY LINDA M. SHIRES

The Ohio State University Press
Columbus

Copyright © 2016 by The Ohio State University.
All rights reserved.

Library of Congress Cataloging-in-Publication Data

Names: Knoepflmacher, U. C., author. | Shires, Linda M., 1950– editor.

Title: Victorians reading the Romantics / essays by U. C. Knoepflmacher ; edited by Linda M. Shires.

Description: Columbus : The Ohio State University Press, [2016] | Includes bibliographical references and index.

Identifiers: LCCN 2016019527 | ISBN 9780814213117 (cloth ; alk. paper) | ISBN 0814213111 (cloth ; alk. paper)

Subjects: LCSH: English literature—19th century—History and criticism. | Romanticism—England. | Romanticism—Great Britain.

Classification: LCC PR461 .K66 2016 | DDC 814/.6—dc23

LC record available at https://lccn.loc.gov/2016019527

Cover design by Mary Ann Smith
Text design by Juliet Williams
Type set in Adobe Garamond Pro

♾ The paper used in this publication meets the minimum requirements of the American National Standard for Information Sciences—Permanence of Paper for Printed Library Materials. ANSI Z39.48-1992.

9 8 7 6 5 4 3 2 1

CONTENTS

Preface	Rereading Knoepflmacher Now LINDA M. SHIRES	vii
Acknowledgments		xvii

	Introduction	1
1	Mutations of the Wordsworthian Child of Nature	21
2	Genre and the Integration of Gender: From Wordsworth to George Eliot to Virginia Woolf	56
3	On Exile and Fiction: The Leweses, the Brownings, and the Shelleys	76
4	Projection and the Female Other: Browning and the Romantics	95
5	Dover Revisited: The Wordsworthian Matrix in the Poetry of Matthew Arnold	118
6	Arnold's Fancy and Pater's Imagination: Exclusion and Incorporation	130
7	Revisiting Wordsworth: Lewis Carroll's "The White Knight's Song"	144
8	The Return of a Native Singer: Keats in Hardy's Dorset	162
9	Kipling as Browning: From Parody to Translation	180
10	The Victorianism of Strachey's *Eminent Victorians*	201
11	Endings as Beginnings: Woolf and Nineteenth-Century Women Novelists	213
Works Cited		227
Index		241

PREFACE

REREADING KNOEPFLMACHER NOW

Linda M. Shires

U. C. Knoepflmacher, known to his friends as "Uli," is my husband. It is perhaps odd, though not unprecedented, for a wife to edit a husband's essays. Forty years ago Uli's reputation preceded him in my life. His decency toward women students and colleagues, and not just his remarkable interdisciplinary intellect or his artistic talents, had caused the buzz. In my circles he was considered an ally, a nonpatriarchal scholar of nineteenth-century literature, known as a fighter for equality—for women, for African Americans, for Hispanics, for Jews, for gays and lesbians, and for the poor.

In the mid-1970s, when his name was first mentioned to me, he was a professor of English at Berkeley. He had witnessed the Free Speech Movement, civil rights marches, and the Vietnam War protests, and he had become part of second-wave feminism at a time when male allies were few. His professional support then and later proved important for both men and women. He actively helped younger scholars and peers on their essays, book manuscripts, and grant applications. Both at Berkeley and later at Princeton, he defended deserving candidates for tenure and promotion, bristling against all kinds of prejudice. In addition to teaching generations of undergraduates and graduate students, including those in summer programs at Bread Loaf, Tulsa, and Harvard, he led numerous NEH summer seminars for college and high school teachers. He also served on the editorial boards of academic journals and university presses, where his reports were valued for their precision, detail, and high standards. His gifts of helpful readings, professional ethics, and generosity continue to shape the humanities today through those whose lives he touched.

Uli was born as an only child to Hilde (née Weiss) and George Knoepflmacher in Munich, Germany, in 1931 during the rise of the Nazi party. His father's engineering job took them back to Vienna before he was three. After many attempts to obtain exit visas from Austria, the family secured passage to Bolivia in 1939. Uli grew up in Oruro, Bolivia, as an exile. Although he had not felt overtly different from others in Europe, he was obviously so in South America. He was taller, lighter in skin color, German-speaking, and Jewish. Crossing boundaries was to shape his life and career.

After obtaining a BA in architecture from the University of California, Uli was persuaded by his English professors to obtain an MA in English literature at Berkeley. He subsequently secured his PhD at Princeton University under the direction of E. D. H. Johnson and returned to teach at Berkeley, an institution he deeply loved, from 1961 to 1978. He moved rapidly through the ranks, while he and his first wife, Cecilia, raised three children: Julie, Paul, and Daniel. Uli won the Distinguished Teaching Award in 1978, and he garnered numerous fellowships and other prizes over the years, including the ACLS Fellowship, Rockefeller award, two Guggenheim Fellowships, two NEH grants, and a fellowship at the National Humanities Center in North Carolina. In 1979 he joined the faculty at Princeton University, where he was subsequently named the William and Annie S. Paton Foundation Professor of Ancient and Modern Literature. We were married in 1988 and raised a son, Alexander. In his year of retirement, 2006, Uli received the Anne Devereaux Jordan Award for Outstanding Achievement in Children's Literature and Princeton's Howard T. Behrman Award for Distinguished Achievement in the Humanities.

This nutshell version of a career gives little indication of the depth of Knoepflmacher's facility with expression, his love of literature, or his range of expertise. As a crosser of boundaries both national and linguistic, with fluency in German, Spanish, and English, he might have become a comparatist. Indeed, his published work has ranged among different time periods, nations, genres, and authors besides those reflected in this volume: others include Chaucer, Pope, Shakespeare, Louisa May Alcott, Mark Twain, Francis Newman, Henry James, D. H. Lawrence, Madame D'Aulnoy, Charles Perrault, the Brothers Grimm, George MacDonald, Juliana Horatia Ewing, Jean Ingelow, Christina Rossetti, Robert Louis Stevenson, Anne Thackeray Ritchie, E. Nesbit, E. B. White, Kenneth Grahame, Mary Norton, Anne Sexton, Randall Jarrell, and Maurice Sendak.

All of his work reflects a sheer love of literary creativity and a commitment to its importance for civilized peoples.

A specialist in Victorian literature and culture, nineteenth-century poetry, the British and American novel, British and American children's literature, and the Jew in English literature, he is the author of over one hundred academic articles and five academic books published between 1965 and 2016: *Religious Humanism and the Victorian Novel*; *George Eliot's Early Novels*; *Laughter and Despair: Readings in Ten Novels of the Victorian Era*; *Emily Brontë: 'Wuthering Heights'*; and *Ventures into Childland: Victorians, Fairy Tales and Femininity*. He has edited or coedited ten books, including *The Endurance of 'Frankenstein'*; *Nature and the Victorian Imagination*; *Forbidden Journeys: Fairy Tales and Fantasies by Victorian Women Writers*; and *Victorian Hybridities: Cultural Anxiety and Formal Innovation*. Additionally, he has published a self-illustrated children's book, *Franny, Randy, and the Over-the-Edge Cat Person,* and recently completed a memoir, "Oruro: A Boy's Holocaust Refuge in the Bolivian Andes."

Knoepflmacher is best known now, perhaps, for his work on children's literature, the novel, and writings by women authors. Yet the scores of essays he wrote over decades in different areas of nineteenth-century studies deserve to be better known and to be reread together in units. As postmodernist (soon posthumanist) critics and theorists explore different kinds of historicisms, reexamine surface/depth reading or distant/close reading, and examine modes of textual attachment, it is time to review a body of work that implicitly and explicitly argues against any singular critical approach as well as against binary thinking, while at the same time avoiding a senseless plurality of meanings.[1] The essays collected here further illustrate the operation of an integrative literary mind, a gift that is critical to the survival of the humanities in an increasingly fast and fragmented culture.

I

Certain core traits run throughout Knoepflmacher's work. These include his rabbinic respect for the words on the page before him (words that move in his imagination rather than staying fixed in one place); his love of the visual; his response to the senses—the shape, color, and texture of

---

1. Other critics of this generation are being reread for today or revising their criticism for new readers. James Phelan and David H. Richter have edited the late Ralph Rader's essays, and J. Hillis Miller recently reread George Eliot and published *Reading for Our Time: Adam Bede and Middlemarch*.

things; his respect for the imagination of every writer he studies; a humility before the authorial presence who crafted the text; his sense that biography matters but does not determine or limit meaning; his belief in subjectivity as androgynous and fluid; and his trust in a covenant between author and reader: a shared responsibility for meaning-making in which a reader activates the text. Knoepflmacher assumes multiple directions of influence within the act of writing and reading, not least of all, of course, the historical moment of writer, imagined readers, and actual readers. Yet equally important to him are temporal relationships of anticipation and memory in the act of reading; horizontal and vertical modes of reading across and down a paper or digital page; and what I would call *seminal reading,* where individual phrases, images, or words emerge as nodal points of meaning in a creative engagement with text. Balance, connection, webs of relationship, and integration interest him immensely, as do works or authors that take up such issues—within individual texts, across texts, and across ever-changing canons. Perhaps this emphasis on connectedness is attributable to a life of exile, loss, and relocation. It may also stem from his natural optimism as a stay against existential despair. Whatever the reason, his interest in connections is exercised with faith, self-irony, and skepticism.

Given his belief that all of us apply retrospective constructions that narrativize the ambiguities of our lives in order to control uncertainty and rationalize the irrational, it is hardly surprising that Knoepflmacher should hold strong views about a literary criticism that attempts to "explain" the actual messiness of texts. Every reconstruction, in his view, is subjective and temporary—his own included—no matter the degree of objective grounding. Every name, tag, type, or method thus only serves the ends of explanation devised at particular historical moments. Yet our human tendency to frame life events and the critical tendency to tame textuality do not erase, in his view, the chaos, ambiguity, impurity, or imperfection of the original. One interpretation can build on another and may turn out to be far more convincing, but an ultimate "truth" in life or any "finality" in interpretation will persistently elude us.[2] Moreover, the value of a memorable text, whether *Middlemarch* or "Ode to Autumn," is partly due to its ability to survive reinterpretations. Disassembling, reassembling, contextualizing, and redescribing of a literary text are essential as part of cultural process.

Unlike, say, the Chicago School, prominent at Berkeley when he started teaching there, Knoepflmacher has never believed in the purity of literary forms (from realism to dramatic monologue). Instead, he strongly favors

---

2. See Alexander Nehamas's thorough exploration of critical pluralism and textual monism.

interpretive processes that stress the impurity of form. He delights in frictions—of styles, words, discourses, and ideologies. Form and content shape each other but do so in a fluid process for both producer and consumer. Critics, he believes, must allow for that kind of multiplicity in the text and, while acknowledging their own cultural framings, should not adhere to any preset formula, typology, or ideological line. Some texts lend themselves better to certain kinds of criticism than others do—say, to class or race analysis or to remediation theory. But Knoepflmacher believes that the best literary texts allow multiple types of interpretation precisely because of their capaciousness. All readings are partial. He is a close reader and an inductive thinker, working up from details to larger deductions and insights, not down from predetermined structuring typologies.

The governing trope for Knoepflmacher's work is the metaphor, where one thing is like another but not the same as another. He believes that the nature of the specific literary text suggests, to a large degree, how and what kind of criticism emerges. While we can't know an author's intentions, we draw upon contexts that help us understand what an author could have intended as creative artist while focusing on what the text presents. Moreover, the specific cultural and temporal framing of the critic affects interpretive choices and emphases. Knoepflmacher also believes, as do poststructuralists, that a literary text holds virtual potentialities for how it will be realized and how activated in the future, as well as in its own time (see Colebrook), for he views writing as a fluid process and as a product that one inductively disassembles through criticism and reassembles for new readers with pleasure. Thus we pass cultural issues and values on to the next generation. We reanimate—through empathetic analysis—the beauties of the original text (as in this volume he claims Pater succeeds in doing with Wordsworth's poetry).

A belief in complex pleasure undergirds every aspect of Knoepflmacher's scholarship. It is a pleasure that, as in Jewish tradition, partakes of pain and difficulty. He would agree that readers work both with and against a text—a reader can accept the invitation into the text to participate in the mode of representation, relying on learned responses while remaining open to new experiences; but, as there is no pleasure in merely being an observer/redescriber of a text, a reader, he maintains, looks for points of distance as well as points of identification. Knoepflmacher analyzes where he is drawn into and repelled by a text. So, too, there is no full pleasure in relying only upon learned responses or traditional heuristic categories; one must be open enough to let a text shock or surprise or overpower. Knoepflmacher appreciates up to a point the 1985 advice Gilles Deleuze gave students in a Foucault seminar: "You must trust the author you are studying. Proceed by feeling your way. One must ruminate, gathering and regathering the notions. You must silence the voices of objection within you" (Colombat 204 qtd. in Bewes 25). Knoepflmacher would add that after trusting the author and silencing your objections, you also need to distrust both in order to allow a debate.

There should be risk involved in reading—a challenge to the known. This is precisely why the best literary readers must also be creators rather than fill-in-the-blank repeaters or mere appliers of the already known. We need to find new foci; invent new ways of reading; see never-before-noticed details; note new connections across texts and traditions; and experience surprises, allowing interruptions up and down and across a page and a book. Only by allowing new constellations of multiple affects and ideas can one be said to be reading at all. This is true of a first reading and all subsequent readings, since the text is new each time, translated, as it were, by each new reading.

The following essays often return to William Wordsworth. The Poet Laureate's 1800 *Preface to Lyrical Ballads* may be considered a touchstone for Knoepflmacher's understanding of the emotional knowledge afforded by reading, writing about, and teaching literature. In the following iconic quotation Wordsworth refers to meter in poetry but also pays tribute to the special delight the mind gains from analysis of likeness and difference:

> The pleasure which the mind derives from the perception of similitude in dissimilitude . . . is the great spring of the activity of our minds, and their chief feeder. From this principle the direction of the sexual appetite, and all the passions connected with it, take their origin: it is the life of our ordinary conversation; and upon the accuracy with which similitude in dissimilitude, and dissimilitude in similitude are perceived, depend our taste and our moral feelings. (Wordsworth 1966, 740)

II

The essays reprinted here can be productively related to several current debates in literary criticism. In what follows, I refer to just two such debates. Both critical reading vs. uncritical reading, and surface reading vs. depth reading, are, in my view, versions of the same limited binary thinking. Other specific critical schools of thought—empathy studies, affect studies, cognitive studies, distant or close reading—are also related to these larger binaries, for all are concerned with the modes and depth of a reader's engagement with texts.[3]

Michael Warner's essay on Uncritical Reading has generated numerous responses.[4] There he argued that the academy labels as "uncritical" and naive any forms of reading—including those based in identification, sentimentality, enthusiasm, liberalism, and aversion—that are apparently neither "reflective nor analytic" (15). Academic practice, he argues, has little to do with how the majority of readers actually read. Influenced by Marxism, psychoanalysis, deconstruction, postcolonialism, and other theoretical schools, much literary criticism of the last thirty-five years, Warner notes, has emphasized distance, suspicion, the uncovering of ideologies latent in the text, and faith in the efficacy of exposure which often goes by the name of *critique*.[5] If we rethink the dominant mode of critique, we might better see that *all* reading practices have a history and embed certain ways of forming subjectivity. In examining the binary of critical and uncritical, though, Warner repeats the binary of mentalist and affectual or active and passive criticisms without recommending any dialogue. Critical reading, he notes, seems socially conscious, or "purposeful" as Caroline Levine would term it (n. pag.), while uncritical reading seems private, naive, and devoted to simple emotional pleasures.

In the fall 2009 *Representations* special issue, Stephen Best and Sharon Marcus suggested the weakening hold that symptomatic reading has on critics who had formerly sought "hidden, repressed, deep" (1) meaning of texts. Valuing surface reading that rejects such "wresting meaning from a resisting text" (Jameson as qtd. 5), they prefer a reading method of "minimal critical agency" (17) but hardly tag it as naive. Contributors to the special issue instead offer contemporary variations on surface reading. In these variations the binary no longer separates a first emotional reading from second thoughtful reading (as if they could be so divided) or an appreciation from a critique. The binary now involves distancing from vs. digging

---

3. See Jurecic, Mitchell, and Keen on various limits of empathy theory; Leys on limits of Eve Sedgwick's affect theory; and Vincent on the limits of Leys's critique of Sedgwick.

4. Among the numerous responses, see those by Caroline Levine, Stephen Best and Sharon Marcus, and Timothy Bewes.

5. Rita Felski helpfully scrutinizes qualities of a suspicious or critical reading practice as a mode of detachment (2011) and explains the popularity in Anglo-American criticism of "critique"—investigating five of its facets (2012). She further notes that the hermeneutics of suspicion and critique share an "investment in a particular ethos—a stance of knowingness, guardedness, suspicion and vigilance" (2012) and advises that we move beyond the "dichotomy of the critical versus the uncritical." The sociopolitical resonances of texts should not rule out other modes of reading.

for meaning. For these thinkers insight is achieved "by distancing" but not by "digging" (see Felski 2012, n. pag.).

Still, Best and Marcus hardly propose much that is new; indeed they acknowledge that many kinds of reading, some old, some new, could be covered by the rubric of *surface*.[6] With their stress on surface vs. depth, though, we still remain stuck in a binary of either/or, belittling the complexity of literary texts, the reading act, and individual readers. We also reinforce the sense that there is only one right way of reading. Binary terms are simply reversed in value[7] or are terms altered in meaning by new binaries. As Ellen Rooney intelligently remarks, Best and Marcus do not indicate *any reason* why what the text is "saying about itself" (assuming such saying exists) would be more visible on its surface than at some depth—why should every text "eschew the possibility of a double game?" Indeed. "Is the metaphorical depth of a text a foreign country, where another language is spoken, not the text's own?" (13). The Best and Marcus literary text seems passive and simple-minded, while its wise reader remains actively in charge. Claiming to know what the text says on its "surface" is just as authoritative and immodest as the charge Best and Marcus level against suspicious depth theorists who dig for what is buried.[8]

While reading literature may increase empathy, as George Eliot surely hoped, Knoepflmacher's criticism indicates that he does not believe that reading necessarily provokes social action. As Ann Jurecic puts it: "readerly empathy differs profoundly from social empathy" (15). Awareness of alterity can just as easily lead to storing up more prejudice, not less. While Knoepflmacher's work supports Georg Lukács's idea that the "form of a social work is integral to its moral, social, and political meaning" (Armstrong 197), he would also agree with his Princeton colleague Susan Wolfson that

---

6. After explaining that they are not talking about paper or book bindings, Best and Marcus suggest that *surface* could mean materiality (see Scarry); it could mean the intricate verbal structures of literary language and form, recalling some of the aims of New Criticism, Old Formalism and New Formalism (see Otter); it could mean a type of reader response that Best and Marcus would consider ethical and affective (see Sontag). *Surface* could also mean practical criticism: the point is to consider no external theory but what a text says itself about its form, structure, or meaning (see Fineman). Or *surface* might mean identifying patterns across texts (see Siskin). Finally it might mean reading for literal meanings rather than symbolic ones (see Stoler). Overall, Best and Marcus argue for the potentialities and the agency of the text itself vs. a critical agency that reduces a text to "instrumental means to any end" (16). Such critical activities, they maintain, best preserve the complexity of literary surfaces. Whether or not such critical activities best preserve the complexity of literature is another matter.

7. Audrey Jaffe also noted a persistent retention of the binary in "Face Value: Victorianism and the Status of Surface Reading," presented at NAVSA, Pasadena, October 2013.

8. At the same time, Ellen Rooney shows where Best and Marcus's own surface reading of Louis Althusser fails descriptively and thus reveals its own ideological interestedness (15).

formalism's legitimacy goes well beyond its enmeshment in networks of social and historical conditions. Form creates its own value and pleasures.

The more aesthetically complex, the more "mixy," the more challenging a text's form, the more engaging it becomes for Knoepflmacher. While the politics of form may not be his main concern, he fully recognizes the emancipatory, progressive, and repressive elements that a text's form can simultaneously embody. Indeed, literary forms often achieve their most powerful effects by satisfying—and at the same time questioning—a reader's normative expectations (see Jauss as qtd. in Armstrong 213).

Rather than hierarchize or ghettoize affect *or* reason, or focus a reader at surface or depth, or demand closeness or distance, Knoepflmacher tries in his criticism, as Wordsworth did in his poetry, to find a momentary synthesis of opposites.[9] Emotion recollected in tranquility, after all, involves a transaction between affect and reason. It demands close, pleasurable observation and distant thought, surface, and depth. Emotion is felt deeply, raised to consciousness, controlled by the intellect, and reprocessed as affect to be shared intellectually and feelingly with others.[10] What happens in the speaker occurs ideally in the reader, as the text invites and enacts the very same process formally. Knoepflmacher is drawn to Wordsworth because of the poet's high standards for a literature that goes beyond mere entertainment, but even more because his poetry enacts what it is about: it is itself *about* a balancing of intellect with emotion. The reader's response to Wordsworth's poetry might ideally be emotional, intellectual, and syncretic. Such a reader is able to move among historical and personal situations, among forms, at the surface and at the depths, in multiple directions of spatial, verbal, and imagistic attention, across and down a page, and most of all *in the passageways* between surface and depth—in the embodied translation of affect to thought and back to affect and again to thought.[11]

Knoepflmacher is drawn to later nineteenth-century literature because it wrestles with the increasing *problems* of such a translation. Various kinds of problems are evident in the writings of numerous "Victorians," canonical and noncanonical, and those who address both adults and children

---

9. See individual poems by Wordsworth, for instance, "A Night Piece" (lines 8–13); "I Wandered Lonely as a Cloud" (lines 19–24); "Lines Composed a Few Miles Above Tintern Abbey" (lines 146–59); and "The Idiot Boy" (lines 447–53).

10. Many recent literary critics chart the histories of affect and reason in philosophers and theorists from Plato to Nietzsche to Kant to Ricoeur to Deleuze to Latour. Most comment on the supremely mentalist bias informing much contemporary criticism and theory (see Littau 20), while others comment on the rise of affect theory.

11. For related research into multimodal processing instead of bipolar verbal and visual cognitive attention, see Blazhenkova and Kozhevnikov.

by *cross-writing* (in the term coined by Mitzi Myers in collaboration with Knoepflmacher). In too many studies to mention here, scholars of the nineteenth century have shown how the rise of science and the increasing split between the imagination and fact-based disciplinary cultures shaped and reshaped literature. The difficulty of blending reason and emotion, already fully acknowledged in Wordsworth's writing, appears in thousands of nineteenth- and twentieth-century literary texts, some of which engage Knoepflmacher here.

Translation is a word I have used earlier to represent Knoepflmacher's early diasporic life and what I first took to be his mode of reading. In thinking further about my usage of the word in both a metaphoric and a literal sense, I am reminded of Hans Robert Jauss's description of pleasurable aesthetic experience. Only by surrendering to the object sensuously and contemplatively can we constitute the aesthetic object (30–31). The literary text, like a symphony or a painting, comes into its fullest being through a recipient's feelings and mental interpretation, through the pleasure of a dialectic. This is why Knoepflmacher's work is still critical for our time. It challenges modes of reading and thinking that increasingly rely on oppositional extremes.

ACKNOWLEDGMENTS

This project would not have been possible without Sandy Crooms, former senior acquisitions editor at The Ohio State University Press; Lindsay Martin, current acquisitions editor; and Malcolm Litchfield, former director. Their unwavering support and patience meant a great deal to us. We are grateful as well to Professor William N. Rogers of San Diego State University for his timely editorial response to the preface and introduction. We also thank Amy Kaufman of Portland, Oregon, and Gila Yarmush of New York City who aided us with some of the conversion from print to digital formatting. The book was completed with the help of Research Leave granted by Stern College, Yeshiva University, in fall 2013; Linda M. Shires thanks Dr. Morton Lowengrub, then Provost, and Dr. Karen Bacon, The Dr. Monique C. Katz Dean of Undergraduate Faculty of Arts and Sciences, Stern College for Women, Yeshiva University.

We are also deeply grateful to librarians of the Princeton University Firestone Library, particularly Linda Oppenheim and Andrea Immel, for their time and friendship.

All essays here have appeared in earlier versions in the following journals and collections. They are reprinted with permission:

Chapter 1 "Mutations of the Wordsworthian Child of Nature," *Nature and the Victorian Imagination*, ed. U. C. Knoepflmacher and G. B. Tennyson. Berkeley: University of California Press, 1977, 391–425.

Chapter 2 "Genre and the Integration of Gender: From Wordsworth to George Eliot to Virginia Woolf," *Victorian Literature and Society: Essays Presented to Richard Altick,* eds. James R. Kincaid and Albert J. Kuhn. Columbus: The Ohio State University Press, 1984, 94–118.

Chapter 3 "On Exile and Fiction: The Leweses and Shelleys," *Mothering the Mind: Twelve Studies of Writers and Their Silent Partners,* ed. Ruth Perry and Martine Brownley. New York: Holmes and Meier, 1984, 102–21.

Chapter 4 "Projection and the Female Other: Romanticism, Browning, and the Victorian Dramatic Monologue," *Victorian Poetry* 22.2 (Summer 1984): 139–59.

Chapter 5 "Dover Revisited: The Wordsworthian Matrix in the Poetry of Matthew Arnold," *Victorian Poetry* 1.1 (Winter 1963): 17–26.

Chapter 6 "Arnold's Fancy and Pater's Imagination: Exclusion and Incorporation," *Victorian Poetry* 26:1–2 (Spring and Summer 1988): 103–15.

Chapter 7 "Revisiting Wordsworth: Lewis Carroll's 'The White Knight's Song'," *Victorians Institute Journal* 14 (1986): 1–20.

Chapter 8 "The Return of a Native Singer: Keats in Hardy's Dorset," *Influence and Resistance in Nineteenth Century English Poetry,* ed. G. Kim Blank and Margot K. Louis. London: The Macmillan Press, Ltd., 1993, 112–30.

Chapter 9 "Kipling as Browning: From Parody to Translation," *Victorian Poetry* 50.4 (Winter 2012): 605–23.

Chapter 10 "The Subject of Biography: The Victorianism of *Eminent Victorians,*" *Victorians Institute Journal* 18 (1990): 1–15.

Chapter 11 "Afterword: Endings as Beginnings," *Famous Last Words: Changes in Gender and Narrative Closure,* ed. Alison Booth, with Afterword by U. C. Knoepflmacher. Charlottesville: University of Virginia Press, 1993, 347–68.

INTRODUCTION

I

Originally published in different venues and over a wide span of years, the eleven essays collected in this volume now serve as chapters of a continuing critical narrative that examines the intricate textual modifications undertaken by three successive generations of writers born in the nineteenth century. These poets, novelists, and essayists persistently reassessed and revised the foundational work undertaken by their Romantic forebears. Born as late as 1882, even Virginia Woolf, the youngest and most radically innovative of these revisionists, still enlisted Romantic poetry and the romances of sister-novelists such as Charlotte Brontë in her modernist fiction.

The dilemma faced by a literary critic who reprints a selection of earlier articles resembles that of an editor charged with the task of fashioning a volume out of a creative writer's early and later work. Should the arrangement be chronological in order to allow a reader to chart the "growth" of that author's "mind"? Or should the arrangement rely on subsidiary units to convey different aspects of the collection's overall concerns? I quickly decided that, in my case, the latter option was preferable by far. It seemed pointless to reprint these essays in the order in which they first appeared. I therefore decided to fit them into a sequence that would allow me to highlight interrelations.

Given those interrelations, I would urge my readers to read the eleven chapters in their sequential order and to consider the links within each of the three clusters formed by chapters 2 to 4, 5 to 7, and 8 to 11. The first and longest chapter in the collection can act as a gateway to these clusters. It analyzes the "mutations" created by no fewer than sixteen Victorian writers who transformed William Wordsworth's investment in the child's powers of imagination. Several of these writers (Matthew Arnold, Robert Browning, George Eliot, Thomas Hardy, Rudyard Kipling, and Walter Pater) play prominent roles in the later essays. Yet other major figures considered here (such as Charles Dickens, Gerard Manley Hopkins, John Ruskin, and Alfred Tennyson) will not reappear.

I resisted the temptation to enlarge the first chapter even further by adding George MacDonald, Christina Rossetti, and other figures amply analyzed in my 1998 *Ventures into Childland* or by showing how Charles Lamb's "Dream Children" and Thomas De Quincey's account of his encounters with the ghost-child Catherine Wordsworth infiltrated the fictions of George Eliot and Emily Brontë. But to insert any new materials—whether primary or secondary—into any of these essays would have deprived them of their former cohesion.

To retain the collection's integrity, I also abandoned the idea of fashioning entirely new chapters to supplement the eleven essays reprinted here. One of these would have contrasted the 1822 "Romantic" version of *Confessions of an English Opium Eater* to its 1856 "Victorian" revision. A discussion of De Quincey's creation of a bulky volume of reminiscences to replace his fragmentary account of a quest fueled by mighty opium dreams certainly could have reinforced this collection's demonstration that generic changes actually helped to perpetuate literary continuities.[1] Not only Victorians were engaged in this transformative activity. As I will suggest later in this introduction, the second generation of Romantics had already experimented with forms that went beyond those Coleridge and Wordsworth had fashioned.

Gender issues are taken up in each of the essays placed in the first of my three clusters. Chapter 2, "Genre and the Integration of Gender," lays out the difficulties met by writers who tried to fuse separate brother and sister selves into an androgynous whole. Already inherent in poems written by male Romantics such as Wordsworth, Byron, and Shelley, these difficulties were compounded in the plots devised by women novelists. The

---

1. Given Virginia Woolf's (and her Wordsworthian father's) interest in De Quincey, such a discussion would also have been tangentially relevant to the discussion of *To the Lighthouse* in chapters 2 and 11.

chapter therefore positions George Eliot's *The Mill on the Floss* as a median between Wordsworth's insertion of sororal selves into his poetry of remembrance and Virginia Woolf's representation of irreconcilable gender divisions in *To the Lighthouse*. George Eliot figures even more prominently in chapter 3, "On Exile and Fiction." If the metaphorized unions of male and female halves discussed in chapter 2 were purely wishful, the bi-gendered partnerships that replaced what had produced the 1798 *Lyrical Ballads* were beset by all-too-real inequities. Thus, George Eliot's highly fruitful creative union with George Henry Lewes is set in apposition to the inequalities of Mary Godwin's subservience to Percy Shelley as well as to the adjustments the Shelleyan Robert Browning had to make after his elopement with a fully established woman poet. Browning's reformulation of the roles that a Female Other had played in Romantic poetry is taken up in chapter 4. His disengagement from Shelley and affiliation with Keats helped transform idealizing Romantic lyrics into dramatic monologues spoken by males whose suppression of an animating female force signifies their incompleteness. Browning's tribute to Elizabeth Barrett, his adoption of a female voice in "James Lee's Wife," and his repudiation of younger contemporaries like Dante Gabriel Rossetti (whose "Jenny" he loathed) are all in keeping with his later identification with Caponsacchi, the soldier-priest who acts as Pompilia's paladin in *The Ring and the Book*.

The three essays in the next cluster resume the focus on Wordsworth introduced by chapters 2 to 4. Chapter 5, "Dover Revisited" (the oldest of the essays in this volume), returns to Matthew Arnold's appropriation of Wordsworth's poetry, first tackled in chapter 1. Arnold's intended preservation of "feeling" in an age dominated by evolutionary thinking resulted in over-intellectualized verses such as the early "Resignation," published in 1849, a year before Wordsworth's death, and the posthumous publication of *The Prelude*. Wordsworthian touchstones are more cleverly embedded in "Dover Beach," which appeared after Arnold had assumed the role of a cultural critic. His 1880 essay "Wordsworth" is next contrasted to Walter Pater's earlier appreciation of the poet in chapter 6, "Arnold's Fancy and Pater's Imagination." Here, the younger writer's familiarity with *The Prelude* enables him to grant Wordsworth imaginative powers that Arnold still qualifies in his criticism and curbs in the pared-down verses he now edits. In chapter 7, it is another young Victorian, Lewis Carroll, who can bend Wordsworth's imagination to suit his own objectives in the interaction between the nostalgic White Knight and the forward-moving Alice.

The four essays in the last cluster transport my narrative into the twentieth century. In chapter 8, "The Return of a Native Singer," Thomas

Hardy, who had already used Wordsworth's and Shelley's skylark verses as foils for his own avian poems, turns to Keats as he surveys the desolation of a darkling new century. By 1921, however, the octogenarian poet fully reclaims the twenty-five-year-old "comrade" who had perished a century earlier. Hindsight allows Hardy to correct the indifference shown in 1820 by a Dorset observer of a youth about to board a ship bound for Italy. This obscure stranger, the witness is told, will be revered as a major poet one hundred years later. Chapter 9, "Kipling as Browning," begins with "Wireless," a short story in which still another unsuspecting witness is brought into contact with Keats's poetry; it ends with the 1934 story "Proofs of Holy Writ," a story in which Kipling impersonates the self-effacing Shakespeare whom Keats had upheld as a model. Yet it is as a young poet that Kipling began to enlist the "negative capability" of Browning's dramatic monologues in a line that would link both writers to a Shakespeare whose work Coleridge, Hazlitt, and Keats had promoted as an alternative to Wordsworth's Miltonic egotism. Chapter 10, "The Victorianism of Strachey's *Eminent Victorians*," argues that this 1918 foray into a genre that had flourished from Hazlitt's *The Spirit of the Age* and Carlyle's *On Heroes, Hero-Worship, and the Heroic in History* to Arnold's and Pater's own collective biographies actually sympathizes with most of its nineteenth-century subjects. Although Strachey relentlessly satirizes Thomas Arnold, he favorably casts John Henry Newman and General Gordon as Romantic idealists and presents Florence Nightingale as a mighty androgyne, the healer who could have served as a fiercer warrior and shrewder strategist than any one of Queen Victoria's inept generals. Last, chapter 11, "Endings as Beginnings," reintroduces Woolf's 1927 *To the Lighthouse*, a novel whose ending is now read against the closures of the journeys taken in earlier romances such as *Frankenstein, Wuthering Heights, Jane Eyre,* and *Villette*.

II

In a recent discussion of books that focus on the history of the novel, Frances Ferguson alludes to the generic criticism once practiced by our former Berkeley colleague and my dear friend, Ralph Rader. That brand of criticism, she shrewdly notes, was retroactively progenitive. A novel might be accepted into a highly restricted canon only upon the appearance of a worthy "descendant": "Virginia Woolf's stream of consciousness" thus legitimized Defoe's *Robinson Crusoe* (721). Although the essays I have collected here also stress genealogical filiations, they dwell upon texts that were unusually open to mixed forms and generic crossings. This remarkable fluidity is borne out by the retrospective embedding of so many of Wordsworth's major and minor poems in later nineteenth-century lyrics, dramatic monologues, verse narratives, novels, romances, children's books, and nonfictional prose. The work of a writer who saw himself as Miltonic became as progenitive as Milton's own had been.

What accounted for Wordsworth's century-long preeminence? Was it the boldness of his literary manifestos, his inventiveness, the variety and novelty of his copious verses that tantalized later writers? Or was it also, quite paradoxically, his failure to carry out the aims he had so confidently promised to fulfill? If so, the works of both allies and detractors might actually be read as a series of reparative efforts rather than a reflection of a combative Bloomian "anxiety of influence." Contemporaries and successors tried to resurrect, amend, and revitalize the agenda first voiced in the 1800 *The Preface to Lyrical Ballads*. Feeling increasingly displaced after Wordsworth ceased to regard him as a viable partner, Samuel Taylor Coleridge still tried to remind his "friend" of their joint agenda. But even those younger Romantics most sorely disappointed by Wordsworth's blunted purpose were hardly uncooperative. Their efforts to rechannel the poet's objectives can, I think, be read as latter-day collaborations.

The 1814 appearance of *The Excursion* certainly thwarted the expectations of a good many of Wordsworth's growing body of admirers. But their disenchantment was caused not only by the slow-moving, blank-verse narrative in nine parts that recounts an author's discursive encounters with the Wanderer, the Solitary, and the Pastor. There also was the confusion created by a short prose "Preface" and the verse *Prospectus* that followed it.

Though divulging the existence of an unnamed biographical poem on "the origin and progress of his own powers," Wordsworth's "Preface" fails to explain why he had refrained from publishing that "long finished" work. Instead, it merely hints that this "preparatory" poem would someday serve as "ante-chapel to the body" of a much larger, yet to be "constructed," verse-edifice, "of which *The Excursion*" was to become an "intermediate part." The other two parts of the magnum opus to be called *The Recluse*, Wordsworth explained, would consist chiefly of "meditations in the Author's own person" and hence differ from the "dramatic form adopted" in *The Excursion*. But in the interim, the verse *Prospectus* placed after the "Preface" might offer his 1814 readers a foretaste "of the design and scope of the whole poem" (*Poetical Works* 589).

Significantly enough, "the Author" here delegates to an "attentive Reader" (gendered as a "he") much that he refuses to spell out. Familiar with "minor Pieces" that have been "long before the Public," such a reader should be able to detect their "connection" to a "main Work" still in its planning stage, for these earlier pieces, Wordsworth claims, are as integral to the cathedral-like structure of that masterwork as the "little cells, oratories, and sepulchral recesses, ordinarily included in those edifices." Yet the demands this literary architect places on readers asked to complete an invisible master plan escalate as soon as he presents himself as a philosopher-poet who has no "intention formally to announce a system." Once again, Wordsworth delegates that task to a cooperating ideal "Reader" who should "have no difficulty in extracting the system for himself" (*Poetical Works* 589).

The difficulty of extracting any such "system" from the 107-line, blank-verse specimen offered as *Prospectus* was compounded by the counterweight of the seemingly interminable 8,849 lines of *The Excursion*.[2] The discrepancy between the two texts obviously baffled any attentive nineteenth-century reader. For the bold pronouncements made by a Miltonic "I" in the *Prospectus* were palpably at odds with a verse narrative that relied on the long-winded "intervention[s] of characters" whose rhetorical pronouncements the poet's deferential "I" seems content to record (*Poetical Works* 589).

Invoking Urania "or a greater Muse, if such / Descend on earth, or dwell in the highest heaven," the speaker of the *Prospectus* vows to replace the topography of *Paradise Lost* (lines 26–27, *Poetical Works* 590). Professing to be "unalarmed" by "shouting Angels," this assertive speaker promises to shrink the vast cosmos once navigated by Milton's Satan (35, 34). His own descent will penetrate an interior realm by taking him "Into our Minds, into the Mind of Man— / My haunt, and the main region of my song" (41–42). A new Paradise can be recovered, not by religious faith, but through the agency of a universal imaginative power lodged "in the hearts / Of mighty Poets" whose fusion of opposites can set in motion the "blended might" of subject and object (86–87).

Unlike most 1814 readers, Coleridge knew that this *Prospectus* was intended to validate the finished but concealed *The Prelude* rather than the theologically orthodox *The Excursion*. Wordsworth's *Preface to The Excursion* had linked his unnamed work to a similarly unnamed "dear

---

2. Byron astutely seizes on the word *system* when he dissociates himself from Wordsworth in the fourth octet of the "Dedication" in *Don Juan*: "And Wordsworth, in a rather long 'Excursion' / (I think the quarto holds five hundred pages), / Has given a sample from the vasty version / Of his new system to perplex the sages' / 'Tis poetry—at least by his assertion, / And may appear so when the dog-star rages ("Dedication" 25–30).

Friend, most distinguished for his knowledge and genius, and to whom the Author's Intellect is deeply indebted" (589). And indeed, from mid-1806 to early 1807, the poet had spent six months reading aloud, line by line, all thirteen books on "the growth of an individual mind" to a highly grateful Coleridge. Upon that long recital's conclusion, the coauthor of the 1798 *Lyrical Ballads* promptly signified his appreciation with "To William Wordsworth: Composed on the Night After His Recitation of a Poem, on the Growth of An Individual Mind." Coleridge's laudatory poem became a pendant to his earlier, self-derogating "Dejection: An Ode."[3]

The speaker of "To William Wordsworth" claims to have been invigorated by listening to his friend's "long sustainéd Song." The poem's activation of childhood epiphanies has rejuvenated his adult mind. Freed from painful self-consciousness, the rapt auditor feels himself converted into a "devout child" (lines 104, 95, *Complete Poetical Works* 1: 408). Reaffirmed as partner and philosophic adviser, Coleridge also assumes the role of the ideal reader Wordsworth continued to covet. To help keep *The Prelude*'s existence a secret, he even promised to delay the publication of "To William Wordsworth."

That moratorium, however, was short-lived. In March 1815 Wordsworth published a two-volume "collective" edition of his poems headed by a new preface that privileged an "enthusiastic and meditative Imagination" over the "dramatic Imagination" of a Shakespeare whose works remained an "inexhaustible source" for other writers (*Poetical Works* 755). To describe the imaginative power he attributed to "the prophetic and lyrical parts" of the Bible and to a Milton who, despite his classicism, "was a Hebrew in soul," the poet relied on "the language of one my most esteemed friends" (755). Yet the "friend" he now cites is no longer the anonymous "dear Friend" acknowledged as a mentor only a year before. Instead, Wordsworth pointedly identifies his source as "Charles Lamb upon the genius of Hogarth" (755n1). Coleridge has been snubbed.

The reasons for this repudiation may be deduced from an unusually long letter that Coleridge wrote to Wordsworth on 30 May 1815. In it, the shunned collaborator apologizes for not having told his "honored Friend" that he had decided to include "To William Wordsworth" in a future collection of his own poems, yet he also defends himself for having shared

---

3. Although Wordsworth's presence in "Dejection: An Ode" is more obliquely handled, both poems enlist his sure sense of self as a counter to the speaker's insecurities and self-doubts. Not only was the "Lady" addressed in "Dejection" called "William" in an earlier draft, but the echoes of the "Immortality" ode and the conversion of Wordsworth's "sweet Lucy Gray" into a screaming ghost-child signify the imaginative differences that "To William Wordsworth" tries to gloss over.

a critique of *The Excursion* with common friends. Although he had not expected to have his "Dispraise" relayed by a third party, Coleridge insists that his "criticism" merely amounted to a sense that "the excursion, as far as it was new to me," had dashed "the expectations" so greatly raised by Wordsworth's "*former* Poem" [*The Prelude*] (*Collected Letters* 4: 572–73). Worried that the dramatic form of *The Excursion* may signify a departure from the design of *The Recluse,* Coleridge wants Wordsworth to follow the original "Plan I had supposed that you were engaged on" (575).

The later chapters of Coleridge's 1817 *Biographia Literaria* closely scrutinize Wordsworth's poetry to help the poet or any of his acolytes produce "the FIRST GENUINE PHILOSOPHIC POEM" (275; ch. 22). Yet the attempt to wean Wordsworth from the "dramatic form" of *The Excursion* is already evident in an earlier chapter ostensibly devoted to the narrative poems of a young Shakespeare who has yet to find the proper outlet for his genius. Lacking Shakespeare's dramatic strength and imagistic control, Wordsworth seems to have turned into a pseudohistorian by merely cataloguing the tribulations suffered by scores of humble men and women.[4]

Chapter XV of the *Biographia* celebrates Shakespeare's unique capacity for accommodating contradiction and conflict. Only drama could reconcile his "intellectual energy" and "creative power" (179; ch. 15). Coleridge ends the chapter with a peroration that expands Wordsworth's contrast between the powers of Shakespeare and Milton:

> What then shall we say? Even this: that Shakespeare, no mere child of nature; no mere automaton of genius; no passive vehicle of inspiration possessed by the spirit, not possessing it; first studied patiently, meditated deeply, understood minutely, till knowledge become habitual and intuitive wedded itself to his habitual feelings, and at length gave birth to that stupendous power by which he stands alone, with no equal or second in his own class, to that power which seated him on one of the two glory-smitten summits of the poetic mountain, with Milton as his compeer not rival. While the former darts himself forth and passes into all forms of human character and passion, the one Proteus of the fire and the flood; the other attracts all forms and things to himself, into the unity of his own ideal. All things and modes of action shape themselves anew

---

4. As noted in chapter 2, George Eliot's early fictions—her *Scenes of Clerical Life* and *Adam Bede*—owe their conception to *The Excursion.* The novelist who began her career as a supposed chronicler of the tragedies of everyday life may be said to start at precisely the point where Wordsworth left off, but "the author of *Silas Marner* and *Middlemarch*" (as Henry James liked to call her) soon became a weaver of far more intricate fabrics.

in the being of Milton; while Shakespeare becomes all things, yet forever remains himself. O what great men hast thou not produced, England! my country! Truly indeed,

> Must *we* be free or die, who speak the tongue,
> Which Shakespeare spake; the faith and morals hold
> Which Milton held. In every thing we are sprung
> Of Earth's first blood, have titles manifold!
> WORDSWORTH (180; ch. 15)

Coleridge's decision to cap his peroration by citing the last lines of a sonnet in Wordsworth's 1807 *Poems Dedicated to National Independence and Liberty* is extremely clever.[5] Having praised the young Shakespeare for perfecting a mode that he will soon fault Wordsworth for falsely pursuing, Coleridge uses his friend's own words to remind him that he still holds the powers that "Milton held." Even in the very last chapter of the *Biographia,* Coleridge suggests that Wordsworth's adherence to the multitudinousness of a reality composed of particulars has led the poet to lose sight of the whole. Yet the missionary zeal with which he prodded Wordsworth to complete *The Recluse* did not bear fruit. Not only did that work remain unfinished,[6] but even the changes that *The Prelude* underwent suggest that Coleridge's criticism had gone unheeded. Posthumously published in 1850, the thirteen books of "The Poem to Coleridge" were eclipsed by the appearance of Tennyson's *In Memoriam* only few months before.

The shift in sensibility that Coleridge correctly diagnosed and vainly tried to arrest was symptomatic of the much larger generic shifts that Wordsworth bequeathed to his Romantic and Victorian successors. Percy Shelley's 1816 sonnet "To Wordsworth" and John Keats's sonnet "To One Who Has Been Long In City Pent," also written in 1816 but published in 1817, provide an early adumbration of those changes. Each of these young poets adopts a markedly different strategy to signify his simultaneous association and dissociation from Wordsworth.

Like Coleridge's "To William Wordsworth," Shelley's "To Wordsworth" opens by directly addressing his subject. But Coleridge's "comforter and

---

5. The sixteenth sonnet in the 1807 sequence ("It is not to be thought of that the Flood / Of British freedom . . .") was first published by the *Morning Post* in April 1803.

6. See, however, Kenneth R. Johnston's compelling 1984 reconstitution of *The Recluse* as a coherent body of fragmented yet interrelated texts; for Johnston, the collaboration between Coleridge and Wordsworth was actually extended not only through "Coleridge's reappropriation of the *Recluse*-ideal" but also by his reliance on the later books of *The Excursion* for his definition of a "clerisy" (*Wordsworth and 'The Recluse'* 360, 361).

guide" has now been turned into a chronicler of irrevocable loss. What is more, the "I-thou" relationship crucial to both poems has radically altered. Coleridge's speaker had extolled a self-confident poet's ability to infuse others with his strength. Shelley's speaker, however, derives his own strength by separating himself from a depleted prototype.

> Poet of Nature, thou has wept to know
> That things depart which never may return:
> Childhood and youth, friendship's and love's first glow,
> Have fled like sweet dreams leaving thee to mourn.
> These common woes I feel. One loss is mine
> Which thou too feel'st, yet I alone deplore.
> Thou wert as a lone star, whose light did shine
> On some frail bark in winter's midnight roar:
> Thou hast like to a rock-built refuge stood
> Above the blind and battling multitude:
> In honored poverty thy voice did weave
> Songs consecrate to truth and liberty,—
> Deserting these, thou leavest me to grieve,
> Thus having been, that thou shouldst cease to be. ("To Wordsworth,"
> *Shelley's Poetry* 92)

Left "alone" in the present, Shelley's stranded speaker must clear that presence of the obstacles created by a poet bereft of his luster as "a lone star" (6, 7). He begins with a profession of kinship. Not only "woes" but also the sonnet form itself—and, with it, the Petrarchan conceit of a storm-tossed vessel led by a stellar guide—are "common" to both poets.[7] Indeed, as Shelley seems to remember, Wordsworth had invigorated that worn trope by addressing England as a "Fair Star of evening" in "Composed by the Sea-Side, Near Calais" (line 1, *Poetical Works* 241). Yet Shelley's apparent allusion to the opening sonnet of the same *Poems Dedicated to National Independence and Liberty* that Coleridge would cite in his *Biographia* is not complimentary, for the sonnet's speaker accuses Wordsworth of "deserting" the songs to "truth and liberty" he had composed only a decade before (13, 12). The older poet's turn to a political and religious orthodoxy not only has weakened the impact of those sonnets but also has supposedly erased his

---

7. Like young Hamlet, Shelley may well enlist the word *common* to taunt an older addressee whose behavior he will then "deplore" (lines 5, 6). When Hamlet hurls back Gertrude's "common," he turns her intended meaning ("usual" or "shared") into something that has become "tawdry" or "vile."

former identity. Since the poet he once admired has ceased "to be," a fresh mourner must now fill the vacancy (14). Shelley hardly shares Coleridge's eagerness to revive an old poet's dormant powers. Instead, the young poet will soon convert Wordsworth's beneficent breezes into a destructive but regenerative force. By asking the mighty West Wind to be "Me," Shelley can funnel Wordsworth's Miltonic egotism into new directions.

Shelley's sonnet adds Wordsworth to the departed "things" that "never may return." Yet instead of merely slaying a poetic father, "To Wordsworth" also establishes Shelley's dependence on Wordsworth for his self-definition as a writer. The poet who perished in a storm-tossed "bark" eight years after the publication of this sonnet continued to cling to his predecessor's verses even in his most radical compositions. At first glance, the frenzied poet of "Alastor," whose gaze can terrify infants, seems closer to Coleridge's *Ancient Mariner* than to Wordsworth's sober itinerants. Yet the subtitle of "Alastor; or The Spirit of Solitude" signals its Wordsworthian underpinnings.

Phrases culled from "Ode: Intimations of Immortality" and minor poems such as "My Heart Leaps Up" are sprinkled throughout a narrative that begins, as so many of Wordsworth's excursive poems do, by mournfully revisiting a hallowed site. We are asked to contemplate the wind-caressed, "untimely tomb" of a seeker whose journey the poem will painfully retrace, step by step (line 50, "Alastor"). Propelled by "wild" female eyes (264) that are as beckoning as those sister-eyes in which the speaker of "Tintern Abbey" once saw a reflection of his former self, this new pilgrim fails in his quest. Still, all "who remain behind" are asked to honor him, in "a woe 'too deep for tears'," as a most worthy "wanderer" (716, 713, 311). According to Mary Shelley, she and her husband had been "much disapointed [*sic*]" by *The Excursion*, "of which" they "read a part," shortly after its appearance (*Journals of Mary Shelley* I: 25). Nonetheless, Shelley's attempt to convert that 1814 poem into his own 1816 account of an excursive quest for a female epipsyche called "Alastor" demanded a reader as steeped as he was in all of the Wordsworthian antecedents he tried to recombine.[8]

Unlike the open engagement with Wordsworth in Shelley's sonnet, John Keats's 1817 playful sonnet "To One Who Has Been Long in City Pent" covertly tweaks hallowed trademarks. The Wordsworthian "I" on which

---

8. The Shelleys began to read the recently published *Excursion* on 14 September 1814 (a day after their return from France) and finished it in the next two days, but Percy reread the work (as well as Wordsworth's 1815 *Poems*) in 1815. In a list in which she records all their readings for 1814, Mary places *The Excursion* right after her mother's *Letters from Norway* and *Mary, A Fiction* (*Journals* I: 85).

Keats had still relied a year earlier in "To Solitude," his first published poem, has now vanished. Instead, we join an unidentified "he" on a day's mini-excursion to the Hampstead fields outside London. And this figure, who owes his identity to a simile in *Paradise Lost,* acts as an adjunct in a mood poem that relies on literary allusion and artifice to challenge Wordsworth's conviction that one "impulse from a vernal wood" may teach us more than the "meddling intellect" of books and sages (lines 21, 26, "The Tables Turned: An Evening Scene . . . ," *Poetical Works* 377).

> To one who has been long in city pent,
>   'Tis very sweet to look into the fair
>   And open face of heaven,—to breathe a prayer
> Full in the smile of the blue firmament.
> Who is more happy, when, with heart's content,
>   Fatigued he sinks into some pleasant lair
>   Of wavy grass, and reads a debonair
> And gentle tale of love and languishment?
> Returning home at evening with an ear
>   Catching the notes of Philomel,—eye
> Watching the sailing cloudlet's bright career,
>   He mourns that day so soon has glided by:
> E'en like the passage of angel's tear
>   That falls through the clear ether silently. (*The Poems of John Keats* 45–46)

Keats's sonnet relies on a dense network of literary allusions. The surprise felt by a city dweller who ventures into a pastoral space was used by Milton as an analogue to Satan's stupefaction on first encountering the goddess-like Eve; Coleridge had redeployed the trope in both "This Lime Tree Bower My Prison" and "Frost at Midnight." But Keats also recalls Wordsworth's 1800 *Preface to Lyrical Ballads* when his sonnet's sestet converts the seeming celebration of a rural "lair" into a night-piece like Milton's "Penseroso" or Wordsworth's own "A Night-Piece." By likening the pain of one who "mourns" a day's passing to "the passage of an angel's tear / That falls through the clear ether silently" (13–14), Keats defies Wordsworth's assertion that "Poetry sheds no tears 'such as Angels weep,' but natural and human tears; she can boast of no celestial ichor" (*Wordsworth: Poetical* 736). Suspended as a timeless literary icon, a single tear shed by Milton's fallen archangel suffices to hint that a poetry that relies on metaphor can indeed enlist such a "celestial ichor."

Keats here actually anticipates Coleridge's response to Wordsworth's notions about the artificiality of poetic diction.[9] Contending that poetry was "essentially ideal and generic," Coleridge would soon insist that the "language of Milton [is] as much the language of real life, yea, incomparably more so than that of the cottager" (*Biographia* 188). But "To One Who Has Been Long in City Pent" also engages Wordsworth on other fronts. In the opening of *The Excursion* Wordsworth had constructed a "most pleasant" yet remote vernal setting for any dreamer who "on soft cool moss / Extends his caveless limbs along the front / of some huge cave" (*Poetical Works*, Book I, 9–11). The lair of "wavy grass" on which Keats's "fatigued" wanderer has sunk, however, is not used for a communion with Nature but as a convenient resting spot for the reading of a book (lines 7, 6, "To One"). That "tale of love and languishment" (8) may well be as full of pathos as the myth of "Philomel," the nightingale whose "notes" are heard by the city dweller who "mourns" the fleeting passage of an especially pleasant day (10, 12).

That day, however, is not extraordinary. It does not need to be interpreted by a surprised speaker who feels compelled to memorialize an unusual epiphany. Keats's poem, I would argue, confronts Wordsworth's far more famous sonnet, "Composed Upon Westminster Bridge, September 3, 1802." In that poem, a "he" is amazed to discover that the morning's "silent" beauty has blended traditional opposites by opening the city "unto the fields." Converted into an "I" in the sonnet's exclamatory sestet, this awed witness moves from observation to celebration:

> Never did sun more beautifully steep
> In his first splendour, valley, rock, or hill;
> Ne'er saw I, never felt, a calm so deep!
> The river glideth at his own sweet will:
> Dear God! The very houses seem asleep;
> And all that mighty heart is lying still! (lines 9–14,"Westminster
>   Bridge," *Poetical Works* 214)

Unlike Wordsworth, Keats is not engaged in the glorification of a special moment. He deliberately places the verb that Wordsworth had highlighted in the twelfth line of his "Westminster" sonnet into the twelfth line of his own composition to signify that he is replying to the older poet's

---

9. For a fuller discussion of similarities and differences between Keats's and Coleridge's critiques, see Bygrave 38–40.

expostulation. "Will" Wordsworth had invested the river that "*glideth* [my italics] at his own sweet will" with a power he suddenly felt within himself. But the "sailing cloudlet" that Keats's city stroller sees with but one eye (while a single ear listens to Philomel's song) only marks his regret that a pleasant day has so swiftly "*glided* by" ("To One" 11, 12; my italics). Time passes. Though bound to the temporal actuality of a "real" world, Wordsworth dramatically transcended the rare fusion he had witnessed. A special morning could carry intimations of an Edenic timelessness. Keats, however, simply deploys his literary coordinates to mark an everyman's enjoyment of a pleasant but ordinary day. The quotidian reality he is content to embellish is more mundane than that which Wordsworth exalted.

Even more than the pugnacious Percy Shelley, however, Keats would firmly hold on to his Wordsworth for the rest of his short career. Like Shelley, Keats went back to the *Prospectus* of *The Excursion* when, in his "Ode to Psyche," he makes the human mind a "region" that poetry should explore. As Susan Wolfson has wittily pointed out in her refutation of Bloom's reading of that ode, there is no agonistic male struggle here: "Keats's texture of allusion and revision seems less engaged with agon than with shadow boxing" (Wolfson, *Questioning* 311). Indeed, here, as well as in the two *Hyperion* poems, Keats casts himself as a fellow explorer, not as a rival. His much-quoted letter about "human life" as a "mansion of many apartments" elevates "the giant" Wordsworth (*The Letters* I: 280) as a "superior" leader whose "explorative" genius all successors ought to adopt (281). Wordsworth's ability to "think into the human heart," Keats now contends, makes him even "deeper than Milton" (282, 281).

Born in the same year as Thomas Carlyle, a longer-living Keats might well have become Queen Victoria's Poet Laureate in the mid-nineteenth century. But it was Tennyson, of course, whose early verses Arthur Hallam had likened to those of Keats and Shelley, who, dressed in the ceremonial suit that Wordsworth had worn, would replace the eighty-year-old poet in 1850. The "grand march of intellect" that Keats had hoped to join took unexpected turns (282). Wordsworth never completed the grand philosophical poem Coleridge expected. Appearing too late to serve as possible models for progressive poets like Elizabeth Barrett or Robert Browning, neither *The Prelude* nor the fragments of *The Recluse* could offer two generations of post-Romantic writers major signposts for new directions.

Retrospection, however, always Wordsworth's prime mode as well as that of Sir Walter Scott's historical novels, was a legacy that Victorians and Edwardians readily embraced and complicated in their manifold generic innovations. Not only did *In Memoriam, A. H. H.* convert Tennyson into a chronicler of loss very different from the one Shelley had featured in "To Wordsworth," but even the piecemeal composition of his *Idylls of the King* suggests that the shattering of Camelot had to be complemented by a return to its youthful beginnings. Yet retrogression and hindsight had become less joyful. The role played by "Nestling," the woodland baby Arthur and Guinevere cannot keep alive, was as emblematic of lost innocence as the tragic part Thomas Hardy would assign to "Father Time" in *Jude the Obscure* at the end of the century.

III

Before contrasting current reading theories to my own practices as a reader, Linda Shires stressed my predilection for "mixy" literary texts. Hybridity certainly predominates in Victorian reconfigurations of Romantic forms. But the Romantics themselves had steadily reconfigured their own literary antecedents by adopting and modifying earlier forms. Despite tenaciously insisting on his originality, even Wordsworth relied on an extraordinarily wide range of literary echoes and allusions to transport a linked past and present into the future.[10] Indeed, long before Charles Darwin proved that a species was not reducible to a single type with fixed attributes, the evolution of English literature was propelled by the repeated creation of rich hybridic constructs.

It thus seems hardly surprising that critics of the last two decades should have continued to explore the literary and cultural legacies of Romanticism. Stephen Gill's *Wordsworth and the Victorians* (1998) is an influential study that rounds up the usual suspects (Tennyson, Arnold, and George Eliot) but also assesses the poet's significant impact on institutions such as the National Trust and the Anglican Church. A decade later, Stephen Prickett's *Romanticism and Religion: The Tradition of Coleridge and Wordsworth in the Victorian Church* (2008) usefully expanded Gill's discussion of the Romantic move from natural piety to doctrinal religiosity. Wordsworth's centrality is reaffirmed in Richard Gravil's *Romantic Dialogues: Anglo-American Continuities* (2000) and in Joel Pace's and Matthew Scott's collection of essays, *Wordsworth in American Literary Culture* (2004), two studies that stress his relation to nineteenth-century American writers such as Thoreau and Whitman. And twentieth-century appropriations of poems such

---

10. See Edwin Stein's *Wordsworth's Art of Allusion* and Andrew Bennett's chapter on Wordsworth in *Romantic Poets and the Culture of Posterity.*

as "Tintern Abbey" and *The Prelude* are considered by Michael O'Neill in *The All-Sustaining Air: Romantic Legacies and Renewals in British, American, and Irish Poetry* (2007). Finally, even though Joel Faflak's and Julia M. Wright's *Nervous Reactions: Victorian Recollections of Romanticism* (2004) may suffer from a somewhat reductive thesis, their refreshing introduction of figures frequently omitted in similar trans-generational studies is helpful and productive.

The last decades have been especially fruitful by offering new insights into Romantic/Victorian interconnections that restore the importance of poets displaced or "appropriated by a patriarchal poetics."[11] A second wave of feminist scholars have not only revised literary history by reinstating Romantic figures such as Charlotte Smith, Felicia Hemans, Maria Jane Jewsbury, and Letitia Landon, but have also shown how later poets like Elizabeth Barrett, Christina Rossetti, Dora Greenwell, Jean Ingelow, and Augusta Webster persistently defined themselves in opposition to their male forebears and contemporaries. As a result, early studies like Marlon B. Ross's important *The Contours of Masculine Desire: Romanticism and the Rise of Women's Poetry* (1989) have been meaningfully complemented by later works such as Amy Billone's *Little Songs* (2006), an examination of the sonnet tradition created by the female poets who followed Charlotte Smith.

Even the nature of male/female literary collaborations has been profitably reinterpreted. In a prefatory essay to the essays they collected in *Literary Couplings* (2006), Marjorie Stone and Judith Thompson challenge our continued adherence to the Romantic notion of "solitary subjectivities" by claiming that any multi-voiced authorship should be seen as "inherently 'heterotextual'" (Introduction, 19). In a fine contribution to that volume, "The Body of My Father's Writings," Alison Hickey prefers the concept of "polyglotism" to account for the simultaneous presence of "divergence" and "oneness" in Sara Coleridge's attempts to fashion a unified text that might procure a Victorian readership for her father's scattered ideas (140).

Several critics have valuably moved beyond my own forays into the constructs created by a "hermaphroditic" imagination. Here, Susan Wolfson's work (already noted above by Professor Shires and by myself) seems truly indispensible. In *Borderlines: The Shiftings of Gender in British Romanticism* (2006), her close look at the writings of the "masculine" women authors who succeeded Mary Wollstonecraft and Felicia Hemans is complemented by chapters that discuss the Victorian feminizing of Keats and trans-

---

11. E. Warwick Slinn, "Poetry," in *A Companion to Victorian Literature and Culture*, ed. Herbert F. Tucker.

gendering of a "virile" Byron. As always, Wolfson's important revisions of literary history are buttressed by her exquisite close readings of pertinent texts.

Though gender-shifts are not a primary concern in *Byron and the Victorians* (1995), Andrew Elfenbein examines Byron's impact on both the poetry and the fictions of Charlotte and Emily Brontë by showing, for example, that the "feminization of Byronic memory" in Emily's *Gondal* poems relies on repeated verbal echoes of *Childe Harold* (135). Although Elfenbein omits Arthur Hugh Clough's Byronic *Amours de Voyage* and excludes *Oliver Twist* from an all-too-brief discussion of Dickens, he brilliantly links "Byronism" to Carlyle's essays, Tennyson's poems, and the fictions of Bulwer-Lytton and Disraeli.

Textual relations between Romantics and Victorians are taken up by most of the contributors to G. Kim Blank's and Margot K. Louis's collection of essays, *Influence and Resistance in Nineteenth-Century English Poetry* (1993). Shelley is the prime Romantic progenitor here—related to Matthew Arnold by W. David Shaw, to Robert Browning by both Theresa M. Kelley and Mary E. Finn, to Clough by Anne Marie Ross, and to Christina Rossetti by Barbara Charlesworth Gelpi. Christina Rossetti's relation to Blake, Coleridge, Wordsworth, Keats, and the Tractarians is considered by Anthony H. Harrison in an essay that supplements his compendious *Victorian Poets and Romantic Poems: Intertextuality and Ideology* (1992). Eschewing the emphasis on poetry in the Blank and Louis collection's, Keith Hanley's "In Wordsworth's Shadow: Ruskin and Neo-Romantic Ecologies" claims that Ruskin's increasingly pessimistic historicism led to his disenchantment with Wordsworth's exaltation of nature.

The "fixation on childhood" Judith Plotz examines in *Romanticism and the Vocation of Childhood* (2001) was, as she notes, "sardonically" satirized in Max Beerbohm's famous cartoon of the interrogating Wordsworth of "We Are Seven" (xii). Whereas James Kincaid had already looked at some later manifestations of this phenomenon in *Child-Loving: The Erotic Child and Victorian Culture* (1992), Plotz's excellent study takes us back to its early nineteenth-century origins. After discussing Wordsworth's and S. T. Coleridge's deification of the child, she introduces three case studies that analyze the writings of Charles Lamb, Thomas De Quincey, and Hartley Coleridge, the boy-man deformed by his father's designation of him as an instant genius.

Criticism still needs to connect the depictions of childhood introduced by Plotz's Romantic quintet (and by William Blake) to a host of Victorian representations. "How does Romanticism help or hinder the development of theoretically sophisticated children's literary studies in a post modern age?" Mitzi Myers memorably asked in one of the essays that James Holt McGavran collected in *Literature and the Child: Romantic Continuations, Postmodern Contestations* (1999).¹² Several essays in that volume and in an earlier McGavran collection, *Romanticism and Children's Literature* (1991), delve into textual interrelations that deserve to be augmented. Thus, Roderick McGillis's "Childhood and Growth: George MacDonald and William Wordsworth," in the earlier of these volumes, helpfully suggests that, unlike a time-bound Wordsworth and more like Blake or Novalis, MacDonald considers childhood to be an atemporal "state of being which everyone must aspire to" (152). Again, in the same volume, two fine essays by Jeanie Watson and by Alan Richardson on the so-called "Fairy Tale Controversy" that gripped the Romantics remind us that the clash between didacticism and fantasy would continue in later tales such as those that Nina Auerbach and I introduced and reprinted in *Forbidden Journeys: Fairy Tales and Fantasies by Victorian Women Writers* (1992).¹³

But there are a host of rich cross-generic connections that still deserve to be fleshed out by future critics. How did the Romantic recovery of fairy "mythologies"—inspired by the Grimms and conducted by Scottish, English, and Irish folklorists—find its way into Victorian children's books, adult novels, poetry, pantomines, and dramas? How did fairy tales and *The Arabian Nights* seep into different literary forms? And how did a childlike playfulness enter the writings of Victorian sages like Carlyle or Matthew Arnold, the apostle of "High Seriousness" who wanted to do away with Wordsworth's "Poems Referring to the Period of Childhood"? If the "Hyper-Brobdingnagian Wuotan, Woden, Odin" whom Carlyle exalts in his first lecture of *On Heroes* is as fantastic and as magical as a Cheshire Cat, the grinning deity of Wonderland, the opponents of culture whom Arnold satirizes in *Culture and Anarchy* appear to be as deranged as any March Hare or Mad Hatter.

Let me end this introduction with a short personal note. In her generous preface to this volume, Linda Shires has alluded to my recently completed memoir, "Oruro: A Boy's Holocaust Refuge in the Bolivian Andes." Since my work on that narrative coincided with the preparation of this volume, I could not help noticing certain similarities between these two very different exercises in retrogression. In reconstructing what Shires describes

---

12. "Reading Children and Homeopathic Romanticism: Paradigm Lost, Revisionary Gleam, or 'Plus ça change, plus c'est la même chose?'" (McGavran, 45)

13. See, in this connection, my 2003 "Literary Fairy Tales and the Value of Impurity," written as a meditation on the vital endurance of "impure" literary forms and a demonstration of seldom-made intertextual relations.

as my "early diasporic life," I tried to acknowledge the extraordinary debt I owe to my Austrian parents, to my Bolivian and American schoolteachers, and to the small but vibrant and protective community of Jewish European refugees in which I grew up. The influence that these long-gone figures exerted on a boy who had yet to find his vocation in the United States was indeed incalculably diffusive.

Linda Shires has already thanked those who have helped us in the realization of this project. But just as my memoir expressed my deep gratitude to those who shaped a gringo boy's identity, so must this introduction also recede into the past to acknowledge the importance of the mentors and colleagues who helped me hone my skills as a literary scholar. I shall list here only those who are no more: Janet Adelman, Travis Bogard, Philip Collins, Thomas Flanagan, George Ford, Andrew Griffin, James D. Hart, E. D. H. Johnson, John E. Jordan, Coral Lansbury, Louis Landa, Robert Martin, Josephine Miles, Masao Miyoshi, Mitzi Myers, Charles Muscatine, John Paterson, Ralph Rader, John H. Raleigh, Gordon Ray, Alain Renoir, James Rieger, Mark Schorer, Wayne Shumaker, Carole Silver, Henry Nash Smith, Willard Thorp, Ernest Tuveson, and Ian Watt. In rereading these essays, I found that my interactions and conversations with many of these mentors and friends came to life again.

CHAPTER 1

MUTATIONS OF THE WORDSWORTHIAN CHILD OF NATURE

Drawing on a vast range of written documents—from letters, essays, and reviews to poems and novels—Knoepflmacher demonstrates that the internal relations among nineteenth-century writers (contemporaries and predecessors) are crucially important as, themselves, "readings" that alter the history of literature as it is made. Taking the iconic trope of the Wordsworthian Child of Nature, articulated most forcefully in *The Prelude* and in "Ode: Intimations of Immortality," he analyzes the mutations of this figure as formal expressions of deep-rooted historical and ideological changes. Close analysis of numerous Victorian texts leads him to note a revaluing of retrospection; a narrative separation, rather than Romantic integration, of child and adult; and a shifting of cultural power away from imagination toward reason and duty. For many later writers and social critics, the Wordsworthian child served as a key reference point to express ambivalence about the social order in which they lived. Later writers, he shows, critiqued the trope, ridiculing or transforming both its transcendent and literal potential. In so doing, they drew out a powerful but latent self-questioning strand already present in the Wordsworthian ideal. Yet, at the same time, later British writers rearticulated Wordsworth's notion of adult life as a prison house. Although they may have challenged his idealization of the child as blessed seer, they also recapitulated his main beliefs. As a result, his poetry virtually enabled much future literature.

In the summer of 1911, the novelist Mary Augusta Arnold Ward undertook a sentimental pilgrimage to the Westmoreland countryside where she had lived as a child half a century before. The destination of Mrs. Ward was not Fox How, however, the home that had shaped her identity as an Arnold; instead she chose to stay at Rydal Mount, Wordsworth's old home available for summer rental. The poet had died a year before she was born, but her grandmother (Thomas Arnold's widow), her father, and her aunts and uncles exulted in the short-lived friendship that had existed between Wordsworth and the Headmaster of Rugby. Wordsworth, they recalled, had preferred to meet his neighbor on lonely mountain walks rather than be surrounded by Arnold's children and pupils who yelped, according to the great Solitary, "like little dogs" (Ward, *Writer's* 102). Years later, she proudly claimed to remember "vividly" (109) the experience of sitting "on a footstool at Mrs. Wordsworth's feet" (109) around 1856 or 1857. Her description of this event is rendered in diction that is itself Wordsworthian: "I can still recall the childish feeling that this was no common visit, and the house no common house—that a presence still haunted it. Instinctively the childish mind said to itself, 'Remember!'—and I have always remembered" (109). Clearly that early "spot of time" (see Wordsworth, *Prelude* XII: 208–10) influenced her decision to return in 1911 to "the valley of Wordsworth and Arnold; the valley where Arnold's poet-son rambled as a boy; where, for me, the shy and passionate ghost of Charlotte Brontë still haunts the open doorway of Fox How; where poetry and generous life and ranging thought still have their home" (Ward 9–10).

Mrs. Ward's first work of fiction, *Milly and Olly: Or, a Holiday Among the Mountains* (1881), had also involved a return to "the dear mountain country" of her childhood memories. In that book, written for her own children, two citified Victorian children who have "scarcely ever seen a hill higher than the church steeple" (21) are taken to the more elemental natural world known by their mother as a child. Windermere Lake and Rydal Lake and Mount Brownholme impress them with indelible memories. Even during days marred by pouring rain, their minds are fertilized: Milly's mother, Mrs. Norton, stimulates her daughter's imagination by making her copy "some verses of a poem called 'Lucy Gray.'" Using a "big map of Westmoreland" (194), she recreates Wordsworth's *Guide to the Lake Country* by taking Milly on a "pretendy drive" (194).

Yet this childhood journey is not wholly regressive. Although Mrs. Ward wants to immerse Milly and Olly in a landscape suffused by "natural piety"

(Wordsworth, "My Heart Leaps Up" 9), she is also clearly distrustful of the asocial gratifications that such an immersion might produce. Wordsworth's Child of Nature is, for her, no father of the man. Wordsworth's children, she implies, are egoists consumed by their oneness with Nature: Johnny Foy forgets his social mission in his delighted absorption of a moon-bathed landscape; Lucy Gray flees the world of her parents to vanish in the snowstorm; and little Edward in "Anecdote for Fathers," the small girl in "We Are Seven," and the dear child who stands by the seashore in "It Is a Beauteous Evening, Calm and Free"—are all creatures who defy and thwart the alien logic imposed on their experiences by the adult mind. In contrast, Milly and Olly never escape the grasp of their parents. Though allowed to taste Wordsworthian delights, they must be educated as potential adults who are told edifying tales of heroism, self-sacrifice, and repression by their parents and who must witness the conversion of a genuine Wordsworthian child, the sprightly Tina Backhouse, into a penitent little Victorian.

At the end of *Milly and Olly* the children have learned that Nature can be at best a temporary retreat: "Goodbye river, goodbye stepping-stones, goodbye doves, goodbye fly-catchers! Mind don't any of you go away till we come back again!" (351). Mrs. Norton may shed some natural tears—tears not too deep for words, however, for the narrator helpfully explains that "to the old people there is nothing sweeter than to see the young opening their hearts to all that they themselves have loved and rejoiced over" (352). Children must walk on stepping-stones that lead to maturity; the adults who guide their steps can find pleasure by remembering their own toddling. The book's emphasis is on social growth: the Nortons must return to the city, the seat of adult responsibility. Nature and "childish feeling," though important, must be left behind as a mere foundation for the development of higher duties.

Mrs. Ward's recollections of the Wordsworth she associated with her own "childish mind" (*Writer's* I: 109) continued to surface in her later thesis-novels: in *David Grieve* (1892), for instance, the hero proudly displays a first edition of *Lyrical Ballads* amidst his bookstall in grimy Manchester. By the summer of 1911, however, when the exhausted sixty-year-old novelist moved into Rydal Mount, the need to revive the old associations had acquired a new urgency. Wordsworth responded to Mrs. Ward's call; yet, like Cathy in *Wuthering Heights*, his specter appeared, not to the called, but to a surrogate, Mrs. Ward's oldest daughter Dorothy, the Milly of that earlier holiday among the mountains. As in *Wuthering Heights* and in many a Romantic poem, bright moonlight streamed through open casements when a ghostly presence manifested itself. Yet what the awakened

Dorothy saw was not a plaintive waif but the figure "of an old man sitting in the arm-chair by the window" (I: 111). It was William Wordsworth, of course, looking down "straight in front of him with a rapt expression" (I: 111). Next morning the "striking vision" (I: 112) duly reported by Dorothy to her mother was quickly domesticated. Like Lockwood, Mrs. Ward decided that the apparition was but "an example of the influence of mind and association on the visualizing power of the brain" (I: 112)—resorting now less to Wordsworth's diction than to that of T. H. Huxley (her sister's father-in-law). Yet her unbelief could not quite dislodge her wonder. By what strange "coincidence" (I: 112) had her daughter Dorothy unknowingly chosen the bedroom in which her namesake Dorothy Wordsworth had spent her last "sad years of death-in-life" (I: 112)? The apparition itself had an emblematic value on which Mrs. Ward could freely expound: "In that very corner by the window Wordsworth must have sat, day by day, when he came to visit what remained to him of that creature of fire and dew, that child of genius, who had been the inspiration and support of his poetic youth" (I: 112).

As in *Milly and Olly,* child and adult are again in apposition, yet now the emphasis is on mourning rather than on continuity and growth. Mrs. Ward's account of the sad apparition seen by her daughter—herself no longer a child but a matron like her mother—displays a characteristic Victorian ambivalence toward that elementary creature of "fire and dew" that Wordsworth sought in Dorothy, in his own recollections of childhood, in the mythic archetype of the divine Child of Nature. This archetype—which Carl Jung and Karl Kerényi would eventually codify as a symbolic representation of the universal search for an elemental harmony "born out of the womb of the unconscious, begotten out of the depths of human nature, or rather out of living Nature herself" (89)—clearly had its appeal for Mrs. Ward's Victorian mind. Wordsworth's successors, too, had attempted to deify the "child of pure unclouded brow / And dreaming eyes of wonder" (Carroll 135, 1–2 of prefatory poem in *Through the Looking-Glass*). Yet the Victorian eulogies of the natural child remain tentative, qualified by irony, inevitably circumscribed by "the limited range of our conscious mind" (Jung and Kerényi 89). It is no coincidence that the ghost encountered by Mrs. Ward's daughter should appear indoors rather than outdoors and in the shape of an elegiac mourner whose deep distress for a dying sister has both humanized and crippled his soul. He is the author of the "Ode to Duty," so dear to the Victorians, not the writer of "Lucy Gray," the celebrant of the asocial gratifications experienced by the Child of Nature.

As we shall see, Mrs. Ward's description of an old Wordsworth looking with melancholy at lost "inspiration and support" aptly fits those Victorian poets, essayists, and novelists who clung to Wordsworth's elementary creatures in their efforts to redefine the connections between the human and the natural. The Wordsworthian Child of Nature survives in the productions of its Victorian successors, but it survives in altered shapes, mutations that call attention to a new relation between self and Nature. There is a mixture of nostalgia and criticism in the Victorian treatment of the Wordsworthian child; at times the nostalgia outweighs the criticism, while at other times the criticism overwhelms the nostalgia. The nostalgia stems from an unacknowledged kinship with Wordsworth's desire to recover an undifferentiated self—from an appreciation of the symbolic content of his attempts to find wholeness by linking children to Nature and to the world of instinct. The criticism, on the other hand, arises out of skepticism and doubt that have their roots in empirical observation. Nature, after all, may be indifferent or antipathetic to the human urge for integration of self with not-self; children, likewise, far from divine, may be only reduced adults who lack adult understanding.

The conjunction of these two attitudes yields a variety of resolutions. Still, almost all the writers examined in the sections that follow retain the triad of child, landscape, and adult observer found in Wordsworth's poetry. And to this triad they add, significantly enough, a fourth element—William Wordsworth himself. Whether invoked directly or indirectly, whether parodied or adapted, the older poet acts as a point of reference for the Victorian writer, a shade sadly surveying—as in Mrs. Ward's elegiac account—each writer's transmogrification of that earlier child of fire and dew.

———◆———

If Mrs. Wards's association with Wordsworth was secondhand, her uncle Matthew Arnold's familiarity with the poet was more direct. In his 1879 essay on Wordsworth (the preface to his selection of Wordsworth's poetry), Arnold proudly insisted that he had been "brought up in veneration" of this "pure and sage master" and, like his niece, pointedly reminded his readers that he had lived in Wordsworth's "neighborhood, and been familiar with his country" (Preface xxvi). Yet Arnold's "veneration" certainly seems most qualified in one of his earliest poems, written in direct refutation of Wordsworth's exaltation of the divine Child of Nature. His brother Thomas (Mrs. Ward's father) recalled the circumstances of the poem's composition in his obituary of its author: "In 1843 or 1844 the family passed part of the long vacation at Douglas in the Isle of Man. Matthew and a companion were one afternoon on the pier . . . in front of them stood a poor woman; she might have been a gipsy . . . she was looking down at the steamer, and the child in her arms was looking backwards over her shoulder. Its pitiful wan face and dark eyes rested on Matthew for some time without change in expression" (Arnold, *Poems* as qtd. in Allott 22). The poem that was to arise out of this chance encounter was "To a Gipsy Child By the Sea-Shore: Douglas, Isle of Man," first published in 1849 and extensively revised twenty years later.[1]

It is easy to conjecture why this particular scene should have led the young Matthew to write a poem that adopts, yet radically alters, Wordsworth's cherished belief that "in a season of calm weather" ("Ode" 166), the adult mind can recover glimpses of a primordial body of water and "see the Children sport upon the shore, / And hear the mighty waters rolling ever more" (170–71). Wordsworth had attempted to recover this oceanic feeling at the same site a decade before. Nine of the sonnets of the sequence titled "Poems Composed or Suggested During a Tour in 1833" record the old poet's impressions during his sojourn at the Isle of Wight. Of these, sonnets XII, "In the Channel, Between the Coast of Cumberland and the Isle of Man"; XIV, "At Sea Off the Isle of Man"; and XVI, "By the Seashore, Isle of Man" contain tentative reassertions of an old Romantic "Imaginative Faith" (XIV: 10) now branded as a "past illusion" by "Science" and "conquering Reason" (XIV: 1–7). In "By the Sea-Shore, Isle of Man," the best of this sequence, Wordworth resorts to the image of a "sleeping infant's brow, or wakeful eye / Of a young maiden" (7–8) to affirm that the "sparkling Brine" (1) before him, unstained, clear, and crystalline, suggests "something of benign" (5). A return to an undifferentiated world seems momentarily possible:

> Our daily raiment seems no obstacle
> To instantaneous plunging in, deep Sea!
> And revelling in long embrace with thee. (12–14)

We may easily assume that Matthew Arnold recalled these sonnets on revisiting the same scene and encountering the wakeful eye of an actual young maiden. The child's supposed or real gipsy character would have added an

---

1. As the late Geoffrey Tillotson noted, Thomas Arnold's dating of the event may have been incorrect. See Allott's edition of Arnold's poems (22).

extra poignancy to the young poet's eager subversion of Wordsworth's favorite emblem for oneness with Nature. In chapter 22 of *Biographia Literaria*, in a passage immediately preceding that in which he ridicules Wordsworth's idealization of the child as a "seer blest," Coleridge had quoted from Wordsworth's "Gipsies" for another specimen of the "characteristic defects" of his friend's poetry and had faulted Wordsworth for his presumed lack of sympathy with "the poor tawny wanderers" whose indolence is so unfavorably compared to the active motions of Nature (259). Coleridge's point is essentially moralistic: love of Nature has led *away* from love of man.

Arnold's "To a Gipsy Child by the Sea-Shore" intensifies Coleridge's criticism. In "It is a Beauteous Evening, Calm and Free," Wordsworth had employed the child "untouched by solemn thought" (10) to betoken an absorption in Nature no longer possible for the adult speaker. In "To a Gipsy Child," Arnold inverts the emphasis and attributes to the gloomy child his own adult awareness of stoical suffering: "thou has foreknown the vanity of hope, / Foreseen thy harvest—yet proceed'st to live" (39–40). Instead of addressing a child of hope, whose intimations of oneness can give joy to adults alienated from Nature, the speaker recognizes in the "meditative guise" (3) of the gipsy child his own adult despondency over a universe of fragmentation and pain. The eyes of this child, like those of Hardy's soulful Father Time, are precocious, prematurely adult:

> Thou, drugging pain by patience; half averse
> From thine own mother's breast, that knows not thee;
> With eyes which sought thine eyes thou didst converse,
> And that soul-searching vision fell on me. (13–16)

Had Arnold's poem concluded with these lines, his inversion of Wordsworth's "Ode: Intimations of Immortality" would have been effective. The first sixteen lines of "To a Gipsy Child" deftly create a new context for the questions with which Wordsworth concludes the first movement of his famous ode: "Whither is fled the visionary gleam? / Where is it now, the glory and the dream?" (56–57). Arnold, too, opens with a series of questions:

> Who taught this pleasing to unpractised eyes?
> Who hid such import in an infant's gloom?
> Who lent thee, child, this meditative guise?
> Who massed, round that slight brow, these clouds of doom? (1–4)

Wordsworth's unthinking "Child of Joy" has become a pensive child of gloom bereft of all "superfluity of joy" (9); the babe that so eagerly leaped up in its mother's arms is transformed into a stoic thinker who turns away from her "own mother's breast" (14). And Nature herself, which the speaker of the ode tries to reanimate with the former visionary gleam, has become fitful, fallen, indifferent. Wordsworth seeks to isolate a single tree and a single field only to find that "both of them speak of something that is gone" (53). Arnold recalls the line and invests it with an even greater impermanence: "Lo! Sails that gleam a moment and we are gone" (5).

Yet "To a Gipsy Child" is intended as more than a mere extension or reply to the expostulation of the first half of Wordsworth's ode. In lines 17–68 of his poem Arnold needlessly prolongs his apostrophes and rhetorical questions because he is eager to undermine the more mythic second half of the ode. The unending catalogue of fictional stereotypes—a solitary mountain hermit, an exile, a fallen angel, a stoic soul (like Wordsworth, "self-centred, stern" [32]), "some gray-haired king" (33), and "gray-haired scholars" (42)—is recited to counter Wordsworth's own fiction of the child as Mighty Prophet. The "trailing clouds of glory" (65) with which Wordsworth covers the child become, in Arnold's handling, "the soiled glory and the trailing wing" (56). If Wordsworth asserts that the luminous child can lead us back to embers that lie deep in our memory, Arnold rhetorically proclaims that a universal darkness envelops child and adult alike:

> What heavens, what earth, what suns shalt thou discern?
> Ere the long night, whose stillness brooks no star,
> Match that funereal aspect with her pall,
> I think thou wilt have fathomed life too far,
> Have known too much—or else forgotten all. (44–48)

Memory is still preferable to oblivion. But that memory is one of adult experience and sorrow rather than an intimation of childish innocence and joy.

"To a Gipsy Child" fails as a poem because Arnold's attempts to invert Wordsworth's most famous production only led him, ironically enough, to emulate the very bombast that Coleridge had professed to find in portions of the ode. By choosing an actual and particular child for his poem, Arnold tacitly agreed with Coleridge's contention that Wordsworth's mythic Child of Nature was an inadequately universalized emblem. Arnold's gipsy girl, however, never becomes substantial. She is nothing more than an occasion, a mere peg for a young poet's capricious associations. Max Beerbohm's famous cartoon, "William Wordsworth, in the Lake District, at Cross-Purposes," also captures Arnold's own encounters with his soiled Child of Nature. In Beerbohm's cartoon, a bent bespectacled old man stiffly interrogates a little girl standing by the lakeshore; both figures are clearly uncomfortable and have little in common besides the pelting rain from which both seem eager to flee.

The speaker of "To a Gipsy Child" reveals the same stiffness. Like the discomfited narrator of Wordsworth's "We Are Seven," he winds up dissociating himself from the child who has elicited his attention. In "We Are Seven," however, this dissociation is intentional: the speaker who belabors the uncomprehending girl ironically exposes his own, far greater incomprehension. In Arnold's poem, the poet's verbose detachment from the mute child remains unintentionally ironic; his "real," non-Wordsworthian child is but a literary device, an adjunct in a rhetorical effort to discredit Wordsworth's precedent. The "dramatic ventriloquism" that Coleridge found in some of Wordsworth's poems is nowhere more evident than in the young Arnold's use of the gipsy child as a puppet.

In his 1879 selection of Wordsworth's poetry, Arnold pointedly omitted all of the Isle of Man sonnets, although he did reprint "We Are Seven" (which had remained popular and had been illustrated by several Victorian engravers) and included "Anecdote for Fathers." Yet he deliberately placed "Ode: Intimations of Immortality" together with poems such as "Laodamia," "Dion," "Ode to Lycoris," and "Ode to Duty" in a section titled "Poems Akin to the Antique, and Odes," thereby directly and knowingly contravening Wordsworth's express desire to have his ode stand as a separate selection in any edition of his poems. Arnold's introductory essay indirectly explains his motives:

> Even the "intimations of" the famous Ode, those cornerstones of the supposed philosophical system of Wordsworth,—the idea of the high instincts and affections coming out in childhood, testifying of a divine home recently left, and fading away as our life proceeds,—this idea, of undeniable beauty as a play of fancy, has itself not the character of poetic truth of the best kind; *it has no real solidity.* The instinct of delight in Nature and her beauty had no doubt an extraordinary strength in Wordsworth himself as a child. But to say that universally this instinct is mighty in childhood, and tends to die afterwards, is to say what is extremely doubtful. In many people, perhaps with the majority of educated persons, the love of nature is nearly imperceptible at ten years old, but strong and operative at thirty. (Arnold, Preface xx)

As in the poem he had published exactly thirty years before he wrote these remarks, Arnold persists in opposing an adult and "educated" Victorian consciousness to Wordsworth's regressive cult of the Child of Nature.

Matthew Arnold's dissociation from what he caustically dubs "the high instincts" of early childhood was characteristic of other Victorian poets who likewise chose to dramatize the gap between the educated adult and the child tutored by Nature. Despite their frequently sentimental, even saccharine, portraits of divine and innocent children, the Victorians tended to look skeptically at the Wordsworthian child. If "To a Gipsy Child" unconsciously imitates the distance between child and adult that Wordsworth had ironically handled in "We Are Seven" and "Anecdote for Fathers," other poets restored deliberate parody to widen the rift. Charles Stuart Calverley's delightful "The Schoolmaster Abroad With His Son" is one such piece. In "Anecdote for Fathers," Wordsworth had favorably contrasted "little Edward's" (37) illogic to the need for logic of his adult companions; in his parody, Calverley cleverly reverses the emphasis. In his poem the Edward who rambles with his father on a jaunt through Nature is not the "dearest, dearest boy" (Calverley 57) apostrophized by Wordsworth, but, quite to the contrary, a boy who proves a nuisance to his learned parent. The poem begins auspiciously:

> O what harper could worthily harp it,
>   Mine Edward! This wide-stretching wold
> (Look out *wold*) with its wonderful carpet
>   Of emerald, purple, and gold!
> Look well at it—also look sharp, it
>   Is getting so cold. (Calverley 85, 1–6)

Soon, however, the schoolmasterish habits displayed by the speaker turn into an exasperating botany lecture unheeded by his pupil.

> The purple is heather (*erica*);
>   The yellow, gorse—call'd sometimes "whin."
> Cruel boys on its prickles might spike a
>   Green beetle as if on a pin.
> You may roll in it, if you would like a
>   Few holes in your skin.
>
> You wouldn't? Then think of how kind you
>   Should be to the insects who crave

> Your compassion—and then, look behind you
>   At yon barley-ears! Don't they look brave
> As they undulate (*undulate,* mind you,
>   From *unda, a wave*). (Calverley 86, 7–18)

As the poem continues, it becomes increasingly evident that the speaker is as distanced from the child, as both are from a landscape that is being used as a backdrop for a lesson better delivered in a classroom. The "educated" speaker is overeducated; the unconscious child is so unconscious that it promptly falls asleep:

> How it interests e'en a beginner
>   (Or *tiro*) like dear little Ned!
> Is he listening? As I am a sinner
>   He's asleep—he is wagging his head.
> Wake up! I'll go home to my dinner,
>   And you to your bed. (Calverley 87, 31–36)

The poem capitalizes on the same lack of communion and reciprocity dramatized in Calverley's "Wanderers," almost as superb a parody of "Resolution and Independence" as "The White Knight's Song" by Calverley's friend and correspondent Lewis Carroll. It ends with the schoolmaster's abject recognition that his is, after all, not the Wordsworthian mode:

> The splendor of mountain and lake
> With their hues that seem ever to vary;
>   The mighty pine-forests which shake
> In the wind, and in which the unwary
>   May tread on a snake;
>
> And this wold with its heathery garment
>   Are themes undeniably great.
> But—although there is not any harm in't—
>   It's perhaps little good to dilate
> On their charms to a dull little varmint
>   Of seven or eight. (Calverley 87, 38–48)

In a penetrating essay on Calverley, written in 1901, Francis Thompson argued that it was Calverley's Arnoldian reverence for the classics that converted him into "the first of the parodists": "his parodies are likewise criticisms, and very keen criticisms, of a poet's weaker side" (*Literary* 268). The remark is just. Yet Calverley not only pokes fun at Wordsworth's deification of all those little Edwards untouched by thought who wander through Nature's heathery garments; he also acknowledges what Wordsworth himself had stressed: thought and language embody our alienation from the simplicity shared by Nature and the child.

Thompson himself in the early 1890s demonstrated the truth of Calverley's insight. Two poems in the section he titled "Poems on Children"— "The Poppy" and "Daisy"—make a similar point, albeit seriously. Both render the familiar situation: adult and girl walk together through a lush landscape; both contrast the painfully self-conscious and time-obsessed adult to the child immersed in Nature. In "The Poppy," the flower of sleep ironically startles the speaker. He has viewed the poppy erotically "as a swinkéd gipsy" and "mouth wide a-pout for a sultry kiss" (*Poems* 3; 10, 11)[2] But the child's gift of the flower mocks him and her and their association: "I am but, my sweet, your foster-lover, / Knowing well when certain years are over / You vanish from me to another" (5; 55–57). In "Daisy," too, the "tokens" given to the speaker by the little girl painfully remind him of the impossibility of regressing to her sexually innocent world. Deliberately echoing Wordsworth's "She Dwelt Among the Untrodden Ways," Thompson bemoans the difference to him:

> She went her unremembering way,
>   She went and left in me
> The pang of all the partings gone
>   And partings yet to be. (2; 45–58)

"Daisy" concludes on a note of melancholy that is all the more moving because the little girl, unlike Arnold's thoughtful gipsy child, is so oblivious to mutability and pain. The conclusion, too, contains a denial of Wordsworth's yearned-for return to happier origins in Nature:

> Nothing begins, and nothing ends,
>   That is not paid with moan;
> For we are born in other's pain,
>   And perish in our own. (3; 45–48)

---

2. "The Daisy" and "Poppy" were first published in *Merry England* in March 1890 and August 1891, respectively, and reprinted in the 1893 edition of *The Poems of Francis Thompson*.

But the most consummate treatment in Victorian poetry of the Wordsworthian triad of Nature, child, and adult observer does not come in Thompson's mournful poetry of despair but rather in that of his fellow Catholic, Gerard Manley Hopkins. The young girl addressed in "Spring and Fall: *to a young child*" is neither as innocent as Thompson's child companion nor as all-knowing as Arnold's gipsy child. Hopkins empathizes with the child's intimations, not of immortality, but of impermanence, the process of decay she witnesses during her first experiences of autumn; the season becomes proleptic of the child's own impending egress from the Eden of Goldengrove into a fallen world:

> Márgarét, are you gríeving
> Over Goldengrove unleaving?
> Leáves, líke the things of man, you
> With your fresh thoughts care for, can you?
> Áh! ás the heart grows older
> It will come to such sights colder
> By and by, nor spare a sigh
> Though worlds of wanwood leafmeal lie;
> And yet you *will* weep and know why. (*Poems* 88–89, 1–9)

Moved by the child's spontaneous grief, her instinctive ability to care for the fallen leaves of the "unleaving" (2) forest, the speaker knows, as she, not yet leaving ("unleaving") her childhood paradise, cannot know: that both he and she are subject to this cyclical process of natural decay. Although other adults may not "spare a sigh" (7) over Nature's relentless decomposition, she will weep and, like the speaker, will *then* know why.

> Now no matter, child, the name:
> Sorrow's springs áre the same. (89, 10–11)

Although Hopkins here denies Wordsworth's fiction of the joyful Child of Nature, he retains the older poet's faith in the spring or "fountainhead" located in the child's more intense capacity to feel. Unlike Arnold, Calverley, or Thompson, Hopkins imposes no adult emotions on the child; he is content to name and to interpret emotions he shares and understands:

> It ís the blight man was born for,
> It is Margaret you mourn for. (89, 14–15)

The child first addressed as "Márgarét" (the accent-marks recalling margarites, a pearl, as well as a Wordsworthian daisy) becomes, in the last line of the poem, an ordinary "Margaret" (recalling now, through the removed accent marks, the words *mar* and *regret*). She has become, like Margaret in Wordsworth's "The Ruined Cottage" (or like Arnold's Marguerite), an adult destined to become consumed by the flux of the natural world. But her powers of sympathy can survive and be retained by a poet who shares Wordsworth's own acute concern with those "obstinate questionings / Of sense and outward things, / Fallings from us, vanishings" ("Ode" 142–44). In his letters Hopkins derisively lashes out at Swinburne's celebration of infants (in poems such as "A Child's Laughter," "Children," "Child and Poet," and "Étude Réaliste") as "*rot* about babies," a "blathery bathos" that almost "makes a Herodian of me"; yet his attitude toward Wordsworth and the Wordsworthian child is always reverential: he speaks of his own poem "The Brothers," another adult observation of children, as "something in Wordsworth's manner" (*Letters* 304) and elsewhere warmly identifies with those Wordsworthians who prize the "Ode: Intimations of Immortality" without any of Arnold's condescension (*Letters* 86).³

In longer verse narratives, the Child of Nature is also invoked, less as an object of contemplation in itself than as an antithesis to stories about adult experience, for Victorian narrative poetry seldom lingers on the youthful spots of time in Nature that arrest Wordsworth in *The Prelude*. In an essay on Browning's poetry, Francis Thompson maintained that "Nature—meaning thereby the external universe—has for the present day a preponderating poetic importance which is to our thinking quite undue"; Thompson lauds Robert Browning for making Nature nothing more than a "background—a sentient and significant background—for the drama of humanity" (*Literary Criticisms* 154).⁴ Thompson's remark can be applied to Browning's use of a Victorianized Lucy Gray in his poetic drama *Pippa Passes* (1841). If Lucy's solitary song can be heard only at "the break of day" by an equally solitary poet in Nature, the songs of the "little black-eyed pretty Felippa" act as a connecting device to enlighten the lives of Browning's worldly men and women. The speaker of "Lucy Gray" cannot, or does not want to, repro-

---

3. In defending Wordsworth's "Ode" against Canon Dixon, Hopkins asserts that Wordsworth, like Plato, was one of a few men in history to whom something happened that "does not happen to other men"; thus, when he wrote the ode, "human nature got another of these shocks, and the tremble of its spreading. This opinion I do strongly share; I am, ever since I knew the ode, in that tremble" (*Correspondence* 147–48).

4. According to Thompson, Browning's use of Nature merely reflects a "primal interest in man" (*Literary Criticisms* 156).

duce the words of the girl's eerie song. By way of contrast, Pippa's songs are carefully reproduced, even if their essence is presumably nonverbal:

> Overhead the tree-tops meet,
> Flowers and grass spring 'neath one's feet
> There was naught above me, naught below,
> My childhood had not learned to know:
> For what are the voices of birds
> —Ay, and of beasts,—but words, words,
> Only so much more sweet? (IV: 174–80)

Despite this insistence on a primordial world of treetops, flowers, and grass, Pippa's importance lies in her effect on her listeners in the poem. It is their corruption, rather than her inviolable innocence, that gives the poem its dramatic interest.

To most Victorian poets, the Wordsworthian Child of Nature could at best act as a reference point for their ambivalence about social order. In Tennyson's *Idylls of the King* the unspoiled "maiden babe" called "Nestling" is invoked at the opening of "The Last Tournament" (1871). When the knights vie over the ruby carcanet of the child who died after being touched by Guinevere, the "Tournament of Innocence" degenerates into a bloody Darwinian contest in which men "reel back into the beast" (1708, 125). Even in *In Memoriam* (which in 1850 had overshadowed the appearance of *The Prelude*), Tennyson invokes the child only to identify with the precariousness of its strivings for security and certainty. Seen through the "freezing" glare of reason, the world of Nature yields no unified "He, They, One, All" (Tennyson CXXIV: 974, 14; 973, 3). Relief can come through regression, not because a lapse into childishness permits a glimpse of some immortal sea but quite to the contrary: because such a relapse at least constitutes an acknowledgment of man's utter helplessness and dependence. Tennyson's child is no mighty prophet or seer blessed:

> No, like a child in doubt and fear:
> But that blind clamor made me wise,
> Then was I as a child that cries
> But, crying, knows his father wise;
>
> And what I am beheld again
> What is, and no man understands,

And out of darkness came the hands
That reach thro' nature, moulding man. (CXXIV: 17–24)

Like Arnold's gipsy child, or Calverley's Edward, or Thompson's girl companion, or Browning's Pippa, or even Hopkins's Margaret, this figure remains an adult in miniature. Not until Yeats's "Among School Children" would English poets attempt to recover the bonds and the vital sense of unity with Nature that the child had betokened for Wordsworth. For Victorian prose writers and novelists, however, who were able psychologically to probe into the recesses of the child's mind and more minutely analyze its natural environment, the options were far more diverse.

In 1858 John Ruskin, still at work on the fifth and final volume of *Modern Painters* (1860), read "Lucy Gray" in "an exquisitely beautiful manner" to a highly receptive audience, declaring himself aware of "the efforts now being made to depreciate that great poet" Wordsworth. Ruskin vowed that such derogations would "never be successful" (Ruskin, *Works* XVI: 459). The anti-Wordsworthian "efforts" to which Ruskin so obscurely alluded may well have been his very own, for Ruskin openly joined the ranks of Wordsworth derogators in the fifth volume of *Modern Painters* (see Rosenberg 23ff; Landow 232–36). There he rejected the fostering Nature that earlier had for him been the essence of all "purist" art, and, simultaneously, he withdrew the assent he had formerly given to the Wordsworthian ideal of a childhood enriched by that benign Nature. Two decades later, in *Fiction, Fair and Foul* (1880–81), where not only Wordsworth's fictions but also those of Dickens and George Eliot are under severe attack, Ruskin's disenchantment reached an almost vituperative intensity. Apparently stung by "Mr. Matthew Arnold's arrangement" and "his high estimate" of Wordsworth's poems, Ruskin seeks to restore a proper perspective: "though it is very proper that Silver [*sic*] How should clearly understand and brightly praise its fraternal Rydal Mount, we must not forget that, over yonder, are the Andes all the while" (XXXIV: 318). Contrasted to true artists poised on Parnassian peaks, Wordsworth seems but a "pleasant fingerer of his pastoral flute," simply "a Westmoreland peasant, with considerable less shrewdness than most border Englishmen or Scotsmen inherit" (XXXIV: 318).

Like Arnold, Ruskin maintained throughout his life a proprietary interest in Wordsworth, and he returned, significantly enough, to the Wordsworthian mode of retrospection in his *Praeterita,* the truncated autobiography he began in 1885. The young Ruskin, however, had clung to Wordsworth most steadfastly (and far less critically than the young Arnold of Fox How). Wordsworth happened to witness the tremulous Oxford undergraduate's recitation of his prize poem in 1839; he is in evidence, too, in "The Gipsies," a poem that Ruskin had unsuccessfully submitted for the same prize in 1837. In that poem, far more Wordsworthian in its allegiances than Arnold's "To a Gipsy Child," Ruskin does not shy away from entering the persona of a solitary adolescent, a "gentle boy, who shunned his playmates rude, / To seek the silver voice of solitude, / And, by some stream, amidst the shadows grey / Of arching boughs, to muse the hours away, / Smiled" (*Poems* 47, 118–22). Even before his Oxford years, as an eleven-year-old in 1830, Ruskin had modeled his "Iteriad; or, Three Weeks Among the Lakes" on "The Excursion," the same poem from which he chose an epigraph for the first volume of *Modern Painters* (1843), a choice noted and approved by Wordsworth, who even bought a copy of the book. In the "Iteriad," a series of verse-letters written to his parents, the boy recorded his impressions of all the hallowed Wordsworthian sites—Grasmere, Helvellyn, Keswick, Buttermere, Coniston, and Mount Skiddaw. The incomplete childish effusions were to have ended with the crowning sight of "old Mr. Wordsworth at the chapel of Rydal, / Whom we had the honour of seeing beside all" (*Works* II: 315).

Ruskin's rejection of his own youthful Wordsworthianism began, as Francis G. Townsend has recognized, in *Modern Painters* III, where in a chapter titled "The Moral Landscape" he methodically discredits Wordsworth's notion that "the intense delight which he himself felt, and which he supposed other men feel, in nature, during their thoughtless youth" was nothing less than an "intimation of their immortality" (*Works* V: 363–64; Townsend 73). Like the Arnold of the 1879 "Preface," Ruskin doubts whether a youth could feel "so strongly as the man, because the man knows more, and must have more ideas" (V: 364). But unlike Arnold, and very much like a novelist, Ruskin also is willing to conduct a scrupulous psychological "self-examination" to determine whether "this strange delight in nature" (V: 364) deserves Wordsworth's claims. A scrutiny of his own recollections as a Child of Nature, Ruskin insists, is undertaken, not out of egotism, but because of his own special qualifications. He, too, he suggests, was once a Wordsworthian child: "whatever other faculties I may or may not possess, this gift of taking pleasure in landscape I assuredly possess, in a greater degree than most men" (V: 365).

Ruskin hints that, like the "babe in arms" of *The Prelude*, he too has had fair seed-time for his soul:

> The first thing which I remember, as an event in life, was being taken by my nurse to the brow of Friar's Crag on Derwent Water; the intense joy, mingled with awe, that I had in looking through the hollows of the mossy roots, over the crag, into the dark lake, has associated itself with all twining roots of trees ever since. (V: 365)

After recounting two other early memories, Ruskin analyzes their import:

> In such journeyings, whenever they brought me near the hills, and in all the mountain ground and scenery, I had a pleasure, as early as I can remember, and continuing till I was eighteen or twenty, infinitely greater than any which has since been possible to me in anything. (V: 365)

Though sensing in his experiences the same process described by Wordsworth in "Tintern Abbey," Ruskin does not undertake this recreation of his early feelings in Nature for its own sake; instead, he calculatedly enlists his memories in a polemic directed against Wordsworth's separation of the child's mystic feelings from the adult's sobered thoughts. To him, the child brings to Nature the ready-made associations and thoughts of his early reasoning self. There is no immanence in Nature, no definite "religious feeling," to be extracted from mountains and glens. Ruskin insists that it was his own reading of books (particularly Scott's novels) that made the scenery seem "enchanted" to him; it was his birth in London, with "no other prospect than that of brick walls," that conferred on the landscape an unusual charm "which a country-bred child would not have felt" (V: 366). Children bring to Nature the constituent elements of their personality. The pleasure of "pure landscape-instinct" (V: 368) may be safe and good; yet it may also be seductive and evil, a "joy only to the inactive and the visionary, incompatible with the duties of life" (V: 354). Even the element of novelty and surprise, those "interventions" that are akin to the divine for Wordsworth, may be nothing more than "a suspicious or evanescent element":

> I think that what Wordsworth speaks of as a glory to the child, because it has come fresh from God's hands, is in reality nothing more than the freshness of all things to newly opened sight. I find that by keeping long away from the hills, I can in great part still restore the old childish feeling about them; and the more I live and work among them, the more it vanishes." (V: 369)[5]

---

5. That Ruskin had little need for the surrounding hills while he lived and worked among

This new insistence on an empirical "reality" is in full evidence in *Modern Painters* V, where, as John Rosenberg and George P. Landow have shown, Ruskin continuously stresses the "insufficiency of the Wordsworthian view of nature" (Rosenberg 23; also see Landow 232). As Landow points out, Ruskin opposes the quietism of a "Scotch clergyman" who had described a "scene in the Highlands to show (he said) the goodness of God" (*Works* VII: 268). In reexamining the scene from his new Turnerian perspective, Ruskin beholds a far more gruesome landscape. The observer of such misery, Ruskin implies, can no longer be a complacent Wordsworthian: "Truly, this Highland and English scenery is fair enough; but it has shadows; and deeper colouring, here and there, than that of heath and rose" (VII: 270–71).

In *Modern Painters* V, however, Ruskin's most devastating subversion of Wordsworth is directed against the Child of Nature whose early mind is "peopled" by "forms sublime and fair" (*The Prelude* I: 466). It occurs in a chapter in which Wordsworth is never directly mentioned, the celebrated "The Two Boyhoods." In that chapter, Ruskin's Turner is reared among the "booths of a darksome Vanity Fair, busily base" (*Works* VII: 385). Turner's childhood environment thus is not only palpably at odds with that of Giorgione's boyhood, so lavishly described, but also pointedly unlike the self-enclosed basin that sequestered Wordsworth's most precious spots of time.

Ruskin portrays Giorgione's golden Venice through images of water, breeze, and mountain that are suspiciously Wordsworthian; indeed, his prose can almost be scanned as stately blank verse: the Venetian world from which "all ignoble care and petty thoughts were banished" becomes, in Ruskin's ringing description, an airy construct with "winds and fiery clouds ranging at their will;—brightness out of the north, and balm from the south, and the stars of evening and morning clear in the limitless light of arched heaven and circling sea (VII: 375). If the setting of Giorgione's childhood is clear and undisturbed, a city bright and glittering, open to the sky, the cityscape into which Ruskin places the boy Turner is like that "sordor" which twenty years later he would claim only Byron saw: "None of these things very glorious; the best, however, that England, it seems, was then able to provide for a boy of gift" (*Works* XXXIV: 342; VII: 376). The slight is intended. We are invited to recall not only Giorgione but also that other "boy of gift" who roamed the Lake Country—"then," at the same time that the boy Turner makes his way through the cluttered dark city

---

them is demonstrated by the layout of his study at Brantwood, the country house in the Lake District he purchased in 1871. See Ellen E. Frank in Knoepflmacher and Tennyson, 75–77.

and beholds the Thames, "with its stranded barges and glidings of red sail, dearer to us than Lucerne Lake or Venetian lagoon" (*Works* VII: 376–77). Or we may well ask, dearer also now "to us" than that lake Windermere that another boy of gift had celebrated in his "Iteriad" so very long ago?

In "The Two Boyhoods," Ruskin relies on indirection to attack what, in *Fiction, Fair and Foul,* he would eventually brand as Wordsworth's "lacustrine seclusion" (*Works* XXXIV: 317). Unlike Wordsworth, Ruskin's boy Turner does not escape the "meanness, aimlessness, unsightliness of the city" (*Works* VII: 385) but accepts instead the harder burden of a quest for a visible unity. This quest does not lead the boy into hidden valleys of repose such as those in *The Excursion*: "No gentle processions to churchyards among the fields, the bronze crests bossed deep on memorial tablets, and the skylark singing above them from among the corn. But the life trampled out in the slime of the street, crushed to dust amidst the roaring of the wheel, tossed countlessly into howling winter wind along five hundred leagues of rock-fanged shore" (VII: 378).

The same contrast between pastoralism and a dynamic, dusty, and changeful city reality informs the opening of *Fiction, Fair and Foul.* Pretending to yield to a reverie about his "young days" in a green Dulwich, Ruskin begins by alluding to Wordsworth's "To My Sister" and its fantasy of perennial spring: "On the first mild—or, at least, the first bright—day of March, in this year, I walked through what was once a country lane" (*Works* XXXIV: 265). With consummate deception, Ruskin makes the reader believe that he has completely yielded to a reverie about his boyhood in Nature:

> A slender rivulet, boasting little of its brightness, for there are no springs at Dulwich, yet fed purely enough by the rain and morning dew, here trickled—there loitered—through the long grass between the hedges, and expanded itself into moderately clear and deep pools, in which, under their veils of duck-weeds, a fresh-water shell or two, sundry curious little skipping shrimps, any quantity of tadpoles, and even sometimes a tittlebat, offered themselves to my boyhood's pleased, and not inaccurate observation. (XXXIV: 265–66)

But Ruskin loiters in this lane only to shock his readers. The paths where he and his mother "used to gather the first buds of the hawthorn" have become obliterated: "grassless" and "deep-rutted," the lane is now covered by

> mixed dust of every unclean thing that can crumble in drought, and mildew of every unclean thing that can rot or rust in damp: ashes and rags,

beer-bottles and old shoes, battered pans, smashed crockery, shreds of nameless clothes, door-sweepings, floor-sweepings, kitchen garbage, back-garden sewage, old iron, rotten timber with jagged torn-out nails, cigar-ends, pipe-bowls, cinders, bones, and ordure, indescribable" (XXXIV: 266).

Confronted with this chaos, Ruskin asks whether his childhood paradise has ever really existed. And how can "children of to-day," accustomed to the "sight of infinite nastiness," find "food" or "stimulus" (XXXIV: 267) for their own youthful pilgrimages?

In *Fiction, Fair and Foul,* Ruskin not only attacks Dickens for his delight in disorder and violence and George Eliot for reproducing only "blotches, burrs, and pimples" (XXXIV: 377) but also inveighs against the delusive comforts he himself once found in Wordsworth's pastoral bowers. Arnold had preferred Wordsworth's serenity over Byron's discontent as an antidote to the loss of feeling in a mechanical age. But to Ruskin, Scott's presumed religious resistance to natural depravity and Byron's acute awareness of universal pain and evil are superior to the "innocent, unrepentant" mind of a poet who can be "helpful" only to "sinless creatures and scatheless, such of the flock as do not stray" (XXXIV: 320). Like the Ruskin who interpreted Sunday sermons to the little girls at Winnington School, Ruskin's Scott is aware of the child's potential sinfulness, a schoolmaster who can dispense "lessons to his children in Bible history."[6] Ruskin's identification with Byron's "volcanic instinct" is even stronger: "In Byron the indignation, the sorrow, and the effort are joined to death"; they are parts of a nature "from which the piously sentimental public, offering daily the pure oblation of divine tranquility, shrink with anathema" (XXXIV: 344).

In the fourth essay of *Fiction, Fair and Foul,* Ruskin satirized those "bucolic friends" who had chided his preference of Byron over Wordsworth. He excoriates the sentimentalists, the "amiable persons" who, as he once did, "call themselves Wordsworthians," believers "who have read—usually a long time ago—'Lucy Gray,' 'The April Mornings,' a picked sonnet or two, and the 'Ode on the Intimations'" (XXXIV: 349). Earlier, he

---

6. After his unsuccessful attachments to figures of ideal girlhood in Adele Domecq, Effie Gray, and Rose La Touche, Ruskin sought to erect a collective image of an unaging Wordsworthian child; to his "little birds" at Winnington Hall he wrote: "How would you like to be all alike—though you were ever so pretty—ever so good! Fancy coming down in the morning and nobody knowing which was which—nor themselves in the looking glass—having to sew numbers on your sleeves—or tie your hair in different knots—and you know—(there could be only one ideal knot—)—so even that would be unallowable on ideal principles" (letter of March 1859, *The Winnington Letters* 131).

mockingly contrasted Wordsworth's sonnet on Westminster Bridge to some lines from Byron's "Island." Byron is an adult; Wordsworth remains a child:

> While Mr. Wordsworth in irrepressible rapture, calls God to witness that the houses seem asleep, Byron, lame demon as he was, flying smoke-drifted, unroofs the houses at a glance, and sees what the mighty cockney heart of them contains in the still lying of it, and will stir up to purpose in the waking business of it, "The sordor of civilization mixed / With all the passions which Man's fall hath fixed." (XXXIV: 342)

Although by 1884, in *The Art of England,* Ruskin would again become a tentative ally of "Mr. Matthew Arnold and the Wordsworth Society," the man who returned to the satanic "track of Byron" against which his father had warned him in 1837 could no longer abide in Wordsworth's childhood paradise.[7]

If Ruskin's outraged sense of pain and evil made that paradise an impossibility, Walter Pater welcomed the nostalgic process of retrospection by which the adult mind lingers on the child's first word. Pater, too, regards Wordsworth as a quietist who resembled "early Italian or Flemish painters" ("Wordsworth" 44), a purist "tethered down to a world, refined and peaceful indeed, but with no broad outlook" (54). Yet his 1874 essay on Wordsworth delights in those regressive journeys that Ruskin had so ironically rejected:

> It was in this mood that [Wordsworth] conceived those oft-reiterated regrets for a half-ideal childhood, when the relics of Paradise still clung about the soul—a childhood, as it seemed, full of the fruits of old age, lost for all, in a degree, in the passing away of the youth of the world, lost for each one, over again, in the passing away of actual youth." (55)

Pater can thus allow what Ruskin so vehemently denies—the value in everyone's life of remembered childhood Edens, some static abiding place. Demanding *action,* Ruskin had thrust his boy Turner into a hectic and mutable present; contending that "the end of life is not action but contemplation—being as distinct from doing" (62). Pater welcomes Wordsworth's "impassioned contemplation" (60) of an imagined childhood past.

---

7. To Ruskin's father, his son's "evil Genius" was derived from Byron, but John James Ruskin never says whether the "steady and useful light" of John's "good Genius" emanates from Wordsworth. See John James Ruskin, *The Ruskin Family Letters* I: 404.

Whereas Ruskin's "The Two Boyhoods" is both moralistic and reality oriented in its exaltation of Turner's sordid London over the more beautiful, secluded world of Giorgione's (and Wordsworth's) youth, Pater's "The Child in the House" (1878), like the early chapters of *Marius the Epicurean* (1885), resorts to a Wordsworthian exploration of the interaction between outward setting and the child's mind. Yet the environment that stamps the selves of Florian Deleal and of the young Marius is a country house rather than a desolate mountain or lake. Interested in process, rather than in a definable moral influence, Pater admits any external setting:

> For it is false to suppose that a child's sense of beauty is dependent on any choiceness or special fineness, in the objects which present themselves to it, though this indeed comes to be the rule with most of us in a later life; earlier, in some degree, we see inwardly; and the child finds for itself, and with unstinted delight, a difference for the sense, in those whites and reds through the smoke on very homely buildings, and in the gold of dandelion at the road-side, just beyond the houses. (Pater, "The Child" 175)

Ruskin's sharp distinction between an urban world of smoke and dust and a golden world in touch with Nature, Pater seems to say, is meaningless: any external object can serve to help differentiate our childhood selves from the not-self. Thus it is that Pater feels no self-consciousness in *Marius the Epicurean* whenever he connects an imaginary Roman boy to the Cumberland peasants whom Wordsworth actually met (*Marius* I: 5). For Pater, then, who openly acknowledges Wordsworth in his evocations of Florian's and Marius's childhoods, Wordsworth remains a myth-maker whose enduring concerns and archetypes can be of value to all those interested in the formation of character. Pater's insights serve as a helpful bridge for our consideration of the uses of the Wordsworthian child by those bona fide fiction-makers George Eliot and Dickens, whom Ruskin had attacked, together with Wordsworth, in *Fiction, Fair and Foul*. Helpful, too, is Pater's own practice as a novelist. Near the conclusion of *Marius the Epicurean*, Pater has his protagonist revisit his birthplace in the country, an old villa "half-hidden by aged poplar trees" (*Marius* II: 205). Unlike Ruskin's treatment of his return to Dulwich, Marius's revisitation is regarded by Pater as a solemn ritual: soon to die himself, the adult Roman beholds near his mother's funeral urn, the "protruding baby hand" (II: 206) of a boy, long dead, a friend who, like Wordsworth's boy from Winander, "had descended hither, from the lightsome world of childhood, almost at the same time with her" (II: 206). To the brooding Marius, it seems "as if this boy of his own age had taken filial place beside her there, in his stead" (II: 206).

Victorian fiction is full of such revisitations—though not all so lugubrious. At the beginning of *The Mill on the Floss* (1860), the narrator becomes arrested by the "same unresting wheel" (Eliot 8) that hypnotizes the motionless little girl who stands poised "at the edge of the water" (8). Near the end of *Great Expectations* (1860–61), after an eleven-year absence from the forge in the marshes, the adult Pip returns to see a replica of his former self: "there, fenced into the corner with Joe's leg, and sitting on my own little stool looking at the fire, was—I again! (489). In the second book of *The Prelude* Wordsworth had explained that a vacancy between his adult thinking self and his childhood in Nature created a double consciousness:

> The vacancy between me and those days
> Which yet have such self-presence in my mind,
> That musing on them, often do I seem
> Two consciousnesses, conscious of myself
> And of some other being . . . (Wordsworth, *Prelude* II: 29–33)

The Victorian novel in general, and Dickens and George Eliot in particular, exploit this selfsame double vision of an adult self beholding its earlier incarnation. In *Great Expectations,* Pip's "first most vivid and broad impression of the identity of things" among the "marsh country, down by the river" (Dickens 1) is recreated by a remembering adult mind that has painfully traveled far beyond that early state which Wordsworth calls "the eagerness of infantine desire" (*Prelude* II: 24). For Wordsworth, "the fairest of all rivers" (*Prelude* I: 270) could irrigate and replenish the channels of his imagination and become "the river of my mind" (*Prelude* II: 209):

> Oh, many a time have I, a five year's child
> In a small mill-race severed from his stream
> Made one long bathing of a summer's day,
> Basked in the sun, and plunged and basked again. (*Prelude* I: 288–91)

The "bright blue river" that passes along the "margins of our terrace walk" in *The Prelude* remains a therapeutic connection between past and present. For Dickens and George Eliot, however, the dark rivers that connect Pip to Magwitch and reunite Maggie with Tom are laden with far more ominous connotations.

The "peacefulness" (Eliot, *Mill* 8) of the scene described in the opening of *The Mill on the Floss* is highly deceptive: the little rivulet with its "dark, changing wavelets" (7) flows into the mighty Floss that will engulf the Tulliver children. "Nature repairs her ravages but not all" (457). Although *Great Expectations,* too, is set in an earlier, tranquil time, Dickens's imagination never reconstructs a lush pastoral setting such as that which George Eliot uses to lure the reader into sharing little Maggie's obliviousness to time and change. In two successive installments of "The Uncommercial Traveller," written shortly before he began *Great Expectations,* Dickens returned to "scenes among which my earliest days were passed; scenes from which I departed when I was a child, and which I did not revisit until I was a man" (Dickens, "Associations" 274). Like Ruskin, Dickens finds "Dullborough" (Chatham) an irrevocably altered enclave: "the beautiful hawthorn-trees, the hedge, the turf, and all those buttercups and daisies, had given place to the stoniest of jolting roads" (274). In *Great Expectations,* this same stony reality invades Pip's life in the country. We find ourselves in a graveyard, among tombstones that record thwarted expectations. If the narrator and reader of *The Mill on the Floss* must be gently startled to forgo their "love with moistness" (Eliot, *Mill* 8) on a distant February afternoon, Pip and the reader of *Great Expectations* are far more violently jolted. Behind the tombstone springs a "man who had been soaked in water, and smothered in mud, and lamed by stones, and cut by flints, and stung by nettles, and torn by briars" (Dickens, *Great* 2).

In *The Prelude,* Wordsworth had also resorted to terrifying out-of-doors encounters to define Nature's hold on his young imagination; he is startled by shepherds the size of giants "stalking through thick fog" (*Prelude* VIII: 266) and arrested by the sudden appearance of the "uncouth shape" (*Prelude* IV: 387) of the veteran soldier:

>   a more meagre man
> Was never seen before by night or day.
> Long were his arms, pallid his hands; his mouth
> Looked ghastly in the moonlight: from behind
> A mile-stone propped him . . . (IV: 393–97)

Both Dickens and George Eliot appropriated the Wordsworthian Child of Nature to an extent not possible for most of the writers we have so far examined. The George Eliot who wrote *Silas Marner* to offset the grim ending of *The Mill on the Floss* chose to stress the more beneficent aspects of the Wordsworthian vision; Dickens, on the other hand, adapted for his purposes the terror that plays such an important role in *The Prelude*. That George Eliot was even a more confirmed Wordsworthian than Arnold and Ruskin is easily documented: her incorporation of Wordsworth's private mythology in her own pastoral fictions suggests a sympathetic identification perhaps unique among the Victorians. Dickens, though, left little record of any overt indebtedness to the poet who shunned London as a "monstrous ant-hill" (*Prelude* VII: 149) of "modern Merlins / Wild Beasts, Puppet-shows, / All out-o'-the-way, far-fetched perverted things, / All freaks of nature (*Prelude* VI: 713–15). But Wordsworth was hardly uninterested in such freakish mutations. And, as we shall see, the city novelist who promptly bought *The Prelude* on its appearance in 1850 had keen affinities of his own with the bard of Nature.[8]

On 19 October 1860, Wordsworth's contemporary and friend, the eighty-five-year-old Henry Crabb Robinson, recorded the particulars of an "agreeable" meeting with "Miss Evans": "She has quite won on me. . . . I began a course of instruction on Wordsworth's poetry, repeated to her what I could by heart, and . . . devoted several hours to the making out of a list of those of Wordsworth's poems which I thought a beginner ought to read. She will buy his works" (*Henry Crabb Robinson* II: 799). Miss Evans, whose identity as George Eliot had become public knowledge around this time, may not yet have owned her own copy of Wordsworth's collected poems; still, she most assuredly was not the "beginner" Robinson innocently took her to be.

Two decades earlier, Marian Evans had entreated her brother Isaac, on his honeymoon in the Lake District, to bring back "some rose-leaves from Wordsworth's garden" (Eliot, *The George Eliot Letters* I: 99), and thereafter Wordsworth's impact was to endure throughout her literary career. It is manifest in *Adam Bede* (1859), where Arthur Donnithorne's underestimation of a "volume of poems" called *Lyrical Ballads* is ironically exploited by the novelist who adopts the Pastor's words in *The Excursion* as a motto for her own pastoral intentions: "So that ye may [shall] have / Clear images before your gladdened eyes / Of nature's unambitious underwood / And flowers that prosper in the shade" (Wordsworth, *Excursion* VI: 651–54). It is seen again in those eleven sonnets "on the childhood of a brother and sister" and the "mutual influences in their small lives" which George Eliot penned in 1869 (*Letters* V: 403). It is evident in George Eliot's delight in

---

8. Dickens owned an 1836 copy of Wordsworth's *Poetical Works* and an 1850 copy of *The Prelude*.

Modern Painters as an equivalent to "the sublimest parts in Wordsworth" (*Letters* II: 423) and in her regret that Arnold's 1879 selections had omitted some of the "precious lines" she valued as personal touchstones (*Letters* VII: 262). Yet Wordsworth's influence remains most prominent in the childhood portions of *The Mill on the Floss,* which Crabb Robinson had read six months before his meeting with Miss Evans, and in *Silas Marner* (1861), which less than a year later he pronounced to be "a powerful production" (*The Diary of Henry Crabb Robinson* II: 308).

To the octogenarian Robinson, *The Mill* recalled the humor of Jane Austen and the melodrama of Bulwer Lytton but not the rural scene of childhood in Wordsworth's poetry. He was only slightly more discerning in his choice of analogues for the story of Silas—a story of which George Eliot had said that she expected no one to be "interested in it but myself (since William Wordsworth is dead)" (*Letters* III: 382). To be sure, Robinson duly noted the novel's epigraph from Wordsworth's "Michael" ("A child more than all other gifts / That earth can offer to declining man, / Brings hope with it, and forward-looking thoughts" [146–48]). Yet the "motto" only made him ponder the novel's "great affinity to Coleridge's *Ancient Mariner.* . . . A little child, its mother having frozen to death at his solitary hovel, is taken in by Silas. . . . It is to him what the blessing of the animals is to the Ancient Mariner" (*Letters* II: 800–801).

Robinson's locus is correct, even if his particulars remain hazy. Both *The Mill on the Floss* and *Silas Marner* hark back to those poems of severance, loss, and expiation that had haunted the imaginations of Coleridge and Wordsworth at the turn of the century. I have elsewhere suggested that George Eliot wanted to recall Coleridge's Mariner by giving the name "Marner" to the pale, bent, epileptic exile, the gaze of whose "large brown protuberant eyes" terrifies both the adults who accuse him of the "old demon-worship" and the young boys who have left off "their nutting and birds'-nesting" (*Silas* 3). Some Gothic touches also exist in *The Mill,* where the dark-haired little demonist who mutilates her dolls and can expound on the shapes of the Devil goes far beyond her superstitious father's own "rampant Manichaeism" (*Mill* 14). Yet to depict the loss of wholeness and unity, George Eliot preferred to resort to the metaphors of a Wordsworth who never abandoned the safer realm of the real:

> These familiar flowers, these well-remembered bird-notes, this sky, with its fitful brightness, these furrowed and grassy fields, each with a sort of personality given to it by the capricious hedgerows—such things as these are the mother-tongue of our imagination, the language that is laden with

all the subtle, inextricable associations the fleeting hours of our childhood left behind them. (38)

In *The Mill on the Floss* George Eliot depicts the loss of such a fleeting childhood Eden; in its emphasis on the irreversible destruction that accompanies all change and growth, the novel recalls Wordsworth's own elegiac treatment of the adult's alienation from childhood in Nature. In *Silas Marner*, on the other hand, George Eliot attempts to recover a more childlike existence closer to the forms of Nature. Maggie Tulliver bears the name not only of her grandmother, Margaret Beaton, and of her struggling aunt and godmother, Gritty Moss, but also of the protagonist Margaret of Wordsworth's "The Ruined Cottage." In telling Maggie's story, George Eliot's narrator hopes to produce the same effect that the Wanderer induces through his tale of Margaret's suffering and death. Like the Wanderer's listener, the reader of *The Mill on the Floss* is asked to recover out of a panorama of decay:

> That secret spirit of humanity
> Which, 'mid the calm oblivious tendencies
> Of nature, 'mid her plants and weeds, and flowers,
> And silent overgrowings, still survived. (Wordsworth, *Excursion* I: 927–30)

In *Silas Marner*, however, George Eliot retreats to a more restorative world of vegetation to rescue the Paradise lost by the Tullivers. And, like the sick Susan Gale in "The Idiot Boy," the paralyzed Silas Marner is healed through the agency of a child: "There was love between him and the child that blent them into one and there was love between the child and the world—from men and women with parental looks and tones, to the red lady-birds and the round pebbles" (165).

Both *The Mill on the Floss* and *Silas Marner* are strongly indebted to "Michael," the poem from which George Eliot drew the "motto" for the latter work. *The Mill on the Floss* follows the outlines of Wordsworth's story of decay—a secluded pastoral world in which parents and child can briefly fuse gives way to separation, exile, and ruin. *Silas Marner*, on the other hand, reverses this progress. Silas and the reader are taken back to the fusion that existed among Nature, adult, and child when the manly Michael did "female service" for little Luke and "rocked / His cradle as with a woman's gentle hand" (Wordsworth, "Michael" 154–55).

In *The Mill on the Floss*, Mr. Tulliver's oneness with the "little wench" who takes after his "side" (Eliot, *Mill* 12) also betokens his identification with a feminine Nature represented by darkness, water, and the moon. Similarly, Maggie's rare moments of oneness with the masculine brother who will replace her father come only when both children can forget their sexual differences and merge into a primordial and undifferentiated natural world such as the quasi-magical Round Pool: "no one knew how deep it was; and it was mysterious, too, that it should be almost a perfect round framed with willows and tall reeds" (36). Yet, as in "Michael," these cherished moments of harmony give way to discordant intrusions of social demands, which George Eliot, like Wordsworth, identifies with the ways of the "dissolute city," with legal forfeitures, demeaning work. As in "Michael," a natural world of female nurture is broken by the demands of a social system of proprietorship that calls for male aggression: if Wordsworth's Luke slackens in the city and seeks a "hiding place" ("Michael" 449) from his father, Tom Tulliver thrives in St. Ogg's; yet in his obsessive attempts to recover his father's mill, he only manages to widen the gap between himself and his sister and to remove both from the natural world in which she thrived.

The Mill on the Floss shows George Eliot's penetration of the imagery to which Wordsworth habitually resorted to convey the natural child's dispossession. The nutting-crook given by an adult to the little boy who so mercilessly violates "the green and mossy bower" (47) in "Nutting," and the raised "hook" with which Lucy Gray's father snaps "a faggot-band" (19–20) before sending the child on her ill-fated mission, like the "sickle, flail, or scythe" (108) that Michael and Luke try to repair, are male tools of work that become emblems of destruction. The Clipping Tree seen again at the end of "Michael" symbolizes the severance between father and son and their joint severance from the "feelings and emanations" that united them to each other and to the surrounding natural world. In *The Mill on the Floss*, there is a similar clash between the natural, feminine images of water and trees associated with Maggie and the recurrent images of knives, scissors, swords, shears, and machinery associated with the representatives of a male order such as Tom, Lawyer Wakem, Stephen Guest, and Mr. Deane.

The "unfinished" sheepfold ("Michael" 471–72) that Wordsworth places beside the "tumultuous brook of Greenhead Ghyll" ("Michael" 2) stresses the vulnerability of all social structures in the face of an inviolable Nature: "Yet the oak is left / That grew beside their door" (479–80). In *The Mill on the Floss*, however, Nature in the shape of the swollen river hurls "fragments" of some "wooden machinery" (Eliot, *Mill* 456) at Tom and Maggie. The devastation is complete; there is no emblem for nature's continuity: "The uptorn trees are not rooted again; the parted hills are left scarred: if there is a new growth, the trees are not the same as the old" (457).

Unable to end on the serene note with which "Michael" ends, George Eliot seizes on the Wordsworthian myth of childhood at the moment of Maggie's and Tom's violent death. There is a desperation in the narrator's assertion that the drowning brother and sister lived "through again in one supreme moment the days in which they had clasped their little hands in love, and roamed the daisied felds together" (456).

In *Silas Marner* these daisied fields are allowed to permeate the entire novel. If Mr. Tulliver and his children are destroyed by the city across the river from the ancestral mill, Silas abandons the acquisitive city-ethic he has carried into Raveloe as soon as his hoarded gold is replaced by the golden-haired foundling deposited at his door. "Feyther" Marner can reenter the nurturing pastoral world lost to the Tullivers as well as to Michael, and his reentry is made possible by his transformation into a male mother who does "female service" to the natural child of a man who, like Tom, is too obsessed by the need to maintain his social possessions. Eppie reawakens in Silas those same natural feelings that Michael so movingly recalls in Wordsworth's poem: "Never to living ear came sweeter sounds / Than when I heard thee by our fireside / First uttering, without words, a natural tune" (345–47). The feelings that linked Michael both to his child and to Nature are at odds with the "endless industry" (95) for which his and Isabel's household is proverbial—an industry Wordsworth represents early in the poem by the two spinning wheels of "antique form" (83). In *Silas Marner*, the weaver's loom acts even more prominently as an emblem for an excessive devotion to mechanical and alienating work. Eppie, however, rescues Silas from "the monotony of his loom and the repetition of his web" (Eliot, *Silas* 159); as she toddles out of the cottage "to pluck the flowers" or turn her "ear to some sudden bird-notes," he finds his sense reawakening with "her fresh life" and warming him into joy "because *she* had joy" (159). Gradually, Silas remembers his own early childhood in Nature: "Silas began to look for the once familiar herbs again; and as the leaves, with their unchanged outline and markings, lay on his palms, there was a sense of crowding remembrances from which he turned away timidly, taking refuge in Eppie's little world" (159).

Like Wordsworth's "Michael," *Silas Marner* ends with a glimpse of a broken stone barrier. But the emphasis here is on an open access to the natural forms that bind the identity of parents and children: "The garden was fenced with stones on two sides, but in front there was an open fence, through which the flowers shone with answering gladness" (227). This gladness is neither forced nor unreal. Silas's redemption by the child Hephzibah remains a masterly reactivation of Wordsworth's cherished belief in the healing intercourse among adult, child, and Nature.

In an essay written two years before she published her first work of fiction, George Eliot praised Wordsworth, among others, for the powerful sympathies stimulated by his poems; turning to the "one great novelist" also capable of infusing ordinary reality with such intense emotions, she professed to be disappointed by Dickens's "unreality"; only his rich humor, she asserts, can act "as a corrective to his false psychology, his preternaturally poor children and artisans, his melodramatic boatmen and courtezans" (Eliot, "The Natural History" 270–72). George Eliot and Dickens eventually came to respect each other's work highly, but it is most doubtful whether she ever recognized how much her "incomparable Wordsworth" had contributed to *Great Expectations*, a novel never mentioned in her letters.

Victorian reviewers, however, were fond of comparing Dickens to Wordsworth. An anonymous reviewer of *The Cricket on the Hearth* (1845) welcomed the book's attention to "humble life, contemplated in its poetic aspects, and its more romantic crises" (Rev., *Chamber's* 44)—an attention which, to the reviewer, showed Dickens's ambition "of becoming the Wordsworth of prose fiction." Dickens's own contention in the preface of *Bleak House* (1852–53) of having "purposely dwelt upon the romantic side of familiar things" (xxxii) does indeed seem to echo Coleridge's famous explanation of Wordsworth's objective "to give the charm of novelty to things of every day" (Coleridge, *Biographia* 169). Yet the key connection between poet and novelist unquestionably lies in the importance each ascribes to children. Philip Collins rightly begins his *Dickens and Education* by emphasizing that "Charles Dickens was the first English novelist in whose stories children are frequent and central instead of sustaining merely minor roles in the background" (1).

Dickens's few direct references to Wordsworth always occur when he speaks of the shades of the prison house that begin to close on the growing boy. In a speech delivered in 1857 at the Warehousemen and Clerks' Schools, Dickens attacked the sort of schools "where the bright childish imagination is utterly discouraged, and where those bright childish faces, which it is so very good for the wisest to remember in after life, when the world is too much with us early and late, are gloomily and grimly scared out of countenance" (*Speeches* 241). And, in another speech given at the Southwark Literary and Scientific Institution, Dickens held that "if such institutions had existed in times gone by . . . even Wordsworth might have been drawn from the dust of those shelves where until late he had lain unnoticed" (5).

The work that Dickens himself seems to have drawn from those dusty shelves was *The Prelude*. Before the posthumous appearance of Wordsworth's poem, the only true Wordsworthian figure in Dickens's fiction is, as Philip Collins has noticed, the titular hero of *Barnaby Rudge* (1841). Like Wordsworth's Idiot Boy, Barnaby lives in a permanent childhood in Nature; at the end of the novel he regains his "love of freedom and interest in all that moved or grew, or had its being in the elements" and can never again be persuaded "to set foot in the streets" of London (Dickens, *Barnaby* 257). Yet in the novels written after 1850, from *Bleak House* to *Edwin Drood*, Dickens introduces echoes from *The Prelude*. Thus, Esther Summerson's epiphany at the garden gate before she meets Jo is described as a feeling she "ever since" connects "with that spot and that time, and with everything associated with that spot and that time" (Dickens, *Bleak* 326). Again, as P. D. den Hartog has pointed out to me, in *Little Dorrit* (1855–57), the imprisoned Clennam, barred from the golden autumn fields outside, hears through little Dorrit's voice "all that great Nature was doing" and remembers "the harvests of tenderness and humility that lie hidden in the early-fostered seeds of the imagination" (*Little* 884).

But in *Great Expectations* Dickens dispenses with this sentimentalized Mother Nature and invokes instead those "anxious visitations" that beset the child's mind, the "terrors, pains and early miseries, / Regrets, vexations, lassitudes" that Wordsworth deemed a "needful part" in the formation of his self (*Prelude* I: 345–46). Like Wordsworth, Dickens insists on the shaping power of fear: "Since that time, which is far away now, I have often thought that few people know what secrecy there is in the young, under terror. No matter how unreasonable the terror, so that it be terror" (Dickens, *Great* 13). If the child in *The Prelude* hears "Low breathings coming after me, and sounds / Of undistinguishable motion" after he has offended Nature by snaring birds and stealing the "captive of another's toil" (*Prelude* I: 323–25; 320), the boy Pip finds that after stealing the food for the convict "everything seemed to run at me": a dead hare appears to wink, "gates and dikes and banks [come] bursting at [him] through the mist," a black ox stares at him in "an accusatory manner" (Dickens, *Great* 15).

In *Great Expectations* the most vivid of these moments of childhood fear comes at the end of the first chapter and corresponds to the key passage in Book XII of *The Prelude,* in which Wordsworth isolates the two most memorable "spots of time" (*Prelude* XII: 208–10) from his "first childhood" (*Prelude* III: 464). Pip looks at the marshes into which Magwitch disappears: "On the edge of the river I could faintly make out the only two black things in all the prospect that seemed to be standing upright; one of these was the beacon by which the sailors steered—like an unhooped cask upon a pole—an ugly thing when you were near it; the other a gibbet, with some chains hanging to it which had once held a pirate" (Dickens, *Great* 5). As John P. McWilliams has shown, these two images pattern the entire novel: "landscape has established symbols that engross Pip's imagination, but that he cannot explain" (257). Only after the novel's conclusion can we and the adult Pip grasp the significance of these symbols: the illusive light that beckons Pip to his great expectations in London will turn out to be linked to the black gibbet he associates with the disappearing convict.

In Book XII of *The Prelude* the boy Wordsworth, separated from an adult companion, finds himself alone on "the rough and stony moor." He stumbles on the "gibbet mast" where "in former times / A murderer had been hung in iron chains" (*Prelude* XII: 233, 235–37); fleeing in terror, "faltering and faint," he sees a naked pool and a "beacon on the summit" and is seized by "the visionary dreariness" of the entire scene (XII: 249–50; 256). Although Wordsworth does his best to invest this remembrance with a "sublime" radiance, it is significant that he should follow this event by "another" (XII: 286) memorial that stresses the unreasonable guilt that haunted his childish imagination. To him, the spot on which he fixed his "expectations" (XII: 286) of a carriage that would lead him home becomes, after his father's sudden death, forever associated with his anxieties. Guiltily, he regards his father's death as a "chastisement" (XII: 311).

Pip, too, is consumed by irrational guilt. Yet his aggressive wishes become realized when his sister is maimed by a blow from Magwitch's iron manacle. The growing Pip tries to ignore the chains that, as a child, bound him to the convict; he chooses to forget the bond established in the marshes. If Wordsworth tries to harmonize the "inward agitations" (*Prelude* XII: 332) he felt as a child, Dickens relentlessly confronts Pip with the "spot of time" (XII: 208) he has repressed. The gibbet will reassert its powers when Pip forsakes the country for the city. Wordsworth beholds with some amusement his own "migration strange" and the conversion of a stripling "villager" in to a dandified young man in "gentleman's array": "As if the change / Had waited on some fairy's want, at once / Behold me rich in moneys, and attired / In splendid garb" (*Prelude* III: 34–38). For Dickens, however, Pip's transformation into a well-dressed young gentleman is integral to a darker parable and fairy tale. The "plebeian cards" that in *The Pre-*

lude are treated as "cheap matter" dignified by "boyish wit" (*Prelude* I: 522, 529) introduce, in *Great Expectations,* a "laboring boy's" discontent with his identity. Pip, whose name signifies—among other things—the figure on a playing card, is stung by Estella's disdain: "He calls the knaves Jacks, this boy" (Dickens, *Great* 60).

Like Wordsworth, Dickens bemoans the growth that removes the adult man's reason from the more powerful imagination of the child. And, like Wordsworth, Dickens is fascinated by the "dark / Inscrutable workmanship that reconciles / Discordant elements" in the self (*Prelude* I: 341–43). But if in *The Prelude* the child reared in Nature can as an adult draw himself up on Mount Snowden and be consecrated as a prophet, no such integration is possible in *Great Expectations.* Pip the man remains distanced from both the child-man Joe and the new Pip who has replaced him. In the last chapter of *Great Expectations* Pip can at best hope to borrow Joe and Biddy's child: "you must give Pip to me, one of these days; or lend him, at all events" (Dickens, *Great* 489). In the novel's original conclusion, he silently holds up that child to Estella.

The Wordsworthian Child of Nature surfaces in later Victorian fiction as well. In Meredith's *The Egoist* (1879), for example, the boy Crossjay directs Clara and Vernon to the renovating boughs of the double-blossomed wild cherry tree. By the 1890s, however, this figure appears in more startling shapes. In his two *Jungle Books* (1894, 1895) Kipling literalizes Wordsworth's metaphor in *The Prelude* of a bronzed child who stands alone:

> Beneath the sky, as if [he] had been born
> On Indian plains, and from [his] mother's hut
> Had run abroad in wantonness, to sport
> A naked savage . . . (*Prelude* I: 297–300)

Free from the constraints of civilization, Mowgli the wolf-boy can sing his "Song Against People": "I will let loose against you the fleet-footed vines— / I will call in the jungle to stamp out your lines!" (Kipling 164). In Hardy's *Jude the Obscure* (1895) it is civilization that stamps out the line of the Fawleys. As a boy in Marygreen, Jude vainly wishes for an arrested life in Nature: "If he only could prevent himself from growing up! He did not want to be a man" (25). Yet when manhood (and fatherhood) arrives, Jude finds no Eppie to redeem him. Instead, he is undone by the boy called

Father Time who seems as aged and spectral as the ghost of Wordsworth which Hardy, like Mrs. Ward's daughter Dorothy, claimed to have seen "lingering and wandering on somewhere alone in the fan-traceried vaulting" of King's College at Cambridge (Hardy, *Early Life* 184). By the end of the nineteenth century, that earlier child of fire and dew had assumed its last and strangest mutation.

CHAPTER 2

GENRE AND THE INTEGRATION OF GENDER
From Wordsworth to George Eliot to Virginia Woolf

Knoepflmacher holds that the internal relationships of a historical literary field (such as forms, genres, or symbolic codes) are as vitally important as its external or material conditions (marketing, format, sales) in the establishment of creative authority. Still, the complexity of an individual authorial psyche interests him as much as theorizing about a literary field. He thus agrees with authors from Wordsworth to Woolf that the best writers harbor a hermaphroditic imagination. Nineteenth-century authors may take up the particular historical challenge posed by biology and separate-spheres gender ideologies, yet many pursue, with marked struggle, an imaginative ideal of gender reconciliation or fusion. Individual artists struggle toward this ideal in different ways, given the altering conditions of their lives and their writing. In the case of George Eliot, Knoepflmacher argues, the cultural difference between the genres Victorians called "history" and "romance" signified, as it had signified for Wordsworth and would for Woolf, a psychic split between male and female aspects that Eliot's powerful hermaphroditic imagination tried to overcome. Orienting himself in gender criticism and relying on a variety of primary and secondary texts, Knoepflmacher establishes the foundations for a bi-directional, transgendered, transgenre criticism, even while he consciously retains the classifications and self-understandings of the nineteenth and early twentieth centuries. Male, female, romance, history, Romantic, Victorian, modernist—all are categories, but none are fixed.

*A*ll creative artists, Tennyson once observed, possess an imagination that is essentially hermaphroditic. Still, the poet whose passive Marianas, Ladies of Shalott, and Elaines act as surrogates for his own threatened creativity seem to have regarded the full-scale fusion of Hermes and Aphrodite, brother and sister selves, as a desirable but sadly unattainable psychic ideal. In the Victorian era, when gender stereotyping was at its height, men as much as women vacillated between tendencies too rigidly labeled as *feminine* or *masculine.* This vacillation produced rich but one-sided myths (see Auerbach, *Woman and the Demon: The Life of a Victorian Myth*). Fliess and Freud, those scrutinizers of a late-Victorian psyche, noted with almost voyeuristic relish that an excessive suppression of the traits of the opposite sex resulted in a wide array of inhibitions and neuroses (see Adler 32–35).[1]

The full integration of male and female selves, however, preoccupied another major Victorian writer, George Eliot. Unlike Tennyson, and very much like her favorite Wordsworth, the novelist resorted to a myth rooted in her own psychology. Among Wordsworth's many attractions for George Eliot was his expression of the need to recover what he identified as the feminine component of his imagination. That the novelist who wrote *The Mill on the Floss* in 1860 and the "Brother and Sister" sonnets in 1867 was drawn to Wordsworth's repeated celebrations of his sister Dorothy requires no further documentation. George Eliot's lifelong eagerness to find specimens of harmonious brother-sister relations, after all, even led her to exculpate a Byron whose work she intensely disliked yet whose love for Augusta Leigh made him, she felt, "deeply pitiable, like all of us sinners" (Eliot, *The George Eliot Letters* V: 54). Conversely, that same obsession made her unduly harsh to Branwell Brontë, whom she dismissed as "this drunken brutal son and brother." (*Letters* II: 320)

Although the Wordsworthian myth of a childhood paradise of undifferentiated gender held a steadfast appeal for George Eliot throughout her career, she also gave this ontogenetic myth much wider cultural or phylogenetic applications. Margaret Homans has perceptively suggested how, in her revisions of Wordsworth, George Eliot sought to find "a paradigm more suitable than that of the silent sister" in order to accommodate the "limits" of gender that she, as a woman and a realist, could not find in

---

1. It remained for Adler, whose theories on sexuality challenged Freud's, to remove "psychological hermaphroditism" from "any direct dependence on biological" disorders (Adler 285).

Wordsworth's visionary poetry (234). Yet it could be argued that, artistically at least, George Eliot in fact expanded limits that Wordsworth had introduced in his later poetry, for she moved, in her own career, in a direction contrary to that which Wordsworth had taken after *The Prelude*. I have previously noted that *The Excursion* can be seen as a direct progenitor of *Scenes of Clerical Life* and *Adam Bede* (Knoepflmacher, "A Nineteenth-Century" 5). If so, however, that link needs to be qualified, for, with *The Excursion*, Wordsworth had actually moved away from the feminine sensitivity he had once regarded as "the nurse, / The guide, the guardian" of his being" (*Wordsworth: Poetical Works*: "Tintern Abbey" 109–10). As a narrative poet, he yielded to masculine history, to the temporal reality he had earlier tried to counter in his antinarrative lyrics and ballads.

George Eliot, on the other hand, increasingly eschewed the role of chronicler when, after *Adam Bede,* her male pseudonym was pierced and her identity as a woman had become known. Although, like Wordsworth, she moved from pastoral to epic, to broader and more ambitious constructs encompassing ever-wider segments of human history, she also came to regard historical growth as a threat to a mythic memory that she continued to endow, as the early but not the later Wordsworth had done, with female properties and female characteristics. And the preservation of a myth of female origin led her, as it would lead Virginia Woolf, to introduce ahistorical dimensions into her historical narratives. The division between George Eliot the realist—a writer interested in cause and effect, verisimilitude, analysis, and explanation—and George Eliot the creator of romances,—a writer interested in dream, premonition, visionary or empathetic divination, and the fluidity of myth and archetype—has been carefully studied by critics such as Barbara Hardy, George Levine, U. C. Knoepflmacher, Gillian Beer, and John P. McGowan. What has not been sufficiently noted, however, either by these critics or by those who, like Sandra Gilbert and Susan Gubar, have explored the protofeminist directions of her fiction, is the direct correlation between the novelist's attempts to fuse contrary genres and her attempts to harmonize the gender divisions she so persistently sought to reconcile. The split between history and romance signified for George Eliot, as it had culturally signified for Wordsworth and would signify for Woolf, a psychic split between male and female aspects that her powerful hermaphroditic imagination tried to overcome.

In her handling of these divisions, then, George Eliot must be located at the exact midpoint of a continuum that runs from Wordsworth to Woolf, from Romantic to modernist resolutions of the clash between incomplete male and female psychic halves. Just as all three authors tried to go beyond these offsetting halves by triangulating them into a higher fused self, so is the organization of this essay deliberately and self-consciously triangular: in joining a male poet with two female novelists, I deliberately want to break down some of the dualisms to which we all too often succumb. We must not be seduced by the notions that the analysis of poetry has to be kept apart from that of prose fiction, that women writers living in a male-dominated society are best examined as the exclusive cross-fertilizing members of a creative sisterhood, that the labels *Romantic* and *Victorian* or those that presumably set apart *Victorian* from *modernist* are irrevocably fixed. Like George Eliot's efforts, my own are synthetic: the novelist with the male pseudonym is flanked by a literary father and a literary daughter. Though each defines his or her literary predecessor, all three share common concerns.

The materials I examine are necessarily selective. I begin with a look at some early poems by Wordsworth, written before the poet of *The Excursion* would give primacy to history and to a historically inflected, male authorial persona. I shall then take a close look at the opening paragraphs of chapter 12 of *The Mill on the Floss*, with their opposition of two kinds of narrators, in order to make some claims about that novel as a pivotal work that allowed George Eliot to move in new directions. After some brief remarks about certain trends in George Eliot criticism, I shall conclude by showing how Woolf, though retaining a literary concern with gender distinctions in *To the Lighthouse*, subverted, or at least reformulated, both Wordsworth's and George Eliot's myths of unity.

I

George Eliot deliberately evokes "Tintern Abbey" when, at the end of *The Mill on the Floss*, she has Tom Tulliver stare into his sister's flashing eyes. Looking into "the shooting lights / Of thy wild eyes," Wordsworth's speaker welcomed a glimpse of what he once possessed before his painful fall into male self-consciousness: "Oh! Yet a little while / May I behold in thee what I was once, / My dear, dear Sister" (118–21). Tom Tulliver, on the other hand, finds no such confirming reflections of a former self: Maggie's eyes all too belatedly produce "a new revelation to his spirits, of the depths in life, that had lain beyond his vision which he had fancied so keen and clear" (Eliot, *Mill* 455). The bifurcation that Wordsworth accepted yet still tried to delay in his 1798 poem can hardly be overcome in George Eliot's 1860 novel by the violent fusion-through-death of a brother and sister.

Yet Wordsworth had resisted this bifurcation in the short lyrics celebrating Dorothy which he wrote between 1798 and 1802, before his marriage to Mary Hutchinson and the culturally mandated masculine self-assertions that ensued. In poems such as "To a Butterfly," "The Sparrow's Nest," "Nutting," "To My Sister," as well as in the better-known Lucy poems, Wordsworth identified Dorothy with his own intense desire of arresting or reversing a process of separation that he equated with the loss of a much-coveted, presocial, Edenic oneness. The opening words in "To a Butterfly" ("Stay near me—do not take thy flight! / A little longer stay in sight") are not just addressed to the insect whom Wordsworth mock-heroically magnifies as the "historian of my infancy" but also to his onetime female companion, "my sister Emmeline," herself an emblem of that undivided infancy.[2] Again, in "The Sparrow's Nest," those "bright blue eggs together laid" that boy and girl jointly discover come to signify, as well that legendary figure with the ovarian name, Ogg son of Beorl, a primordial oneness that precedes gender distinctions. In each case, little Emmeline is credited with an intuitive capacity for divination similar to that which George Eliot will attribute to female figures such as Dinah Morris or to feminized male seers such as Latimer or Philip Wakem. In each poem, the female child thus proves her superiority both to her older boy-companion as well as to the remembering male adult.

In "To a Butterfly," the boy's response to the insect associated with the human psyche markedly differs from that of his younger sister:

> A very hunter did I rush
> Upon the prey;—with leaps and bounds
> I followed from brake to bush;
> But she, God love her! feared to brush
> The dust from off its wings. (14–18)

That the intended contrast here is not just between female restraint and male aggressiveness but also between a higher and lower imagination is evident from Dorothy Wordsworth's own gloss to these lines. In her journal entry for 14 March 1802, she noted that William "used to kill all the white [butterflies] when he went to school because they were Frenchmen" (D. Wordsworth 101). A schoolboy's immersion into military history results in the fanciful transformation of unoffending butterflies into hostile oppo-

---

2. In the manuscript originally sent to the printer the line was "My sister *Dorothy* and I" (my italics). See Wordsworth, Knight edition.

nents. Here, as in "Nutting" and "Lucy Gray," Wordsworth deliberately subverts a destructive masculine fancy. And, by deprecating that lesser fancy, the ironic male speaker subordinates himself to the superior sororal imagination of an Emmeline (or of that "dearest Maiden" invoked at the end of "Nutting"). Wordsworth thus anticipates in his self-mockery as a "hunter" the characteristics that George Eliot will attribute to Tom Tulliver in *The Mill on the Floss*. He allows what Tom will fail to allow when, in order to impress Maggie with his superior prowess, he disastrously tries to impersonate the Duke of Wellington yet only manages to maim himself with Mr. Poulter's huge sword. It is Philip Wakem, masculine yet also highly feminine, who, only a few pages earlier, had recognized his own incompleteness when, after looking, Wordsworth-like, into Maggie's eyes, "he wished *he* had a little sister" (158).

Neither Wordsworth nor George Eliot ever banished their regressive wishfulness for complementarity and gender fusion: just as the adult Wordsworth celebrated the infant Emmeline or the little girl "untouched by solemn thought" who walks beside the speaker in the 1802 sonnet "It is a Beauteous Evening, Calm and Free" (10), so did the novelist imagine her reincarnation as a half-submissive "little sister" should "another childhood world" become her "share" (Eliot, "Brother and Sister" XI: 13–14). Even in *Middlemarch,* the novel that Woolf deemed suitable for grown-ups, the successful heterosexual relations between Mary and Fred, and Dorothea and Will, are rendered imagistically in terms of the hand-holding girl and boy we see first in the novel's "Prelude," when little Teresa and her brother Rodrigo toddle out from Avila.

Still, both Wordsworth and George Eliot realized the need for finding other modes and contexts for a resolution of their intense desire to counter a split they so acutely felt. Both writers thus ranged far beyond the biographical mode of brother/sister poems. After "To My Sister," a poem of greater sophistication than "To a Butterfly," Wordsworth gradually accommodated the world of history that he, like George Eliot, persistently identified with a male modality. After her half-hearted expiation for breaking with the patriarchal world of Robert Evans she had so painstakingly reconstructed in *Adam Bede,* George Eliot began to move in exactly the opposite direction. She no longer yielded to the pressures of the "hard, unaccommodating" actuality presented in *Adam Bede,* that novel with an epigraph from *The Excursion.* Instead of killing Hetty Sorrel or of forcing Dinah Morris to submit to Adam's masculinist values, she began to find ways to inundate a male reality with mythic moments or "unhistoric acts" that she, like Wordsworth, identified with female figures or with feminized males.

As an effort to superimpose the atemporality of myth on a time-bound world, Wordsworth's "To My Sister" holds a special relevance for what George Eliot would attempt through the myth of Ogg in *The Mill on the Floss*. "To My Sister" significantly differs from "To a Butterfly," "The Sparrow's Nest," and "Nutting" in that the speaker no longer strains to return through recollection to what George Eliot's remembering narrator calls, in her own sonnet sequence, the "primal passionate store" of childhood ("Brother and Sister" V: 3).[3] The poem is set in the present, not in the past; and it relies on exhortation, rather than on memory. Instead of returning to time-mutilated bowers or lost Edens, the speaker urges an adult sister to join him and a little boy on an imaginative journey. Forward-looking rather than regressive, the poem thus expresses a protracted wish: "One moment now may give us more / Than years of toiling reason" (25–26). That moment, mythical and epiphanic, resembles, as we shall see, the wishful transformation that occurs in *The Mill on the Floss* when woman, ferryman, and child are also lifted above years of toiling reason. It also resembles that "one supreme moment" in which Tom and Maggie supposedly gain in death the childhood unity their growing up had sundered. And it resembles, too, that moment in which Woolf's Mr. Ramsay will spring "like a young man" again, onto the rock of the lighthouse, to the amazement of his daughters and son (*To the Lighthouse* 308).

In "To My Sister" the speaker insists that the ordinary sequentiality of time can be, if not totally annulled, displaced, flooded with new meaning: "We from to-day, my Friend, will date / The opening of the year" (19–20). On a special day, linear time (of which novels and verse narratives must partake much more than such short lyric outbursts) can be dissolved altogether. Speech itself, words in sequence, become inconsequential: "Some silent laws our hearts will make" (29). The same kind of mute communion so briefly experienced by a Tom whose "lips were silent" and a Maggie who "could make no answer" (Eliot, *The Mill on the Floss* 455, 456) here does not result in an expedition that leads to death or to a lighthouse that has become an emblem for the specter of Mrs. Ramsay. Instead, the speaker of "To My Sister" simply asks Dorothy to indulge what Mr. Ramsay will refuse his wife and little son. As an imaginative unit of trinitarian wholeness, William, Dorothy, and little Edward, the prepubescent child who acts as an emblem of their former childhood oneness, become cyclical figures.

---

3. Though Wordsworth assigned "To a Butterfly" and "The Sparrow's Nest" to "Poems Referring to the Period of Childhood," he placed "To My Sister" in the category he called "Poems of Sentiment and Reflection." Like "Nutting," however, it could just as well have been included among "Poems of the Imagination."

The poem itself is cyclical. Just as *The Mill on the Floss* begins and ends with a biblical epigraph that enfolds a sequential narrative, so do the concluding lines of "To My Sister" echo and remodulate earlier ones.

The tentative resolution of "To My Sister," however, is as far as Wordsworth can venture in trying to recover the female components of an imagination threatened by the rigid divisions that sunder the masculine from the feminine in a world of growth and socialization. In his later career, Wordsworth continued to pay fulsome tributes to Dorothy. Yet for the pastoralist who now turned to the epic mode, his dear, dear sister began to recede in importance.[4] *The Excursion* may open with the legendary Margaret whose name three Tulliver women come to bear, but "The Ruined Cottage" was, of course, composed long before the completion of the 1814 poem. Despite his empathy with Margaret, the speaker of *The Excursion* prefers to look to male models, the Wanderer and the Pastor, and to a male antiself, the Solitary, for his self-definition. Even in *The Prelude*, that hoarded relic of his earlier imagination, Wordsworth's repeated tributes to the sister whose name George Eliot was to assign to the heroine of *Middlemarch*, though sincere and profoundly moving, are of a different cast. His sister gift-of-God is now at best a worthy helpmeet, like Mary Wordsworth or Mary Garth (or the discarded Mary Burge of *Adam Bede*). Like Dorothea Brooke, the exquisite mate of Will Ladislaw, Dorothy, the sister-mate of Will Wordsworth's youthful imagination, becomes a foundress of nothing. Still, like Dorothea, she will survive as a literary archetype to aid future imaginations—especially the imaginations of women novelists interested in the sororal archetype.

II

Rhetorically, the opening paragraphs of chapter 12 of *The Mill on the Floss* act as a foil to the novel's first chapter, "Outside Dorlcote Mill." In that

---

4. As Judith M. Schelly observes in her doctoral dissertation on the brother-sister relation as a metaphor (Berkeley 1980), a subtle change in outlook already takes place earlier in Wordsworth's 1800 *Poems on the Naming of Places* [Hutchinson and deSelincourt 116–21]: in "Emma's Dell," Dorothy merely acts as a passive recipient of the dell's name without presiding over it as, say, Maggie will preside over the "Red Deeps." The fresh and clear "Rivulet" that comes to meet the male speaker is itself masculine, "delighting in its strength / . . . with a young man's speed" (l: 2–3). It thus is unlike the active, "wild," moon-bathed, mist-drenched Dorothy whom Wordsworth had only two years before associated with the "fair river" Wye; and it is unlike, too, the "little" Ripple that flows with such "lively current into the Floss," a rivulet whose "dark changing wavelets" retroactively remind the reader of the young Maggie Tulliver (Eliot, *Mill* 7).

first chapter the novelist-dreamer who began by describing the linear flow of the "broadening Floss" had become arrested by and drawn into a more quiescent, moist, and "softening" pastoral scene. In Wordsworthian fashion, the narrator, who stands on a stone bridge, spans an adult present with a childhood past; and, like the early Wordsworth, too, the narrator identifies that past with the figure of a little girl. As "rapt" as the child, the narrator tries to screen out, as the girl apparently does, the dry activities of "the world beyond" (8). Yet the narrator has promises to keep. She cannot lose herself in a Wordsworthian moment of lyrical ecstasy. She is a novelist and not a poet, and, as such, she must tell a story that requires sequential unfolding. She thus reproves herself for her reverie and sets out on her appointed task to inform her readers "what Mr. and Mrs. Tulliver were talking about, as they sat by the bright fire in the left-hand parlour, on that very afternoon I have been dreaming about" (8–9).

The first four paragraphs of chapter 12, "Mr. and Mrs. Glegg at Home," each longer than the preceding one, move in a direction that reverses that of the five paragraphs that make up the first chapter. Lured by the domestic title, we expect an uninterrupted resumption of the plot that has been unfolding ever since we overheard what Mr. and Mrs. Tulliver were talking about in their own home. Yet, instead of being introduced to the Gleggs at home, we are conducted on a broadening excursion through time and space.

The first paragraph, itself an elongated single sentence, insists that in order to see the Gleggs at home we must become reacquainted with the same "fluted red roofs" and "black ships" first mentioned in the book's opening sentences (7). As the sentence progresses, its tone becomes increasingly mocking. Addressed as "my refined readers" (103), we are made uncomfortable by the narrator's insistence that we confront a larger world from which we, like Maggie in the previous chapter, had expected to be sheltered. We do not enter a domestic enclosure but observe a wider socioeconomic panorama in which products from "the far north" are exchanged for "precious inland products" (103). The shift in setting is disconcerting. For the "refined readers" who associate "inland products" such as wool and cheese with "the medium of the best classic pastorals" will again find their expectations thwarted. The novelist is about to shift her own medium by moving away from the eclogue (103).

The soothing natural images that start the long and complex sentence that opens the second paragraph (104) seem, on the surface, still auspiciously pastoral; so, too, ostensibly does the quotation from Wordsworth's *The Excursion* that takes up half of the short sentence ("It is a town 'familiar with forgotten years'") (*Mill* 104; Wordsworth, *Excursion* I: 276). Yet if the old, old town carries "traces of its long growth and history like a millennial tree" (*Mill* 104), that tree proves to be severely scarred. The linear succession of cruel and rapacious invaders suggests a continuity of strife. As we soon discover, defeated Roman legions turn their back on the civil order they had once tried to impose with their swords; greedy Vikings look with "fierce eager eyes at the fatness of the land"; male ghosts, a lustful "Saxon hero-king," and a "dreadful heathen Dane, who was stabbed in the midst of his warriors" (*Mill* 104), carry little of the aura of male heroism with which Carlyle invested his Norsemen in the first lecture, "On Heroes, Hero-Worship, and the Heroic in History."

Quite to the contrary, history is a nightmare from which the narrator would like to, but cannot, awake. Eager to soften that nightmare, the narrator tries to find some palpable relic that, like Shepperton Church or the Hall Farm in George Eliot's earlier fictions, might offer a partial reassurance by its very solidity. The narrator thus welcomes the fusion of a Norman "old hall" with a later Gothic structure and asks the reader to show "loving pardon" at the crass "inconsistencies" of such "widely-sundered generations" (104). Still, historical progress yields few such "loving" tokens. The old town's evolution only reveals its instinct for survival, the hard masculine ethos that Tom will later learn there under the tutelage of Mr. Deane. Even the allusion to *The Excursion* turns out, on closer inspection, to have been a decidedly hard touchstone, a reference to that "tall crag" or mountain peak by which the poet's male tutor, the Wanderer, learns the measure of austere and granitic truths, "the history of many a winter storm" (I: 278).

Unable to find refuge in a pastoral world, unwilling to yield to the crushing forward momentum of history, the narrator reaches out for still another "medium" in the chapter's third paragraph (*Mill* 104–5). He (for I am convinced that the speaker of chapter 12 is a *he* and not the feminine presence of the book's opening chapter) reverses the onward progress he has followed by retreating into an era perhaps "older than this old hall." From that era, the narrator seizes, not just another shard of masonry, but a fluid legend, a timeless myth. Self-consciously, he thus turns to a totally different sort of "history" than that alluded to in the previous paragraph. He chooses one of several versions, he jocularly explains, because it is the briefest. And he professes to believe in it even "if it should not be wholly true." Like Lockwood in *Wuthering Heights,* this narrator thus relinquishes his narrative to another storyteller. The civilized voice of a self-conscious rationalist and antiquarian collector of manuscripts becomes submerged, drowned out by a fabulist's simpler and more archaic speech rhythms. Like the speaker in the novel's opening who lost herself in a moist, female Eden, away from "the drier world above," and like the Wordsworth who conducted his sister to "the banks of this delightful stream" (*Wordsworth: Poetical Works*: "Tintern Abbey" 150), this "private hagiographer" (*Mill* 104) invites us to cross over into the undifferentiated world of myth. Indeed, the myth this anonymous and genderless new speaker proffers is itself a myth of crossing, a return to primitive kernels of truth that must be rescued from the ossified layerings of history, the sedimentations that followed each overspill of the angry floods.

The myth of St. Ogg recounted in the remainder of the chapter's third paragraph represents George Eliot's efforts to render in narrative and cultural terms what had been presented as a wishful, lyrical moment in Wordsworth's "To My Sister." The trio of man, woman, and child are set apart from the ordinary men who rudely question the ragged female stranger. By opposing these questioners, Ogg detaches himself from the order of reality that had dominated in the previous paragraph and, by doing so, also manages to detach himself from the questioning male narrator and that narrator's limited notions of truth. Ogg defies the current of history and thereby furthers a magical transformation in which a mournful and seemingly powerless female figure assumes her full potency and beauty. The ferryman not only contributes to her translation but also is himself translated. As someone who successfully bridges alternate realities, he assumes the identity the female narrator had lost in the book's opening chapter when a bridge turned into a domestic armchair and an Eve "in love with moistness" became a male historian.

The female narrator of chapter 1 recognized the seeds of her own creative powers in the nameless little girl she glimpsed by the water's darkening edge. The vanished male narrator of chapter 12 allows himself to be momentarily displaced by the luminous female radiance who sheds light on the water. Like Wordsworth's Dorothy or Keats's Cynthia, like Jane Eyre, like the magical women in Victorian fairy tales, the radiant figure in the prow is twice identified with the moon, that Romantic emblem of a higher imagination.[5] Invested with her powers, Ogg can henceforth "save the lives both of men and beasts" (105). The Raphael Madonnas whose "blond faces and somewhat stupid expression" the narrator had ridiculed in chapter 2 (13) now undergo a transformation similar to that which Anna Jameson

---

5. See, for instance, George MacDonald's fairy tales "Little Daylight," in "At the Back of the North Wind" and "History of Photogen and Nycteris." The rejuvenation of a withered old woman dates back, of course, to Chaucer's "Wife of Bath's Tale," a story I have linked to George Eliot's myth-making in "Unveiling Men: Power and Masculinity in George Eliot's Fiction."

effected when, in her *Legends of the Madonna,* she chose "to change the scene" and contemplate the Virgin, not as "the glorious empress of heaven," but as "the mere woman, acting and suffering, loving, living, dying, fulfilling the higher destinies in the humblest state" (154).

"Ogg son of Beorl" is not the first male figure whom George Eliot feminizes as a worshiper of an earthly Madonna. But the Amos Barton who belatedly worships Milly, the Seth Bede who becomes content as uncle to Dinah's children, even the Philip who mourns at Maggie's grave—are all constrained by the harsh patriarchal world of male history. Ogg, on the other hand, is allowed to enter a metaphoric, ahistorical matriarchal world of myth such as the one into which Romola will be transported when she glides away from Florence, the city of history, or Daniel Deronda when he finds Mirah on the banks of the Thames. As a female male or a male nurturer, he is chosen, as Silas Marner will be in George Eliot's next novel, as the agent for a novelist divided between male and female modalities, male and female narrators, masculine Dodsons and feminine Tullivers, a masculine pseudonym and a female name. He helps keep in suspension the polarities that George Eliot has so frantically tried to bring into psychic harmony. His own ovarian name is, as I have already suggested, highly significant. In a novel that mocks Mrs. Tulliver as an ineffectual hen; that shows the infertility and death obsession of Mrs. Pullet; that, later in this same chapter, shows the equally infertile Mrs. Glegg to be much harder than her tender, garden-nurturing husband, Ogg's naming is hardly coincidental.[6] In still another gender reversal, he is, in effect, the egg fertilized by a woman. Transplanted to Raveloe, Silas Marner will be stirred by maternal memories suppressed during his sojourn in Lantern Yard. In St. Ogg's, however, the inhabitants forget the matriarchal origins that have led to Ogg's canonization and to their town's name; they therefore also

---

6. See Charlotte Yonge: "The root of the name Oegir is, in fact, *og* or *uok,* the same as our awe. Thence come many words, such as . . . the verb *eggan,* to incite, still common in the North; while we have *to egg on*" (323). Yonge also notes: "Also known as Agir or Ygg, Oegir was a Jotun or giant originally called Hier, a demigod of the sea or wave known to raise storms and drown sailors" (322). By calling the mythical ferryman "Ogg," George Eliot seems to have wanted to conflate the destructive pagan figure of Norse mythology with the Christian chivalric figure of "Ogier le Danois," known in Italian romances as Oggieri or Oggero. Yonge (whose etymological *History* first appeared in 1863, three years after the publication of *The Mill*) notes that "this Oggier was without doubt a contribution from the stores of Norman tradition; for Holger, or Olger Danske is the grandest national hero of Denmark" (402). Yonge speculates that Oggier, too, originally had been a god or "mythical king" from the "sacred island" of Heligoland; his "name itself," she therefore concludes, connotes "*holy,* our very word holy—the *hellig* of the North, the *heilig* of Germany, and these words sprang from those denoting health; as the Latin *salve,* hail, *salvus,* safe, and *salvatio,* safety, are all related to soundness" (403).

unlearn what Silas must be forced to remember—female sources through which they might sustain the "lives of men and beasts" and attain a secular salvation.

Thus drawn into the myth of female origins, female power, and female renovation and fusion, the reader is invited to forget the harsh world of history. But not for long. We are jolted out of our reverie in the next paragraph. The self-conscious male narrator hastily returns. All he purports to see in the legend of Ogg is the factual evidence for an early appearance of the intermittent floods: "This legend, one sees, reflects from a far-off time the visitation of the floods, which, even when they left human life untouched, were widely fatal to the helpless cattle" (Eliot, *Mill* 105). No symbolist, no explicator of metaphoric meanings, the narrator chooses to underplay the legend's moral. The floods may have spared human lives, but as the history-obsessed narrator now shows us, "the town knew worse troubles" (105) than such natural disasters: a new succession of warriors who kill in the name of religious justification and historical right returns us to the earlier cycles of slaughter.

The ruthless process that the myth of St. Ogg has momentarily halted reasserts itself with a vengeance. In the succeeding years, we discover, the town became "a continual fighting place, where first Puritans thanked God for the blood of the Loyalists, and then Loyalists thanked God for the blood of the Puritans" (105). Not Ogg the believer but those hard-hearted men who declared a needy woman to be foolish are the perpetuators of history. A single "aged person" can still remember how "a rude multitude had been swayed" by John Wesley, the mild preacher whom Dinah Morris had so vividly recalled in *Adam Bede* (Eliot, *Mill* 106). Yet life in St. Ogg's remains mundane, historical, uninundated, and unfertilized by the spontaneous overflow of a mythic imagination. Only with this sobering realization in mind are George Eliot's "refined readers" finally allowed to enter the domicile of the Gleggs.

III

In "The Turn of George Eliot's Realism" John P. McGowan contrasts the modes of *The Mill on the Floss* and *Middlemarch* to suggest that in the former novel George Eliot herself clings too stubbornly, as the inhabitants of St. Ogg's do, to a hard and intractable notion of reality. Maggie's creator, he argues, thus blames her heroine for her very own dilemma when she upbraids Maggie for divorcing imagination from the real. By way of contrast, McGowan shows that in *Middlemarch* George Eliot achieves a fluid new realism by altering her notions of what a *referent* is. She now recognizes the metaphoric texture of all human aspirations and allows that such a metaphoric process can be as veracious as factual knowledge. Arguing against J. Hillis Miller's readings of *Middlemarch* and endorsing my own contention that the rhythms of that novel blend fact and ficticity (Knoepflmacher, "Fusing Fact and Fiction"), McGowan insists that in her greatest novel George Eliot does not deconstruct an unknowable sociohistorical reality but is primarily interested, instead, in "how socially held meanings are created" (189).[7] She displays, he holds, "a new interest in visionary or metaphoric language, the direct means by which new meanings are introduced" (189).

Though in full agreement with McGowan on *Middlemarch*, I would quibble with his treatment of *The Mill on the Floss*, fully aware of the inadequacies of my own previous discussions of that novel (which McGowan rightly faults) (180). Where, exactly, at what point in her development, did George Eliot's realism "turn"? Can we really dismiss *The Mill on the Floss* so easily? And, if, as agreed, the turn of George Eliot's realism achieved its high point in *Middlemarch*, what precisely brought that turn about? To the first question, McGowan gives essentially the same answer I offered in *George Eliot's Early Novels*: it is in *Silas Marner* that George Eliot first harmonizes the conflicting orders of reality at war in *The Mill on the Floss*. On the second question, McGowan proves to be harsher to *The Mill* than Barbara Hardy, George Levine, or I am. On the third question, McGowan is as silent as I was in *George Eliot's Early Novels*.

The preceding analysis of the shifts in mode in the first and twelfth chapters of *The Mill* call into question McGowan's notions about the essentially fixed, nonmetaphoric "realism" of *The Mill*. It suggests a closer contiguity between *The Mill* and the legendary fable of *Silas Marner*. And it suggests that George Eliot's increasing experimentation with alternating narrative modes, interpenetrating genres, double plots, and conflicting orders of perception directly stemmed from her needs to integrate the discordant male and female elements at war within her own creative psyche.

Silas Marner can be read as a sequel to the one-paragraph myth of St. Ogg analyzed in the previous section. Silas unwillingly enacts what Ogg has done willingly. Subject to the same cataleptic dreaminess that besets both Maggie and the narrator of chapter 1 of *The Mill*, the asexual Silas is ejected from Lantern Yard by a rival suitor who exploits his passivity.

---

7. See J. Hillis Miller, "Narrative and History" and "Optic and Semiotic in *Middlemarch*."

Although in Raveloe he continues to be victimized by a rapacious male, his passivity now becomes an asset. The male narrator of *The Mill* can at best find a temporary refuge in the dreamlike legend of Ogg, woman, and child: Silas, ferried back into a matriarchal world, can, with Dolly Winthrop's help, become fully feminized as a male mother to Eppie. Told by a narrator as genderless or double-gendered as the narrator of *Middlemarch* will be, the fable that George Eliot claimed only William Wordsworth (beside Lewes) would have appreciated brings together the trio of woman, feminized man, and small child. The novel thus provides a step-by-step enactment of what is merely adumbrated by Ogg, woman, and child in *The Mill*. If the flood that claims Maggie and Tom is necessary to remind their survivors that there is a higher reality than that represented by Ogg's harsh countrymen and their descendants throughout history, the draining of the stone pit reveals the skeleton of a phallic male: still clutching his brother's gold-handled "hunting-whip" and Silas's hoard, Dunstan is found "wedged between two great stones." "Do you think he drowned himself?" asks Nancy. "No, he fell in," replies her husband (*Silas Marner* 201–2).

Without delving further into the relations between *The Mill* and *Silas Marner*, I would submit that George Eliot had already begun to repudiate the realism still evident in *Scenes of Clerical Life* and in *Adam Bede*, fictions told by a distinctly male narrator. The visionary world that George Eliot identified with a predominantly female sensibility is asserted in *The Mill*. Indeed, the book's conclusion—though flawed, as readers keep insisting—stems from the author's compelling need to assert the primacy of symbolic myth. Maggie has become the radiant female figure in Ogg's boat; Tom, who "could ask no questions" (455), has become an Ogg who was "blessed in that thou didst not question (105). The reiteration is obviously deliberate. And so is the description of Maggie's superhuman "energies" when she rows against the tide in what suddenly becomes "a story of almost miraculously divinely-protected effort" (455). The emblem of the child, too, reappears to signify the reconciliation of female and male polarities: in drowning their separate adult identities, the gender-divided brother and sister can return to an undifferentiated childhood. To demand, as I once did in *George Eliot's Early Novels*, that Maggie and Tom take their place in the adult world they have inherited is to subvert a closure that, George Eliot feels, can be represented only in the mythic terms of romance. Brother and sister must acquire a legendary or emblematic status for those who remain behind in a world of time—narrator and reader, Stephen and Lucy, and the lonely Philip Wakem.

Read in this fashion, the ending of *The Mill* becomes far more palatable, certainly more important, than most of us have allowed over the years. It is a Wordsworthian moment lifted out of the temporal world with its hurling, fragmenting, dead, and "wooden machinery." It belongs to the metaphoric world of Romantic realism to which George Eliot would now turn with renewed zest, a world closer to that of a Charlotte Brontë, whose metaphoric excess she had previously eyed with considerable suspicion. Brontë, too, had striven to harmonize male and female energies through the maiming of Rochester or by drowning M. Emmanuel. Yet George Eliot fundamentally differs from Charlotte Brontë, as even Gilbert and Gubar somewhat reluctantly admit when they separate the bulk of her work from that of their Gothic satanists. If George Eliot, too, occasionally turned male sadism on the male, she nonetheless remains primarily interested in inwardly harmonizing female tendencies with the male tendencies that she, like other women novelists, had introjected. Like those other daughters of domineering fathers—Fanny Burney, Maria Edgeworth, Mary Wollstonecraft Shelley, the Brontës, and Virginia Woolf—she resorted to acts of exorcism that involve more than a gallery of overtly and covertly angry female characters, the victims of male history. If Professors Gilbert and Gubar allow that George Eliot *is* Latimer (447) (whose name becomes transposed in that kinder, but still sterile, self-projection called Nancy Lammeter in *Silas Marner*), why not allow that she also "is," as she herself signified, a Casaubon or a Lydgate? Latimer, after all, was created because the novelist was unsatisfied with the excessive suppression of her female side in *Adam Bede*. Her turn from realistic pastoralism in *Adam Bede* to supernatural horror story in "The Lifted Veil," like her many other generic shifts both from fiction to fiction as well as within a single work of fiction, must be read in terms of gender divisions such as those I have briefly tried to sketch.

IV

I began this essay with Wordsworth as a reminder that male poets see themselves as possessing an imagination composed of interacting male and female elements. I want to conclude with Woolf to remind ourselves that women novelists within an ever-more-discernible "female tradition" are, for all their sympathy and acute understanding of their precursors, constantly forced into revising and redefining the fictional tropes they inherit from other women. Just as it was unnecessary to document George Eliot's

Wordsworthianism, so does it seem unnecessary to document the Eliotism of Virginia Stephen, the daughter of a man who misread both Wordsworth and George Eliot.[8]

It is in *To the Lighthouse,* a novel embedded with allusions to Wordsworth and George Eliot, that Woolf shows herself to be every bit as self-conscious of her literary, as well as of her biological, parentage. Given her need to achieve distance, it is hardly surprising that many of these allusions should be faintly ironic or that the irony should be primarily directed at Mr. and Mrs. Ramsay, the incarnations of Leslie and Julia Stephen. William Bankes nostalgically recalls Mr. Ramsay as a fallen Wordsworthian Solitary, once capable of striding on a Westmorland road with a "natural air," yet betraying his impending socialization when, showing "his sympathy with humble things," he stopped before a "hen, straddling her wings out in protection of a covey of little chicks, upon which Ramsay, stopping his stick . . . said, 'Pretty—pretty'" (34). And Mrs. Ramsay, too, though no henlike Mrs. Tulliver but an earthly Madonna who out-radiates the "picture of Queen Victoria" (25) illustrates the pitfalls of that Wordsworthian sympathy which George Eliot had tried to strip of all residue of romantic egotism: "She praised herself in praising the light, without vanity, for she was stern, she was searching, she was beautiful like that light. It was odd, she thought, how if one was alone, one leant to inanimate things; trees, streams, flowers; felt they expressed one; felt they became one" (97).

When Minta Doyle remembers how "frightened" she had first been by Mr. Ramsay's "really clever" talk about George Eliot, "for she had left the third volume of *Middlemarch* in the train and she never knew what happened in the end" (148), Woolf does more than merely expose the flaws of both Minta and Mr. Ramsay. As her 1919 essay on George Eliot hints, that last third of *Middlemarch,* with Dorothea Brooke's "seeking wisdom and finding one scarcely knows what in marriage with Ladislaw," strikes Woolf as an inadequate compensation for the cherished recreation of a world of "fields and farms" in the earlier novels ("George Eliot" 157, 156).[9] Instead of pastoralism and humor, there remain only those "great emotional scenes" that clearly embarrass Woolf and the talkativeness of dialogues that, since no longer in Midlands dialect, she finds to be "tediously slack" (158). Woolf protests that George Eliot "allows her heroines to talk too much . . . She

---

8. See Elaine Showalter, "The Greening of Sister George," for a valuable discussion of the ways in which Woolf corrected the male prejudices (including those of Leslie Stephen, her father) that had clouded George Eliot's reputation by 1919, the centennial of her birth.

9. Woolf wrote two further essays on George Eliot, one in the *Daily Herald* of 9 March 1921 and another in the *Nation* and *Athenaeum* of 30 October 1926.

lacks the unerring taste which chooses one sentence and compresses the heart of the scene within that. 'Whom are you going to dance with?' asked Mr. Knightley at the Westons' ball. 'With you, if you will ask me,' said Emma; and she has said enough. Mrs. Casaubon would have talked for an hour and we should have looked out of the window" (159).

If Minta Doyle has, like Virginia's stepbrother George Duckworth, never finished reading *Middlemarch,* Woolf has. And in *To the Lighthouse* she sets out, among other things, to rewrite that unfinished third of a novel she respects, for all her strictures, as "magnificent." The figure of Mrs. Ramsay reenacts the dilemma of Dorothea Casaubon and, by extension, the dilemma, too, of Julia Stephen and of Mary Ann Evans Lewes, the loving "Mutter" of the Lewes's children, the presiding presence at those Priory gatherings: "Nothing seemed to have merged. They all sat separate. And the whole effort of merging and flowing and creating rested on her" (126). The figure of Mr. Ramsay reenacts the dilemma of the Reverend Edward Casaubon and, by extension again, the dilemma of a Leslie Stephen overeager to disengage the "unfeminine" habits of mind of a masculine George Eliot. But the dilemma is also that of a writer forced, but unwilling, to separate what Woolf calls in her 1919 essay "the ordinary tasks of womanhood" and "wider service of their kind" (159) from the amassed learning and overwhelming mastery of dry facts that she persistently associated with a purely masculine domain. Oppressed by the motions of the historical flux, Mr. Ramsay, who can so eloquently and heroically discourse on Locke, Hume, Berkeley, "and the causes of the French Revolution," becomes as "timid in life" as the timid Mr. Casaubon (70).

Read in this fashion, *To the Lighthouse* emerges as a critical homage to Woolf's antecedents—antecedents she both embraces yet feels compelled to reject. And her rejection becomes most manifest in her refusal to provide a mythical fusion for the gender distinctions she so insistently retains. Like Wordsworth and George Eliot, Woolf abhors a world of flux and severance, a reality that destroys sisters and brothers, a Prue as well as an Andrew Ramsay. But she also resists the fusions desired by an androgynous imagination. This resistance is partly evident through Woolf's evocations of Wordsworth and George Eliot. Walking by the shore with Paul Rayley and Minta Doyle, Andrew and Nancy feel a momentary oneness; sharing the boat with their father and the Macalisters, James and Cam briefly join in a silent alliance. But Woolf relentlessly sunders that fusion with the sharp wedge of gender division.

Nancy and Andrew are not the children who played by "that immortal sea / Which brought us hither"; we may see them "sport upon the shore,

/ And hear the mighty waters rolling evermore," but we derive no intimations of either immortality or oneness (*Wordsworth: Poetical Works*: "Ode" 167–68, 170–71). United at first in their antagonism toward the adult Paul and a Minta who still exhibits, in Andrew's opinion, "sensible," unfeminine habits, brother and sister soon grow apart. Once alone, Nancy crouches Eve-like over the surface of pools she imaginatively wants to possess as her "own," while Andrew wanders off to a craggy promontory. Like the dreamy Maggie Tulliver hypnotized by the mill's churning water or the little sister who, in the "Brother and Sister" sonnets, converts the brown canal into a floating "dream-world," Nancy yields to a reverie that shuts out the world beyond: "Brooding, she changed the pool into the sea, and made the minnows into sharks and whales, and cast vast clouds over this tiny world by holding her hand against the sun, and so brought darkness and desolation, like God himself, to millions of ignorant and innocent creatures, and then took her hand away suddenly and let the sun stream down" (114–15). But this Eve-like aspiration to godhead is short-lived. From a Coleridgean "Infinite I AM" (*Biographia Literaria* 167; my italics) Nancy returns to her finite ego. It is Andrew who shouts that the sea is about to rush in, just as Tom Tulliver and a "boyish Will" interrupt a little sister's watery reveries.

What is more, both children now witness Paul and Minta embracing, "kissing probably." Outraged, indignant, yet "in dead silence, Nancy and Andrew feel more apart than before":

> Indeed, they were rather sharp with each other. She might have called him when she saw the crayfish or whatever it was, Andrew grumbled. However, they both felt, it's not our fault. They had not wanted this horrible nuisance to happen. All the same it irritated Andrew that Nancy should be a woman, and Nancy that Andrew should be a man, and they tied their shoes very neatly and drew the bows rather tight." (Woolf, *To the Lighthouse* 116)

Like the scene in *The Mill* in which Maggie, stung by Tom, pushes Lucy into the mud, this brief episode depicts a mock-heroic version of the Fall. But whereas George Eliot, like Wordsworth, still tries to recover a childhood paradise, Woolf regards the severance of miniature Eves and Adams as an emblem of an alienating reality in which the prime fluidity is that of time. Her narrator, correspondingly, can have no fixed identity or fixed gender but must flit from consciousness to consciousness. To try to envelop, as Nancy so briefly did, an entire cosmos is a Miltonic impossibility. As Lily Briscoe later observes while speculating about Mr. Carmichael's attachment to Andrew, "this was one way of knowing people, she thought: to know the outline, not the detail" (289).

In Section II of "Time Passes," Woolf again revises literary precedent. She deliberately evokes *The Excursion* by depicting a female abode that, like Margaret's ruined cottage or Maggie's Dorlcote Mill, is about to succumb to the unmending ravages of nature. And she rescues it from corruption:

> Then the roof would have fallen; briars and hemlock would have blotted out path, step, and window; would have grown, unequally but lustily over the mound, until some trespasser, losing his way, could have told only by a red-hot poker among the nettles or a scrap of china in the hemlock that here once some one had lived; there had been a house. (208–9)

But no trespassing Wanderer and Poet, Lucy Deane and Stephen Guest, or solitary Philip Wakem, are allowed to extract thoughts that lie too deep for tears. The catharsis is spread out, and it carefully avoids that emotionalism that Woolf so distrusted in her predecessors.

First the snorting Mrs. McNab; then a Lily Briscoe who must keep at bay the ghost of Mrs. Ramsay as well as the flesh-and-blood Mr. Ramsay who finds such unexpected comfort in his boots; and, finally, the pilgrimage to the Lighthouse—all subvert a Wordsworthian or Eliotic closure. An epiphany occurs. But it is acknowledged as impermanent: "But what did it matter? she asked herself, taking up her brush again" (310). And in the boat, though it reaches its goal, the fusion is similarly qualified. Cam, peeling her "hard-boiled egg," is no radiant Madonna, but remains at odds with brother and father and Mr. Macalister and the Macalister boy who, in defiance of all Wordsworthian notions of childhood, mutilates a fish and throws it back into the water. Nor is Mr. Ramsay idealized. Though executing at last his dead wife's wish, though as unquestioning now as Ogg son of Beorl had been, he is not a feminized male out of some ancient legend: "He was shabby," Cam notes, "and simple, eating bread and cheese; and yet he was leading them on a great expedition where, for all she knew, they would be drowned" (305). Yet no such apotheosis occurs. Unlike Tom and Maggie—and unlike Virginia Woolf herself—Cam does not drown.

CHAPTER 3

ON EXILE AND FICTION
The Leweses, the Brownings, and the Shelleys

During the nineteenth century, misogynistic myths of male genius often constructed woman as passive and secondary. Yet, at the same time, with a fertile mother on the English throne, Victorians saw an increase in legal rights and literary opportunities for women. As professional women writers demanded equality, creative couples faced special challenges and opportunities. In this essay Knoepflmacher counters the emphasis on sexed giftedness by examining the collaborations of three couples. He sets the romantic myths that rose up around both the Shelleys and the Brownings in apposition to the creative struggles faced by George Eliot in her domestic partnership with George Henry Lewes. Drawing on the novelist's "How I Came to Write Fiction," and on letters and biographical details of all three couples, he stresses the differences in their parallel exiles. Known for his appreciation of the female imagination, Knoepflmacher hardly downplays Mary Ann Evans's extraordinary talents. Still, by focusing on Eliot's emotional traumas and their impact on her self-doubts as a writer, he stresses the importance of the self-sustaining, protective interdependence fostered by Lewes. It was a domestic situation in which art had to envy life for what they achieved as partners.

———•———

*A*s a major novelist's retrospective attempt to account for the freeing of her imagination, George Eliot's "How I Came to Write Fiction" fully deserves the attention of her readers. In reproducing this document, biographers from J. W. Cross in 1885 to Gordon S. Haight and Ruby Redinger in our times have rightly stressed its importance. Yet "How I Came to Write Fiction" still demands further analysis.[1] In it George Eliot not only casts considerable light on the process of her creativity but also underscores the role played in the liberation of that creative process by George Henry Lewes, the partner whose first name she incorporated in her male pseudonym. This double aim also links, whether consciously or not, "How I Came to Write Fiction" to the account in which another female novelist looked back at the "origin" of her fiction-making and at the "inciting" influence of her own partner—the 1831 Introduction to *Frankenstein*. Despite efforts to connect George Eliot to Mary Shelley, our minds seem determined to keep the two writers apart.[2] George Eliot has been cast as the preeminent emblem of a mature and thoughtful realism, the author of works, as Virginia Woolf put it, written for grown-ups. Mary Shelley, on the other hand, seems frozen as the author of *Frankenstein*, that product of an adolescent's fixed fears and fantasies. Though helpful, the juxtaposition remains oversimplified and needs to include a fuller consideration of the roles played in each novelist's development by their respective partners, Percy Shelley and George Henry Lewes.

Male collaborations such as Wordsworth's and Coleridge's work on *Lyrical Ballads* broke down whenever one of the partners was required to subordinate his ego to the other. Creative equality and interdependence became even more problematic when an aspiring younger female writer like Mary Wollstonecraft Godwin, living with an established male author, sought to develop her literary creativity. Given the fixity of nineteenth-century gender roles, she was then in danger of subordinating her budding imagination to that of her male partner. This essay seeks to show how Mary Ann Evans, the future George Eliot, and her partner, George Henry Lewes, an author who had promoted the genius of Jane Austen and Charlotte Brontë, broke with the precedent of the Shelleys. Their partnership will be also likened and contrasted to that of another pair of Shelleyans, Elizabeth Barrett and Robert Browning.

George Eliot begins "How I Came to Write Fiction" on the same note of self-deprecation and doubt that marks Mary Shelley's 1831 Introduction. She admits, as her predecessor did, her long-standing ambition to write a novel. But, unlike Mary Godwin, not yet nineteen and still a "young

---

1. Eliot's essay can be found reprinted in *The George Eliot Letters* II: 406–10.
2. See Gilbert and Gubar 455–58; George Levine, "Ambiguous" 23–25; U. C. Knoepflmacher, *George Eliot's Early Novels* 138–43.

girl" (M. Shelley 222) when she turned to her first long work of fiction among the Swiss Alps, the Mary Ann Evans who had eloped to Germany with Lewes in 1854 at the age of thirty-four was no neophyte. She was a skilled translator, editor, and essayist. It was her creative imagination that remained blocked, as she later realized, upon looking back at the "shadowy conception of what [her intended] novel was to be . . . from one epoch to another" (Cross, *George Eliot's Life*, 6 December 1857; Eliot, *Letters* II: 406). Her despondency, she insisted, was endemic: "I lost any hope that I should ever be able to write a novel, just as I desponded about everything else in my future life" (II: 406).

At this point in "How I Came to Write Fiction," George Eliot shifts, rather abruptly, to her exile in Germany after her elopement with Lewes. An early sketch, she relates, "*happened to be* (my italics) among the papers I had with me in Germany, and one evening at Berlin, *something* (my italics) led me to read it to George" (II: 407). The vagueness and passivity George Eliot attributes to her former self suddenly gives way to an account of Lewes's gentle but determined intervention; he is, we are told, "struck" by the "concrete" power of her descriptive abilities but warns her that he distrusts, indeed disbelieves in, "my possession of any dramatic power," thus implicitly seeming to confirm her self-estimation (II: 407). And yet Lewes also begins to think "that I might as well try, some time, what I could do in fiction" (II: 407). Portrayed as an empiricist, Lewes thus seems to be willing to wait for further evidence before he will be ready to pronounce, "It is worthwhile for you to try the experiment" (II: 407). Only after his companion has shown a "greater success than he had ever expected in other kinds of writing" does he encourage her "to see how far my mental power would go towards the production of a novel" (II: 407). Though still quite guarded, he now chooses to speak "very positively" for the first time (II: 407). His mate, however, reverts to her earlier resistances. After beginning her first story, she procrastinates, "after my usual fashion, with work that does not present itself as an absolute duty" (II: 407).

One morning, while "lying in bed" and "in a dreamy doze," George Eliot—or rather Mary Ann Evans, still—takes a distinct step forward: "I imagined myself writing a story of which the title was—'The Sad Fortunes of the Reverend Amos Barton'" (II: 407). Ever alert, Lewes seized the opportunity for a stronger dose of encouragement: "I was soon awake again, and told G. He said, 'O what a capital title!'" (II: 407). The approval proves to be exactly right, "and from that time on I had settled in my mind that this should be my first story." It is noteworthy that the female dreamer should immediately associate being "awake" with Lewes (who was probably lying next to her in bed). Although a determined antifantasist who had recommended to Charlotte Brontë that she saturate herself in the works of Jane Austen, this realist knew exactly how to mediate between a dreamy projection and its actualization. He enthusiastically applauds the chosen title yet also reminds the reassured dreamer that the story itself still remains to be written. For all his encouragement of her creativity, he will not betray the reality principle to which she, like himself, must subscribe. He therefore carefully spreads out for her all possible contingencies. The story, he warns her, "may be a failure . . . Or perhaps it may be just good enough to warrant your trying again. . . . You may write a chef d'oeuvre at once—there's no telling" (II: 407).

George Eliot's decision to reproduce the various stages of development in this genetic account is as noteworthy as the account itself. In its apparent faithfulness of detail, "How I Came to Write Fiction" adopts the "sincerity" which her coexperimenter, Lewes, had upheld both as the literary critic who, in his very first essay, professed to admire Percy Shelley "because he was eminently sincere" ("Percy Bysshe Shelley" 313) and as the empirical physiologist who, in those "Seaside Studies" that ran in *Blackwood's* concurrently with George Eliot's first fictions, insisted on a rigorous process of documentation and verification. By the time Lewes appeared in Mary Ann Evans's life, "sincerity" had also assumed a personal significance for him. No longer the dandy who once boasted himself "next to mad with love and its fallacies" (Scott I: 133 as quoted in Hirshberg 22), Lewes had shed the flippancy and theatricality that marked some of his earlier incarnations—the garrulous drama critic "Slingsby Lawrence"; the irrepressible *farceur* in Dickens's company of "splendid strollers"; and the wishfully self-dramatizing author of *Ranthorpe* (1847), which, as his first novel, he had dedicated to his wife Agnes, for lightening the "burden of an anxious life" (*Ranthorpe*, n. pag.). By 1854, however, Agnes Lewes had greatly contributed to his anxiety, as well as to a more mature notion of "sincerity." When she presented him with several children fathered by Thornton Hunt, the same friend whom Lewes had once urged to write down his early recollections of Percy Shelley, whom both men worshipped, Agnes's infidelity led her husband to reconsider his earlier enthusiasm for a community based on free love.

Lewes seemed to grasp that his new relationship with Mary Ann Evans had to be cemented on absolute frankness. The woman who had on her own resolved to see life without any opiates of self-delusion demanded nothing less. His refusal to yield to falsification or to brush away her very own doubts about her "dramatic power" thus helped her, paradoxically, to overcome her mistrust of the gifts so apparent to others and allayed her intense fear of her creative energies. Interested in play as well as in the psychology of the imagination, Lewes seems to have fully fathomed the relation between creativity and regression. He regarded the portions on "Childhood" and "Schooltime" as the finest sections of Wordsworth's *The Prelude* and implied that the "marvelous vividness" of Dickens's imagination stemmed, like the novelist's "overflowing fun," from a childlike capacity to believe in the fantastic and hallucinatory (Hirshberg 11, 90). Yet he also derided the philosophical underpinnings of *The Prelude* as absurd and deplored Dickens's presumed lack of intellect. It thus seems unsurprising that he should emerge as a sober adult superego in "How I Came to Write Fiction." Only the exuberant exclamation "O what a capital title!" suggests some of the playfulness that others continued to notice in Mary Ann Evans's vivacious yet "sincere" mate. The childlike qualities that George Eliot would later impute to male nurturers of adopted daughters, such as the grotesque Silas Marner and the droll Rufus Lyon of *Felix Holt*, are notably absent in her characterization of "George."

Sickly, despondent over his adulterous wife, Lewes gratefully leaned on the sympathy his new mate so fully extended to him after she had pierced the veneer of his Bohemian reputation. In return, as "How I Came to Write Fiction" eloquently shows, he was also fully capable of being "primary caretaker" for her own unfulfilled imagination. His caring supervision of his three legitimate sons and his steady devotion to his long-lived mother, Elizabeth Ashweek Lewes William (she died in 1871 at the ripe age of eighty-three), suggests Lewes's appreciation of, and capacities for, the necessity of "mothering." Yet unlike the position of superiority that Percy Shelley had adopted in urging the daughter of Mary Wollstonecraft and William Godwin to prove herself "worthy" of her "parentage" and improve her "ideas in communication with his far more cultivated mind" (M. Shelley 222–23), Lewes never infantilizes his "Polly" in urging her to try the identity of a novelist. Hardly a recusant child, she is a clear-eyed adult whose diffidence might be justified. A "chef d'oeuvre" will require the full use of her mature powers, as the author of the immature novels *Ranthorpe*, and *Rose, Blanche, and Violet* (1848) could attest.

Some elements in George Eliot's "How I Came to Write Fiction" remain deliberately screened, of course. When John Cross reproduced her account of the "dreamy doze," he stripped it of all sexual overtones by prudishly deleting the phrase "as I was lying in bed." In so doing, he may well have detected an inference that later biographers, not privy—as Cross was—to George Eliot's marriage bed, have just as discreetly avoided. Still, the likelihood that George Eliot herself relates her latent creativity to her sexual intimacy with Lewes cannot be discounted in her description of the dreamy doze. The tiny, ugly, pockmarked man, so un-Victorian and seemingly un-English in his lack of reticence, at first struck Barbara Leigh Smith as an "extremely sensual man" (Smith as qtd. in Redinger 299). Smith, who distrusted her own passion for John Chapman (Mary Ann Evans's seducer), and who would soon marry the cold Eugène Bodichon to escape that passion, welcomed George Eliot's reassurance that "in their intimate relationship [Lewes] is unsensual, extremely considerate" (Smith as qtd. in Redinger 299–300).[3] But the reassurance, proffered to a friend whose loyal friendship was essential to George Eliot, and veiled, as it is, by a triple layer of transmissions, only seems to suggest that the "intimate relationship" of the couple was extremely healthy.

More tantalizing, however, is George Eliot's elliptical suggestion that her elopement with Lewes had reactivated emotional traumas that her fiction would both tap and master. The phrase appearing early in her account, "just as I desponded about everything else in my future life," remains unlocalized in time and hence may seem descriptive of a self-doubting tendency that manifested itself even after each of her immense successes. Still, since the phrase is followed by an account of her 1855 stay in Berlin, several months after her elopement to Weimar, the effect is to yoke the general despair she felt about ever becoming a novelist with the specific anxieties about her future identity as Lewes's companion in exile. In 1855 the identity of a London journalist, editor, translator, and valued member of the Victorian intelligentsia that Mary Ann Evans had so strenuously fashioned for herself had suffered a profound setback. The shock threatened to be even more damaging to her than all her previous crises.

Each of George Eliot's earlier ruptures with the past had been severe. Her father's death and the dubious freedom that ensued proved to be as painful as the previous conflicts with both Robert and Isaac Evans on the issue of her break with Christianity. But just as traumatic, if we are to believe Ruby Redinger, was her estrangement as a small child from an ailing mother. Though Redinger, like Cross, forgets that Christiana Pearson Evans's decline was probably accelerated by the birth and death of twin sons in 1821, sixteen months after Mary Ann's own birth, there is no need to discount the likelihood that the girl magnified her "role in her mother's prolonged illness" (45). It is true that George Eliot's guilt never

---

3. That the relationship was hardly "unsensual" is suggested by the description of the couple's contraceptive practices in a letter destroyed by Marie Adelaide Belloc Lowndes in 1942 (see Haight, *Biography* 203).

assumed the proportions of Mary Shelley's self-castigation for having been the unwitting cause of her own mother's death. Still, by attributing Mrs. Evans's neglect to invalidism and by blaming herself as its cause, the child could deflect from the more painful inference that her mother did not really much care for either of her two daughters, for, even while healthy, Mrs. Evans had shown a similar indifference toward her older daughter and namesake Christiana (or "Chrissey"), born in 1814. Whereas both girls were promptly sent off to boarding school at the early age of five, their brother Isaac, born in 1816, and "his mother's pet" (33), was allowed to remain at home until the age of eight. Unable to obtain her mother's love, and separated from her older sister, Mary Ann transferred her attachment to the two male members of her immediate family. Both her father and Isaac apparently returned her love. And by eliciting her brother's love, the little girl could at least indirectly identify with her mother. It was a psychic pattern that would allow her to accept similar substitutions in her later life.

Nonetheless, as her portraits of deficient mother figures would later show, George Eliot never fully weathered the withdrawal, at such an early stage of her development, of that maternal "warmth" she poignantly dramatized in "Self and Life," a poem that Redinger rightly reads as "one of her most personal utterances" (40–41; see also Zimmerman and Knoepflmacher, "Unveiling" 130–45). In that dialogue, "Life" insists on a symbiotic fusion between mother and child: "I was thy warmth upon thy mother's knee / When light and love within her eyes were one; / We laughed together by the laurel tree." But an individuated adult "Self" bemoans its separation and exile: "Soon I knew thee more by Fear / And sense of what was not, / Haunting all I held most dear; / I had a double lot: / Ardor, cheated with alloy, / Wept the more for dreams of joy" (Eliot, "Self and Life" 7, 19–24).

Both as a girl and as a growing woman, Mary Ann Evans struggled to accept the "alloys" of compensation for the early severance she had suffered. Yet the child who first turned to her rigid father and older brother as surrogates for the withdrawing Christiana, Evans continued, as an adult, to find her emotional needs thwarted by a series of deficient male mentors and suitors. In 1854, at the age of thirty-four, she had at last discovered a man who could amply satisfy those needs. Ironically enough, however, her elopement with Lewes also reactivated her earlier sense of loss. Although she had entered a relation ideal in its finely balanced interdependence, elopement raised anew the old specter of a solitude as devastating as that which besets the loveless Shelleyan protagonist of her 1859 horror story, "The Lifted Veil."

Though Redinger properly stresses the blissfulness of the "dual solitude" that George Eliot would find after her elopement with George Henry Lewes, she also severely underestimates, I think, the depth and intensity of the fears unleashed by the decision to share his life. Once again, fusion was followed by separateness, the monster that an alienated little girl had never fully learned to slay. All past gains seemed in danger of becoming obliterated. By eloping with a married man, not only had Mary Ann Evans become irrevocably estranged from her brother Isaac, her father's stolid and conventional heir, and from her timid, tubercular sister Chrissey, her mother's namesake and fellow invalid; she also seemed to have deprived herself, just as irrevocably, of the much-coveted recognition of older friends such as Harriet Martineau, whose biography she now was never to write, as she had previously intended.[4] Would she—could she—ever again be accepted by Victorian society, when even some of its most free-thinking members seemed eager, in Barbara Bodichon's words, to "spit at" her (Eliot, *Letters* III: 56). All evidence seemed to deny that likelihood. The readership she had gained as thoughtful reviewer and editor at the *Westminster Review* might now also be lost. It was for this reason, apparently, that Lewes advised her to persist "in other kinds of writing" before venturing into the new province of fiction.

That George Eliot should choose, amidst these dire and uncertain circumstances, to show Lewes the draft that somehow "happened to be among [her] papers" during their sojourn in Berlin thus seems doubly significant. Her phrasing strikes the only chord of disingenuousness, however slight, in "How I Came to Write Fiction." Surely both she and Lewes, expert weighers of consequences that they were, had carefully anticipated that their projected flight to the Continent might result in a resurfacing of old torments. Their decision to go had hardly been a matter of thoughtless impulse. The possible recurrence of her earlier anxieties must thus have called for some precautionary measures. It therefore seems deliberate that, whether consciously or only half-consciously, George Eliot chose to scoop up the old manuscript, "an introductory chapter describing a Staffordshire village and the life of the neighbouring farm houses" (*Letters* II: 406). As an imaginative fragment of a lost but recreatable past, it could be a talisman against impending change.

---

4. When the hypochondriachal Martineau circulated the rumor that she was near death, George Eliot asked John Chapman to allow her to become Martineau's official biographer. Martineau's *Autobiography*, an unduly neglected masterpiece, appeared in 1877, a year after her actual death.

The fragment had unquestionably been written to resist some earlier bout of dejection. If Gordon Haight is correct in his conjecture that it dates from 1846, it was composed at a time when Mary Ann Evans was finishing her influential translation of David Friedrich Strauss's *The Life of Jesus, Critically Examined*. At the time she reportedly told her friends the Brays that "she was Strauss-sick—it made her ill dissecting the beautiful story of the crucifixion, and only the sign of her Christ-image [a cast of Thorwaldsen's *Risen Christ* in her study] . . . made her endure it" (*Letters* I: 206). Not only the visible cast of Thorwaldsen's Christ but also her mental recasting of a solid Midland locality may have been needed on that occasion to allay her "dreadfully nervous" state, her worries about the book's impending publication and about her father's rapidly failing health. Despite her "pale, sickly face and dreadful headaches," she was, significantly enough, also reported to look "very happy and satisfied at times with her work" (I: 206) Writing—whether the translation of "leathery Strauss" or the composition of her "introductory chapter for a novel"—had clearly become a welcome means of defense. In her later career as a novelist, her habitual migraines would miraculously cease whenever her pen began to flow.

It is not at all unlikely, therefore, that Lewes himself had actually encouraged her to take along the eight-year-old descriptive fragment. It was a portable bit of space, "a paradise within," to which the would-be pastoralist and lover of Wordsworth's poetry-of-return might therapeutically resort. It was soon to be extended, as the "dramatic power," doubted and despaired of, gradually began to assert itself through Lewes's careful coaxing and through his mediations with *Blackwood's* magazine, upon their return to England. In his own *Blackwood's* piece, "The Novels of Jane Austen," Lewes loyally puffed "the works of Mr. George Eliot," a writer whose "culture, reach of mind, and depth of mind" ("Novels" 104) he avowed, exceeded Austen's. Although George Eliot must have relished his solicitude, she could also count on Lewes's characteristic candor. Ever the truth-teller, he allowed that "in the art of telling a story" the new novelist still "seems to us inferior" to Austen (104). His sincerity paid off. If the static quality of the description he had read in Berlin was still evident in "Mr." George Eliot's evocation of Shepperton Church in "Amos Barton" or of Chevrel Manor in "Mr. Gilfil's Love-Story," her rendering of the Hall Farm and its dairy in *Adam Bede* was far more dynamic (and impressed Queen Victoria so greatly that she commissioned a painting of Hetty Sorrel and Arthur Donnithorne next to the churning butter vats in the dairy).

By the time she wrote *The Mill on the Floss* (1860), when her gender and identity could no longer remain hidden, George Eliot had fully learned how to infuse description with drama. In the masterly opening of the novel, the solid and inert structures of the earlier fictions have been replaced by the ever-moving river. The little girl who stands on the bridge that connects Ripple to Floss may think herself shut off "from the world beyond," as sheltered and immune as the ducks "dipping their heads into the water here among the withes, unmindful of the awkward appearance they make in the drier world above" (8). But if the child stands arrested on that "one February afternoon many years ago," the adult intelligence of the narrator who witnesses the scene must bestir itself into motion (8). The narrator cannot lose herself in the landscape that proves to be so hypnotic. In diction that reminds one of the "dreamy doze" in "How I Came to Write Fiction," George Eliot makes the narrator of *The Mill on the Floss* conscious of having "dozed off" in a reverie, of having "been dreaming" (8–9). Though tempted to linger with Maggie, her fellow dreamer, the narrator must bestir herself to acknowledge a painful world of change, alienation, and loss.

If a harsh world of change will claim Maggie the dreamer, Maggie's creator managed to complete the metamorphosis denied to her heroine. We know that George Eliot wept bitterly while writing the last pages of *The Mill on the Floss*. Yet in depicting the drowning of Maggie and Tom, the novelist also signified a transcendence of the stifling ties that stunted the growth of this incarnation of her earlier self. She had at last found the freedom to move beyond a fixation with the past and beyond her attachment to a Tom-like brother whom she regarded as her link to that past. The newly integrated identity she had fashioned for herself could be shared with an alert partner far more supportive than the Stephen Guest who reproaches Maggie for seeing "nothing as it really is" (420). The long-delayed "dramatic power" unleashed in *The Mill on the Floss* was freed by the fellow exile who had aided Mary Ann Evans's transition from a dreamy doze to that dream's realization. Unlike Maggie, the exiles in her next two novels, *Silas Marner* and *Romola,* would, like their creator, find the strength to survive.

On 2 August 1863, Robert Browning impulsively dashed off a short note to "My dear Mrs. Lewes." He had just finished reading the second volume of *Romola* and wanted to express his "gratitude for the noblest and most heroic prose-poem I have ever read" (see Eliot, *Letters* 96). Possibly aware that George Eliot's eagerness to be acknowledged as "Mrs. Lewes" was matched only by her desire that Mr. Lewes be accorded the same respect she was now receiving, Browning made sure to add his parting "regard to your Husband" (96). On reading the final installment of *Romola,* a sobered Browning would privately retract his high estimate of the novel. But the gracefulness of his tribute could hardly have failed to produce the desired effect: deeply as she must have valued finding *Romola* praised by a fellow artist known for his own imaginative incursions into the Italian Renaissance, George Eliot would have also cherished Browning's parting salutation. Although her literary reputation was by now more than secure, there were still those who privately harbored doubts about the reputableness of "Miss Evans" and "her elective affinity" (Cooper 257–59). One of these doubters, until won over by *Adam Bede* and *The Mill on the Floss,* had been Elizabeth Barrett Browning. Her widower's letter, sent two years after Barrett Browning's death, thus carried an added poignancy.

By 1863, the companionless Robert Browning was well able to appreciate the benefits the Leweses had reaped from their creative partnership. In a further gesture of kinship, two years later, he invited the couple to 19 Warwick Crescent. George Eliot's journal for 15 October 1865 conveys her profound emotions: "15. Sunday. In the evening walked home with Browning, went into his house, and saw the objects Mrs. Browning used to have about her, her chair, tables, books, etc. An epoch to be remembered. Browning showed us her Hebrew Bible with notes in her handwriting, and several of her copies of the Greek dramatists with her annotations" (*Letters* IV: 205).[5] George Eliot's response to these memorabilia seems deeper even than Browning's own excitement at one who once saw "Shelley plain" (R. Browning, "Memorabilia" 1, *Poems* I: 643). It was around this time that Eliot, who had once praised *Aurora Leigh* as a "work exhibiting all the peculiar powers, without the negations, of our sex" (*Letters* II: 278), had begun to entertain the notion of casting *The Spanish Gypsy,* that other woman-centered epic, as a verse-novel.

But it was the domestic setting of that October evening that must have made it, for George Eliot, a ritual "to be remembered." For a writer so wonderfully attuned to all shades of human relationships, a writer whose fiction relied on the continuous transposition and modification of the major relationships in her own life, a literary mother-sister was kept alive through the loving devotion of a surviving brother-mate. The copresence of Browning and Lewes was thus essential for her own fullest identification with the

---

5. George Eliot reviewed *Aurora Leigh* in the opening of her "Belles Lettres" section in the *Westminster Review* 67 (January 1857): 307, and apparently reread it with Lewes thereafter.

dead Barrett. Without these male figures, who were at once as capable of extending as of receiving a mothering of the mind, George Eliot's heightened sense of the affinities between her artist-sister and herself would have remained incomplete.

Neither Browning nor his two visitors had to be reminded that Elizabeth Barrett's 1846 elopement with him to Italy had yielded strikingly similar results to the Leweses' own flight to Germany in 1854. As Dorothy Mermin has argued, both *Aurora Leigh* and Barrett's later poems owe much to Robert Browning's impact (Mermin qtd. in Perry, "The Domestic Economy" 82–101). But, unlike Barrett, who had been a famous poet long before her elopement, Mary Ann Evans had not really tapped her true creative powers during her years as translator, editor, and essayist. Whereas Barrett resembled the later Aurora Leigh in her emotional subjectivism and lyrical unselfconsciousness as a poet, the *Westminster Review* intellectual had only, like the younger Aurora in her years of apprenticeship "learnt the use / Of the editorial 'we' in a review" (Barrett Browning, *Aurora Leigh* III: 312–13; *Works* IV: 88). Her creative identity thus depended far more fully on the chemistry of her exile with Lewes.

There were, to be sure, some notable similarities between these two female exiles. Like Mary Shelley, both women had been forced to process the loss of a mother as well as that of the beloved brother who had taken that mother's place. Moreover, both had come into conflict with Victorian domestic mores: just as Isaac Evans cut off all communication with his straying sister, so did Edward Moulton-Barrett bitterly sever all familial ties to his oldest daughter; the same Harriet Martineau who so acidly denounced Lewes and George Eliot had already withdrawn her friendship from the Brownings on hearing of their flight. But life for the Brownings was relatively frictionless. As Mermin reminds us, they were more financially secure and did not require a market for their writing. The Leweses, on the other hand, were professional writers who had to rely on their pens, not just for their own living, but also to support Lewes's three legitimate children as well as Agnes Lewes. Unlike the Brownings, they could not afford to stay abroad in a foreign haven but had to reestablish themselves in London's literary marketplace. Nor could they resort to the games, creative but often hyperbolical, that the Brownings loved to act out with each other. The Brownings delighted in mythical poses, but the Leweses were forced to face sobering consequences unknown to the other pair. There was no possibility for them to cast Lewes as a rescuing St. George or of pretending that they were a reincarnation of Perseus and Andromeda. While the Brownings rummaged through archetypes, George Eliot and Lewes confronted facts. Mary Ann Evans had not eloped with a wealthy bachelor, as Barrett had, but with a married man weighed down by responsibilities and disappointments. The Brownings could have a child of their own to join them as playmate in their Florentine bower. George Eliot, however, could not afford further affronts to Victorian propriety. She was obligated to remain the surrogate *Mutter* to Lewes's three growing sons.

The feelings of kinship that connected the Leweses to Browning as they inspected his dead wife's mementos were undoubtedly genuine and finely felt. Yet beneath this bond lay another tie that would have remained suppressed, for to acknowledge it would have complicated even further their respective images of a realized marriage of true minds. That link was to Percy Shelley and Mary Wollstonecraft Godwin, whose own elopement to the Continent on 28 July 1814 had furnished the joint precedent for both Victorian couples.

The Shelleys provided Browning and Barrett with one further mythic wrapping in which to envelop their romantic relationship, as their letters to one another in 1845 and 1846 so eloquently show. Eager to emulate the "sun-treader" (Browning, *Pauline* 151; *Poems* I: 10) he had so steadfastly worshipped since his youth, Robert saw himself as reenacting the chivalric behavior of a Percy obsessed with tyrannical fathers and imprisoned daughters in distress. (Shelley had married his first wife, Harriet Westbrook, when she was sixteen years old, to shield her from her father's outrage at the atheist opinions she had adopted.) As a young poet's muse, Elizabeth Barrett could, in turn identify with the Mary Shelley whose *Frankenstein* and *The Last Man* she so greatly admired (see R. Browning and E. Barrett, *Letters* I: 179ff; 189ff; 218–19, 278). In the letter written on the very eve of his elopement, Robert made sure to include an obligatory reference to Shelley's poetry; earlier, in opting for Italy as their destined haven, he had borrowed Elizabeth's copy of Mary Shelley's *Rambles in Germany and Italy* (1844) and noted his disappointment on finding that their heroine, "'the Mary dear' with the brown eyes, and Godwin's daughter and Shelley's wife" had become a "commonplace journalist" (*Letters* I: 189). Elizabeth, for her part, teased Robert when she found Shelley's youthful novel *St. Irvyne* to be a rather banal production, yet she also noted that it had been written before the poet had reached "the maturity of his genius" and had not yet secured the help of "Godwin's daughter," the better novelist (I: 218–19). It was one of their poses.

It was not until 1851, according to Betty Miller, that a horrified Browning would discover the full facts of Percy's desertion of Harriet and their children. After eloping with Mary, Shelley had proposed that all three should live together, with Harriet as his sister and Mary as his wife, an offer Harriet had refused before her suicide (Miller 169–70).[6] The Shelleys had still acted as a mythical archetype when the Brownings' cast their son Pen, born in 1849, as a reincarnation of that other Florentine child, Percy Florence Shelley, the only survivor of Percy's seven children. Though never repudiating his onetime idol, Browning's 1852 essay on Shelley no longer exalted the subjectivism of the Romantic lyric but privileged the objectivity of the more ironic and depersonalized dramatic poetry he had adopted.

For the Leweses in 1854, the exile of the Shelleys offered a far more disturbing precedent that neither of them, and especially George Eliot, was particularly eager to acknowledge. Unlike the Brownings, both fully understood the darker implications of the analogue. Like Mary Shelley and unlike Elizabeth Barrett, Mary Ann Evans had eloped with a man legally married to another; but whereas the drowning of Harriet Westbrook Shelley allowed Mary Godwin to assume the name of "Mrs. Shelley," George Eliot had to drown her own rebellious, Maggie-like self in order to earn a tenuous acceptance as the undivorced Lewes's new wife. For her, as for the still unwed author of *Frankenstein,* fiction could appease yet also exacerbate a deep sense of disconnection. "Was I then a monster, a blot upon the earth, from which all men fled, and whom all men disowned?" asks the Creature before pleading with Frankenstein that he create a "creature of another sex, but as hideous as myself," to join it in "exile," cut "off from the world" (M. Shelley 142). That this plea—and the emotions behind that plea—had a special resonance for George Eliot is evident from her own experiment with the mode of the horror story "The Lifted Veil," which she wrote between *Adam Bede* and *The Mill on the Floss.*

When George Eliot sent John Blackwood, her publisher, the manuscript of what she called a "dismal story," she was unusually self-deprecating. It was, she insisted, "a slight story of an outré kind—not a *jeu d'esprit* but a *jeu de melancholie.* . . . I think nothing of it, but my private critic says it is very striking and original" (Eliot, *Letters* III: 41). Supportive as always, Lewes, her "private critic," must nonetheless have been shocked. George Eliot had not only completely contravened the canons of realism that both he and she had espoused but also had depicted the same sense of desolation that shaped *Frankenstein* after a lonely Mary Godwin discovered that her mate was as un-nurturing as her father (see Knoepflmacher, "Thoughts" 88–119; Scott, "Vital" 172–202). Latimer, the male protagonist of "The Lifted Veil," is as irrevocably alienated as Shelley's Monster. Indeed, some

---

6. See Griffin and Minchin (185) for a different dating of this event.

of Latimer's wails of self-pity seem directly lifted from *Frankenstein*: "I have never unbosomed myself to any human being," he complains; "I have never been encouraged to trust much in the sympathy of my fellow-men" ("The Lifted Veil" 2). When Latimer laments that "I have near no relatives who will make up, by weeping over my grave, for the wounds they inflicted on me" (4), he echoes the Frankenstein Monster's complaint: "I am an unfortunate and detested creature; I look around and I have no relation or friend upon earth" (M. Shelley, *Frankenstein* 129). If the Monster is born as motherless, as Mary Shelley was, Latimer is, like George Eliot, deprived of a "tender mother" while still a "sensitive child" ("The Lifted Veil" 4). If the Monster is rejected by the father-creator who escapes his "detested form" (M. Shelley 96), Latimer is at odds with an "unbending" father who prefers his complacent older son to this abnormal child ("The Lifted Veil" 5). If the Monster kills a brother figure in little William, Latimer profits from the death of the brother whose "small patronizing ways" had "irritated" him as much as Isaac Evans's ways had irritated George Eliot (30).

George Eliot invokes Mary Shelley's *Frankenstein* in the Genevan setting of "The Lifted Veil," the story's Shelleyan title, and the portrayal of an experiment in animation. Yet she goes beyond Mary Shelley by denying Latimer a nurturing maternal surrogate. Bereft of kinship, the motherless Monster, who has admired the portrait of Victor's dead mother, asks Frankenstein to "create a female" for him (M. Shelley 140). "*Grant* my prayer" (my italics), he vows, and promises to live in peaceful exile with his monstrous mate (144). It is George Eliot, however, not Mary Shelley, who grants such a mate; but Bertha *Grant,* whom Latimer desires as much as the Monster had desired a female mate, only confirms the impossibility of such a fusion. George Eliot's sudden doubts about the possibility of joining, not just the male and female genders, but also the male and female components of her own psyche, are dramatized by the predicament of her "half-womanish" protagonist ("The Lifted Veil" 20).

I have elsewhere noted that the localities Latimer and Bertha visit—Munich, Vienna, Prague, and Dresden—correspond exactly to the itinerary that George Eliot and Lewes followed after their own departure from Munich, where she had written much of *Adam Bede*. Even the crucial description of the Jewish cemetery at Prague, which ends the first half of the story, contains details factually recorded by the two tourists in their respective journals (Knoepflmacher, *George Eliot's Early Novels* 133–35). But the full emotional import of this analogy has remained unanalyzed. Upon returning to England, George Eliot seems to have questioned once again the protective interdependence that had converted an isolated "single self" into two "united selves" (Redinger 292). That her doubts, soon laid to rest by Lewes's continued support of her creativity and by her continued rise to fame, were encased in a Shelleyan story leads us back to the significance that the failed relationship of the Shelleys had held for Lewes as well as for herself.

In his youth Lewes had been as ardent an admirer of Shelley as Robert Browning. In 1841, a bare six weeks after his marriage to the beautiful Agnes Jarvis, not yet perceived as a Bertha Grant, he published a forty-one-page essay on the poet in *Westminster Review*. Though Lewes's ostensible aim was to review Mary Shelley's 1839 edition of Percy's poems and essays, it also seems more likely that he wanted to impress the poet's widow with his qualifications as Shelley's ideal biographer. He repeatedly compliments her and naively praises Shelley's presumed feminism, which, in still another compliment, he rather dubiously attributes to the influence of "Mary Wolstencraft" [*sic*] (Lewes, "Percy Bysshe Shelley" 330). His praise of that "high-minded woman" (quite different from George Eliot's own later essay on Wollstonecraft and Margaret Fuller) is designed as a tribute, not just to Wollstonecraft's daughter, but also to Agnes Lewes, whose father (Swynfern Jervis) had shared Byron's and Shelley's belief in free love unconstrained by legal or religious trammels. Lewes's paean to Shelley's presumed perception that "women are neither slaves nor angels—but women" thus was intended for the eyes of his young bride: "if a wife be meant to be a partner of your life—a sharer in your spiritual hopes and successes, as well as in your material ledger successes, then it is in Shelley that you will find the true ideal woman" (331).

In 1841 Lewes selected Shelley as a model because, like Browning, though in a different way, he was eager to enact Shelley's presumed role as a champion of femininity. There were personal reasons for his promotion of "the philosophy of Love and Hope" he attributed to the writer he regarded as "par excellence" the "poet of women" (312, 330). Lewes saw Agnes as a fellow-writer, a productive journalist who could help their "material ledger" with translations from French and Spanish. Yet his bride hardly resembled the editor and translator he would, years later, help convert into "George Eliot." By 1851, the year in which Mary Shelley died and in which Mary Ann Evans published her first *Westminster Review* essay, Lewes had closed his Shelley and was more than ready to open his Goethe. He could now join Byron and Shelley in the list of "unhappy husbands" cited in his 1841 essay (311). The erotic pluralism that had once fascinated a Percy Shelley who tried to have T. J. Hogg share a common "treasure" in Mary bore fruit when Agnes Lewes gave birth to the first of several children by Thornton Hunt. What is more, Percy's image had itself become badly tarnished. He was no longer the "gentle, loving, loveable" angel memorialized in his widow's "sympathizing, and affectionate notes" (310). Victorian reality had replaced Romantic mythology.

Thus, when Lewes eloped with Mary Ann Evans, almost exactly forty years after Percy had fled with Mary Godwin and Claire Clairmont, his partner also differed markedly from the young bride he had so idealistically celebrated in 1841 by implicitly linking her to Mary Shelley. Agnes had long ago ceased to resemble the "true ideal woman" who, according to Lewes, Shelley had always celebrated in his best poetry. Though not sixteen, as Mary had been, nor as beautiful, his second partner was truer to Lewes's now matured ideal. Yet the elopement was also cruelly parodic: the two exiles were not Percy and Mary speeding across the Continent with Byron and Claire Claremont in tow. Instead, at last awarded his desired mate, a cuckolded husband settled exhaustedly in Goethe's sedate Weimar.

A consciousness of their Shelleyan antecedents seems to have been engraved in the minds of the newest pair of exiles as much as it had been present in the minds of the two Brownings. Like the Shelleys and unlike the Brownings, however, the Leweses returned to England some months after their elopement to face the same malicious calumnies that, according to Lewes's 1841 essay, were heaped on Shelley by "men calling themselves Christians" (306). Yet it was the new "Mrs. Lewes" and not her "husband" who was the target. As a Shelley-like agnostic and as a woman who had offended Victorian codes of conduct, Mary Ann Evans rightly feared a clash with the patriarchal society in which, for all his feminism and unconventionality, Lewes could still freely move.

Small wonder, then, that in 1858, just before *Adam Bede* secured the reputation of the pseudonymous "Mr. Eliot," George Eliot should have become greatly unsettled by a strident attack—in the very *Westminster Review* to which she and Lewes had contributed—on Shelley's detractors.[7] Her prompt rejection of the author's clumsiness and "false sarcasm" betrays her need to distance herself from the Shelleyan precedent that she and Lewes had redefined. Yet her fears of total isolation, as the fable of "The Lifted Veil" so eloquently shows, were not easily allayed. Only Lewes's con-

---

7. The essay on Shelley (*WR* 59 (1858): 97–131) was authored by John Richard de Capel Wise; his glib handling of the relation between Shelley and the society that had ostracized him offended a George Eliot eager to become reconciled to the readership of her early fictions: "I have long ceased to feel any sympathy with mere antagonism and destruction," she wrote to her friend Sara Sophia Hennell after reading Wise's piece (*Letters* II: 421).

tinued support (even of that "dismal story" and her ever-widening readership permitted her to continue to expand her creative genius.

George Eliot's diary entries after Lewes's death on 30 November 1878 are most painful to read. And painful, too, for her Victorian admirers, was her hasty marriage to the younger John Cross. A widowed state was not as possible for her as it had been for Robert Browning. Nor could she, as Gertrude Stein would, find the masculine component she needed within her own self. Stein, who drew on *The Mill on the Floss* for the title for one of her earliest essays, "Red Deeps," could move, as Catherine Stimpson has shown, from mother love through brother love to sister love (122–39). In 1880, the year of her marriage and death, George Eliot seems to have deliberately rejected such a possibility when she discovered that the young Edith Simcox, who had posed as her quasidaughter, demanded more than mother love. When Edith kissed her repeatedly and "hung over her caressingly," she gently chided her as a "silly child" (Simcox as qtd. in McKenzie 97). As Simcox later reported:

> Then she said—perhaps it would shock me—she had never all her life cared very much for women—it must seem monstrous to me—I said I had always known it. She went on to say, what I also knew, that she cared for the womanly ideal, sympathized with women and liked for them to come to her in their troubles, but while feeling near to them in one way, she felt far off in another—the friendship and intimacy of men was more to her. (Simcox as quoted in McKenzie 97)

Read in one fashion, this graceful rebuke was a justification for George Eliot's preference for the young John Cross as an object of her own mothering. But it was also one last tribute to the dead Lewes and to the economy of their relationship. Lewes's special sympathy for women had led him to nurture and care for "the womanly ideal," a sensibility George Eliot attributed to several male characters in her fiction.

Mary Shelley's *Frankenstein* ends in an orgy of male destructiveness. At the end of *The Mill on the Floss,* however, the "strength, inspired by mighty emotion" which allows Maggie to rescue her brother leads to a sense of reconcilement (*Mill* 453). Although Maggie and Tom can, like the mateless Monster and Victor Frankenstein, only be joined in death, their apocalyptic drowning allowed George Eliot to affirm the integrated powers of an imagination she had questioned in "The Lifted Veil." In *Middlemarch,* a novel embedded with Shelleyan allusions (Duerksen 23–31; D. Carroll 77–84), the novelist went even further. If Maggie clasps Tom's hand as they go down in "an embrace never to be parted" (*Mill* 456), Will Ladislaw clasps Dorothea's "hand with a spasmodic movement" (*Middlemarch* 593). A "vivid flash of lightning" illuminates their faces; "and so they stood, with their hands clasped, like two children, looking out on the storm, while the thunder gave a tremendous crack and roll above them, and the rain began to pour down" (93).

Love, for George Eliot, happened in those moments of overcoming the separateness she intensely felt. Like a Dorothea who overcomes her momentary alienation from the mercurial Will Ladislaw, George Eliot may have, at certain junctures of her life, been beset by doubts about the steadfastness of the relation that had shaped her creative identity. That identity depended on her determination to fuse with the male mate who had replaced parents, brothers, sisters, and tutors. The "ardent" Dorothea Brooke who misplaced her affection on Mr. Casaubon can attain fulfillment with a reformed Shelleyan worshipper of the feminine, a Will whose Slavic surname is pronounced "Lady's Love." Yet Dorothea, whose creativity is spent in "channels which had no great name" (613), must efface herself and subordinate herself to her male companion. The novelist whose "great name" incorporated that of her "husband," George, fared considerably better.

CHAPTER 4

PROJECTION AND THE FEMALE OTHER
Browning and the Romantics

Tennyson is often thought to be the most "feminine" poet of an age in which literary creativity became increasingly feminized and lyric itself was gendered female. But Knoepflmacher here illustrates the ways in which Robert Browning, whom early Victorians had still regarded as Elizabeth Barrett's subordinate, challenged the masculinist myth of a female Muse that Byron, Shelley, and Keats had bequeathed to later nineteenth-century poets such as Tennyson. Knoepflmacher argues that Browning exposes that myth as a death-dealing masculine fantasy. The irony inherent in the dramatic monologue form, as fully developed by Browning, allowed him to expose the male's use of the female. In these ironic constructs, the Female Other has becomes a mere object and prop for male completion, not a subject or artist in her own right. Browning's skepticism about the very process of projection means that his poetry is actually far more respectful of the opposite sex than male-authored literature that colludes with the stifling of a female voice.

We shall become the same, we shall be one
Spirit within two frames, oh! wherefore two?

—Shelley, *Epipsychidion* 583–74

> What I see is that I have become Total-Image, which is to say, Death in person; others—the Other—do not dispossess me of myself, they turn me, ferociously, into an object, they put me at their mercy, at their disposal, classified in a file, ready for the subtlest deceptions.
>
> —Barthes, *Camera Lucida* 14

Robert Browning's 1864 monodrama "James Lee's Wife" contains a remarkable passage in its ninth and last section, "On Deck." The "ill-favored" female speaker has "conceded" the failure of her union with James Lee, the object of her desire (344, 338). The speaker accepts her self-exile from the apathetic "mind" of the man she continues to worship: "Nothing I was" will, she has now come to realize, ever find a "place" in that masculine mind (336–37). And yet, boldly and unexpectedly, she imagines a future moment in which a depleted James Lee "might" fade into

> . . . a thing like me,
> And your hair grow these coarse hanks of hair,
> Your skin, this bark of a gnarled tree,—
> You might turn myself! (368–71)

The metamorphosis the speaker envisions here is neither the natural outcome of aging nor a wishful act of supernatural witchery. Her visionary casting into the future is a projection (from *pro-iacere*: to throw ahead). But what is involved is not the kind of projection that led a Paracelsus or an Agrippa, those alchemist-transformers with whom Percy Shelley and Browning identified, to cast powders into a crucible. It is, instead, a purely mental act.

What James Lee's Wife, the woman without a name of her own, envisions, then, is nothing less than a mental restoration of the identity she has lost. Though physically alive, she has become obliterated in James Lee's mind and hence has become more radically excluded than the extinguished Porphyria and Last Duchess whose outward forms are at least remembered by the male minds who drained their vitality. Like Browning's other martyred female, Pompilia, James Lee's Wife requires an acknowledgment of kinship to take place in the mind of her denier. She can be animated only through such a rebirth of consciousness. She thus assigns herself a role somewhat like that played by the mute Dorothy whose "wild eyes" allow her brother to behold "in thee what once I was" (Wordsworth, "Tintern Abbey" 119–20). But James Lee is not an eager Wordsworth. To conquer his obdurate resistance, his Dorothy does not merely wax silent but also resolves to place herself out of the reach of any "word" or "look" from him. She understands that only by evading him can she ever hope to force him to grasp her true import. Her removal may cause James Lee to reimagine—and reimage—his own selfhood; only then will he be able to take the next step and recognize his wife's image as a speculary analogue or epipsyche of himself:

> Strange, if a face, when you thought of me,
>   Rose like your own face present now,
> With eyes as dear in their due degree,
>   Much such a mouth, and as bright a brow,
> Till you saw yourself, while you cried "Tis She!" ("James Lee's Wife" 353–57)

The young Browning who more than thirty years earlier had addressed the figure of Pauline as the equivalent of Wordsworth's Dorothy or of Shelley's Emilia Viviani had also tried to see himself in a female mirror:

> And then I was a young witch whose blue eyes,
> As she stood naked by the river springs,
> Drew down a god: I watched his radiant form
> Growing less radiant, and it gladdened me. (*Pauline* 112–15)

Still, the female impersonations of the *Pauline* poet who repeatedly likens himself to a "girl" were but a spasmodic expression of yearnings after a complementary Otherness which, like Shelley's search for an inconstant "Intellectual Beauty," were destined to remain unfulfilled. Although James Lee's Wife despairs of fusion as much as the *Pauline* poet, her self-removal frees her from the impotence that marks his mental agitations. She thus resembles Pauline, the fictional Frenchwoman who distances herself from the male speaker's Romantic effusions in a footnote. She hence is even closer to Browning's own distancing intelligence, especially as it had begun to operate, significantly enough, in "Porphyria's Lover" (1836) and "My Last Duchess" (1842), where the motifs of *Pauline* are ironically exposed through a male speaker's inadequate attempts mentally to possess a Female Other.

When Browning renamed as "James Lee's Wife" the poem he had four year earlier titled "James Lee," he signified his full understanding of the reversal he had produced through the creation of still another layer in a multilayered sequence that went back from poems in *Men and Women* (1855) to earlier dramatic monologues such as "Porphyria's Lover" and "My Last Duchess," and from these to his youthful *Pauline* and beyond, to the Romantic conversation poem and to the lyrics and narratives by Shelley and "by a Mr. John Keats, which were recommended to [Browning's mother] as being very much in the spirit of Mr. Shelley" (Cooke 204, quote by Gosse *Personalia*). To understand the genesis of the dramatic monologue and to appreciate also the impact that Browning's development of the monologue had on latter-day Romantic seekers of a female Muse—Rossetti, Morris, and Swinburne—the critic must carefully unravel each of these strands and assess their full interrelation.

I

It is no coincidence that "James Lee's Wife" should have been conceived after the death of Browning's own wife, that female "moon of poets," only one of whose "two soul-sides" her worshipful, Endymion-like mate had been able to extol "out of my own self" in "One Word More," at the end of *Men and Women* (188, 185, 193). Both in her poetry as well as in her own person, Elizabeth Barrett had tried to maintain that Keatsian "central self" that she has Aurora Leigh adopt. Barrett thus furnished Browning with a further link to the Romantic idealization of a female complement who might restore an incomplete male self. She was his Mary Godwin, his Emilia Viviani. As noted in the previous essay, his elopement with Elizabeth was a self-conscious reenactment on the part of both lovers of Percy Shelley's own flight abroad, thirty-two years before, with another daughter shackled by a father. Yet long before the famous letter of 10 January 1845, in which he offered his worship to the unseen "dear Miss Barrett," Browning had been what, around the same time, George Henry Lewes called Shelley, "*par excellence,* the 'poet of women'" ("Percy Bysshe Shelley," 330). The elopement, after all, merely confirmed him in the role of liberator of an imprisoned Muse he had all along assumed in his verses. It was a fantasy come true. He could become a Perseus destined to "save" the alluring Andromeda-figure whom the impotent *Pauline* poet had coveted: "But change can touch her not—so beautiful / With her fixed eyes, earnest and still" (*Pauline* 658–59). He could be the manly Count Gismond, a St. George figure, who rescues a damsel from opprobrium and defamation. Pauline's successors had proliferated in the 1842 *Dramatic Lyrics*. In the same volume in which he reprinted "Porphyria's Lover" and for the first time published "My Last Duchess," "queen-worship" (a joint title for "Cristina" and "Rudel to the Lady of Tripoli") vies with the depiction of thwarted lovers. With the publication in 1845 of the *Dramatic Romances and Lyrics*, their number had greatly multiplied.

Yet Browning's lifelong urge to represent the imaginative possession of a female epipsyche was punctured, in true Romantic fashion, by severe doubts. And these doubts were exacerbated by dissatisfactions with the lyric and narrative forms he had also inherited from his precursors. In his own lyrics and romances, severance and betrayal abound. Incompleteness is far more prominent than the fusion of complementary selves. But only in the form of the dramatic monologue first developed in "Porphyria's Lover" was Browning able to scrutinize that incompleteness without the melodramatic overtones that made "In a Gondola" so inadequate a revision of Keats's "Isabella" and without the sentimentality that marred an otherwise unimpeachable lyric such as "The Lost Mistress." And, whereas his early female speakers remained two-dimensional (one would never think of "Count Gismond" as "Count Gismond's Wife," despite its female voice), it was in those monologues in which Browning parodied his own male desire to flatten women into the "fixed" and immovable Andromedas of graphic art—in poems such as "Porphyria's Lover" and "My Last Duchess," once again, but also in "Andrea del Sarto," "The Bishop Orders His Tomb," and even "Fra Lippo Lippi"—where his own art suddenly became powerfully and magically three-dimensional.

"Porphyria's Lover" and "My Last Duchess"—more closely analyzed in the next section—feed on the very incompletion they depict. They still render the appropriation of a Female Other who is portrayed as elusive and silent; at the same time, however, they introduce a critical distance that was still absent in the lyrics and the dramatic romances. Removed as either lyricist or narrator, Browning now ironizes the act of projection by which a devouring male ego reduces that Female Other into nothingness. Animations of a process of deanimation, these monologues thus self-consciously mock the poet's very own enterprise. Though an ironist, the poet also acts as abettor and accomplice, for he too flattens a female anima into a mere image, a representation, an object of art.

Still, if the Browning who exposes the pathological windings of the Lover's and the Duke's minds partakes of their suppression of the Female Other, he simultaneously maneuvers the reader into becoming that suppressed Other's chief ally. Even more than Andrea del Sarto's Lucrezia or the dying Bishop's long-deceased, yet still jealously hoarded, mistress, Porphyria and the Duchess are deformed into static images. They thus assume the inertness of those frozen and "fixed" photographic stills that Roland Barthes reads as emblems of a cruel art of depersonalization first introduced in the nineteenth century (14–15).

Porphyria and the Duchess have lost more than a freedom of motion. Imprisoned as they are within a male's rhetoric of justification, they also are bereft of a voice of their own. It is their very voicelessness, however, that stirs in us the process of identification that James Lee's Wife hopes to produce, through her absence and silence, in her husband's mind. It is because they are mute that the reader is prompted to adopt the same role of liberator that Browning delegated to chivalric surrogates such as Count Gismond. Unless rescued by the reader, Porphyria and the Duchess remain the perennial captives of masculine speech.

Thus, just as Barthes the reader of fading photographs is provoked into restoring to the photographer's subjects the motions and identities that they have lost, so is the reader of "Porphyria's Lover" and "My Last Duchess" stimulated into reanimating what Browning's speakers have deanimated. We are drawn into a process of restitution and reconstitution. Whether consciously or not, Browning thus cleverly delegates to his readers a task that neither he nor his Romantic predecessors had been able to carry out to their full satisfaction.

It was a brilliant solution to a plaguing problem that went back, before *Pauline,* to the beginnings of the century. As a lyric poet manqué, Browning was able to profit from the experimentations of those Romantic subjectivists who had sadly discovered that their desire for fusion with another could all too easily convert that Other into a mere projection of the lyricist's male self. Hence, before we can assess the full achievement of "Porphyria's Lover" and "My Last Duchess," we must wind back to those earlier beginnings and try to unravel some further layers in this complicated genealogy.

Robert Langbaum was surely correct when, in *The Poetry of Experience,* he stressed the "movement toward objectivity" inherent in the productions of Romantic poets for whom "subjectivity was . . . the inescapable condition" (28). Yet whereas in 1957 Langbaum still felt compelled to rescue Romanticism from the "charges" made by modernists overeager to signal their "independence" from their nineteenth-century roots, we no longer need to mount such a defense. Indeed, in the intervening half century, the emphasis has shifted in exactly the opposite direction. The influence of critics such as Harold Bloom has made us too disposed to read the poetry from Blake to Stevens as a smooth, uninterrupted continuum. If, as Bloom repeatedly would have it, Browning is a latter-day Shelley (175–204), there are nonetheless highly important formal differences that sharply separate

Browning's from preceding efforts at overcoming the "inescapable condition" that Langbaum so well describes: the plight of a male ego whose isolation "within himself," deprives him of an "objective counterpart" for his subjective will and feelings (28). These differences become most notable when we look at the Romantic search for a counterpart of the opposite gender, a topic that strangely interested neither Langbaum nor Bloom, for all its centrality to their respective concerns.

"Be thou me!" an "impetuous" Shelley urged the "Maenad"-like West Wind ("Ode to the West Wind" 62, 62, 21). The famous apostrophe could just as well have been uttered by all those equally impetuous Romantic seekers who coveted an Eve in order to replenish the vacancies experienced by a solitary Adamic self. Whether factual or mythified, alive or dead, human or immortal, the Romantic epipsyche became an increasingly problematic emblem that allegorized the male's unsatiated desire for fusion. In his very first conversation poem, Coleridge could ask "pensive Sara" ("The Eolian Harp" 1, 3) to act as a counterweight for his flights of fancy by having her recline her cheek against him in their "Cot" (a posture that Browning was to reverse carefully in his macabre parody of this idyllic scene in "Porphyria's Lover"). Soon, however, the silent helpmeet on whose "more serious eye" (50), Coleridge's speaker projects his own misgivings about the unbridled use of the imagination (in Miltonic double negatives that might have been used by admonishing archangels but hardly by Sara Fricker) fades out altogether. So much "at rest" (4) in "Frost at Midnight" that her restless mate can appropriate her maternal role by bestowing a new Edenic birth on their infant son, she has become replaced as a "woman beyond utterance dear" (4) by her namesake in "To Asra." Yet she and that namesake altogether lose their individuality in "Dejection: An Ode," where the subjective capacity for projection (as in Browning's "'Childe Roland'") has become a curse. The speaker of that powerful poem now parades the isolation produced by his dubious gift before a "Dear Lady" ("Dejection" 138) who, in earlier drafts, Coleridge had given the names of William and Edward.

This pattern of denying to the female the position to which she had first been exalted was to become a paradigm. If in Wordsworth's earlier poems, as Margaret Homans has perceptively suggested, "the quietude" not just of Dorothy the living sister but also of dead sister-spirits such as Lucy Gray or Margaret in "The Ruined Cottage" "verifies the power of the poet's performative words" (224), his later poetry dissipates the feminine pagan sources of that power. Once again he turns the Female Other into a male Christian deity. In "She Was a Phantom of Delight," the gleaming "Apparition" that glides, Porphyria-like, into the poet's field of vision dissolves into a mundane woman engaged in "household motion," who can at best retain "something" of the "angelic light" formerly conferred on her by the poet's recoiling imagination (3, 13, 30). Masculine history and masculine religion take over in the later books of *The Excursion* and in the "Victorian" revisions of the 1805 *Prelude.*

In Byron's poetry, too, whether in the obsessive lyrics of parting such as "Fare Thee Well" and "To Augusta," or in dramas like *Manfred* (where the male protagonist can receive nothing more than an echo of his own name from Astarte's shade), and, most persistently, in *Don Juan,* where all romantic liaisons come to naught, the desired Female Other can never be embraced. Haidée, whom Juan still worships as his lodestar before he is forced to enter a harem in woman's clothing but whom he quickly forgets thereafter, can neither live nor expire in his arms. The only fusion possible is between Haidée and another male, the piratical father who causes her death:

> I said that they were alike, their features and
>   Their stature, differing but in sex and years;
> Even to the delicacy of their hand
>   There was resemblance (Byron, *Don Juan* IV: xlv)

Female victim and male victimizer can blend in death, equally forgotten by memory, resting in unvisited tombs. In Byron's masculine world, the Female Other must necessarily be sacrificed. Not until "James Lee's Wife" and its pendant-piece "Dîs Aliter Visum," significantly subtitled "Le Byron de nos Jours," and, most significantly in "Pompilia," would Browning counter this dispiriting vision by restoring to Byron's silent Haidée a genuine voice of her own.

It was the immediate precedent of the younger Romantics, however, as Harold Bloom rightly insists, that was most forcefully engraved in the mind who moved from *Pauline* (modeled after confessional romances such as *Alastor, Epipsychidion,* and *The Fall of Hyperion*) to the dramatic monologue spoken by Porphyria's deranged lover. Bloom perceptively recovers some of the Shelleyan "subtexts" that lurk in Browning's poetry. But his oedipal emphasis on masculine rivalry leads him to miss one of the chief attractions which Shelley, that "poet of women" (Lewes, "Percy Bysshe Shelley" 330), held for the young Browning. It also leads him to underestimate the significance of a Keats he casts as Tennyson's, but not Browning's, poetic "father" (Bloom 177, 143–74 *passim*).

Let us consider first the case of Keats. "Porphyria's Lover" can be seen as a deliberate revision of "The Eve of St. Agnes"—or, to indulge in Browning's macabre joke, what might be called an "Eve of St. Agnes" with a twist. The ironies and ambiguities embedded in Keats's semiallegorical treatment of projection are sharpened by the psychological realism of a poem in which the active Porphyro turns into Porphyria and the illusions of the hoodwinked Madeline turn into the delusions of a mad male fantasist. But it is not just Keats's single poem that provides a Bloomian "subtext" for "Porphyria's Lover." The Boccaccian Porphyro who penetrates Madeline's bower is merely one of many "Lovers" whose recurrence throughout Keats's entire canon Browning also rescrutinizes.

Whether it is the Endymion with whose search for Cynthia the early Keats had already identified in "I Stood Tip-Toe" ("He was a Poet, sure a lover, / Who stood on Latmus' top" [193–94]); or the "Bold Lover" on the Urn who must remain content with a "She" who cannot fade ("Ode on a Grecian Urn" 17, 19); or the ever-smitten Hermes who can blend with the nymph who, "like a moon in wane, / Faded before him" ("Lamia" 136–37); or the acolyte who wrests Psyche away from Cupid's embrace in order to place her into "some untrodden region of my mind" ("Ode to Psyche" 51), the figure of the Lover persistently acts as Keats's chief agent for the satisfaction of his desire to blend sexual consummation with the stasis of immortality. That stasis is associated either with godhead (as it also will be in the closure of "Porphyria's Lover") or with the permanence of art (as it will be in "My Last Duchess"). Yet the lyrical reconciliation of the mutable and the permanent can be expressed only as a subjective wish fulfillment. Only wishfulness can combine, in Keats's last great sonnet, a simultaneous enjoyment of the "steadfast" and "unchangeable" qualities of the distanced "Bright Star" and of the breathing motions of a living woman's warm, white "breast" against which the reposing lover can lie "pillow'd" (the original version read "*cheek*-pillow'd") (Keats, *The Poems of John Keats*: "Bright Star" 9).

Browning must have recalled some of these Keatsian touchstones in "Porphyria's Lover" where Porphyria makes the Lover recline his "cheek" against her bared "white" shoulder (19, 17). But he invokes them more directly in the sixteenth section of "One Word More," where he questions the fulfillment of the wish that Cynthia might "turn a new side" to her mortal gazers (Browning 161). "Unseen" (162) by herdsman, huntsman, and steersman, the other face of that female moon remains

> Blank to Zoroaster on his terrace,

Blind to Galileo on his turret,
Dumb to Homer, dumb to Keats—him, even! (162–65)

Browning's doubts, however, were fully anticipated by Keats himself. His skepticism is evident in the ironic treatment of a Porphyro who violates the "chamber of maiden thought" (Keats, *Letters* 107) or of a Lycius incapable of sustaining the vision that is Lamia.[1] Keats was as aware as Browning of the dangers of subjectivity. If that subjectivity could happily result in Endymion's transfiguration or in the internalization of Psyche, it could also deanimate and kill. The "palely loitering" "knight-at-arms" who fails to read the "language strange" of a Belle Dame sans Merci, the entranced Lycius who must die depleted, or the weak "dreaming thing" apostrophized by Moneta are all exemplars of the self-destructiveness inherent in a desire based on projection (Keats, *Poems*: "La Belle Dame Sans Merci" 2, 1, 27; "The Fall of Hyperion" I: 168). In "Porphyria's Lover," Browning simply reverses the process by having the Lover kill the very object of his desire.

Although in "Porphyria's Lover" Browning was able to accentuate ironies already inherent in Keats's narratives, his infatuation with Shelley's own cult of the woman was not easily shaken. Not until after the 1852 "Essay on Shelley" did he discover the full record of the infidelities of the Sun-Treader whose idealizations of the Female Other he had earlier emulated. Browning's reluctant dissociation from *Alastor* and *Epipsychidion* in *Pauline* had been artistic, not emotional. Yet in the 1855 "'Childe Roland to the Dark Tower Came,'" that hallucinatory and "de-idealizing" monologue (Bloom 175), the dissociation had become more profound. It is significant that no females appear in that poem of pure projection. The knight who journeys to the Dark Tower is not charged with the mission of rescuing an immured female. He is no St. George about to free a chained maiden, no Perseus rescuing Andromeda, no chivalric Count Gismond or a Gareth or Lancelot (as in Tennyson's or Morris's poems). Yet it is precisely the *absence* of a female object that makes the quest so gripping as an exercise in pure projection.[2] Absence *is* Presence, as Browning would have James Lee's Wife discover.

---

1. That skepticism is already in evidence as early as "Sleep and Poetry" in the deliberate infantilizing of the speaker who relies on "fancy" in order to catch the nymphs, play with their fingers, and touch "their shoulders white / Into a pretty shrinking with a bite / As hard as lips can make" (Keats, *Poems* 104–8).

2. Bloom holds that "'Childe Roland' exposes the Romantic imagination" by the speaker's induction in a "visionary company of loss" (199, 200); his insight might have been extended by a consideration of the failures of the speaker's two precursors in "The Band," Giles and Cuthbert, veiled embodiments of Wordsworth and Shelley.

By the time Browning came to write "James Lee's Wife," a poem which, by his own account, interestingly enough, was to dwell on "people newly-married," trying futilely "to realize a dream of being sufficient to each other, in a *foreign land* (where you can try such an *experiment*) and finding it break up,—the man being *tired* first, and tired precisely of the love" (Browning and Wedgewood, Browning as qtd. in Curle 109; only final italics are Browning's), the repudiation had become complete. He could at last see Shelley plain. Browning was now wholly disenchanted with the experimental love-ethic of a poet who had tried to share Harriet Westbrook and Mary Godwin; or, later, Mary and Emilia Viviani; or, later still, Mary and Jane Williams. It was an affront to the widowed Browning's Victorian respectability. But it was more. Despite its negative emphasis, "James Lee's Wife" reinstates the Female Other that Browning now felt Shelley had tarnished. Browning had already fashioned critiques of a male's denial of the feminine in "Porphyria's Lover" and "My Last Duchess." But whereas Lover and Duke had at least tried to possess a Female Other, the "tired" James Lee rejects fusion altogether. As Browning now knew, a wearied Shelley too had abandoned his quest for an ideal he despaired of finding in any living woman.[3]

Like James Lee, and unlike the poet who clung to a remembered happiness with Elizabeth Barrett, Shelley had never been satiated in his search for Intellectual Beauty. The Alastor poet who impales himself on the thresholds of consciousness could at best encounter a reflection of his own eyes. The speaker of *Epipsychidion*, who also dies in the course of his quest, similarly despairs of a female projection of his own self: "I measure / The world of fancies, seeking one like thee, / And find—alas! Mine own infirmity" (*Shelley's Poetry and Prose* 69–71). Neither Emilia the Sun nor Mary the blotted Moon "whose pale and waning lips" shrink "as in the sickness of eclipse" (*Epipsychidion* 309–10), nor even Clare Clairmont, that other astral body so abruptly introduced as a Comet "beautiful and fierce" (368), could satisfy an ever-hungry Astrophel. But if Keats questioned that hunger, Shelley relished it as a means of propulsion until, wearied, he turned away from the Female Other with something of the same disgust with which Victor Frankenstein destroys the half-completed Monstress he had tried to fashion. In one of the last letters he was to write before he immolated himself like the seekers of *Alastor* and *Epipsychidion*, he provided a fitting epitaph for his culmination of the Romantic quest for an epipsyche:

---

3. By adopting a female point of view, Browning attacked the weariness and lack of commitment of a male Romantic egotism, much as Mary Shelley had done in *Frankenstein*, the novel that, significantly enough, always remained one of Elizabeth Barrett's favorites.

The "Epipsychidion" I cannot look at; the person whom it celebrates was a cloud instead of a Juno; and poor Ixion starts from the centaur that was the offspring of his own embrace. If you are anxious, however, to hear what I am and have been, it will tell you something thereof. It is an idealized history of my life and feelings. I think one is always in love with something or other; the error, and I confess it is not easy for spirits cased in flesh and blood to avoid it, consists in seeking in a mortal image the likeness of what is perhaps eternal. (Shelley, *Letters* II: 434)

In "James Lee's Wife," Browning gave a voice to that "something or other" Shelley treats as yet another abstraction. In part VIII of the poem, he added a stanza in which the Wife adopts Shelley's bitterness as well as some of his phrasing:

I have my lesson, understand
    The worth of flesh and blood at last.
Nothing but beauty in a Hand?
    Because he could not change the hue,
    Mend the lines and make them true
To this which met his soul's demand,—
Would Da Vinci turn from you? ("James Lee's Wife" 294–300)

Leonardo the artist, she conjectures, would not dismiss a spirit cased in "flesh and blood" for an unrealizable ideal. But James Lee has dismissed his mate. And so, as Browning now reluctantly came to admit, would have Percy Bysshe Shelley.

II

In "Porphyria's Lover," as in Keats's "The Eve of St. Agnes," we are presented with a contrast between a cold outside world and a warm interior. In each poem, it is the passionate outsider penetrating that interior who brings warmth to the immobile dreamer within: just as Porphyria immediately kneels to make "the cheerless grate / Blaze up, and all the cottage warm" (*Robert Browning: The Poems* I: "Porphyria's" 8–9), so does her namesake, "burning Porphyro," with "heart on fire," try to melt the "chilly nest" he has invaded (*The Poems of John Keats*: "Eve" 159, 75, 235). Their efforts, however, are half-successful at best. If Browning's Porphyria cannot thaw her unresponsive lover by placing his "arm about her waist" and by pillowing his cold cheek on her "smooth white shoulder bare" ("Porphyria's" 16–17), Keats's Porphyro cannot rouse the sleeping Madeline by sinking "His warm, unnerved arm" on her "pillow" ("Eve" 280, 281).

The coldness of the outside world and its instability somehow cling to each of these intruders. Death's pallor envelops them, for all their warmth and vigorous movement. Kneeling before Madeline, Porphyro sinks "pale as smooth-sculptured stone"; when, on awakening, she sees him as "pallid, chill, and drear!" he is associated with the "pallid moonshine" in which her taper "died" (*The Poems of John Keats*: "Eve" 297, 311, 200). Even after he springs back into motion, Madeline's fears seem borne out by ominous details wedged into the narrative: the blowing "frost-wind," iced gusts, and setting moon undermine Porphyro's "impassion'd" (*The Poems of John Keats*: "Eve" 316) professions of eternal devotion. Yet Porphyria's Lover is warier than Madeline. Though Porphyria assures him that the "thought of one so pale / For love of her" has caused her to brave the elements and try to free her "struggling passion," the Lover finds insufficient comfort in the knowledge that "passion *sometimes* would prevail" (*Robert Browning: The Poems* I: "Porphyria's" 28–29, 23, 26, italics added). Instead, he stares guardedly at Porphyria's damp clothes and "soil'd gloves" (12) before deciding to convert that "sometimes" (26) into a forever, a moment of eternity. He will not risk the fate of his Romantic predecessor.

Hence, while Madeline resorts to trustfulness, Porphyria's Lover remains suspicious. Madeline accepts Porphyro's assurance that what he calls an "elfin-storm from faery land" ("Eve" 343) sanctions their joint removal from the "bloated wassaillers" at the feast (346). She thus submits to her abductor and vanishes in the chilly exterior: "And they are gone: aye, ages long ago / These lovers fled away into the storm" (370–71). Porphyria's Lover, on the other hand, will not venture beyond his mental cell. He fears that he will no more be able to "restrain" an impulsive Porphyria than did the "gay feast" she has abruptly left ("Porphyria's" 27). If Madeline comes to disregard the blowing "frost-wind," Porphyria's Lover considers the "sullen wind" to which he has listened "with heart fit to break" as an emblem of the instability that might destroy this brief "moment" of communion (2, 5, 36). The woman who found it so difficult to "dissever" herself from the stormy world without may prove to be as unreliable as Porphyro; while alive, she can at best momentarily "shut the cold out and the storm" (24, 7). Thus, only by freezing her into a stony permanence can this pale Lover preserve her temporary fire. Though he will tell us that the "cheek" of the woman he has strangled still blushes "bright beneath [his] burning kiss," he has conferred on her his own deathly pallor (47, 48). The

Lover who resembles Madeline has transformed himself into Madeline's possessor.

Browning's poem thus inverts Keats's narrative: the external coldness into which Porphyro ominously transports "so pure a thing" ("Eve" 225) becomes internalized by the Lover who wants to preserve Porphyria's purity by making her permanently "mine, mine, fair, / Perfectly pure and good" ("Porphyria's" 36–37). Yet Browning also has the Lover internalize the skepticism which in Keats's poem is presented through a "negative capability" that relies on imagery and multiple points of view. Porphyro's name (as well as Porphyria's) is derived from the Greek word for *purple* (as Keats knows when he alludes to the "purple riot" in Porphyro's heart, 138); as such, the name suggests a warm hue, as well as a high station.[4] But the vermilion dye of porphyry is obtained by pulverizing ("porphyrizing") a hard red shell or equally hard red slab of rock (as Keats again suggests when he describes Porphyro as a "smooth-sculptured stone," a "throbbing star," a "vermeil dyed" shield for Madeline's beauty (297, 318, 336). Madeline's warm lover, regarded by Angela as "liege-lord of all Elves and Fays" (121), may thus well be a cold-blooded immortal like Lamia or Merlin's "Demon" (171).

What Porphyria's Lover fears, however, is not the draining of his lifeblood by a vampiric immortal but rather the mutability of the mortal woman he identifies with the raging wind. Stony and still, unresponsive to her overtures, he awaits the moment in which he can rob Porphyria of her animated movements. Porphyro devises a quick stratagem to bypass the revelers at the feast and enter the "maiden's chamber": "Sudden a thought came like a full-blown rose" ("Eve"139, 187, 136). Similarly, a "sudden thought" has prompted Porphyria, according to the Lover's account, to leave the gay feast and venture into his chamber ("Porphyria's" 28). But her "thought" was a mere impulse, destined to be—or so he fears—short-lived. It is his own mind that searches for a stratagem as he, outwardly still passive and virginal, debates "what to do" until he lights upon the "thing" that might allow him to preserve her (35, 38). By draining Porphyria of her life, he can assume the mental control of a Porphyro. The "Bold Lover" forever frozen on Keats's stony Urn can never kiss his unfading "She": "though thou hast not thy bliss, / For ever wilt thou love, and she be fair!" (Keats, "Ode on a Grecian Urn" 19–20). In the stony tableau devised by Porphyria's Lover, however, that "bliss" becomes attainable. The necrophilic

---

4. For these and subsequent connotations see *The Compact Edition of the OED* II: 2242–43.

Lover kisses the dead woman; but, what is more, he can now impose his own mental processes on the mind whose inconstancy he had earlier feared:

> I propped her head up as before,
>   Only, this time my shoulder bore
> Her head, which droops upon it still:
>   The smiling rosy little head,
> So glad it has its utmost will,
>   That all it scorned at once is fled,
> And I, its love, am gained instead! ("Porphyria's" 49–55)

Converted into an "it," Porphyria's head no longer has the power of volition; instead, "its . . . will" is that of her subjective interpreter. She has become an object for the Lover's projection, for he can now impute to her his own wishes without any fear of contradiction.

This mechanism of projection was also at work in Keats's "The Eve of St. Agnes," where Porphyro played on Madeline's wishful and childish trust in the "visions of delight" promised to virgins on St. Agnes's Eve. Yet Madeline had come to sense a disparity between subject and object, wish and reality. Moreover, her misgivings were reinforced by a narrator who casts doubts upon her "shaded" dream by his frequent interventions and by juxtaposing her fantasies to those of the Beadsman and Angela ("Eve" 47, 282). There are no such narrator and no such subsidiary characters in "Porphyria's Lover." As in the companion piece to this poem, "Johannes Agricola in Meditation," we are from start to finish within the "madhouse cell" of the Lover's screened-off mind.

As an exercise in the subjectivism of projection, "Porphyria's Lover" thus raises certain questions that validate the earlier contention that Browning devised a parody of the Romantic quest for a Female Other. Whom is the Lover addressing? Where is he located? Given the absence of a verifiable interlocutor and a verifiable setting such as Browning was to provide six years later in the poem usually considered to be his first bona fide dramatic monologue, "My Last Duchess," how trustworthy, ultimately, is the Lover's account? We have the authority of Keats's narrator that Porphyro entered Madeline's chamber and exploited her dream. We cannot at all be sure that a Porphyria actually sought out the egocentric speaker who, at the very outset of his monologue, projects his internal turmoil on the "vex[ing]" (4) storm outside.[5] Has this speaker, whose very identity depends on his act of

---

5. Like Keats, Browning seems acutely aware of Coleridgean antecedents: if the storm tends to "vex" the Lover by its unruliness, it is the opposite state of "calm," not helped by "any

projection (the poem was originally called, quite simply, "Madhouse Cell, No. II"), truly killed Porphyria? Indeed, does a "Porphyria" really exist in a shape other than in his mind?

The similarity in the names of "Porphyro" and "Porphyria" may, after all, involve more than the reversal traced above. It may well suggest that not only Browning but also the deranged speaker whom he animates is a latter-day Romantic who knows his Keats. The "story" of "Porphyria's Lover" could hence be read as a pure fantasy told by a reader of "The Eve of St. Agnes" who, after identifying with Madeline's desire for the phantasm of a lover, does not want to share her disenchantment. That male reader thus feels free not only to reverse the gender of Keats's protagonists but also to devise a different outcome to gratify his crazed need for "pure" possession. In this sense, the Lover's confident assertion, "No pain felt she; / I am quite sure she felt no pain" ("Porphyria's" 41–42), actually would be true. The strangling of a purely imaginary object of desire can cause no pain to an actual human being "cased in flesh and blood" (Shelley on "Epipsychidion," *Letters* II: 434).

By the untrustworthiness of his speaker, Browning teases the readers of "Porphyria's Lover" into trying to provide a "story" of their own. But the scenarios we may concoct are just as untrustworthy. We may want to visualize a murderer who, surprised by the guard, still hovers gleefully over the body of an actual victim; or, if we accept the murder as imaginary, we may prefer to glimpse a madman in a cell. We may also be tantalized into furnishing some antecedent narrative of star-crossed lovers or one in which a passive visionary who has seen a nameless, high-born lady from afar (one "born in purple," a "porphyrogenite") dreams that this "She" will visit and worship him (*Compact OED* II: 2243). The possibilities are multiple, but all such conjectures are destined to remain futile. Our need to entertain them, despite that futility, only helps to sharpen Browning's ironic emphasis. Our mental narratives delude us into thinking that we can confer permanence and objectivity on what remains erratic and subjective. By inventing alternative "stories," we may try to distance ourselves from the grotesque Lover.

---

wind," that "vexes meditation" for another cottage dweller in "Frost at Midnight" (Coleridge 8, 9). Coleridge's speaker moves from inward paralysis to a dynamic animation of the landscape he devises for his child: Browning's Lover draws Porphyria into the frosty stillness of his mental cell. "Dejection: An Ode," Coleridge's other "midnight" poem, is also recalled in "Porphyria's Lover." Unable to find fuel in "that inanimate cold world" his imagination projects, Coleridge's agonized speaker seeks vainly to remove the "viper thoughts, that coil around my mind" by listening "to the wind" (51, 94); Porphyria's Lover, beset by similar anxieties, prefers to relieve his agony by coiling his thoughts around Porphyria's "little throat" (Browning 40).

Instead, however, we share his need to master a problematic instability through some spurious fiction.

It is precisely such an assumption of a spurious godlike immutability that links "Porphyria's Lover" both to its 1836 pendant poem "Johannes Agricola" and to the 1842 "My Last Duchess," with its own dramatization of the displacement of a Female Other by a male figure playing the role of God. The last two lines of "Porphyria's Lover" jar the reader almost as much as the strangling acknowledged in line 41: "And all night long we have not stirred, / And yet God has not said a word!" (59–60). God's voicelessness recalls the Lover's own deliberate silence when "called" by Porphyria. He and God and now she remain unstirred; they are at one. If Johannes Agricola the Antinomian professes "night by night" (Browning, "Johannes" 1) to be able to reach the abode of a deity who has exempted him from damnation, so does the Lover exult in his newly gained invulnerability. In the seventeenth century, the theologian Ralph Cudworth had inveighed against those "Porphyrianists" (the followers of Arius and Porphyrius) who made "their Trinity a foundation for creature-worship and idolatry."[6] Though not a follower of Porphyrius, the third-century neoplatonist, the Lover is nonetheless a "Porphyrianist" in his own way. His "creature-worship" of a woman of "flesh and blood" has resulted in her deanimation into a cold idol. By appropriating her mentally, he has become, he thinks, immune and immovable, like God. In the "night" of his own mind, he has shaped a new triune Identity. Whether Porphyria is his dead victim or merely a figment of his imagination thus does not matter. She remains in either case an eidolon whose possession he regards, in true Romantic fashion, as licensing his elevation to godhead. Like the artist-figures in the later monologues, who can confer life as well as arrest it, Porphyria's Lover professes to be actuated by his desire for another. Yet his love stands exposed as a monomaniacal self-love.

A similar self-love obviously operates in "My Last Duchess," a poem discussed by Browning critics, and ably so, far more often than "Porphyria's Lover," yet seldom seen in its own pendant relationship to the earlier poem. The similarities between the two works are significant, but so are the differ-

---

6. The citation is from Cudworth's *True Intellectual System* (1678), as qtd. in the *Compact OED* II: 2242. It is noteworthy that in the so-called Porphyrian scale or tree (also reproduced in the *OED*), the "Animate" should be identified, not with an "Incorporeal" substance such as the Christian soul, but with a "Corporeal" substance as much prized as its "Sensible" and "Rational" analogues. Long ago, C. R. Tracy pointed to the theological slant of the *Monthly Repository*, where "Johannes Agricola" and "Porphyria's Lover" originally appeared, in order to account for the religious satire of the former poem (618). The same case should be made for its companion piece, not usually recognized as a similar incursion into a heretical theology.

ences. The Lover who must dominate the "stooping" Porphyria by freezing her into a posture of submissive dependence resembles the Duke of Ferrara who chooses "Never to stoop" ("Porphyria's" 19; "My Last Duchess" 43). The Duke, too, deanimates a Female Other who threatens his need to remain in absolute control of his rigid mental world. But this calculating aesthete, though every bit as monstrous (and possibly more so), is not a crazed, improvising, pale Lover whose words are subject to doubt. Unlike that dehistoricized speaker's voice, his own carries the authority of a specific time and place, the staples of Browning's future monologues.

We do not know whom the Lover addresses and why, or whether he addresses anyone at all. We do know the identity of the Duke's interlocutor and know, moreover, that other viewers have previously been shown the portrait he ritually unveils "by design" ("My Last Duchess" 6). Indeed, it is the Duke's compulsive need for repetition that belies his efforts at composure and control. A new Duchess may be his current "object" (53), but his previous effort to objectify a living woman into a frozen painting still seems to unsettle him. The "curtain" (10) he removes for the Count's emissary thus gradually unveils a mind that is more disturbed than it would admit. If the reader of "Porphyria's Lover" becomes a voyeur at Bedlam who ultimately can no more "dissever" ("Porphyria's" 24) truth from fantasy than the subjective Lover himself, the reader of "My Last Duchess" becomes a detective who wrests away the control the Duke desires by seizing on the "objective" clues that have been provided. These clues permit us to judge the Duke far more unequivocally than we could ever judge the Lover.

The chief clue is provided by the Duchess herself. Like Porphyria, she exists solely within the speaker's words. Yet Browning permits the reader to free the Duchess from the Duke's possessive "My" in ways that Porphyria could never be disengaged from her Lover's strident "she was mine, mine" ("Porphyria's" 36). There is a further difference. It is his yearning for an Ideal that prompts the Lover to drain a woman's "flesh and blood." The Duke, however, has failed to grasp that such a feminine Ideal had actually animated his own world. If the blush on Porphyria's dead countenance was purely imaginary, the "spot of joy" preserved in Pandolf's painting still confounds the Duke's literalism ("My Last Duchess" 21). He will never understand how "such a glance came there" (12).Yet the details he furnishes carry symbolic meanings that continue to defy him. The "white mule" (28) on which his lady was wont to ride, the offering of a "bough of cherries" (27) brought to her by a worshiper, are iconographic details traditionally associated with the Virgin Mary. An earthly Madonna has gone unnoticed by a mind determined not to stoop. The "approving speech" with which this democratic mediatrix kindly received all those who greeted her has been extinguished, like her original "blush" (31). Empowered by Browning's art of inference, however, the reader can reactivate her receptivity, adopt the mediating role that she has lost, and thus restore to her what the Duke continues to deny.

Unlike the Duchess and Porphyria, Browning's later women are allowed to speak: of these, Pompilia, a full-blown version of the earthly Madonna, modeled, as Nina Auerbach has shown ("Robert Browning's Last Word" 161–73), after Barrett's Marian Earle (and Barrett herself), certainly is the most notable. Even when dead or silenced, however, Browning's later incarnations of the Female Other continue to confound the male's attempts at mental possession. The fair "she" appropriated by that other art collector, the Bishop of St. Praxed's (a church named, significantly enough, after a female martyr) will find avengers in her sons. In "Andrea del Sarto" Lucrezia enacts the inconstancy that Porphyria's Lover had feared. But her behavior defiles her would-be possessor more than herself. She is an unchaste Cynthia whom he must share with others: "My face, my moon, my everybody's moon" ("Andrea del Sarto" 29). Her mobility sets in relief the impotence of this half-man (see "Andrea del Sarto" 140). Although Andrea would, like Porphyria's Lover, dearly want to restrain the woman's movements, he can only paralyze himself. His self-loathing strangles his very dream of artistic immortality in a New Jerusalem where he, as the elect decorator of a fourth great wall, might join Leonardo, Raphael, and Michelangelo, "the three first without a wife" (264). He remains walled in by the mental prison that Lucrezia can flee. If she acts as Andrea's foil, so does Fra Lippo Lippi, who also breaks out of the confinement of mental and physical cells, for Lippo knows that Ideal and flesh cannot be "dissevered." Accordingly, at the end of his monologue, he suddenly defers to the female voice of "the sweet angelic slip of a thing" ("Fra Lippo" 370) whom he casts in the role of rescuer. She embodies the paradox he cannot resolve. She is an image, a Saint Lucy, a type in a painting; yet she is also the Prior's niece, a married woman, very much alive, and, as such, one who arouses Lippo's desire.

III

In *Jocoseria* (1883), one of his last volumes of poetry, Browning movingly recalls his dead mate in the fine lyric "Never the Time and the Place." The writer of dramatic monologues once more assays the Romantic lyrical mode he had been forced to relinquish. Whether consciously or not, however, he resorts to the same imagery he had used in "Porphyria's Lover" almost half a century before. And he does so now without the defensive ironies that had marked his earlier, seminal incursion into timelessness and placelessness. "Where is the loved one's face?" ("Never" 5) the speaker asks plaintively, and then proceeds to answer his own question:

> In a dream that loved one's face meets mine,
>   But the house is narrow, the place is bleak
> Where, outside, rain and wind combine
>   With a furtive ear, if I strive to speak,
> . . . .
>   Outside are the storms and strangers: we—
> Oh, close, safe, warm sleep I and she,
>   —I and she! (5–9, 20–22)

James Lee had yet to mature before he could glimpse a female face like his own. But the seventy-year-old Browning was more than ready to exclaim, "Tis She!" ("James Lee's Wife" 357). No "half-man" like Andrea ("Andrea del Sarto" 140), he had given expression to a feminine self. And in *Jocoseria* he once more strove to speak in the female voice. In his poem "Mary Wollstonecraft and Fuseli," Mary Shelley's mother utters an artistic credo that is unmistakably Browning's own. Fuseli can sublimate emotions into his controlled compositions, but she toils "at a language" (12) that in its very roughness retains her "strong fierce" passionate core (29). Elsewhere in *Jocoseria,* in the Talmudic tales of Balkis and Solomon, and Lilith and Eve, Browning blends his feminism with his growing philo-Semitism, the product of a similar identification with the victims of a cultural oppression that relied on mental projection as much as prejudice.

It is significant that *Jocoseria* was originally supposed to include "Gerousios Oinos," Browning's attack on the later Tennyson, Morris, Rossetti, and Swinburne. What prompted Browning to cast his contemporaries as "mere servingmen," unrestrainedly quaffing the diluted "true wine" of the elder English poets, thinking it "bettered and bittered" by "mixing it with beer" ("Gerousios" 14, 41, 42)? He had become defensive about his own stature after Alfred Austin's attack; yet Tennyson had been just as shabbily treated by Austin, and, moreover, younger poets like Swinburne had indignantly rallied to Browning's side. As his letters to Isa Blagden show, Browning genuinely disliked the supposed dilutions of meaning in the later *Idylls of the King,* the later poems of Morris, and the verses of Swinburne and Rossetti, all marred by "the *minimum* of thought and idea in the *maximum* of words and phraseology" (Browning to Isabella Blagden as qtd. in Browning, *Dearest Isa* 333). Yet even this artistic difference seems insufficient to account for the excessive vehemence of Browning's attack in "Gerousios Oinos"—an excessiveness he seemed to acknowledge when he suppressed publication of the poem.

It was not mere difference that so disturbed Browning but a shocked recognition of kinship. Tennyson's most Browning-like dramatic monologue, "Lucretius," had appeared in 1868. And the trio of younger poets had also adopted Browning's central theme of the Female Other—from Morris's 1856 "The Defence of Guenevere" to Rossetti's 1870 "Jenny" and "A Last Confession." To be sure, his impact on these younger poets was far from exclusive. Their female portraits were also indebted to a Tennyson who had, after all, published "Mariana" and "The Lady of Shalott" even before Browning printed—and withdrew—his *Pauline* (which Rossetti was to rediscover) and who had written "Tithon," the original version of "Tithonus," around the very same time that Browning composed "Porphyria's Lover." Still, the Female Other whom the Pre-Raphaelites represented on canvas and in verse, like Swinburne's Proserpines and Sapphos, owed as much, or more, to Browning.

"One face looks out from all his canvasses," Christina Rossetti wrote in an implicit criticism of her brother's work ("In an Artist's Studio" 1). Whether queen or "nameless girl," or angel or saint, the Female Other now allowed a younger generation of artists to "feed" upon "her face by day or night." Browning agreed: "Yes,—I have read Rossetti's poems," he wrote Isa Blagden; "you know I hate the effeminacy of his school,—the men that dress up like women,—that use obsolete forms, too, and archaic accentuations to seem soft" (Browning, *Dearest Isa* 336). Did not these lovers of the Female Other resemble his own Porphyria's Lover? Rossetti had even indulged in necrophilia by wresting his poems from Lizzie Siddal's corpse. Looking at the faces that glanced at him from their paintings in pen and pencil, a shocked Browning saw not the flush of joy of a Last Duchess, as if she were alive, but the grimaces of ladies of pain, adulteresses, femmes fatales, prostitutes, and vampires. The younger nympholepts were not just "feeding" off the representations of England's elder poets. These hungry "servingmen" were also consuming the very substance of the elderly Browning's own poetry.

In "John Jones's Wife," a Swinburne who had become disenchanted with Browning did, in effect, just that. By writing a parody of "James Lee's Wife," the younger poet could openly appropriate Browning's mode and subject matter and go one better. In his attack on Browning in "The Chaotic School," the essay he left in manuscript, Swinburne denies Browning the skill of impersonating a true woman:

> How does it fare with his Colombes, Constances, Mildreds, Phenes, who are visibly fleshless and senseless? Analyze the doings and saying of the wife of Jules or the mistress of Norbert; the utter mechanical absurdity of the monstrous parts they have to play is equalled by the tight, hoarse, intermittent, hard, febrile manner of their utterances: as far from emotion as from reason. (Swinburne 53)

Swinburne thus transforms the voice of James Lee's Wife into the voice of a Female Other wronged by Browning's art; his speaker's quarrel is not just with "John Jones" but with her original creator:

> My skin might change to a pitiful crone's,
>   My lips to a lizard's, my hair to weed,
> My features, in fact, to a series of loans;
>   Thus much is conceded; now, you concede
> You would hardly salute me by choice, John Jones? (Swinburne, *Complete* V: 268)

Like the Keats who wrested Psyche away from Cupid, Swinburne the parodist has become a rival lover. Yet his rivalry stems from an acknowledgment of the very kinship that the older poet so eagerly tried to suppress.

Browning had come to see himself as the jealous preserver of both the memory and the voice of Elizabeth Barrett, his female "moon of poets." He could not accept this "effeminate" competitor, whose "florid impotence" he denounced (*Dearest Isa* 333). Any yet Swinburne's criticism was an act of generosity. "I do *not* count Browning a lyric poet proper," he wrote, "nor properly a dramatic, as he breaks down in dialogue; but his greatness as an *artist* I think (now more than ever) established to all time by his *monodramas*. I say *artist,* or poet, as well as thinker."[7] It is significant that this tribute should have come shortly after Swinburne's close reading of the monodrama of "James Lee's Wife." It was a tribute he was to extend in his elegiac "Sequence of Sonnets on the Death of Robert Browning" in 1889. There, he celebrated Browning for his capacity to "see / The heart within

---

7. To William Michael Rossetti, 1869 October 26; *The Swinburne Letters* II: 46–47; Swinburne's italics. In the same letter Swinburne expresses his outrage at Austin's attack on Browning.

the heart that seems to strive" (Swinburne, *Complete* VI: 148). And that innermost heart remained, for both poets, always essentially female.

This attempt at a chapter in literary history would not be complete without my calling attention to the centrality, in all Victorian poetry, of the patterns of projection I have described. In "The Voice" (1912), Thomas Hardy, that relic from the Victorian Age, still tried to animate a dead Female Other: "Woman much missed, how you call to me, call to me, / Saying that now you are not as you were" (Hardy, *Complete Works* 1–2). Browning's contribution to English poetry was both his attempt to give voice to a Female Other as well as his persistent skepticism about the process of projection that such a voicing involved. Like Keats, who might have become the greatest of Victorian poets, Browning knew that poetry, like all art, can distort the Female Other into what she is not. It was that skepticism which gave rise to the dramatic monologue and which led to a mode simultaneously ironic and idealistic that Browning came to perfect and to bequeath to later poets.

CHAPTER 5

DOVER REVISITED

The Wordsworthian Matrix in the Poetry of Matthew Arnold

Subjecting paired poems by Wordsworth and Arnold to close analysis, Knoepflmacher shows that even though the latter's poetry bemoans a loss of faith in nature and religion, it still seeks to preserve the "feeling" Arnold deems to be Wordsworth's central legacy. Only feeling can prop up and help balance intellect. Arnold is convinced that nineteenth-century poetry can no longer be expected to harmonize "the still sad music of humanity" into a universal chorus of faith. He therefore opts to do the second best thing. Unable to assert "joy," he can at least cling to the "eternal note of sadness" itself. Thus, paradoxically enough, the Victorian poet can engender feeling by bemoaning the loss of Romantic feeling. In his own poetry and in his later editing (and rearranging) of Wordsworth's poetry for readers, Arnold aimed to preserve Wordsworth's emotional core.

*M*uch has been written on Matthew Arnold's qualification of Romanticism, on his fluctuating estimates of the English Romantic poets in general and of William Wordsworth in particular. Such studies are generally limited to Arnold's critical opinions (see James; Jamison). Only occasionally, and then very succinctly, have students of Arnold's poetry dwelled on his creation of what a perceptive critic has called "ironic echoes of

Wordsworth": "a version of Wordsworth which is also a criticism and a rejection of Wordsworth's view" (see W. Stacy Johnson; Baum 25ff; Trilling 75ff; E. D. H. Johnson 152–53).

Arnold's poetry is, to a large extent, derivative. It draws on the classics for much of its mythic substance and the stateliness of its rhythm; on Goethe for intellectual content; on sources as remote as the *Bhagavad Gita* for that "wider application" which Arnold felt was "the one thing wanting to make Wordsworth an even greater poet than he is" (Arnold, *Lectures and Essays* III: 262). But the core of Arnold's emotional power is Wordsworthian, and it is so by intent and not by mere coincidence. Arnold's poems avail themselves of situations that are Wordsworthian, images that are Wordsworthian, and phrases that are Wordsworthian. This Wordsworthian matrix is enlisted in what essentially amounts to a denial of the vision of Arnold's predecessor, although, at the very same time, it is relied upon to preserve Wordsworth's ability "to make us feel" (Arnold *Poems*, "Memorial Verses" 67). I shall try to illustrate the quality and extent of Arnold's use of this matrix in the two sections that follow by examining two poems, "Resignation" and "Dover Beach," in light of their counterparts in Wordsworth. I shall conclude by discussing the reasons that prompted Arnold to conserve Wordsworthian elements in his poetry in face of the almost impossible gulf that separated his convictions as a Victorian poet from those of his Romantic precursor.

I

Arnold's "Resignation" is his version, or, more properly, his inversion, of Wordsworth's "Tintern Abbey." The parallelism between the two poems is deliberate. It enables Arnold to employ his predecessor's work as a frame of reference, an ironic "touchstone" essential to his own meaning.[1] "Resignation" is almost twice as long as "Tintern Abbey." It abounds in erudite allu-

---

1. In their otherwise excellent commentary on the poetry of Arnold, C. B. Tinker and H. F. Lowry, though dwelling extensively on the Goethean sources of "Resignation," strangely failed to point out that the poem is above all a rebuttal of Wordsworth, who, according to his youthful critic, "should have read more books, among them, no doubt those of Goethe whom he disparaged without reading him" (Arnold, *Complete* III: "The Function of Criticism at the Present Time" 262). Although Paull F. Baum noted the analogues between "Resignation" and "Tintern Abbey," he dismissed them cursorily by remarking that the "exhortations" of the two poets are after all "quite unlike" each other, thus underestimating the importance of this "unlikeness" for a reading of Arnold's poem, 25–26, fn. 3.

sions and echoes from sources as varied as Lucretius and Goethe. But the core of the poem is unmistakably Wordsworthian: the setting is the Lake Country of the Romantics; the situation, a return to the earlier associations of the scene by a matured poet and his sister; the import, a creed handed down by the poet to his listener.

In "Tintern Abbey" Wordsworth and Dorothy stand "here upon the banks of this fair river" (*Wordsworth: Poetical Works* 114–15). The poet mourns his lost childhood oneness with Nature but derives joy from the knowledge that his sister still possesses the power he has lost. The poem ends on a triumphant assertion of his belief in a matured and "sober pleasure" (139) based on the "wild ecstasies" (138) of youth. Memory becomes a source of joy: "Nature never did betray the heart that loved her" (122). The poet, "a worshiper of Nature" (152), can readily become its priest.

In "Resignation" the speaker and the sister he addresses as "Fausta" also stand "on this mild bank above the stream" amidst a lush natural landscape that has remained unaltered despite changes they have suffered. "The loose dark stones" (*The Poems of Matthew Arnold* 100) have not moved; "this wild brook" (104) runs on, undisturbed. The scene's permanence sharpens the poet's awareness of mutability. He, too, hopes to derive a creed based on his observation of Nature. But while the speaker's yearning for sobering "thoughts" (203) suggested by the surroundings is not unlike Wordsworth's, his interpretation of these surroundings is markedly different. Indeed, the ethical creed that he charts out for his sister and the poetic creed he indirectly prescribes for himself are based on a complete redefinition of a Wordsworthian faith in Nature. To Wordsworth, the communion between Nature and man is in itself an abundant compensation for life's mutability—it can bring about a communion between brother and sister, man and man, and confirms the poet in his role of Nature's high priest. To Arnold, on the other hand, the utter impersonality of the scene before him only accentuates the need for a response toward a natural world that can no more provide the "tender joy" ("Tintern Abbey" 145) that Wordsworth was capable of extracting from it than it can stimulate the heightened sensations sought by his Faustian sister. Arnold must therefore explain to the Romantic Fausta the limitations suggested by landscape and, simultaneously, delimit his own functions as new kind of poet, a poet deprived of the "rapt security" (246) inherent in the Romantic vision.

To Arnold the landscape is but an emblem of "the general life" (191), an impersonal power that demands human submission. But rather than becoming a mere object subjected to the capriciousness of "chance," humans can at least find some dignity in the rule of "fate" by accepting their position within the "dizzying eddy" of life. This acceptance can come only through detachment. Instinctively achieved by gypsies plodding in their "hereditary way," it must be consciously achieved by those trained to discern "what through experience others learn."

In outline, Arnold's schematization is not unlike Wordsworth's. He has identified the landscape before him with an order or plan that he, as a detached observer, is able to perceive; he has maintained that this order can be understood instinctively by some and consciously by others; he has established the need for an acceptance of this plan, "the general life." But, of course, it is the valuation that Arnold places on these elements which is entirely opposed to Wordsworth's. Children unconsciously in touch with the divine have become hardened gypsies instinctively attuned to the buffets of life; the redeeming Dorothy has become the unredeemable Fausta; the isolated poet who converts the "still, sad music of humanity" into a joyful faith has become a detached stoic contemplator, content with a "sad lucidity of soul" (198).[2] What has changed, above all, is the order perceived by the poet and the manner in which the poet's perception has been achieved.

The divine "presence" Wordsworth perceives in the landscape he sees also resides in himself. It is:

>   a sense sublime
> Of something far more deeply interfused,
> Whose dwelling is the light of setting suns,
> And the round ocean and the living air,
> And the blue sky, and in the mind of man;
> A motion and a spirit, that impels
> All thinking things, all objects of all thought,
> And rolls through all things. (95–102)

---

2. Arnold's choice of gypsies as a prime example involved nothing less than a direct rebuttal of the position taken by Wordsworth in his 1807 poem, "Gipsies." In this little-known poem, Wordsworth regards the gypsies he has met during an excursion as subhuman, almost devilish creatures who remain unaffected by the laws of man and Nature. Shunning their fellowmen during the day, totally oblivious of their natural surroundings, Wordsworth's gypsies raise "bolder" fires at night and thus defy the "mighty Moon" and the "very stars" that "reprove" them for their negligence as much as the poet himself. Arnold's gypsies likewise "crouch round the wild flame" (118). But their purpose is simple: they merely want to stay warm in order to "rub through" life. For, unlike Wordsworth's gypsies, they *are* affected by time and change. Their indifference to Nature therefore is not, as with Wordsworth, a reprehensible act of defiance, but, quite the contrary: an expression of their triumph over a natural world that has, in turn, become wholly indifferent toward them. Arnold's gypsies wait stoically "Till death arrive to supersede, / For them vicissitude and need" (143).

To Arnold, on the other hand, "the something which infects the world" is not an invisible *primum mobile*. It is the aggregate of all that is visible, an impersonal and tyrannical power that offers "not joy, but peace" to those who apprehend its operations:

> Before him he sees life unroll,
> A placid and continuous whole;
> That general Life, which does not cease,
> Whose secret is not joy, but peace;
> That life, whose dumb wish is not miss'd
> If birth proceeds, if things subsist;
> The life of plants, and stones, and rain,
> The life he craves—if not in vain
> Fate gave, what chance shall not control,
> His sad lucidity of soul. (189–98)

Nature has provided Wordsworth with a "holy love"; yet it merely confirms Arnold's saddened intellectual awareness.

"Tintern Abbey" and "Resignation" rely on the modulation of conflicting moods; both poems conclude on the speaker's subjection to a discipline based on Nature. Wordsworth emphasizes the beneficence of this discipline; Arnold emphasizes its grim necessity. In each case, the landscape has acted as a guide. But while, for Wordsworth, Nature is an active teacher and comforter who readily reveals "a presence that disturbs me with the joy / Of elevated thoughts," ("Tintern Abbey" 94–95), Arnold's "thoughts" are addressed rhetorically to the impassive landscape before him so that it might teach "Fausta" a well-rehearsed lesson in the art of "bearing":

> Enough, we live!—and if a life,
> With large results so little rife,
> Though bearable, seem hardly worth
> This pomp of worlds, this pain of birth;
> Yet, Fausta, the mute turf we tread,
> The solemn hills around us spread,
> This stream which falls incessantly,
> The strange-scrawl'd rocks, the lonely sky,
> If I might lend their life a voice,
> Seem to bear rather than rejoice. ("Resignation" 259–76)

Though no longer a "thoughtless youth," Wordsworth can recover his "former pleasures" through the younger sister whose absorption in the landscape he greatly values ("Tintern Abbey" 90, 117). "Nature," he tells her, will continue to "feed" and "inform the mind that is within" (127, 125–26). For Arnold, however, Nature is impervious to the emotional demands of its students. The speaker of "Resignation" who derides Fausta for her immersion in the landscape insists that the language he ascribes to the scene before them is really his own. The turf is "mute," the hills are "solemn," even the rocks are enigmatic and "strange-scrawl'd." The poet thus is forced to superimpose his own order on the scene he sees before him. He can at best attribute an imagined "voice" to the life he sees around him; he can only assume that the landscape would "seem" to teach him how "to bear."

Wordsworth's vision is transcendent and symbolical: ocean, air, and sky contain the same spirit that dwells "in the mind of man" (99). Arnold's vision is analytical and allegorical: the mind of man can tentatively impose its understanding upon what it apprehends through the senses. Therefore, while Wordsworth's poet is a medium for the divine plan of Nature, Arnold's poet is merely the interpreter of the "dumb" (193) wishes of a neutral universe. Whereas Wordsworth becomes infused and intoxicated by the centrifugal power of Nature, Arnold must stand aside and examine his own relative position in time and space in order to preserve his "lucidity of soul" (198). The scene before him is meaningless in itself. It must be related to Mohammedan pilgrims and Gothic warriors, to Orpheus and to Homer. Intensity is replaced by extensiveness: "Not deep the poet sees, but wide" (212). The resolution of Arnold's poem therefore depends entirely on his a priori survey of the "general life," a survey brought about by that cultural view which he claimed that Wordsworth lacked to make "his thought richer and his influence of wider application" (*Lectures and Essays, Complete* III: 262).

"Resignation" thus represents Arnold's attempt to give a contemporary application to Wordsworth's Romantic poem. In a characteristically Victorian juggling, an emotional faith in Nature is qualified by the wider intellectual view afforded by scientific skepticism, historicism, and "Culture." But Arnold's qualification also alters Wordsworth's poetic method. The symbolically exalted "green pastoral landscape" ("Tintern Abbey" 158) becomes an allegorized "green hill-side" ("Resignation" 59) arbitrarily invested with qualities corresponding to the human situation. This same process would be carried over, eighteen years later, into "Dover Beach" (1867), a poem in which Arnold again relies on a Wordsworthian matrix to record his own dissentient Victorian vision.

II

While Arnold's "Resignation" stands squarely in the line of "Tintern Abbey," the dependence of "Dover Beach" on Wordsworth's two famous sonnets, "It is a Beauteous Evening, Calm and Free," and "Near Dover, September, 1802," is far more oblique, for Arnold draws on the situation, the imagery, and the phrasing of both of Wordsworth's Romantic sonnets to build up the essentially anti-Romantic impact of "Dover Beach."

In "A Beauteous Evening" Wordsworth interprets the scene for "the dear girl" at his side by asking her to listen to the thunder of the tide: "Listen! the mighty Being is awake, / And doth with his eternal motion make / A sound like thunder—everlastingly" (6–8). Arnold's command to his companion echoes that of the sonnet, but, significantly enough, his interpretation of the sound is almost exactly the opposite of Wordsworth's:

> Listen! you hear the grating roar
> Of pebbles which the waves draw back, and fling,
> At their return, up the high strand,
> Begin, and cease, and then again begin,
> With tremulous cadence slow, and bring
> The eternal note of sadness in. ("Dover Beach" 9–14)

To Wordsworth the sound of the sea suggests a "solemn thought" ("A Beauteous Evening" 10) which, though important for his own edification, is unnecessary for the child who, like Dorothy in "Tintern Abbey," is in direct communication with the divine order of Nature. Arnold likewise finds "in the sound a thought," but he must translate his thought to his companion, who has, like the poet himself, been deceived by the illusory beauty of the calm evening scene ("Dover Beach" 19). Thus, while the "thunder" of the sea suggests to Wordsworth the beneficence of Nature's plan and fills him with that harmonious sound described in "Tintern Abbey" as "The still, sad music of humanity, / Not harsh nor grating," it is precisely the "grating" quality of the tide's "roar" that causes Arnold to reflect on the "ebb and flow of human misery" heard long ago by Sophocles.

Arnold makes use of Wordsworth's second sonnet, "Near Dover," to an even larger extent. At first sight, however, only the similarity in location would seem to link both poems. While "A Beauteous Evening" and "Dover Beach" share a common situation provided by the seaside setting, the evening, the relationship between the speaker and his female companion, and by the interpretation of what the poet *hears* rather than sees, in

"Near Dover" the poet is alone out in the open; it is daylight, and the poet's interpretation is based exclusively on the unusually sharp visual clarity that projects the French coast into an unexpected proximity: "Inland, within a hollow vale, I stood, / And saw, while sea was calm and air was clear, / The coast of France how near!" ("Near Dover" 1–3). Only the calmness of the sea is identical in both poems: "The sea is calm tonight. / The tide is full, the moon lies fair / Upon the straits;—on the French coast the light / Gleams and is gone" ("Dover Beach" 1–4). The sharply delineated "coast of France" of "Near Dover" has become a shimmering "French coast." Moonlight haze has been substituted for daylight clarity. And, what is more, the heightened, quasi-Wordsworthian feelings produced by the sight of the "tranquil bay" are abruptly replaced by the thoughts produced by the "grating" roar. For "Dover Beach" inverts the experience depicted in "Near Dover" just as much as "Resignation" inverted "Tintern Abbey."

Wordsworth's poem is about belief. The contracting channel brings the coast of France into a "frightful neighborhood," but the span of waters that divides the two countries acts as a protective ring which speaks to the poet of the unseen protection of God:

> I shrunk, for verily the barrier flood
> Was like a Lake, or River bright and fair,
> A span of waters; yet what power is there!
> What mightiness for evil and for good!
> Even so doth God protect us if we be
> Virtuous and wise. ("Near Dover" 5–10)

The sonnet posits faith in the invisible which is based on a faith in the visible. "Dover Beach" laments the impossibility of such a faith. Just as in "Resignation" Arnold discredits the "healing power" of a Wordsworthian landscape, so in "Dover Beach" he stresses the unreliability of a Romantic belief in the visual.

Wordsworth's sonnet is neatly divided. The octave renders the poet's surprise at the sudden proximity of the French coast; the sestet, beginning with "even so," reproduces the intuitive faith that the awareness of the "barrier flood" has produced. The opening of "Dover Beach" mimics Wordsworth's harmonious vision. Like Wordsworth's octave, the first eight lines of "Dover Beach" rely exclusively on the poet's visual appreciation of the scene before him. The smooth alliteration and balance of Wordsworth's "and *s*aw *wh*ile *s*ea *w*as *c*alm and air *w*as *c*lear" find their counterpart in Arnold's "The tide is *full*, the moon *lies fair*." Just as the sight of the water provokes from Wordsworth an enthusiastic outcry over its "power," so does the view of the bay cause Arnold to indulge in a romantic exclamation. But the evidence of the senses is soon dispelled. The poet's raptures are qualified by a hesitant "only" in line 7 and by a sudden pause after line 8, as the full force of the "thought" provoked by the "grating roar" has asserted itself. From that point on, discordance enters into the poem. The rhyme scheme and rhythm become highly irregular and regain only some regularity in the conclusion.

For Wordsworth, the optical trick that transforms the channel into a "river bright and fair" provides an instantaneous revelation, a realization of God's decree. But for Arnold, the momentary deception produced by the "fair" moon and the glimmering coastal lights only confirms his anterior suspicion of the senses. For neither a visual sense, as in "Near Dover," nor an auditory sense, as in "A Beauteous Evening," can be relied upon, since these senses may very well be at odds. Thus sight is replaced by sound, but sound must be replaced by thought, by the poet's self-conscious allegorization of the retreating waters into a "Sea of Faith." The emotional Wordsworthian surge of feeling has been displaced by the ebb of intellect. Wordsworth's analogy between the bright "barrier flood" and God's armor has been instinctive; Arnold's analogy between the sea and the "bright girdle" that was once furled around the shores of humanity is derivative and intellectualized. The "thought" that he has found in the harsh sound of the tide is not the product of a sudden inspiration but is based instead on his lulled, but now reawakened, consciousness of historical determinism, the decay of religion, of Sophocles' metaphoric description of human misery, and, indirectly, of that other poet who stood before him "by this distant northern sea" (Arnold, "Dover Beach" 20). Once again Arnold has inserted the "Culture" he found absent in Wordsworth.

For Wordsworth, the contraction of the channel causes him to "shrink" with it into a more direct contact with unseen divinity. For Arnold, the channel spreads out endlessly through time and space leaving him stranded on "the naked shingles of the world" (28). Wordsworth regards the winds and waters of the channel as messengers of God's "decree." "In themselves," he asserts, they "are nothing" (12). Arnold must cling to this "nothing." The value he ascribes to the "bright girdle" (3) of water is the same value given to it by Wordsworth. But the emblem has only an antiquarian importance. It has lost its immediacy and become a thing of the past. Resigning himself to life in a "land of dreams" (30), the poem's speaker can at least bemoan his inability to believe in the dream itself, the dream of the Romantics. In his catalogue of lost qualities—joy, love, light, certitude, peace, and help for pain, Arnold enumerated all the qualities that Wordsworth was still able to obtain in 1802, near the very same beach. The view from Dover had changed considerably over the short span of sixty years.

III

"Resignation" and "Dover Beach" are perhaps the most obvious examples of Arnold's use of a Wordsworthian matrix in his poetry. But they are by no means the only ones. Arnold's "To a Gipsy Child by the Seashore" reverberates with echoes from "Ode: Intimations of Immortality" (see W. Stacy Johnson 47–51); his "East London" and "West London" sonnets are the Victorian counterparts of the London sonnets written by Wordsworth in 1802; the conception of the "Marguerite" poems owes much to Wordsworth's use of his "Lucy." There are correspondences in situations and phrases. Images, such as the elm tree in "Thyrsis" (which recalls the oak of "Michael"), or the "sea of life" in "To Marguerite," are invested with Wordsworthian properties.

The introduction of these elements into Arnold's own poetry represents more than a mere negation of Wordsworth's vision. There is a definite effort at conservation on the part of a poet, who, according to Quiller-Couch's witticism, had a notable tendency to regard himself as Wordsworth's widow (as qtd. by Bush 359). The younger man, whose boyhood "had been spent in the Lake Country and under Wordsworth's affectionate eye" (Trilling 19), tried to knit his own experience unto that of his predecessor. Indeed, not only Arnold, but a host of other eminent Victorians, regarded Wordsworth with a curious ambivalence. Intellectually, they deplored the simplicity of his natural faith, yet, at the same time, the skeleton of this faith provided them with a vicarious emotional gratification. Wordsworth was able to do what his successors could no longer achieve. He could convert grief and pain into joyous affirmation; he could draw this affirmation from the element which he called "the still sad music of humanity" (91) and which Arnold was to rename "the eternal note of sadness" (14). This is the pattern of some of Wordsworth's greatest poems: "Tintern Abbey," the "Immortality" ode, and the opening of *The Prelude*. Even in "Elegiac Stanzas," written in bereavement over the tragic drowning of his brother, he managed to draw "hope" from "deep distress" and to derive humanizing emotions from irreparable loss (60, 36). To the Victorians such a feat was definitely worth observing.

Arnold particularly admired this Wordsworthian power of transforming individual grief into a statement of universal affirmation. In his "Memorial Verses, April 1850," he pays homage to his dead predecessor by ranking him above Goethe and Byron. The attitude Arnold takes toward the Laureate is very similar to that which, ninety years later, W. H. Auden was to take toward Yeats. The deceased poet stands for a definite period of history, a simpler worldview that his successor cannot revive. But Wordsworth also stands for something else:

> Ah! since dark days still bring to light
> Man's prudence and man's fiery might,
> Time may restore us in his course
> Goethe's sage mind and Byron's force;
> But where will Europe's latter hour
> Again find Wordsworth's healing power?
> Others will teach us how to dare,
> And against fear our breast to steel;
> Others will strengthen us to bear—
> But who, ah! who, will make us feel? (58–67)

Others can adopt a "prudent" Goethean renunciation or teach us to resist despair through a Byronic defiance. But Wordsworth's "healing power" is as irretrievable as the shining armor of the Sea of Faith. The question of the hour, therefore, is not only "*who* will make us feel?" (67) but the implicit "*what* will make us feel?" Arnold never doubts that the power "to make us feel" must be kept alive at all costs, but from where is this feeling to be drawn? Nature no longer offers a religion. The Victorian poet can no longer expect to harmonize "the still sad music of humanity." He must therefore do the second best thing by merely clinging to the "eternal note of sadness" he can share with Wordsworth. By lamenting his own inability to replace this sadness with new feelings of joy, Arnold can at least acknowledge the superiority of "Wordsworth's healing power" (63). Thus, paradoxically enough, the Victorian poet can engender feeling by bemoaning the loss of feeling.

Arnold eventually realized that such a diminished conservation of Wordsworth was not a conservation after all. By reiterating an elegiac "note of sadness" (14), Arnold had transgressed his own rules for "the right Art" (Arnold "Preface" 1853, in "Culture and Anarchy" I: 2). The joy so deeply felt by Wordsworth was denied to Arnold in both "Resignation" and "Dover Beach." Renouncing poetry, Arnold turned to the dissemination of Culture. But even in his new role, he remained faithful to his desire to blend Wordsworth's feeling with the intellectualism of his own age. In 1879, nine years before his death, Arnold offered a selection of Wordsworth's poetry to the Victorian reading public. His revision of entire lines and phrases was regarded by some as a sign of editorial irresponsibility. It suggests, however, the extent to which Arnold had taken upon himself the cultural responsibility of preserving Wordsworth as an emotional fount for his age, a task he had already set for himself, long before, in the creation of his own poems.

CHAPTER 6

ARNOLD'S FANCY AND PATER'S IMAGINATION
Exclusion and Incorporation

In this rethinking of the relation between Arnold and Pater as prose writers, Knoepflmacher rejects distinctions based on value judgments. Instead, he contrasts Arnold's uncomfortable parryings and ironic disengagements to Pater's unabashed identification with the Other as the object of criticism. Pater, he argues, not only engages deeply with the subjectivity of the creative artists about whom he writes but also enlists the energies of an implied reader, thus producing a psychic and emotional fusion of writer, reader, and object. Analyzing each Victorian thinker's assessment of Wordsworth as his prime example, Knoepflmacher illustrates how Arnold creates the Wordsworth he would prefer, whereas Pater molds his prose to recreate for his own reader the power of reading Wordsworth's poetry. Pater's essay thus becomes an exercise in affinity, the product of a sympathetic imagination that can translate into prose the same "pleasure" that Wordsworth's 1800 Preface to *Lyrical Ballads* had upheld as the chief aim of all poetry. Whereas the pleasure of reading Arnold lies in the vitality of his witty antagonisms and oppositions, that of reading Pater lies in an experience of union.

---

*I*n the second paragraph of his 1873 Preface to *The Renaissance,* Walter Pater invokes Matthew Arnold, not once, but twice. After adopting Arnold's memorable phrase, "To see the object as in itself it really is," only to give it a decided twist of his very own, Pater seems to recall Arnold again as he poses a series of questions for the "aesthetic critic" (xix) to ponder: "What is this song or picture, this engaging personality presented in life or in a book to *me*? What effect does it really produce on me? Does it give me pleasure? And if so, what sort or degree of pleasure?" (xix–xx). In annotating this passage, the editor Donald L. Hill spotted an Arnoldian echo in its phrasing. Pater had apparently remembered a question asked in "Heinrich Heine," the essay that first appeared in 1863 and then became the fifth selection in Arnold's *Lectures and Essays in Criticism* (1865). There, eager to counter Carlyle's attachment to figures like Tieck, Novalis, and Richter, Arnold tried to establish an "affiliation" (*Complete* III: 108) between Goethe and Heine as fellow skeptics. Goethe, he therefore insists, habitually challenged those who would fall back on mere "authority and custom" by asking "with Olympian politeness, 'But *is* it so? Is it so to *me*?'" (III: 110).

Arnold puts to a very different use the italicized "me" which Pater, his fellow Goethean, would appropriate, for in "Heinrich Heine," that "me" acts as a bridge between Arnold and Heine. If, at the beginning of the paragraph in which this passage appears, an authorial "I" assures us of Arnold's credentials as a Goethean loyalist ("My voice shall never be joined to those who decry Goethe" [III: 110]), that "I" will be replaced by Goethe's own "me" only to make room for the discordant voice of a more radical surrogate—"a young man of genius, born at Hamburg, and with all the culture of Germany, but by race a Jew; with warm sympathies for France, whose revolution has given to his race the rights of citizenship" (III: 111). It is through the agency of this foreigner that Arnold is able not only to invalidate "the self-will and eccentricity of a genuine son of Great Britain" such as the deluded "Mr. Carlyle" (III: 108) but also to question, much more imperceptibly, the very Goethe whose "mantle" (III: 108) he covets for himself. Indeed, a destructive Heine can show himself to be as disrespectful of his presumed mentor's cautious gradualism as he is of that "ächt britische Beschränktheit," which his translator eagerly renders as "the genuine British narrowness" for the ready edification of any English reader unable to savor the foreign phrase (III: 112). A new "affiliation" has clearly been formed before our very eyes.

If Mr. Carlyle, "the living writer who has done most to make England acquainted with German authors," had placed "far too much importance" on the cloudy "romantic school of Germany," which "Heine was to destroy," the cosmopolitan critic of culture can produce allies whose power is more readily demonstrable (III: 107, 108). In the battle with

"Philistinism," Matthew Arnold enlists Goethe and Heine as fellow questioners willing to ask, "But is it so?" One must, however, be wary of such helpful allies. The function of the critic is to reject as much as to embrace. The Olympian politeness which Arnold noted in Goethe (and which he employed himself by graciously praising Mr. Carlyle before denouncing his true-British eccentricity) will eventually allow him to detach himself from a Heine whose satirical excesses and lapses in taste can betray a dangerous "want of moral balance" (III: 132). Arnold must thus distance himself from Heine as much as Heine had presumably distanced himself from the Goethe whose "mantle" (III: 108) he briefly wore. Like any one figure in Arnold's ever-shifting portrait gallery, Heine can at best act as a partial "me," activated, used, but finally discarded. No Carlylean heroes are available for a total and submissive identification. The distance is all. Heine thus remains but one of the many partial selves whose busy, warring, intellectual interplay allows Arnold to produce the network of juxtapositions that can dazzle and delight the reader of *Essays in Criticism* (see III: 108–12; 132).

The italicized "me" that Pater borrows from Arnold for his own Preface to *The Renaissance* is similarly enlisted as an emblem for a process of questioning he strongly endorses. Yet for Pater this process is associative rather than disjunctive. Instead of tracing the descending "influence" of a Goethe on rival followers/antagonists who may or may not be his literary heirs, Pater is concerned with the idiosyncratic confluences of self and not-selves. What is at stake for him is the relation that exists between any intense "it"—be it a "song" such as a Du Bellay chanson, a "picture" such as *La Gioconda,* or a "book" (xix)—and a receptive "me" who is both generic and yet also highly individualized. Listener, viewer, reader, even the observer of an "engaging personality" in actual life, are therefore capable of being collapsed into that singular, concrete-universal "me." And Pater's "it" is even more compendious and all-embracing since it can comprehend all pleasurable products of art as well as life: "the picture, the landscape, the engaging personality in life . . . are valuable for their virtues, as we say, in speaking of a herb, a wine, a gem; for the property each has of affecting one with a special, a unique, impression of pleasure" (xx). The task of the "me" is to isolate that indwelling impression: "How is my nature modified by its presence, and under its influence?" (xx). If Arnold must disengage himself from "personalities" (xx) he introduces only to reject, Pater engages what might seem disengaged. As allies, implied author and implied reader can "bring into connexion" what "the narrowness" of lesser minds (whom

Pater refuses to call Philistines) "constantly tends to oppose" (*Renaissance* 2). Fusion, not opposition, is Pater's aim. Although Arnold professes to seek the "central source" of a "main stream" from "which many rivers flow," it is the diversity of these tributaries that *Lectures and Essays in Criticism* charts (III: 108). In *The Renaissance*, however, the imagistic emphasis on the fluidity of water and music contributes to our belief in the flow of a movement that can supersede all differences between periods, types, temperaments, nationalities, and forms. Opposites dissolve. It is a "strange blending" that Pater professes to find in the work of the same Heine whom Arnold enlisted for his sharp polemical antagonisms (24).

This essay is based on two propositions: first, that something can still be said about the relationship between Arnold and Pater; second, that it remains valuable to insist that literary texts, whether poems or novels or nonfictional prose such as *Lectures and Essays in Criticism* and *The Renaissance*, should not simply be read for detachable ideological messages. These two propositions are closely related, for if there is indeed space for further remarks about the relation between Arnold and Pater, it is precisely because most existing discussions of that relation are almost exclusively couched in simplistic ideological terms. By overlooking acute differences in strategy, arrangement, voice, and self-personation, these existing discussions are, in David J. DeLaura's words about Arnold himself, "remarkably innocent of any developed treatment of the relationship between form and matter" (*Hebrew and Hellene* 194).[1] That this should be so is partly attributable to Arnold's own precedent. His vivid presentation of a "criticism of life" (III: 209) has led us to read his prose more for its content than for the "dramatic quality" on which the successful presentation of the content relies (see Farrell 123). If we have similarly been too disposed to read Pater as but a quasi-

---

1. David DeLaura furnishes what will remain the most thorough and well-informed discussion of Pater's appropriation of Arnoldian concepts such as "criticism" and "culture" in *Hebrew and Hellene*. Still, though wonderfully attuned to the full resonances of all those Arnoldian phrases that recur through Pater's prose, though rightly noting how "Winckelmann" redefines the essay-lecture "Pagan and Christian Moral Sentiment," or how the famous "Conclusion" to *The Renaissance* had been sanctioned by Arnold's "Maurice de Guérin," DeLaura's exclusive attention to intellectual history leads him to an emphasis which a closer look at form and texture would have strongly contradicted. DeLaura still follows T. S. Eliot's emphasis by seeing Pater as a diluted, limiting, and circumscribing version of a many-more-sided Arnold: "If 'criticism' is redefined and restricted, 'culture' is even more drastically diminished from Arnold's comprehensive assessment of the modern world" (194). Though enormously indebted to DeLaura's insights into the relation between Arnold and Pater, this essay questions his emphasis by asking, with Olympian politeness, "But is it so?" For other discussions of the Arnold-Pater relation see T. S. Eliot "Arnold and Pater"; Wendell V. Harris, "The Road"; and DeLaura "The 'Wordsworth' of Pater and Arnold."

Arnoldian purveyor of a "criticism of life," it is because Pater's own sense of how best to read both his writings and Arnold's has gone unheeded.

In the 1873 Preface, Pater upholds "the writings of Wordsworth" as a challenge or test case for the aesthetic critic, whose task he sees as one of imaginative recovery of the pleasurable essence, the "virtue" or "active principle" of poetry itself. Pater's choice of Wordsworth's poetry is deliberate, for in his characterization of the unfinished quality of "that great mass of verse," he both accepts, and yet also invalidates, Arnold's own complaint about its incompleteness and lack of variety ("Wordsworth" xxii). Thus, when Pater invites critics of Wordsworth to "follow up that active principle, to disengage it," he unmistakably is addressing Arnold, who, in "The Function of Criticism at the Present Time" had singled out Wordsworth's poetry for its presumed deficiency in thought (xxii). If Arnold's prescription for Wordsworth to become "an even greater poet" was "that he should have read more books, among them, no doubt, those of that Goethe whom he disparaged without reading him" (*Lectures and Essays* III: 262), Pater wants the critic of Wordsworth to participate far more fully in the "energy" and "creative force" that Arnold grants but judges to be insufficiently balanced by "thought" ("Wordsworth" xxii).

Instead of waiting for Arnold, however, Pater met his own challenge when, a year later, he produced his 1874 essay on Wordsworth, an essay sharpened by the insights he had gained in putting together his *Studies in the History of the Renaissance*. "The office of the poet," Pater now insists, "is not that of the moralist, and the first aim of Wordsworth's poetry is to give the reader a peculiar kind of pleasure" (59). The statement, like so many in Pater's and Arnold's prose, deserves a careful translation. It is more than a new gauntlet flung at an Arnold whose continued tendency to read poetry as a criticism of life would be intensified by his own 1879 essay on Wordsworth to come five years later; it is also a description of the very medium that Pater and Arnold had jointly come to develop. The office of the essayist, too, and especially of the critic whose prose tries to activate the pleasure inherent in the creative energies he wants to recover for his readers, is not that of the moralist or the ideologue, the assayer of criticism who acts as a mere arbiter or judge. Instead, the first aim of critical prose is to give the reader a peculiar kind of pleasure. It seems proper to follow Pater's suggestion. If we have subjected for too long both Arnold and Pater to readings that stress content over form, it seems high time to reverse that emphasis. A Paterian reading of Arnold and Pater alike, paying closer attention to the distinct "pleasure" each man's rhetoric can produce, may well be overdue.

I

Pater's essay on Wordsworth seems the proper starting point for discriminations that need to be applied to the larger constructs of *Essays in Criticism* and *The Renaissance*. It is an ideal starting point because it was written immediately after the imaginative achievement of *The Renaissance* gave Pater the credentials that Arnold had won with *Essays in Criticism*. In the Preface that Pater wrote after he had emulated Arnold by compiling his eight essays and the Conclusion,[2] he seized on Wordsworth's poetry as a prime instance of an elusive, shifting, half-crystallized, and heterogeneous substance that, like the varied spirit of the Renaissance itself, required the exercise of a receptive temperament to do full justice to "the action of [its] unique, incommunicable faculty" ("Preface" xxii). Having just ended an imaginative search through the multiple manifestations of an "action" dispersed and dissipated over six centuries of art, Pater returned in "Wordsworth" to the similarly "perplexed" and perplexing "mixture" afforded by a body of poems written over the span of six decades (41). By combining old and new essays in *The Renaissance,* as Arnold had done in his *Essays in Criticism,* Pater had perfected the mode he so self-consciously shared with his predecessor. He had arrived at a fuller sense of his own critical identity and of its similarities to and differences from Arnold's own. He was now ready to communicate this understanding in a more compressed form.

Pater's 1874 essay on Wordsworth, however, also furnishes a desirable starting point because the sheer fact that it precedes Arnold's 1879 essay on the poet rescues it from the subsidiary position Pater is habitually forced to hold in all discussions of his relation to Arnold. Even in DeLaura's fine "The 'Wordsworth' of Pater and Arnold," the emphasis falls squarely on Arnold. For DeLaura, Pater's piece at best holds an amphibian position: shaped by Pater's awareness of Arnold's previous dicta on Wordsworth, the essay is seen to contribute to Arnold's later thought by providing the polemicist of the 1880s with the necessary fuel to sharpen "at once his condemnation of aestheticism and his furthest accommodation to the new formalism" (667). Here, as in *Hebrew and Hellene,* Pater acts as but a "competent" continuator of Arnold whom DeLaura, following the precedent of T. S. Eliot (though not of Yeats or Woolf, writers who could read Pater without having to unflesh his ideas from their lyrical mythopoeic presenta-

---

2. Pater would match the number of essays Arnold had collected when he added a ninth piece in 1877, "The School of Giorgione."

tion), much prefers as a "friend." Yet a close look at the two Wordsworth essays brings into question DeLaura's Eliotic notion of Pater as one who "restricted" Arnoldian culture. Such a look reveals that, in its inclusiveness and flexibility, Pater's essay certainly exceeds that of an Arnold who, much like T. S. Eliot himself, builds his authority by relying on techniques of exclusion, structures of antithesis, reduction, and elimination, in order to arrive at an elegantly pared-down version of the preconceived "essences" he upholds for his mesmerized reader.

Both Arnold and Pater begin their respective essays on Wordsworth by placing the poet squarely within a temporal frame. Pater notes that "some English critics at the beginning of the present century had a great deal to say concerning a distinction, of much importance, as they thought, in the true estimate of poetry, between the Fancy, and another more powerful faculty—the Imagination" (Pater, "Wordsworth" 39). In the absence of a distinct speaker in this opening sentence, we remain unsure whether Pater agrees or disagrees with the unnamed critics he invokes. The qualifying phrase, "as they thought," may suggest a faintly ironic hindsight, an attempt at distancing. But it soon turns out that even if the distinction between Fancy and Imagination was "perhaps not always clearly apprehended by those who talked about it" after borrowing it from the metaphysical writings of "German philosophers," it can still be valuably reactivated by a later borrower in 1874, for the speaker now insists that the original distinction contains within it a "far deeper and more vital distinction" that goes beyond metaphysics—"the distinction, namely, between higher and lower degrees of intensity." It is that distinction, we now discover, that is as essential for a full appreciation of a Wordsworth "who made the most of it, assuming it as the basis for the final classification of his poetical writings," as it is for the full exercise of "all true criticism." Imagination and Fancy thus act as coordinates that will allow the reader of Pater's essay to penetrate a "poet's perception of his subject" and, at the same time, to penetrate also the intensely imaginative mode of a critic who seeks to recreate that earlier perception as fully as possible (39).

Whereas Pater thus moves, in three long sentences, by converting a metaphysical distinction into a vehicle that will allow him to be true to Wordsworth's "perplexed," dualistic mixture of higher and lower degrees of lyrical intensity, Arnold does not directly grapple with Wordsworth's poetry until the middle third of his essay. Moreover, whereas Pater elides any self-presentation as commentator or guide, Arnold vividly dramatizes himself as a public defender, an appraiser. He begins in a relaxed, anecdotal manner and immediately makes us aware of the ease and pliability of a well-informed and well-connected man of letters: "I remember hearing Lord Macaulay say, after Wordsworth's death . . ." (*Complete* IX: 36). But if this worldly speaker can pose as Macaulay's familiar, he is also quick to detach himself through his wit and irony: "Lord Macaulay had, as we know, his own heightened and telling way of putting things, and we must always make allowances for it. But it is probably true that. . . ." The phrase, "as we know," inserted with such seeming casualness, establishes a familiarity that aligns the reader with the speaker who no longer needs to proclaim his familiarity with a Lord. Used but discredited, Macaulay now can give way to the speaker's recollection of what Wordsworth had actually said to him: "But I have myself heard him declare . . ." (IX: 36). The reader is in Arnold's hands: surely we are eager to be connected to one who can boast such connections; we would not think of questioning his authority. We trust the veracity of his ensuing remarks about Wordsworth's difficulties in achieving his reputation because we have been induced to believe in his own reputation. His credentials are obviously of the highest order.

Thus, at a point in which Pater is already deep into his assessment of the uniqueness of Wordsworth's "perplexed" imaginative mixture of contrary impulses, Arnold is still busy establishing his own unique credentials: "I cannot think, then, that Wordsworth has, up to this time at all obtained his deserts. 'Glory,' said Mr. Renan the other day, 'glory after all is . . . '" (IX: 38). It is in the power of this watchful, self-conscious speaker to grant or to deny glory: by scaling Wordsworth's reputation against those of Byron, Scott, Coleridge, and Tennyson, by ranking the poet among "our chief poetical names," by devising elaborate roll calls of poets English, poets Continental, and poets English-and-Continental, Arnold rhetorically shores fragment upon fragment not just to place Wordsworth but also to affirm and reaffirm his own special qualifications. As a witness who can remember what Macaulay and Wordsworth have said, who has overheard what M. Renan has said just "the other day" across the Channel, he can also call attention to his own earlier dicta as an authoritative preserver of the ancients: "Long ago, in speaking of Homer, I said . . ." (IX: 44). His mind is a refining filter that sifts, rejects, and retains only the purest residues, the choicest morsels.

In the second third of his essay, where he ventures an estimate of Wordsworth's actual poetry, Arnold presumably comes closest to what Pater has, in his own essay, undertaken from the start. Both men concern themselves with the variety, the multitudinousness, of Wordsworth's poetry. It is Pater who halfheartedly proposes what Arnold will later enthusiastically execute: "Of all poets equally great, he would gain most by a skilfully made anthology" ("Wordsworth" 40). Yet the suggestion is made only to be again retracted. Pater insists upon the irrefragability of a poetry that demands that its readers follow each and every alternation between imagination and fancy, activity and passivity, higher and lower moods:

> And the mixture in his work, as it actually stands, is so perplexed, that one fears to miss the least promising composition even, lest some precious morsel should be lying hidden within the few perfect lines, the phrase, the single word perhaps, to which he often works up mechanically through a poem, almost the whole of which may be tame enough. (41)

Whereas Arnold emphatically rejects as "ingenious but far-fetched" what he calls the "scheme of mental physiology" by which Wordsworth chose to classify his poetry (*Complete* IX: 43), Pater not only insists that this scheme is the very key for a true appreciation of the poetry but also tries to mold his own style so that it can remain true to the mental operation in Wordsworth "of a power not altogether his own, or under his control, which comes and goes when it will, lifting or lowering a matter, poor in itself" ("Wordsworth" 41).

If Wordsworth is to be valued for a receptivity that allows him to submit himself to and recreate the workings of a mysterious power outside himself, so must Pater make his own prose subservient to the poet's "special and privileged" faculties by becoming as "finely scrupulous" in his choice of "visible imagery" and "in the noting of sounds"; "He has a power likewise of realising, and conveying to the consciousness of the reader, abstract and elementary impressions—silence, darkness, absolute motionlessness: or, again, the whole complex sentiment of a particular place, the abstract expression of desolation in the long white road, of peacefulness in a particular folding of the hills" (45). By mixing the abstract with the concrete, Pater's diction imitates what it describes. Whereas Arnold filters and screens, Pater diffuses in order to recreate through the liquidity of his prose the very qualities he prizes in Wordsworth. Wordsworth's poetry, we are assured, provides "an excellent sort of training," instilling in "those, who, coming across him in youth, can bear him at all, a habit of reading between the lines." Requiring a mind thus trained "to look beyond the surface," Pater's essay becomes an exercise in affinity, the product of a sympathetic imagination that wants to translate into prose the same "pleasure" that Wordsworth, in his 1800 Preface, upheld as the chief aim of his poetry (41–42).

Arnold, who had already conceived his 1853 Preface as a partial rejoinder to Wordsworth's 1800 Preface to *Lyrical Ballads,* is not at all interested in respecting the full contours of Wordsworth's imagination. In order to preserve Wordsworth as an enduring classic, he therefore must, quite to the contrary, remove, sever, cut away all excrescent impurities and obstacles that might stand in his way. As anthologizer-preserver he feels entitled, moreover, to discard, rearrange, and even change actual lines of individual poems. Rejecting "the supposed unity of mental origin, which was Wordsworth's reason for joining" poems that Arnold much prefers to regroup, he can adduce against Wordsworth a higher authority, the "infallible tact" of the ancient Greeks: "We may rely upon it that we shall not improve upon the classification adopted by the Greeks for kinds of poetry: that their categories of epic, dramatic, lyric, and so forth, have a natural propriety, and should be adhered to" (*Complete* IX: 43).

The idiosyncrasies that appeal to Pater thus impede, according to Arnold, an acceptance of Wordsworth. The poet who wrote about common life "classified his poetry not according to any commonly received plan of arrangement" (IX: 42). Wordsworth's insistence on psychological labels such as "poems of the fancy, poems of the imagination, . . . and so on," lacks "the natural propriety" of the Greeks that Arnold values (IX: 42). In great need to "be relieved" of much of "the poetical baggage which now encumbers him," Wordsworth seems almost as unnatural as Sir Charles Adderley or Mr. Roebuck, the politicians Arnold had juxtaposed to Ionia and Attica. Elsewhere in his essay, Arnold again introduces the wisdom of the Ancients to discredit the "alleged systematic philosophy" that some unnamed modernist sympathizers have professed to find in the "intimations" of the famous Ode. A touchstone from Thucydides concerning the dubiousness of claims for the "early achievements of the Greek race" can lay to rest these latest pretensions. If Thucydides can dismiss such early achievements as "no very great thing," so can a witty *krites* able to appeal to "the majority of educated persons" similarly laugh at the awe that "these high instincts of early childhood" have produced in many an uncritical Wordsworthian (IX: 50).

With the removal of all such impurities and obstructions, with Wordsworth's poems "freed" from his own "arrangement" and "grouped more naturally" by a Victorian editor who knows that Wordsworth's "shorter pieces" are his "best work" (IX: 43, 42), polemics can fade away. Thus, Arnold's persona can undergo its final transformation. The ironic "I" and classically minded "we" now give way to the earnest disciple: "No Wordsworthian has a tenderer affection for this pure and sage master than I, or is less really offended by his defects. But Wordsworth is something more than the pure and sage master of a small band of devoted followers, and we ought not rest satisfied until he is seen to be what he is" (IX: 55). The critic who can now declare, with Wordsworth's own simplicity, "But I am a Wordsworthian myself," has once again won us over. His sincerity is disarming; his affection all the more convincing when he admits that he can "read with pleasure and edification . . . everything of Wordsworth, I think, except Vaudracour and Julia" (IX: 55). It is this nearly total note of conciliation, this wonderfully seductive fiction of a relaxed open-mindedness, that presumably still lures intelligent readers into believing Arnold to be more "comprehensive" than Pater.

Read closely, however, Arnold's essay has actually stressed, not what Wordsworth is, but rather what Arnold does not want him to be. The sudden shift in tone at the end, the professed "veneration" for a man "so truly worthy of homage," has the same effect as the sudden shift, at the end of the wonderfully ironic Preface to *Essays in Criticism*, to "venerable Oxford" as a maternal bulwark against the Philistines. It builds on the previous ironic cancellations and excisions, acts as a release from the dissociative tactics so relentlessly used, and makes us gratefully welcome the discovery that there may indeed be something left to revere. We cling to that something. But it remains ineluctable nonetheless.

Pater's procedure is totally different. It is the very ineluctability of Wordsworth which, like the ineluctability of the Renaissance, fascinates him from the start. Whereas Arnold separates Wordsworth from rival Wordsworthians and from fellow Romantics such as Byron, Shelley, and Keats, Pater prefers to startle us by discovering unexpected points of contact: Wordsworth's peculiar consciousness of natural things, he says, can be found, though more fitfully, "in so different a poet as Shelley"; his acute sensitivity to "sights and sounds" and the "fullness of imagery" of a poem such as "Resolution and Independence" may "be compared to Keats's "Saint Agnes' Eve"; his pastoralism can be likened to the work of novelists such as George Sand, George Eliot, and Thomas Hardy: "A sort of biblical depth and solemnity hangs over this strange, new, passionate, pastoral world, of which he first raised the image, and the reflection of which some of our best modern fiction has caught from him" ("Wordsworth" 44, 53).

Arnold's fancy relies on yoking and unyoking fixities; it is his own protean activities as joiner and disjoiner that give his prose its vitality, movement, and interest. Pater's imagination, on the other hand, dissolves and dissipates barriers in order to detect sameness in difference without overlooking difference in sameness. Whereas Arnold sees no difference between *The Prelude* and *The Excursion* as long philosophical poems he wants to discard in the process of "freeing" Wordsworth's reputation, Pater does see differences. And while Arnold dismisses the "Ode: Intimations of Immortality" because he finds it deficient in "poetic truth of the best kind" (*Complete* IX: 49), Pater strains to create a metaphoric equivalent for the universality of the poem's effects:

> It was in this mood that he conceived those oft-reiterated regrets for a half-ideal childhood, when the relics of paradise still clung about the soul—a childhood, as it seemed, full of the fruits of old age, lost for all, in a degree, in the passing away of the youth of the world, lost for each one, over again, in the passing away of actual youth. ("Wordsworth" 55)

This sentence, with its carefully modulated cadences, its rises and falls and suspensions, is not saved for the very end of the essay, like Arnold's artfully delayed peroration. Instead, Pater's piece is, from start to finish, a sustained attempt to reanimate Wordsworth. If at the end of Arnold's lively performance we applaud the animated critic who persists in seeing Wordsworth from without by placing him in a panorama, we have been led throughout Pater's appreciation to savor the paradoxes into which we have burrowed, contradictions which we are asked to recognize as essential to the "perplexed mixture" of Wordsworth's Romantic poetry.

II

In distinguishing between the modes of Pater's and Arnold's essays on Wordsworth, I have tried to prepare the ground for more complicated discriminations between each critic's larger ventures into the genre of "collective biography" undertaken, earlier in the century, by Hazlitt and by Carlyle. Such discriminations are beyond the scope of a short essay, but they will have to be made by future critics if we are to assess the relationship between *The Renaissance* and *Essays in Criticism* from a vantage other than that of intellectual history. The actual process of composition of each of these serial constructs is itself indicative of the profound difference between them. Originally, each writer began with the prose portrait of a figure who could act as a kind of surrogate or analogue, Arnold with Maurice de Guérin the failed Romantic poet, and Pater with Winckelmann the Nordic seeker of Hellenic beauty. But as each writer began to devise his larger series, their purposes began to diverge. Each of Arnold's subsequent portraits was a fragment of the writer who once bemoaned that he was all fragments; though aspiring to find wholeness, his work remained composed of sets of antitheses, the largest of which remained the gap separating the present from the past. Whether retreating into the immediate past by looking at recently deceased near-contemporaries such as the de Guérins or Heine or into the remoteness of second-century Rome or into the "Renascence" and its "return towards the pagan spirit" (*Complete* III: 226), Arnold remains burdened by the present. He can at best point to the century of Pindar, Aeschylus, and Sophocles as a model for balance, "thinking-power," the religious sense. Pater's Winckelmann similarly finds it impossible to translate himself into the Greece he wants to recover; "his plan for a visit to Greece 'remains' unfulfilled" (*The Renaissance* 155). But Pater enlists Winckelmann as a bridge builder who can connect us to a fluid network of similar strivings and yearnings, to earlier wanderers and pilgrims of the imagination, a Pico who comes to rest in Florence after "many wanderings" of intellect and body, a Leonardo who "sinks to rest" after "nineteen years of wandering," and a Du Bellay who voyages from France to Rome. Whereas the mobility in *Essays in Criticism* is provided by Arnold's elastic narrator, the movement in *The Renaissance* is provided by historical figures stirred by a spirit still manifest in modern life.

The temporal progression in Arnold's collection spirals backwards from present to near-past to earlier eras of belief. Pater, on the other hand, begins at the farthest remove in "Two Early French Stories," his first selection, only to deposit the reader at the end before the threshold of the nineteenth century, with the death of Winckelmann in 1768, two years before the birth of Wordsworth. Goethe, English Romanticism, and the many voices of the Victorian present that Arnold assumes as his own starting point, though evoked and implied, are kept outside Pater's temporal framework. The nineteenth century is the future toward which Winckelmann, a Moses figure who, like Arnold's modern critic, must die in the wilderness, can only point. Yet by stopping before the advent of his own century, Pater not only avoids polemical skirmishes but also can guarantee continuities that Arnold, marooned among disputing contemporaries, can merely wish for. The sequence of spatial settings presented in each book offers a similar contrast. Arnold's version of the present relies on repeated oppositions between British and French (and German and British) realities; when he retreats into the more distant past in the second half of his collection, he roams through Italy and Greece, Spinoza's Holland, and Marcus Aurelius's Rome. Pater, however, arranges his essays to anticipate the final movement from North to South undertaken by Winckelmann at the end. Pater thus begins in France, rests in Italy for most of the essays, and then returns north again, with Du Bellay's France, Winckelmann's

Germany, and his own England. The reader's own journey thus becomes similarly rounded. Fruition, rather than restlessness, is a possibility for the modern traveler.

Arnold begins his collection with an epigraph from Edmund Burke: "Our antagonist in our helper" (*Complete* III: 2). And it is antagonism, discord, the clash of contraries that gives his work its distinctive vitality and pleasure. Pater, however, carefully chooses for his epigraph one of the psalms in which David is not inveighing against "mine enemies" but rather asserting a vision of perfected wholeness: "Though ye have lain among the pots, yet shall ye be as the wings of a dove covered with silver, and her feathers with yellow gold." Pater's subject as well as his mode involves transmutation, metamorphosis. At the end of Arnold's last essay, Aurelius, philosopher-king, man of culture, still remains agitated, "stretching out his arms for something beyond" (III: 157). But at the end of "Winckelmann," Pater proffers the possibility of completion; he has traced, he says, "the growing revelation of the mind to itself" (*The Renaissance* 184). For the modern reader both Arnold and Pater have each a distinct value and a distinct pleasure. Their talents, as Pater seemed to have recognized when he decided to discuss the "vital" distinction between Imagination and Fancy, remain essentially complementary: the lyrical Wordsworthian imagination of the one blends what the other's fanciful wit resolutely insists on sundering.

CHAPTER 7

REVISITING WORDSWORTH
Lewis Carroll's "The White Knight's Song"

Whereas Knoepflmacher's chapters on Arnold and Browning illustrate why and how Victorians writers appropriated and revised the work of their predecessors, here he shows how parody, a popular nineteenth-century literary form, also relied on a rhetoric of revisitation. By virtue of its own "motions retrograde" (Wordsworth, 1805 *Prelude* IX: 8), parody inevitably respects the antecedents it ironizes yet feeds upon. In Wordsworth's poetry of selfhood, Knoepflmacher argues, "an insistence on progress, on the presumed *growth* of a poet's mind, is constantly checked by regress, a nostalgic longing for the traces of an earlier, lost oneness." Analyzing Lewis Carroll's parodies of Wordsworth, he suggests that Carroll perfectly understood the Romantic origins of his own Janus-like consciousness. Moreover, his "White Knight's Song" performs a characteristically Victorian, self-ironizing tribute to Wordsworth, even while, in terms of plot, it is paired with the socialization of Alice. Only later in life, as a nostalgic adult, can the forward-looking girl who energetically leaps to the eighth square retrospectively sentimentalize "The White Knight's Song."

> How shall I seek the origin? where find
> Faith in the marvellous things which then I felt?
>
> —William Wordsworth, 1850 *The Prelude* II: 346–47

"The Eighth Square at last!" she cried as she bounded across.
—Lewis Carroll, *Through the Looking-Glass*, edited by Gray, pp. 190–91

I

Nineteenth-century verbal structures rely on revisitations. Like their Romantic predecessors, the Victorians devised forms that inevitably involved a backward or retrospective movement. If *The Prelude*, that Romantic relic published in the mid-Victorian era, eddies back in "motions retrograde" like a backward-turning "River," part yielding to "old remembrances" and "Part sway'd by fear to tread an onward road" (Wordsworth, 1805 *Prelude* IX: 1–8), so do Victorian productions, hovering, Janus-like, between two worlds, likewise recede in order to progress or push forward. Wordsworth's retrograde River, flowing back in order to avoid the "devouring Sea," is lyrically recalled in the opening of *The Mill on the Floss*, where the voice of a speaker lingering in the past must eventually yield to the forward-looking exigencies of a linear narrative. That voice also operates in the dramatic monologue, where the words of Renaissance men and women long silenced by time are reanimated and ironically carried into modernity. And it speaks to us, too, at a crucial juncture in *Through the Looking-Glass*, through the ventriloquism of Lewis Carroll's White Knight. It is hardly coincidental that Carroll should invoke Wordsworth just before Alice moves onward to the eighth square. The Knight vainly tries to detain the resolute girl; she, in turn, just as vainly expects to find her progression to be crowned by power and maturity.

The clash between the Knight's retrospection and Alice's anticipation dramatizes the dialectic that Anne K. Mellor attempts to define in the opening chapter of her *English Romantic Irony*. There, Mellor turns to Schlegel, Schiller, and Kant to provide her with a paradigm for the "opposing psychic drives" that gave rise to the "variety of formal structures" she then ably traces in the works of Byron, Keats, and Carlyle and, far more succinctly but much less felicitously, in Lewis Carroll's Alice books (29, 30). When Mellor dismisses "The White Knight's Song" as but "a vicious parody of Wordsworth's 'Resolution and Independence,'" she betrays an inadequate understanding of the romantic-ironic operations of parody. Moreover, when she asserts that Carroll does nothing more than "undercut" an "overly naive faith" that he found embedded in a Wordsworthian "romantic moral code," she indirectly calls attention to the drawbacks of a method that deduces from German philosophy the paradigm that might have been inductively extracted from the poetic practice of the central figure among the English Romantics (177–79).

Parody, that quintessential nineteenth-century form, by the very virtue of its "motions retrograde" (Wordsworth, 1805 *Prelude* IX: 8) inevitably respects the antecedents it ironizes yet feeds upon. Like Byron and Keats before him, Carroll thus merely intensified ironic tensions already fully enfleshed in Wordsworth's poetry. As Coleridge shrewdly noted as early as 1817, Wordsworth's verses had from the very start led to a rash of "parodies and pretended imitations" (*Biographia* XIV: 170). Yet such parodies of the "simple Wordsworth" only helped to enlarge—wittingly or unwittingly—the ironic gaps between innocence and experience he had himself skillfully exploited. In poems such as "We Are Seven" (which was soon issued as a chapbook under the title "The Little Maid and the Gentleman") and "Anecdote for Fathers," Wordsworth relied on the interaction between child and adult to mock the mental projections of a time-oppressed, adult self-consciousness.

Unlike Mellor, then, I much prefer to situate Romantic irony at the threshold of that double consciousness that Wordsworth bequeathed to contemporaries as well as to his successors and that he most fully incarnated in *The Prelude*. There, an insistence on progress, on the presumed *growth* of a poet's mind, is constantly checked by regress, a nostalgic longing for the traces of an earlier, lost oneness. A prime result of this friction is irony. The clash produces a paralyzed self-consciousness that either stresses its impotence or replicates mental movements which, like the jerky motions of Carroll's chessboard Knight, can never be straight or linear: "Thus my days are past / In contradiction; with no skill to part / Vague longing, haply bred by want to power, / From paramount impulse not to be withstood" (Wordsworth 1850 *Prelude* I: 237–40). Eager to tread (like Alice) the road that lies plain before him, the adult self nonetheless is checked (like Carroll/Knight) by the residues of an "eagerness of infantine desire" that still "covets" a primal "Union that cannot be" (*Prelude* II: 26, 24). Unable thus either wholly to progress or wholly to regress, the mind may prefer to hover over the gap separating past and present selves:

> so wide appears
> The vacancy between me and these days
> Which yet have such self-presence in my mind,
> That, musing on them, often do I seem

Two consciousnesses, conscious of myself
And of some other Being. (II: 28–33)

Wordsworth's successors accentuated the ironies he had himself brought to bear in many of his self-debates and ironic dialogues with some such Other. If he could shape antinarratives as richly diverse as "The Idiot Boy" (1798), "Michael" (1800), and "Laodamía" (1815), prose writers could dramatize the same clash between "two consciousnesses" in even more varied ways by carrying it into the inherently ironic mode of the novel. Mellor admits that Romantic irony operates most fully in the realm of nineteenth-century fiction. It is displayed not only through a disenchanted Byronic narrator looking at a still naive Don Juan but also by a Thackerayan showman whose hindsight ironically undermines the forward-looking thoughts of a Dobbin or Amelia or by an adult Philip Pirrip watching his earlier incarnation as Pip.

In Victorian fiction, Romantic irony frequently manifests itself in the tonal shifts that dramatize the clash between childlike innocence and adult experience. At the beginning of *The Mill on the Floss,* for example, the lyrical dreamer mesmerized by the "unresting wheel" (Eliot 8), also watched by the little girl she had been describing, must abruptly distance herself from this child-surrogate. A lyrical immersion gives way to narrative hindsight. Similarly, the Lewis Carroll who apostrophized another Wordsworthian "dream-child" (prefatory poem to *Alice in Wonderland* 3), situated by still another river, must drop his poetic recreations of a lost moment in time as soon as he unfolds his ironic prose narrative. In fictions that display a double consciousness, the child who acts as a surrogate for the author's own "eagerness of infantine desire" (Wordsworth 1805 *Prelude* II: 22–26) finds that its powers decline as it starts to share the adult world the author inhabits.

Like the "little Actor" who so doggedly persists in imitating fallen adults in Wordsworth's "Ode: Intimations of Immortality" (*Wordsworth: Poetical Works* 103), so do the child Maggie and the child Alice remain unaware of their impending fall into a linear world of growth, decay, and death. A tribute to their power thus ironically turns into an anticipation of their loss of power. Only if wrested away from the actuality of flux and transported, like Wordsworth's Lucy Gray, into an arrested world of myth might such growing beings retain their lost omnipotence. Treated with an irony that always borders on self-irony, the child-character thus remains enveloped by the narrator's adult self-consciousness; what is more, the growing child encounters further authorial personations who only accentuate its plight.

Whether sympathetic (a Philip Wakem or a White Knight) or sarcastic and angry (a Mr. Tulliver or a Humpty Dumpty), these grown-ups only mirror the protagonist's own powerlessness through their own inability to negotiate an adult world.

Whether impersonating a White Rabbit clutching his timepiece while luring Alice into the timeless underground she will reject or a White Knight vainly trying to retard Alice's forward progress on the chessboard, Lewis Carroll perfectly understood the Romantic origins of his own double consciousness. Laughter became for him, as for other Victorian ironists, a mode of defense, lest it dissolve into a tearful nostalgia. Like Thackeray and George Eliot, he resisted potential sentimentality. He knew that if one were to yield to floods of tears, one could easily drown, as the dwindling Alice almost does in her own pool of tears, or one might become transformed into an impossibly eccentric, bi-conscious, amphibian creature such as the ever-weeping Mock Turtle. The Turtle's "heavy sobs" (99) are still heard by Alice's older sister as she looks backward and forward at the end of the 1865 *Wonderland*. In the earlier version, it was a river, the very "stream" on which Dodgson has told his original story that dominated the ending.

Far from denigrating his Romantic predecessor's "overly naive faith" (Mellor 177), then, Lewis Carroll fully grasped the nature of his kinship with Wordsworth. His decision to assign to the White Knight the parody he had earlier published betokens Carroll's recognition of the Wordsworthian "under-sense" of both of his Alice books. His revisitation of "Resolution and Independence" must be construed, not as the "vicious parody" Mellor finds (177), but rather as a characteristically Victorian, self-ironizing tribute to the "motions retrograde" (Wordsworth, 1805 *Prelude* IX: 8) of a similarly fluid imagination.

II

It seems fitting to start this survey of Carroll's relation to Wordsworth with a visit to an auction, for auctions, as the narrator of *Vanity Fair* helpfully volunteers, are themselves likely to produce a Romantic irony that stems from the interplay of recollection and anticipation. At those spectacles, "which Satire and Sentiment can visit arm in arm together" and where "you light on the strangest contrasts laughable and tearful," the shards of the past lead to a crippling fear of the future (Thackeray, *Vanity Fair*

200). The speaker of Wordsworth's "Resolution and Independence" had anxiously regarded his own future after surveying the fate of his predecessors: "I thought of Chatterton, the marvelous Boy, / The sleepless soul that perished in his pride" (*Wordsworth: Poetical Works*: "Resolution" 43–44). The "Vanity-Fairians" attending an auction are similarly beset by "a sensation . . . not a little startling . . . of the day when their turn shall come too" (*Vanity Fair* 200). When Lewis Carroll's personal library was auctioned a few months after his death, there were at least five lots of Wordsworth items for bargain hunters to pounce upon. There was a seven-volume edition of Wordsworth's *Poetical Works,* half-morocco and with gilt edges; three more two-volume editions of the poems in separate lots (paired with items as discrete as Shakespeare's works and an early edition of *Frankenstein*); and, finally, a first edition of *The White Doe of Rylstone; or, the Fate of Nations* (Carroll, *Library* 18, 22, 26). Any Vanity-Fairian familiar with Carroll's own adroitness in mixing Satire and Sentiment would have wanted, if present at that 1897 auction, to hunt for the volumes containing "Resolution and Independence." What lines, if any, did Carroll mark? Did earlier markings, in copies he might have purchased as a young man, differ from later ones? For Carroll's involvement with a poem that so vividly depicts Wordsworth's "two consciousnesses" was itself multilayered. He had, after all, revisited it, not only in the 1871 *Through the Looking-Glass,* but also in the original *Alice's Adventures Underground* in 1864 and, before that, in 1856.

Like the poet who revisited the spots "in which my childhood walked" (Wordsworth 1850 *Prelude* II: 3), Lewis Carroll was obsessed with the loss of a power that he too located in the passing of childhood. The White Rabbit that rushes past Alice in the opening of his most famous book introduces events that need to be assessed from the same double perspective at work in a poem in which another observer beholds, not a male rabbit, but a female hare "running races in her mirth" (Wordsworth, "Resolution" 11). The speaker of "Resolution and Independence" tries to lose himself in a dreamy reverie to abolish the "Dim sadness—and blind thoughts, I knew not nor could name" (28). Yet his lyrical reverie must itself be rendered as a narrative in the past tense: "I was a Traveller then upon the moor / I saw the hare that raced about with joy; / I heard the woods and distant waters roar; / Or heard them not, as happy as a boy" (15–18). The speaker's adult self-consciousness can no more be allayed than the ironic adult voice whose parenthetical interjections persistently qualify the experiences of Carroll's own eager "dream-child." The primal joy of childhood cannot be sustained:

> I heard the sky-lark warbling in the sky;
> And I bethought me of the playful hare:
> Even such a happy Child of earth am I;
> Even as these blissful creatures do I fare;
> Far from the world I walk, and from all care;
> But there may come another day to me—
> Solitude, pain of heart, distress, and poverty. (29–35)

The speaker's "summer mood" is broken (37). A regressive communion with "blissful" animal creatures is no more possible than a "friendly chat with bird or beast" is possible in Carroll's first Alice book, a "tale begun in other days, / When summer suns were glowing" (verse proems to *Alice in Wonderland* and *Through the Looking-Glass*, 23, 13–14).

Yet it was in 1856, long before he decided to have Alice confront the not-so-blissful creatures of Wonderland, that Carroll had first turned to "Resolution and Independence." The timing was significant, for he had suddenly found himself situated in a threshold position quite similar to that dramatized in Wordsworth's 1802 poem. A year earlier, he had still been able to characterize himself as "a poor bachelor student, with no definite plans or expectations" (Collingwood 65). But he was now a tutor and a master of the house at Christ Church, "with an income of more than £300" (65). His new responsibilities, however, made him question the value of socialization and led him to yearn, with a new intensity, for a lost freedom he continued to associate with childhood. When the Oxford undergraduates proved unresponsive to his tutoring, he tried to teach boys and girls at St. Aldate's school nearby. Yet here, too, he was made to feel inadequate, unable to teach mixed classes, and incapable of disciplining boys he found to be far more aggressive and sophisticated than the placid country children he had enjoyed teaching in Yorkshire.

In March of 1856, the new tutor published an elegiac lyric titled "Solitude." This earnest poem, the first work to bear the pseudonym of "Lewis Carroll," contains a stitchwork of phrases and sentiments culled from both "Resolution and Independence" and "I Wandered Lonely as a Cloud" (Carroll, *Humorous* 417–18):

> I love the stillness of the wood:
> I love the music of the rill:
> I love to couch in pensive mood
> Upon some silent hill. (1–4)

Like Matthew Arnold's near-contemporary "Lines Written in Kensington Garden," Carroll's poem seeks a Wordsworthian landscape as a makeshift refuge:

> Here from the world I win release,
> Nor scorn of men, nor footstep rude,
> Break in to mar the holy peace
> Of this great solitude. (9–12)

Yet Carroll cannot activate the pleasure that Wordsworth's speakers inevitably reclaim. The "pleasant noise of waters" of "Resolution and Independence" has turned into the "scarce heard" sound of distant ripples; the "roaring" wind that preceded the sounds of birds has become diminished into a "breeze" that barely "whispers among the grass" ("Resolution" 7, 1; "Solitude" 5, 7–8). No sprightly daffodils are fluttering and dancing in that breeze. Moreover, whereas Wordsworth insists that he can recover "the bliss of solitude," though removed from daffodils or splashing hares, when lying on his couch, in "vacant or in pensive mood" ("I Wandered" 22, 20), Carroll regards solitude as but a temporary anodyne. The mere "fragrance of a lonely flower"—of a single daffodil, as it were—cannot compensate him for the lost "fairy-dream of youth" ("Solitude" 31, 36). He remains paralyzed between the extremes of innocence and experience.

Though "happy as a boy," the speaker of "Resolution and Independence" turned to a man in "his extreme old age" to regain his original cheerfulness. Whereas in his childlike reverie the speaker had rejected "all the ways of men, so vain and melancholy," he gratefully accepts his maturation by internalizing the "old man's shape, and speech" in his "mind's eye" ("Resolution" 18, 66; 21, 128, 129). Carroll, on the other hand, cannot bring himself to relinquish the "golden hours of Life's young spring" he sentimentally apostrophizes ("Solitude" 33). Though weeping the "silent tears" of "infants" who "sob themselves to sleep / Upon a mother's breast" ("Solitude" 13, 15–16), Carroll's speaker somehow adopts the wearied voice of an aged, aged man in his concluding stanza:

> I'd give all wealth that years have piled,
> The slow result of Life's decay,[1]

---

[1]. Cf. line 125 of "Resolution and Independence": "But they have dwindled long by slow decay."

> To be once more a little child
> For one bright summer-day.

Carroll published "Solitude" in the little-known journal *The Train*. It was not republished in book form until after his death. Yet unalloyed sentiment was hardly Carroll's best mode of defense. His 1856 parody of "Resolution and Independence" also appeared in *The Train*, under the title, "Upon the Lonely Moor." This pendant response to Wordsworth's poem greatly complicated the dialectic already embedded in "Solitude." And, whereas that early poem would remain nearly forgotten for the next forty-two years, Carroll reclaimed the parody of "Upon the Lonely Moor" (see Carroll, *Humorous* 44–46) fifteen years later when he assigned it, in altered and expanded form, to the White Knight in *Through the Looking-Glass*. Though different in emphasis, both versions of the poem revivify the double consciousness dramatized in their Wordsworthian original.

Before writing "Solitude" and "Upon the Lonely Moor," Dodgson (not yet "Lewis Carroll" and not yet a photographer) had published an essay called "Photography Extraordinary." In it he suggested that "ideas of the feeblest intellect" might profit from a refining process similar to that involved in the production of photographic prints (Carroll, *Complete* 1231). The mental operations of a decidedly feeble-minded young man, as well as any infelicitous lines of poetry, could thus be greatly improved. Byronic excesses, as well any too prosy passage from Wordsworth, would miraculously turn into "strong, sterling poetry" (1234–35).

In "Photography Extraordinary," Dodgson provided three stylistically different versions of the selfsame passage by thrice dipping "into various acids" the feeble thoughts of his prosaic young man, who, like the later Dormouse, "seemed incapable of anything but sleep" (1231). Carroll soon began to expose "Resolution and Independence" to a triple process of intensification. "Solitude," with its self-indulgent question marks, had been the product of a mind much like that of the essay's trite young man;

> For what to man the gift of breath,
> If sorrow be his lot below;
> If all the day that ends in death
> Be dark with clouds of woe? (25–28)

But by dipping "Resolution and Independence" two more times into the acid of parody, Carroll was able to produce something infinitely more suitable than his original Wordsworthian stitchwork. His final product became not only a revisitation of his own revisitation of Wordsworth's poetry of revisitation, but also a reprojection of his self-projection onto a poem of projection.

III

I have suggested that Carroll's "Solitude" dramatizes a gap between the speaker's nostalgic longing for a pristine childhood and the wearied tone of adult disenchantment adopted by a twenty-four-year-old who questioned the resolutions achieved by his recent independence. As such, the forty-line poem merely corresponds to the first seven stanzas of Wordsworth's "Resolution and Independence," with its own tonal shifts between primal "gladness" and the threats of "despondency and madness" ("Resolution" 48, 49). By way of contrast, "Upon the Lonely Moor," Carroll's comic pendant to an earnest "Solitude," turns to the second half of Wordsworth's poem.

Instead of dramatizing the gap between childhood and adolescence as he had done in "Solitude," Carroll now recreates an encounter between youth and extreme old age. Yet whereas in "Resolution and Independence" Wordsworth's "I" recovered a happy and childlike "summer-mood" from such an encounter, Carroll's "I" confirms solipsistic self-absorption. His new speaker still refuses to make a transition from childhood narcissism to adult socialization. Although, in the manner of Wordsworth, this solipsist thrice asks his aged interlocutor to tell him how he lives, it is obvious that he remains blissfully screened from those "rude" intrusions that had so badly "marred" the inviolable solitude desired by Carroll's earlier personation. The "arching trees" in Carroll's previous poem offered little protection to a self no longer capable of burrowing back into the "fairy-dream of youth" ("Solitude" 5, 36; *Complete* 958–59). Now, however, such a shelter has been found by a mind which, like that of Wordsworth's Idiot Boy, allows no access whatsoever to the old Other with whom he professes to interact.

Though ostensibly a "gentleman" ("Upon the Lonely Moor" 3; *Complete* 813), Carroll's new speaker is deliciously infantile, fully ensconced in fantastical pursuits that have no basis in a sober adult reality. These pursuits, as well as his antisocial treatment of the old man he dismisses as a "boor" (4), allow the speaker to cling to a childish behavior now treated wholly without the sentimental pathos that Carroll had poured into "Solitude." Satire has replaced mawkish Sentiment. And comic aggression can enlist that "eagerness of infantine desire" (Wordsworth, *Prelude* II: 22–26) that Carroll had so reluctantly relinquished in his lyric elegy.

"Upon the Lonely Moor" reveals Carroll's astute understanding of his Wordsworthian original. "Resolution and Independence" is a poem of projection in both senses of the word: the speaker relinquishes his fixation on a primal past by allowing his imagination to carry him forward into an imaginary future of extreme old age; he carries out this design by eagerly absorbing the shape, speech, and situation of the old Man. Leech-gatherer, staff, pond, all become symbolic self- projections for a poet who drains the identity of his interlocutor as much as the clinging leeches drain the old Man's blood. A dialogue thus becomes a monologue:

> The old man still stood talking by my side;
> But now his voice to me was like a stream
> Scarce heard; nor word from word could I divide;
> And the whole body of the Man did seem
> Like one whom I had met with in a dream;
> Or like a man from some far region sent,
> To give me human strength, by apt admonishment. ("Resolution" 106–12)

If Wordsworth's meditative imagination feeds on the Leech-gatherer, Carroll's parody leeches off the earlier poem, retaining its essence yet swelling it into new shape. By actually rendering an old man's speech that Wordsworth had obliterated, Carroll reopens the very gap that "Resolution and Independence" had set out to breach. Indeed, the old man's catalogue of his pursuits—which Carroll retained in the later version of "The White Knight's Song"—becomes so absurd that he seems to partake of the very "madness" Wordsworth's poem had tried to resist. Yet the old man's inoffensive lunacy, his "accents mild," and his pathetic pleas for a small tip,[2] make him a far more sympathetic figure than the self-absorbed speaker. That speaker is still another version of the trite young man mocked in "Photography Extraordinary." His own list of mental pursuits—which Carroll significantly altered when he assigned the poem to the White Knight—seems even more trivial than the old man's. Whereas the old man can at least relate to the speaker by vowing to drink his health in beer, the self-intoxicated speaker cuts himself off from all acts of relation.

"Upon the Lonely Moor" provides more than an "apt admonishment" to Romantic egotism. It also contains, as does Wordsworth's own poem, a self-admonishment. Behind the "I" of "Upon the Lonely Moor" stands the

---

2. As Dorothy Wordsworth noted in her journal entry for 3 October 1800, the actual leech-gatherer she and William had met "lived by begging."

same self-scrutinizing yet now fully ironic Lewis Carroll whose despondency had led him to compose "Solitude." The "gentleman" who regards his interlocutor as "but a boor" is someone who can no more communicate with this rustic than the new Oxford don in mathematics could communicate with boorish students:

> But I was thinking of a way
> To multiply by ten,
> And always, in the answer, get
> The question back again.
> I did not hear a word he said,
> But kicked that old man calm,
> And said, "Come, tell me how you live!"
> And pinched him in the arm. ("Upon" 17–24)

The speaker's aggressive behavior reactivates that childhood "wilderness" that Carroll lamented having lost in the mournful lyrics of "Solitude." He would eventually magnify that wilderness by unleashing the mean and sadistic underground creatures who assault an Alice who wants to grow up rather than remain arrested in childhood. Like those Wonderland creatures, the speaker of "Upon the Lonely Moor" is but a pseudo-adult. Though a grown-up gentleman and mathematician, he still wants to return to a verdant and wishful childhood Eden:

> But I was thinking of a plan
> To paint one's gaiters green,
> So much the colour of the grass
> That they could ne'er be seen.
> I gave his ear a sudden box,
> And questioned him again,
> And tweaked his grey and reverend locks,
> And put him into pain. (33–40)

Whereas the speaker of "Solitude" had paraded his own pain for having lost a childhood paradise, this speaker inflicts pain on a figure intended to represent, as in Wordsworth's poem, the very process of aging. He compensates for his loss by indulging in a satirical revenge. Not only is that revenge directed at an analogue of Wordsworth's emblematic Leech-gatherer, who is now preposterously engaged in hunting for soap-bubbles or haddock's eyes; it is also pointed at Wordsworth himself. The poet who had celebrated childhood again and again seemed to have betrayed Carroll by finding strength in decrepitude and decay. In a prose note introducing "Upon the Lonely Moor," Carroll reversed the chronology of parody and original by purporting that he had found an antecedent for Wordsworth's poem: "It is always interesting to ascertain the source from which our great poets obtained their ideas: this motive had dictated the publication of the following: painful as its appearance must be to the admirers of Wordsworth and his poem of 'Resolution and Independence'" ("Upon," *Complete* 813). The implications are clear: it is Wordsworth and not Carroll who has presumably deviated from an original by converting a humorous exchange between two childish grown-ups into a serious celebration of the process of growth and maturation.

Nonetheless, despite its liberating comic anarchy, "Upon the Lonely Moor" conceals the same nostalgic attachment to childhood lost that had been so much more evident in "Solitude." It is noteworthy that Carroll's aggressive speaker can hear the aged, aged man only after he has mentally completed "my design / To keep the Menai bridge from rust / By boiling it in wine" (58–60). Charles Lutwidge Dodgson refused to let the passage of time rust away his joyful memory of crossing the Menai suspension bridge, as a small boy, during a family holiday in Northern Wales. As in "Solitude," he still hoped to bridge innocence and experience. But now that bridging had to be achieved through "contrasts laughable and tearful." At the end of "Resolution and Independence," Wordsworth's speaker "laughed myself to scorn" (137) his excessive fears of maturation, decay, and death. At the end of Carroll's parody, laughter deflects thoughts that lie too deep for tears.

IV

No tears come into Alice's eyes as the Knight sings her the song that constitutes his and Carroll's farewell to a girl on the threshold of womanhood. If the song's four names call attention to Carroll's interest in the arbitrariness of signifiers and signification, they also signal his awareness of the quadruple layering involved. Beneath this new version lie "Upon the Lonely Moor," "Solitude," and the original "Resolution and Independence." The frame-story itself recasts the situation dramatized in Wordsworth's poem: a young traveler in "life's pilgrimage" ("Resolution" 67) from youth to maturity meets an older figure in a dreamlike setting. The Leech-gatherer had been immobile, his body "bent double, feet and head / Coming together" in the stagnant pool (66–67); the Knight cannot negotiate motion—as he tumbles off his horse, his head gets stuck beneath "the soles of his feet" (Carroll, *Alice* 185). Both men are presented as "mild" ("Resolution" 90; *Alice* 187), yet "gentle" and "grave" (*Alice* 187; "Resolution" 97); both seem unusual, "above the reach of ordinary men" ("Resolution" 95–96); and both are ineffectual in their pursuits. The pond that the Leech-gatherer stirs with his staff produces hardly any leeches; the fantastic mixture of ingredients the Knight stirs in his mind fails to produce the very clever "pudding" (186) he hopes to concoct.

Yet if such similarities are intentional, they are meant, once again, to underscore highly ironic differences. Wordsworth's Adamic speaker seeks out the ungainly old Man as a Miltonic monitor who can ease his acceptance of a fall into maturity and therapeutically show him the way to overcome "dejection" and "sadness." Alice, on the other hand, is a small Eve who, though as yet unfallen, does not wish to be detained by the garrulous child-man who accompanies her to the wood's end. She wants to be crowned Queen. The sadness that the White Knight perceives in Alice thus is his very own. He is a projector. He misreads Alice's ruminations about the impossible pudding:

> Alice could only look puzzled: she was thinking of the pudding.
> "You are sad," the Knight said in an anxious tone: "let me sing you a song to comfort you."
> "Is it very long?" Alice asked, for she had heard a good deal of poetry that day.
> "It's long," said the Knight, "but it's very *very* beautiful. Everybody that hears me sing it—either it brings the *tears* into their eyes, or else—"
> "Or else what?" said Alice, for the Knight had made a sudden pause.
> "Or else it doesn't, you know. . . ." (Carroll, *Alice* 186)

When Carroll reinscribed "Resolution and Independence" into *Through the Looking-Glass,* he still tried to fend off sentimentality. By assigning a milder version of his earlier parody to the Knight, he hoped to undercut the Knight's nostalgia—and his own. He was trying to accept the inevitable progress from childhood to maturity, a maturity he still equated with the loss of the very powers the forward-looking Alice will have to relinquish in her drive toward the illusory goal of queenly might. Yet the sentimentalism that had dominated in "Solitude" and had been checked in "Upon the Lonely Moor" now could not be wholly contained by laughter. The book's narrator assures us that as an adult, Alice would remember as "in a half-dream" the "melancholy music" of "The White Knight's Song" (*Alice* 187). Carroll here reinstates the Wordsworthian acceptance of growth he had earlier rejected. He is willing to consider Alice as a fellow adult. A later Alice, such as the actual Alice Liddell who was almost twenty when the book appeared, might lyricize this separation scene and retrospectively pick up the sadness that overwhelms the Knight. The adult Alice projected here thus approximates the speaker of "Resolution and Independence" who can appreciatively remember his own encounter with one who also "did seem / Like one whom I had met with in a dream" ("Resolution" 109–10).

If Carroll struggles to overcome his resentment of the child who refuses to linger on the seventh square by converting her into a fellow nostalgist who will someday similarly look back and treasure what she is about to squander, he also tones down the satiric treatment of his ineffectual Knight. The "mild blue eyes and kindly smile" of Alice's would-be protector make him a far more sympathetic projection than her previous monitor in the book, the equally fragile but irascible Humpty Dumpty (*Alice* 187). And, since the venerable Knight now becomes the speaker of the poem formerly assigned to an aggressive young "gentleman," his interactions with the aged, aged man had become considerably softened. In his song, he no longer questions the old man "roughly" or pinches and tweaks him and puts him "into pain" ("Upon" 5, 40). Instead, he merely thumps and shakes him, much as Alice herself will shake the black kitten she loves.

Still, as I have elsewhere argued ("Balancing" 515), such softening touches belie Alice's impatient, even irritated, responses to the White Knight's delaying tactics both before and after his song.³ By having the Knight falsely assume that Alice is sorrowful about leaving him behind on the chessboard, Carroll mocks his own self-pity upon parting, not only from Alice Liddell, but from all the other little girls whose growth into womanhood left him feeling deserted. After singing his song, the Knight ruefully notes that Alice "didn't cry so much as I thought you would" (*Alice* 190). Indeed, she had not cried at all. By attributing his own emotions to a child, the Knight now reenacts the role played by still another Wordsworthian type. The speaker of Wordsworth's "We Are Seven"—himself a mathematician of sorts who insists that five cannot be seven—vainly tries to foist his adult awareness of the difference between life and death on the "little Cottage girl" ("We" 5) he encounters. Wordsworth was aware that his ironic treatment of the adult speaker would be missed and that his poem,

---

3. An expansion of a talk on Carroll and Wordsworth given at the 1984 MLA Convention in Washington, DC, this essay may also be read as a "revisitation" of the three pages I devoted to Alice and the White Knight in "The Balancing of Child and Adult" (1983).

if published, would make him "everlastingly ridiculous."[4] Carroll undoubtedly had become acquainted with some of the many parodies of "We Are Seven," and among the chapbook collections sold at the auction of his library there may well have been a copy of "The Little Maid and the Gentleman; or, We Are Seven," an earnest attempt to print the poem, "embellished with engravings," for a child audience.[5] Whether parodied or read "straight," Wordsworth's poem became increasingly popular, for it appealed to the Victorian obsession with childhood. Carroll surely understood the ironies other readers persistently missed (well into the twentieth century). Given his interest in looking-glass inversions and self-inscriptions, he might even have noted how Will Words-"throw" injects himself into the poem's conclusion:

'Twas *throw*ing *words* away; for still
The little Maid would have her *will*.
And said, "Nay, we are seven!" ("We" 67–69)

Like the eight-year-old, "wildly clad" cottage girl ("We" 10), the seven-and-a-half-year-old Alice has her will by repudiating her interlocutor. She moves from square seven to eight. She cannot be arrested.

Carroll's decision to assign to the White Knight an adaptation of his earlier parody thus carries a fresh set of resonances. Unlike the summer mood of his first Alice book, *Through the Looking-Glass* partakes of the season of frost and snow in which it is set. If, in 1856, a young Carroll was rather preposterously wishing himself a suckling infant, the Carroll of 1871 could with far less license exaggerate his own decay. The bald and white-bearded White Knight (to whom John Tenniel gave his own features) is, like the frail Humpty Dumpty, the disappearing Gnat, or the impotent Red King, a personation of the book's author, a version of the same "I" who, in the prefatory poem, magnifies his separation from the child of the pure, unclouded brow by noting that they have grown "half a life asunder." In Tenniel's illustration for "The White Knight's Song," it is unmistakably the Knight who bodily seizes the tottering figure no longer encountered upon a lonely moor but perilously perched (as Humpty Dumpty was) on the gate of a boundary. The Knight's interlocutor is no longer the "boor" who was the Leech-gatherer's ironic counterpart. His face is curiously concealed in the drawing. Is he a figure even more aged

---

4. Wordsworth's note to "We Are Seven" can be found in most scholarly editions of the poem.

5. The chapbook, printed by J. Kendrew, is undated but probably appeared as early as 1820.

than the White Knight? Is he thus a last *memento mori* for the girl who is so determined to push through that gate into the realm of experience? Or is he an emblem of innocence, a figure who, in his senility, shares an almost infantile regressiveness with the Knight and all the other dream-creatures Alice has rejected?

The Knight begins his song with a new opening: "I'll tell thee everything I can: / There's little to relate" (*Alice* 187). And indeed as a "relation," or story, "The White Knight's Song," though expanded, exploits the same unrelatedness and discontinuity apparent in Carroll's earlier version. Yet if that version had emphasized the speaker's unwillingness to relate to the ancient man, "The White Knight's Song" ironically undermines the old knight's extreme eagerness to relate to the dream-child who is about to elude his grasp. The long expansion of the ninth and concluding stanza of the poem thus no longer mocks only the implied solipsism of "Resolution and Independence" but also those nostalgic tears that the Knight—and Lewis Carroll behind him—fail to induce in the impatient and wholly unsentimental Alice. If the earlier version, by stressing the pain the young "gentleman" imposes on the "boor," had also claimed that its "appearance" would prove to be "painful" to the "admirers of Wordsworth," the final stanza now stresses the speaker's own pain ("Upon," *Complete* 813). An aggression bordering on sadism has turned into something resembling masochism:

> And now, if e'er by chance I put
>   My fingers into glue,
> Or madly squeeze a right-hand foot
>   Into a left-hand shoe,
> Or if I drop upon my toe
>   A very heavy weight,
> I weep, for it reminds me so
> Of that old man I used to know—
> Whose look was mild, whose speech was slow,
> Whose hair was whiter than the snow,
> Whose face was very like a crow,
> With eyes, like cinders, all aglow,
> Who seemed distracted with his woe,
> Who rocked his body to and fro,
> And muttered mumblingly and low,
> As if his mouth were full of dough,
> Who snorted like a buffalo—

> That summer evening long ago
> A-sitting on a gate. ("The White Knight's Song" 65–83)

Laughter and Sentiment would eventually split asunder in Carroll's *Sylvie and Bruno* books. Here, however, fun and pathos could still be intertwined and still produce "the strangest contrasts laughable and tearful" (*Vanity Fair* 200).

CHAPTER 8

THE RETURN OF A NATIVE SINGER
Keats in Hardy's Dorset

"Echoes and citations from Wordsworth and Shelley" are "abundant in Hardy's oeuvre," Knoepflmacher maintains, "because their ideology and poetic practice furnished him with foils against which he could redefine his own Romanticism." Through a close analysis of bird poems about poetic singing, Knoepflmacher shows how Hardy's ironic borrowings from such lyrics signify his inability to reproduce the joy that he admires in his Romantic predecessors. Keats, on the other hand, strongly appeals to the Dorset poet for his "negative capability." The art of embracing uncertainty and living with doubt and mystery resonates deeply with Hardy's own understanding of the writer, not as prophet or as truth-teller, but as a witness. Hardy understands that an acceptance of reality's un-knowingness can also lead to inspiration. Moreover, Keats's "imaginative partnership with dead poets such as Shakespeare and Milton," which resulted in some of the finest poetry of the English language, is not lost upon Hardy. His own imaginative partnership with Keats is emotionally, intellectually, and even geographically grounded.

———•———

*I*n June of 1921 Thomas Hardy received from a group of "younger comrades in the craft of letters" a copy of the first edition of Keats's *Lamia, Isabella, The Eve of St. Agnes and Other Poems*. The occasion was Hardy's eighty-first birthday. As Michael Millgate wryly notes in his biography of

Hardy, the gift seemed "more obviously appropriate" than the model of a full-rigged ship which John Masefield, another younger "comrade," presented to an octogenarian no longer interested in the vessel he had coveted as a romantic young boy (537).

The gift of Keats's 1820 volume was indeed appropriate. After all, 1921 not only was the year in which Hardy celebrated entering the eighth decade of his long life but also happened to be the centenary year of Keats's death. As the donors of the book well knew, Hardy had only recently joined a national committee to purchase Wentworth Place, the Hampstead house in which Keats composed his 1819 odes and narratives. To help raise money, Hardy had sent a memorial poem, "At a House in Hampstead," as his personal contribution to *The John Keats Memorial Volume,* which appeared on 23 February 1921, exactly one hundred years after Keats's death in Rome. What is more, Hardy's "younger comrades" may also have known that the poet had returned to Keats in two other recent poems, "The Selfsame Song" and "At Lulworth Cove a Century Back," both of which he would place together with "At a House in Hampstead" in his 1922 volume, *Late Lyrics and Earlier.*

Much has been written on the bearing of both Wordsworth's and Shelley's work on the fiction and poetry of Thomas Hardy.[1] But beyond the generally accepted sense that "Ode to a Nightingale" somehow lurks behind "The Darkling Thrush," little has been done to flesh out more fully the imaginative relation between Hardy and Keats (see, however, Harris; May; and Perkins). Hardy's 1887 visit to the graves of Shelley and Keats, commemorated in the poem "Rome: At the Pyramid of Cestius Near the Graves of Shelley and Keats," may suggest that the two younger Romantics were equally "pre-eminent in Hardy's poetic pantheon" (Millgate 281). Yet it is Shelley and not Keats with whose ideas and poetic precedent Hardy always seems more eager to engage. Thus, whereas the 1887 poems of pilgrimage also include "Shelley's Skylark," there seems to be no matching involvement with a Keatsian antecedent.

I intend to show that it was Keats, however, whom Hardy eventually came to perceive as his prime Romantic partner or "comrade." If echoes and citations from Wordsworth and Shelley are far more abundant in Hardy's oeuvre, it is because their ideology and poetic practice furnished him with foils against which he could redefine his own romanticism. Keats,

---

1. All quotations from Hardy's poems are from Thomas Hardy, *Complete Poetical Works,* 1982–85. Quotations from Wordsworth, Shelley, and Keats are taken from Perkins, *English Romantic Writers.* I have used the abbreviations "H," "W," "S," and "K" (Hardy, Wordsworth, Shelley, and Keats) whenever such clarification seems desirable.

on the other hand, eventually was perceived as an alter ego, a poet as self-educated and self-obscuring as Hardy, yet similarly tough-minded in his mixture of idealism and skepticism. Hardy's eventual attribution of Dorset origins to Keats—his belated recollection of "a family named Keats" who had lived a few miles from his home in Max Gate—represents a deliberate attempt to implant the poet's shade in his own immediate environs.[2] Wordsworth's "Nature" or Shelley's "Intellectual Beauty" was, for Hardy, ultimately less trustworthy than the formulations of the ordinary man who could fashion extraordinary verses by entering into an imaginative partnership with dead poets such as Shakespeare and Milton. The sequence of poems in which Hardy engages, surreptitiously at first and then more openly, with the ghost of Keats—a sequence that itself spans a time period of greater duration than Keats's life—culminates when Hardy wrests an English poet away from his tomb in Rome and returns him to a native soil. Like the specter of Emma Hardy, Keats becomes a returning native whose shade can be embraced by a survivor as fragile, common, tiny, and yet also as defiant in flinging his own sound and soul against a "darkling" world.

I

Hardy's 1887 "Poems of Pilgrimage"—first printed as a group in the 1901 *Poems of the Past and Present*—included "Shelley's Skylark" and "Rome: At the Pyramid of Cestius Near the Graves of Shelley and Keats," but, as noted above, the volume lacked any poem exclusively devoted to Keats. The Shelleyan coordinates are quite overt. Ostensibly, the first of these two poems involves an "idealizing" engagement with Shelley's own "To a Skylark" (1820), while the second can be construed as a looser revision of Shelley's 1818 "Ozymandias" (McSweeney 93). Yet, as I shall try to argue in this section, even these two poems anticipate—through their subtexts—an identification with Keats that would become more pronounced in the poems considered in the next section.

If Hardy's skylark poem is placed, not just against Shelley's "To a Skylark," but also against Wordsworth's two poems by the same title, the notion, entertained by both Kerry McSweeney and by James Richardson, that this 1901 poem is a "flimsy, sentimental," and "uncharacteristically precious" construct (McSweeney 92–93; Richardson 3) seems rather ques-

---

2. Florence Hardy's recollection is more fully quoted in "Hardys and Keatses" in the 1928 *Dorset Year-Book*. See Bailey 442.

tionable. Hardy, characteristically self-conscious about his poetic antecedents, seems to enter quite knowingly into a much earlier debate that had involved Wordsworth and Shelley, as well as, indirectly, Keats.

In his original "To a Sky-Lark" (composed in 1805 and printed in 1807), Wordsworth set up a dialectic that would be adopted in Shelley's 1820 poem, reworked in Wordsworth's 1825 "To a Skylark" and recast once more in Hardy's own 1887 "Shelley's Skylark." By contrasting the planes occupied by the vaulting skylark and a plodding human "traveler" bound to a horizontal realm, Wordsworth distinguishes between two kinds of song, and hence also between two types of poets. In the poem's opening line, "Up with me! up with me into the clouds!," skylark and poet are so indistinguishable from each other that it almost seems as if it were the bird who exhorts an earthbound wanderer to rise with it. Soon, however, the "me" become recognizably human:

Lift me, guide me, till I find
That spot which seems so to thy mind. (6–7)

The ecstatic erasure of self and not-self of Wordsworth's exclamatory opening gives way to a gradual splintering in the increasingly reflective remainder of the poem. The spot that "seems so" to an alien, nonverbal "mind" cannot be reached by a poetic mind bound to words and ideas; it is a "banqueting place in the sky" (15) in which an earthbound imagination cannot aspire to feast. In a phrasing that both Hardy and Keats would surely remember, Wordsworth's speaker utters a wishful impossibility:

Had I now the wings of a Faery,
Up to thee would I fly. (10–11)

The separation between skylark and speaker is completed when the bird is perceived as "scorning" his human antitype: "thou wouldst be loth / To be such a traveler as I" (17, 20–21). The final stanza of the poem accentuates the human wanderer's inferiority by stressing the horizontal plane to which he is bound. "Alas! my journey, rugged and uneven, / Through prickly moors or dusty ways must wind" (26–27). The embers of joy that Wordsworth can rekindle at the end of "Poems of the Imagination" that similarly mediate between an atemporal ecstasy and a tempered self-consciousness ("Resolution and Independence," for example, or "Nutting") are dimmed as he closes this "Poem of Fancy" on a deliberately flat and stoic note: "But hearing thee, or others of thy kind, / As full of gladness and as free of heaven, / I, with my fate contented, will plod on, / And hope for higher raptures, when life's day is done" (28–31).

As both Wordsworth and Hardy seem to understand, the 21 five-line stanzas of Shelley's "To a Skylark" constitute a sequel or reply to the 31 lines of Wordsworth's 1805 poem.[3] Shelley keeps Wordsworth's exclamatory opening, stresses the same "joy" Wordsworth had imputed to the bird; retains the contrast between vertical and horizontal planes; and, even more overtly than Wordsworth, likens an airborne singer to a higher type of poet. The "scorning" for those who "must wind" their earthly journeys through "prickly moors or dusty ways" (W 17, 26–27) is retained when Shelley, too, characterizes his skylark as a "scorner of the ground" (S 100). But the differences underlying even these similarities nonetheless remain profound, for, unlike Wordsworth's overly self-conscious traveler, Shelley's speaker ends on a deliberate note of "creative suspension" (Blank 190). The skylark's unselfconsciousness may not be attained by humans, yet its scornful obliviousness to all forms of meditation can nonetheless be held out as a worthy model for earthbound singers.

Shelley wants to narrow the gap between skylark and speaker that Wordsworth opened. He therefore dispenses with Wordsworth's highly individualized speaker. Whereas Wordsworth's omnipresent "me" or "I" increasingly distances us from an alien "mind" whose ecstasy remains untranslatable, Shelley uses the first person sparingly through his much longer poem. Indeed, even when Shelley's "I" makes its first appearance in line 20, he acts as a mere vessel for "strains of unpremeditated art" (5), the "unbodied" joy he tries to reproduce through language that is itself antimeditative: "Thou art unseen, but yet I hear thy shrill delight" (4, 20).[4] Whereas Wordsworth conceded that his dependence on "rugged and uneven" contours made his own measures decidedly weaker than the bird's "strong song," Shelley tries to devise a form of expression that will allow him to emulate the lark's vocal fluidities.

Wordsworth's effort to retain his skylark as a source of inspiration is impaired by his representation of the bird as superior rival to a plodding "I." Shelley's similar goal, however, is aided by his avoidance of a contest between a "Thou" and an "I." He achieves his end in two ways: by deper-

---

3. As Kim Blank reminds us in his discussion of the many verbal echoes that demonstrate Shelley's playful "poetic mastery of the master," the younger poet supposedly was "fond of repeating" Wordsworth's first skylark poem (189).

4. In his remarks on the "instinct and intuition of the poetic faculty" in *A Defence of Poetry*, Shelley reminds his audience that Milton claimed to have automatically produced his "unpremeditated song" in *Paradise Lost* (Perkins 1084). It is this same intuitiveness he celebrates in the skylark's "unpremeditated art."

sonalizing his speaker and subsuming him to a "we" who comes to stand for a universal human awareness of time and space; and by treating the bird-who-never-was as an ineffable presence that can be represented only through the limited human constructions of simile and analogy. Shelley's insistence on such verbal and conceptual limits allows him to stress the intensity of his desire. It matters little whether the creature that inflames his imagination is "Sprite or Bird." Minds who must strain to grasp "What is most like thee?" (31–32) may never shed their painful self-consciousness. Nonetheless, unlike Wordsworth's stoical "I, with my fate contented," such minds can become energized by their very discontent:

> Yet if we could scorn
> Hate, and pride, and fear;
> If we were things born
> Not to shed a tear,
> I know not how thy joy we ever should come near. (91–95)

The "I" that returns here after a seventy-line absence now converts the lark's unpremeditated joy into a potential model for poetic intoxication:

> Better than all measures
> Of delightful sound,
> Better than all treasures
> That in books are found,
> Thy skill to poet were, thou scorner of the ground.
>
> Teach me half the gladness
> That thy brain must know,
> Such harmonious madness
> From my lips would flow
> The world should listen then—as I am listening now. (96–105)

If Shelley had come across the "Ode to a Nightingale," composed exactly a year earlier, before he finished his own poem, then it would seem likely that he had conceived "To a Skylark" as a rejoinder not only to Wordsworth's guarded 1805 verses but also to Keats's more powerful alternation between the contrary moods of escape and self-imprisonment. That Keats himself recalled Wordsworth's "To a Sky-Lark" in his ode among other antecedents (Milton's "Penseroso," say, and Coleridge's "The Nightingale") is borne out by several unmistakable echoes. The "wings of a Faery" which Wordsworth's speaker had vainly hoped to sprout in order to fly "Up to thee," for example, are evoked when the ode's speaker determines "I will fly to thee" and reach the moon and all her "starry Fays" (K 31, 37). But it is through his sharpening of the painful separation between thoughtless ecstasy and a thought-burdened solipsism that Keats most poignantly reworks his predecessor's poem.⁵ Keats's "I," though as prominent as Wordsworth's, no longer traverses prickly moors or dusty ways. Instead, his speaker has become immobilized, passively grounded in his plot of "embalmed darkness." He cannot venture into "near meadows," let alone travel into imaginary landscapes, "faery lands forlorn"—in the phrase that tolls him back to his immured "sole self" (43, 70, 72).

Written after the deaths of both Keats and Shelley, Wordsworth's second "To a Skylark" (1825), a mere twelve lines long, is best read as a quasi-allegorical tribute to younger "comrades." Here again there is a contrast between two kinds of poetry and two types of poet. But Wordsworth has removed the self-conscious speaker of his 1805 poem and of Keats's "Ode to a Nightingale." The opening exaltation of the skylark, now addressed as an "Ethereal minstrel! pilgrim of the sky!" (1), therefore is maintained in the rest of the poem. Wordsworth even accepts Shelley's notion of a fiery mentor when he chooses to convert the bird into a "Type of the wise who soar, but never roam" (11). Yet, at the same time, by humanizing Shelley's "blithe Spirit," Wordsworth also seems eager to inject a certain distancing from a pilgrim-minstrel whose very intensity, like Shelley's own, might prove alienating.

Wordsworth clearly has the younger poet in mind when, picking up Shelley's characterization of the lark as a "scorner of the ground" (S 100), he asks the bird whether it does "despise the earth where cares abound?" (W 2). Can the aloof skylark stay faithful to its kind by maintaining a watch over its "nest upon the dewy ground?" (4). The speaker eventually decides that the bird can be true to both "Heaven and Home," to private ecstasy and domesticity. But the reconciliation is undermined when Wordsworth suggests that nesting may require a stilling of the music he celebrates. Shelley's skylark—and Shelley himself—seek a "privacy of glorious light"; singers confined to their worldly nests, however, can admire but not emulate such self-abandon. Deliberately invoking the night bird Keats found "pouring forth" in "such an ecstasy" (K 58), Wordsworth reactivates the dialectic he had initiated in his earlier poem:

---

5. Keats's entire third stanza, with its protracted account of the "weariness, the fever and the fret" (K 23), reads like a painful elaboration of Wordsworth's two lines: "I have walked through wilderness dreary, / And to-day my heart is weary" (W 8–9).

> Leave to the nightingale her shady wood;
> A privacy of glorious light is thine;
> When thou dost pour upon the world a flood
> Of harmony, with instinct more divine. (7–10)

Playing his two successors against each other, Wordsworth purports to give primacy to the soaring singer who defies boundaries and enclosures. And yet, for all his homage to such aspiration, his sympathy still rests with the "heart and eye" that stay affixed to nesting places on the dewy ground. By 1825, Victoria's future Laureate had moved away from the radicalism of his youthful poetry. Fifty-five years old, Wordsworth treats Shelley with the same mixture of sympathy and detachment that also characterizes the attitude that Hardy will adopt when, also in his fifties, he must confront Shelley and Keats (and Wordsworth himself) as a late-born Romantic poet.

A consideration of the four poems I have examined is necessary, I think, if we are not to misread Hardy's poem of pilgrimage, "Shelley's Skylark." Hardy goes out of his way to ground a singer on whom his three predecessors had conferred such unearthly powers. Shelley lifted his skylark far above the "earth" from which it sprang (S 7); Wordsworth wondered if an aerial pilgrim deigned to return to its nest on the ground; Keats contrasted the "immortal Bird" not born for death to his own mortal "sod" (K 60). Despite their differences in emphasis, however, all three speakers were equally animated by the music they overhear. Not so Hardy. His speaker is deaf to the harmonies that so thrilled his predecessors. What is more, the bird "unseen"-yet-heard by Shelley has decayed into a "pinch of unseen, unguarded dust" (H 4). The vertical and horizontal planes that Hardy's predecessors contrasted have completely collapsed. There remains only the horizontal plane through which a speaker turned archeologist now rummages with microscopic zeal: "Somewhere afield here something lies" (1). The irony is grim. The material order the Romantics tried to pierce has become an ash heap, a repository of vestigial wastes.

"Shelley's Skylark" is hardly shaped by "idealising whimsy," as Kerry McSweeney holds; nor can it be said that Hardy finds himself "unable to engage himself" with antecedent texts (93). Quite to the contrary, Hardy dramatizes his engagement by creating a Shelleyan speaker who finds himself ironically compelled to reverse Shelley's emphasis. Whereas Shelley, in his concluding stanzas, upheld the bird's lyrical power above "all treasures / That in books are found" (S 98–99), Hardy's speaker—unable to hear the sounds that so stirred his Romantic predecessors—can find such treasures only through the printed record of another's words. Hardy's speaker thus is forced to side with Keats, the poet who allowed that an immortal Bird not born for death may have been nothing more than a product of his own feverish desire (K 61). The Keatsian nightingale that Wordsworth introduced as a foil to a Shelleyan skylark is even more prominent in Hardy's poem. When his pseudo-Shelleyan speaker acknowledges that only a poet's brain could make "immortal through times to be" a bird that "lived [and died] like any other bird," he goes to Keats to undermine the climactic credo of the poem he ostensibly sets out to celebrate (H 6, 7). The very effort to find some remnant of a "little ball of feather and bone" (10) after more than six decades of decomposition is as grimly comical as Jude Fawley's attempts to animate the impassive stones of Christminster with the voices of dead idealists.

But Hardy goes further in his ironic relic hunt. The fourth stanza of "Shelley's Skylark," in which the speaker vainly evokes the ideas of transmutation expressed in Shelley's "The Cloud," undercuts even more radically the attempt to find on a horizontal plane some vestige of the airy energies tapped by an earlier "pilgrim" two-thirds of a century before. The animated "Thou" whom the Romantics had apostrophized has wizened into an inert "it":

> Maybe it rests in the loam I view,
> Maybe it throbs in a myrtle's green,
> Maybe it sleeps in the coming hue
> Of a grape on the slopes of yon inland scene. (13–16)

Shelley, whom Hardy's speaker describes as a poet moved "to prophecies" when engaging the material world (3), could fashion the "trumpet of a prophecy" ("Ode to the West Wind" 69) from unextinguished ashes and sparks. But a speaker who hopes to extract some semblance of a Shelleyan energy from the "coming hue" of an unripe grape must cling to the dubious notion that the vines of Leghorn are still being fertilized by a speck of ashes dispersed sixty years earlier. His litany of "maybes" only accentuates his doubt. This modern votary of Shelley demands an act of faith which he is incapable of sustaining. His own verses, therefore, cannot ripen. Indeed, the grapevines of Leghorn cannot even furnish him with that "draught of vintage" that Keats had hoped to drink in order to leave the world unseen (K 11).

Keats and Wordsworth nonetheless can aid this latter-day Shelleyan. If cheating Fancy rather than pure Imagination is to be this earthbound speaker's lot, then he can at least avail himself of those "wings of a Faery" and "faery lands forlorn" that Wordsworth and Keats had invoked as a compensation for their inability to be transported into realms of thoughtless ecstasy. The speaker's abrupt construction of a fairy tale to encase unobtainable wishes stems from the limits his more skeptical Romantic predecessors had also acknowledged:

> Go find it, faeries, go and find
> That tiny pinch of priceless dust,
> And bring a casket silver-lined,
> And framed of gold that gems encrust;
>
> And we will lay it safe therein,
> And consecrate it to endless time;
> For it inspired a bard to win
> Ecstatic heights in thought and rhyme. (17–24)

Unable to find traces of the "it" that Shelley still hailed as a "Thou," the impotent "I" of Hardy's poem can hardly presume to address directly either Shelley or his skylark. Instead, the speaker anachronistically resorts to an outmoded machinery when he asks "faeries" to help him find what he could not unearth on his own. His request is a mark of his desperation. The elves to whom he is forced to appeal are as much the product of a cheating Fancy as Keats's "deceiving elf" was in "Ode to a Nightingale." Unable to reproduce the vital partnership that animated Shelley's poem, the speaker must align himself with an imaginary host of gravediggers. Joined as "we," he and they will try to rebury a lost pinch of dust in a jeweled casket. Yet even if such dust could be found, the symbolic action would remain futile. Just as the dead "it" does not require to be preserved in a new container, so does Shelley's feat in making a lark "immortal through times to be" (6) hardly require another's second effort to reconsecrate it "to endless time" (22). The poem's closure thus is heavily ironic. By dwelling on the dust-filled casket he wants to seal, Hardy's speaker acknowledges his inability to scale the "Ecstatic heights in thought and rhyme" he celebrates in the very last line.

Yet it would be a mistake to read "Shelley's Skylark" as a total negation of its Romantic original. Hardy's tribute takes the shape of a deliberate deformation that is intended to signify his inability to follow a precedent he genuinely admires. Closer to Wordsworth's first skylark poem than to Shelley's text, and closer to Keats's "Ode" than to either Wordsworth or

Shelley, Hardy's negations here take Keats's negative capability one step further. The questions entertained at the end of "Ode to a Nightingale" ("Was it a vision, or a waking dream? / Fled is that music:—Do I wake or sleep?") are no longer operative. The frenzied music still heard by Wordsworth, Shelley, and Keats altogether eludes Hardy's deafened late-nineteenth-century speaker. He can at best admire their own surviving music and try to preserve its impact in tiny caskets silver-lined. His role is that of a witness, a guide to ecstasies not his own.

A similar irony operates in "Rome: At the Pyramid of Cestius Near the Graves of Shelley and Keats." Like "Shelley's Skylark," this pendant poem (which also consists of six quatrains) relies on an act of deflection. It is the unknown Roman Cestius, whose funeral pyramid stands near the resting places of two "countrymen of mine," who ostensibly preoccupies the speaker far more than those two "matchless singers" (12, 20): "Who, then, was Cestius, / And what is he to me?" (1, 2). The sculptor of Shelley's Ozymandias had at least stamped a boastful inscription on the pedestal of the statue that desert sands converted into a "colossal wreck." But the record of Cestius's identity has been obliterated. His actions are as irrecoverable as the stirring sound of Shelley's skylark. Hence, once again, the speaker must resort to constructions that are purely hypothetical. If he hoped "maybe" to sift the skylark's ashes from the loam, he can only conjecture that Cestius owed his eminence because "in life, maybe, [he] / Slew, breathed out threatening; / I know not" (13–15).

Yet the speaker finds a purpose after all in the life of Cestius the Obscure. And that purpose also underscores the speaker's sense of his own precarious position. Although Cestius's pretensions are mocked by his unvisited tomb, his mausoleum can at least direct "pilgrim feet" to the graves of the two English Romantic poets (22, 17). Reduced to a signpost, pointing with "marble finger high" to the resting place of worthier dead, Cestius fulfils a "finer" design as a marker of achievements not his own (18, 16). The poem's concluding stanza suggests that the speaker recognizes that his own function is not unlike that of Cestius:

> —Say, then, he lived and died
>   That stones which bear his name
> Should mark, through Time, where two immortal Shades abide;
>   It is an ample fame. (21–24)

The poet whose name is affixed to "Shelley's Skylark" and "Rome: At the Pyramid of Cestius" modestly accepts his subsidiary role in a Romantic canon. The verbal structures he has erected in these two poems can at best point to the higher achievement of visionary predecessors. He remains an observer of, not an active participant in, their imaginative achievement. Yet as an outsider, he accepts his subordination with something of the resigned satisfaction that Matthew Arnold tried to express at the end of his essay "The Function of Criticism at the Present Time": to point to the preeminence of others, to salute them from afar, is to partake in their distinction. It is an ample fame for late-born Romantics.

II

"The Darkling Thrush," which Hardy deliberately dated "31 December 1900," partakes of the elegiac mode of "Shelley's Skylark" and "Rome: At the Pyramid of Cestius" in marking the passage of a century that began with youthful hymns of hope and transcendence. Yet by his tentative engagement—in the waning hours of a bitter winter day—with the aged thrush's "full-hearted evensong / Of joy illimited," Hardy now is more willing than before to emulate the experience of the Romantic forerunner who guardedly reacted to another such dusky voice singing "of summer in full-throated ease" (H 19–20; K 10). "The Darkling Thrush" thus anticipates the reanimations of Keats that Hardy will eventually produce, two decades later, in the three poems he printed in his 1922 collection: "The Selfsame Song," "At a House in Hampstead," and "At Lulworth Cove a Century Back."

The first two stanzas of "The Darkling Thrush" are taken up with the speaker's response to a gray landscape that pointedly differs from the lush and perfumed darkness in which Keats placed his melodious night bird. Music seems impossible amidst the "Winter's dregs" that shroud a land likened to a giant "corpse" (H 3, 10). The tangled "bine-stems" that score the sky "Like strings of broken lyres" (5–6) would seem to strangle any lyrical outburst. Whereas the surfeits of a vernal nightscape jointly enveloped Keats's "darkling" listener and singer (K 51), Hardy's speaker assumes that all other creatures on this dry and frozen tundra must share his own "fervourless" response (16).

The speaker's assumption, however, is undercut by the sudden eruption, at the poem's exact midpoint, of a "voice" (17) that defies such dire projections of universal gloom. The "happy good-night air" (30) of the thrush may seem far less justified than the "happy lot" Keats had imputed to his joyous nightingale (K 5). Unlike the unseen nightingale (and unlike

Shelley's unseen skylark), the thrush can be vividly seen in all its crepuscular puniness: "frail, gaunt, and small, / In blast-beruffled plume" (21–22). Nonetheless, the insistent cheerfulness of this latter-day singer poses a challenge Hardy's meditative speaker cannot ignore. The thrush not only may act as a potential corrective for his own gloom but also may call into question the despondency of predecessors equally convinced that in a world of death, "to think is to be full of sorrow / And leaden-eyed despairs" (K 27–28). The mid-Victorian pessimism that led Arnold to convert a "various" and "beautiful" nightscape into a "darkling plain" endowed with "neither joy, nor love, nor light, / Nor certitude, nor peace, nor help for pain" ("Dover Beach" 30–32) had eradicated that capacity to entertain contrary states still possible for Keats's darkling listener. By allowing his speaker to overhear a song of "joy illimited" amidst a landscape he has already equated with the dying century, Hardy introduces the possibility of a perspective antithetical to such joyless Arnoldian gloom.

In "The Darkling Thrush," therefore, Hardy can be said to reinstate—very tentatively, to be sure—something approaching a Keatsian negative capability. His speaker still finds "such ecstatic sound" more difficult to partake in than the Romantic predecessor who yearned to participate in "such an ecstasy!" (H 26; K 58). As a creature of the later nineteenth century, Hardy's sober analyst demands empirical proofs that he can hardly expect to obtain from a bird known to oppose "rough or gloomy weather" by heightening its song of instinctual delight.[6] Yet the speaker's very predicament, his inability to detect any "cause for carolings" in the bleak landscape he has allegorized as a giant corpse, also makes him receptive to an attitude contrary to his own. Might not, he ponders, instinctual joy be as justified as his own mental projections of a cosmic despondency? The speaker thus admits, half-grudgingly, that the frail bird could be a vessel for a tremor of "Some blessed Hope, whereof he knew / And I was unaware" (H 31–32). The possibility raises doubts about his earlier representation. The century he has pronounced to be dead might, in fact, be undergoing a cycle of renovation. If so, "The ancient pulse of germ and birth," far from being "shrunken hard and dry" (13, 14), may throb again with something of its old vitality. Though winter is here, spring may not be far behind. Like the "soft-dying day" Keats animated in "To Autumn," this winter day turns out

---

6. Bailey (167) quotes W. H. Hudson's *Nature in Downland* (1900), which Hardy may have read, on the song thrush's "fine temper" in dire weather; the bird's lyrical assertion of "his pleasure in life," Hudson speculates, "must greatly exceed in degree the contentment and bliss that is ours."

to have its music too—a music that may well restore some of the hope that stirred idealists when the century was still in its youth.

This possibility of cyclical continuity is even more strongly embraced in the three Keatsian poems that Hardy composed two decades after "The Darkling Thrush." Indeed, the first of these, "The Selfsame Song," significantly revises both "The Darkling Thrush" and "Shelley's Skylark." Returning one more time to "Ode to a Nightingale," Hardy now offers an elaboration of Keats's conjecture that a nightingale's song heard "this passing night" might perhaps be "the self-same song that found a path / Through the sad heart" of much earlier exiles (K, 63, 65–66). Hardy simultaneously asserts and denies the notion of an immortal bird not born for death. The song is identical—"Unchanged in a note!"—to that heard by the speaker and his former companions, on the same spot, "Long years ago" (H 8, 4). But although the speaker rejoices in the "pleasing marvel" of finding a nightingale still capable of warbling "the selfsame song, / With never a fault in its flow" (5, 1–2), he also must acknowledge that past and present have not really coalesced:[7]

> —But it's not the selfsame bird.—
> No: perished to dust is he . . .
> As also are those who heard
>   That song with me. (9–12)

In "Shelley's Skylark," a seeker of mute vestiges failed to find the material "dust" of the selfsame bird that had stimulated an immortal lyric. Now, however, a thrilled listener can at least assert the perpetuity of disembodied song in a physical world of severance and death. And what holds true in nature may, in fact, also hold true in art. Just as the "rapturous rote" of one long-dead nightingale is automatically repeated by any one of its successors, so does it seem natural now to find the words of a long-dead poet repeated by one who has come to consider himself as Keats's heir. By wresting the title and opening line of his poem from "Ode to a Nightingale," Hardy can attempt an identification that seems more plausible to him than it had been in the past. Having become a live relic of the nineteenth century, Hardy now feels closer than ever before to the generation before him. The gap has diminished.

---

7. Although the nature of the bird remains as unspecified as the identity of the speaker's former companions, the suggestion that it is a nightingale, "perhaps in the copse near Hardy's birthplace or in the grove at Max Gate," seems persuasive (Bailey 453).

Hardy's speaker ends by memorializing "those who heard / That song with me." The final personal pronoun tolls the speaker back to his own sole self. A past "we" exists no more. And yet by hearing once again the familiar cadences of the selfsame song, a lonely "me" has been able to indulge in a reverie that briefly blended past and present. The suspension of disbelief has allowed him to animate fellow listeners who once moved in his own circle—his dead parents, perhaps, or dead friends, or a dead Emma Hardy. Similarly, by building his own lyric around a single Keatsian phrase, Hardy can reanimate that earlier listener/fashioner of songs.

Hardy's own song, however, must go beyond mere replication. Though indebted to its original, his text is hardly the "selfsame song" Keats had fashioned. Nor, for all his kinship, can Hardy presume to adopt Keats's identity, to become the selfsame poet. Nonetheless, by skillfully borrowing one "strain" from the text of an arch-appropriator of the words and images of others, Hardy displays capacities that distinctly resemble Keats's own. His sympathetic identification owes much to the poet who could assert his ability to enter into the existence of a sparrow "and pick about the Gravel" (Letter to Benjamin Bailey, 22 November 1817, Perkins 1208).

"At a House in Hampstead, Sometime the Dwelling of John Keats," the poem that Hardy contributed to help with the purchase of Wentworth Place, extends that sense of kinship by boldly transporting to England a ghost roused from a "drowse" more permanent than the "drowsy numbness" that had enveloped the torpid speaker of "Ode to a Nightingale" (H 5; K 1). Keats's "Ode" had ended with the speaker's self-questioning. Hardy now adopts that interrogative mode by devoting the first five quatrains of his eight-stanza poem to questions he directly asks of the shade he has disinterred and relocated. Did this specter think he might "find all just the same" in a place in which "streets have stolen up all around, / And never a nightingale pours one / Full-throated sound?" (H 6, 2–4). How will he react to such drastic changes? Will "his umbraged ghost" show resentment by blowing "wind-wafts" on the stairs of Wentworth, by slamming doors, or even by materializing next to the "ancient tree" under which he had composed his famous ode (13, 15)? Hardy rejects these possibilities by striking a more conciliatory note in his last question:

> Or will you, softening, the while
> You further and yet further look,
> Learn that a laggard few would fain
>   Preserve your nook? (17–20)

The reference here is not only to twentieth-century Keatsians eager to maintain Wentworth Place as a memorial site. The octogenarian author, a "laggard" creature of the nineteenth century, clearly regards his own verses as a "nook" in which he might preserve the spirit of his Romantic alter ego.

Hardy therefore rehearses his previous relation to Keats in the remaining three stanzas. He is no longer as tied as he was in his 1887 poems of pilgrimage to material remains and resting places. He remembers having stood at "eventide" at the slope of Piazza steps "and thought, 'Twas here he died'" (22, 24). And he again recalls the "white hand" of the pyramid of Cestius that led him to exclaim "'Tis there he sleeps'" (28). But the speaker of this later poem remembers such utterances only to discredit the literalness of his earlier attachment to a physical order. He is no longer the awed tourist of the "Poems of Pilgrimage," a necrophiliac disturber of ashes. If Keats could build a "fane" to Psyche in some untrodden region of his mind, so is Hardy now fain to create a nook to let Keats in ("Ode to Psyche" 50). His poem's subtitle is poignant: "Sometime the Dwelling of John Keats" refers to Wentworth Place, the location that the speaker and Keats's ghost are professedly revisiting. But like the Roman house near the Piazza or the grave near the pyramid of Cestius, the Hampstead house and its garden were but a "sometime" dwelling for one who can make his habitat in the imagination of a fellow poet:

> Pleasanter now it is to hold
> That here, where sang he, more of him
> Remains than where he, tuneless, cold,
>   Passed to the dim. (29–32)

It is no longer enough to pluck and reimplant isolated Keatsian phrases. Keats himself—or "more of him"—can be plucked away from his Roman tomb. Hardy has at last effected the return of a native singer.

If "At a House in Hampstead" hauls into the present a sleeper who died a hundred years ago, "At Lulworth Cove a Century Back," dated "September 1920," retreats in exactly the opposite direction. To be near Keats, Hardy's "I" now becomes a time-traveler. Had he "but lived a hundred years ago," he conjectures, he might well have gone "as I have gone this year," to the spot on the Dorset coast at which Joseph Severn and Keats presumably stopped in September of 1820 before sailing to Italy (1, 2). Addressed by a personification of the hindsight denied to him, the transported visitor is emphatically thrice asked, "*You see that man?*" (5, 9, 13; italics in original).

But the "commonplace" youth who has just stepped off a boat strikes his observer as unworthy of notice (8). He considers him an "idling town-sort; thin; hair brown in hue," a loiterer gaping in the "evening light" at some "star, as many do" (10, 11, 12). The speaker is annoyed by his questioner's reiteration of an *ecce homo*. He has more pressing business than to take note of some obscure idler: "I have fifteen miles to vamp across the lea, / And it grows dark, and I am weary-kneed: / I have said the third time; yes, that man I see!" (14–16).

Once again, as in "The Selfsame Song" and "At a House in Hampstead," Hardy subverts the literalism that had once led him to scour the "loam" of Livorno and the Roman tombs of his countrymen. Stripped of hindsight, Hardy's time-traveler also becomes dispossessed of an imagination that might have profited from a better acquaintance with the "commonplace" youth who took his last farewell from England by showing his friend Severn a part of Dorset "he already knew" (Severn qtd. in Bailey 454). Back onboard the ship bound for Italy, this idle stargazer will present Severn with a fair copy of his famous sonnet "Bright Star."

In his last stanza, Hardy allows foreseeing "Time" to correct the speaker who has thrice refused to recognize a sublime sufferer much as Peter thrice denied Christ.[8] Foresight and hindsight recombine to allow a fuller grasp of the significance of the life of the obscure young visitor of Lulworth Cove:

'Good. That man goes to Rome—to death, despair;
And no one notes him now but you and I:
A hundred years, and the world will follow him there,
And bend with reverence where his ashes lie.' (17–20)

Though martyred by obscurity, the man to be buried in Rome is bound to gain more worldly acclaim than Jude Fawley. Nonetheless, a reverence toward his ashes now has become a ritual of less consequence than Hardy's own animation of a Dorset compatriot. The "weary-kneed" speaker whom Hardy ironizes fails to recognize that the young city-spark he has dismissed has local ties. He is related to the Keatses "living in the direction of Lulworth," farmers and stablemen like Hardy's own father.[9]

In 1820 the poet who opted not to go onboard an Indiaman reembarked on the ship that would ferry him to an early death. In 1920, however,

---

8. Bailey identifies Severn as the time-traveler's interlocutor (455). Since the speaker claims that it was "Time" who "placed his finger on me" (4), I prefer my own emphasis. Still, the distinction is ultimately irrelevant.

9. See note 2.

Hardy could look back on the seven decades that had passed since he had given up his early infatuation with Romantic seafaring and the four decades that had transpired since he resettled in Dorchester after his own sojourn in Keats's London. Having long ago ceased to define himself against Wordsworth's and Shelley's versions of the egotistical sublime, he had come to recognize the kinship between Keats's capacities for projection and his own. Hardy was ready to welcome a country cousin too long exiled from his vicinity. It was not enough to have brought Keats's ghost back to Hampstead. Lulworth Cove provided a better "nook" for one who had become, not just a neighbor, but another self.

CHAPTER 9

KIPLING AS BROWNING
From Parody to Translation

Knoepflmacher here examines Rudyard Kipling's lifelong reliance on Browning as a fellow perpetuator of a Keatsian "negative capability" to entertain contrary perspectives. Kipling's early mastery of different modes was matched by his Browningesque ability to adopt a multitude of different voices and deploy ironic distancing. Able to imitate the speech patterns of ordinary soldiers and bureaucrats, Anglo-Indians and Indians, ageless rustics and small children, Kipling also expanded Wordsworth's notion of the writer as speaking a wider human language. As Knoepflmacher shows, Kipling's total command of Browning's oeuvre served as a continuing frame of reference for his steady experimentations. His very last short story, "Proofs of Holy Writ" (1934), still enlists Browning's identification with Shakespeare's ventriloquist art and signifies Kipling's own, far more modest, identification with the Bard and his Romantic and Victorian idolaters.

Thou wouldst be king? Still fix thine eyes on mine!
—Robert Browning, *Paracelsus* II: 343

*I*n May 1918 Rudyard Kipling surprised Rider Haggard by minimizing his own literary achievements. He insisted that writers could not take any "credit" for "anything" they did well because such achievements "came from somewhere else: we are only telephone wires" (Cohen, *Rudyard Kipling to Rider Haggard* 100). Kipling here even goes beyond the notion expressed by John Keats that poets cannot be said to possess an "Identity of their own" since they are "continually" standing in for and "filling some other Body—the Sun, the Moon, the Sea and Men and Women" (Keats, *Letters of John Keats* I: 387).

Kipling's adoption of the Shakespearean "negative capability" that Keats and Hazlitt had promoted as a counter to Wordsworth's Miltonic "I" had been preceded by Robert Browning's own gradual repudiation of Romantic egotism (see chapter 4). Hazlitt's description of the characterless poet whose art is "like that of the ventriloquist" ("Lectures on the English Poets," *Selected Writings* II: 211) certainly applies to the creator of the dramatic monologues collected in *Men and Women*. But Hazlitt's notion that Shakespeare was preeminently a reporter fits Kipling even better than Browning: "His characters are like real beings of flesh and blood; they speak like men, not like authors. One might suppose that he had stood by at the time, and overheard what passed" (II: 208, 211).

Kipling's startling analogy between writers and "wires" as coequal conductors of impulses that emanate from "somewhere else" is dramatized in "Wireless," the brilliant short story first published in the 1904 volume of *Traffics and Discoveries*. Ostensibly featuring Morse code communications between two warships, "Wireless" turns out to dwell on the mysteries of a creative process that taps time-and-space-transcending signals. The narrator whom Kipling uses to tell the story is amazed when he witnesses how a lovesick and tubercular apothecary who has never heard of the lovesick and tubercular John Keats, his obvious double, involuntarily taps out on his radio set a series of verbal fragments that soon cohere into recognizable portions of "The Eve of St. Agnes" and "Ode to a Nightingale."

By likening the transmission of radio waves to the process of literary transmission, Kipling here updates Keats's Hazlittian insistence that "the poetical Character itself" lacked both self and character (Keats, *Letters* I: 387). Shakespeare, according to Hazlitt, could temporarily inhabit a character he wished to represent before passing into "another, like the same soul successively animating different bodies" (V: 50). But Kipling goes further when he implies that existing texts can be reanimated through a renovating process of transmission. Although he valued Keats's poetry, stressed the importance of Hazlitt's criticism,[1] and turned to Shakespeare

---

1. Among the books sent to his nephew at Eaton, he stressed the importance of his first

in poems such as "The Craftsman," "The Coiner," and the comic mini-drama "The Marrèd Drives of Windsor," the literary antecedents he most frequently chose to retransmit were provided for him by Robert Browning. He parodied, emulated, supplemented, and resituated Browning's verses and regarded Fra Lippo Lippi, orphaned, flawed, yet endowed with the "gusto" that Hazlitt ascribed to Shakespeare, as a personal alter ego and fellow craftsman. Kipling modestly insisted that he was not a new Browning. But, as he subtly hinted in his very last short story, the 1934 "Proofs of Holy Writ," the Browning who had moved away from Lippo's demotic craft had lost the "negative capability" of a Shakespeare.

Kipling met Browning, his elder by over fifty years, twice. The first encounter took place in the early 1870s at the villa of Kipling's aunt and uncle, Georgina and Edward Burne-Jones. The meeting was hardly memorable. The small boy who held on to the bilingualism of his lost Indian childhood was not yet the avid reader he would soon become. Instead, he valued the clamor of a new society composed of young cousins as well as a host of playful adults: "There was an incessant come and go of young people and grownups all willing to play with us—except an elderly person called 'Browning,' who took no proper interest in the skirmishes which happened to be raging on his entry" (*Something of Myself*, hereafter *SoM*, 9).

Kipling's second encounter, however, was more dramatic and far more productive. When his irascible English and Classics master hurled a volume of *Men and Women* at the adolescent who had tried to impress classmates and teachers with his literary skills, the boy read, reread, and memorized the poems of the old gentleman who had dodged the role of a playful deputy uncle. Kipling would recur to those poems throughout his fifty-year career. From his 1881 *Schoolboy Lyrics* to the 1934 "Proofs of Holy Writ," he would persistently invoke, imitate, refine, and redefine Browning's ventriloquist art. Verbally difficult, erudite, allusive, and elusive, Browning's poems met the creative needs of a schoolboy poet eager to shed his immaturity. But they also served the ambitious young journalist who addressed his Anglo-Indian readers in the seemingly authoritative voice of a colonizer while subversively introducing the countervoices of the colonized and the dispossessed, the misunderstood native and the victimized child. Having learned to juggle, juxtapose, and splice together multiple signifiers and voices in narratives of increasing complexity, a Kipling who soon commanded wider

---

selection: "*Hazlitt* isn't as out of date as he looks. He makes one take notice" (Harold Orel, *Kipling Interviews* II: 301).

transatlantic audiences still could not let Browning go. Despite ideological and aesthetic differences, he needed to retain his predecessor's oeuvre as a sounding board for his own inventions.

The sections that follow place Kipling's appropriations of Browning into three consecutive phases. The first section uses his adolescent imitations and parodies to explain why Kipling considered himself to be a latter-day Fra Lippo Lippi. The second section examines the more serious uses to which the prolific writer of poems and short stories put Browning's major dramatic monologues. Last, the third section shows how Kipling's embrace of Shakespeare ultimately led to a sly distancing from the poet who had come to resemble the erudite and domineering Ben Jonson. Browning had cast "Ben" as Shakespeare's rival in "At the Mermaid." Yet Kipling generously converts Shakespeare's learned contemporary into a collaborator rather than an antagonist.

I

When, in *Something of Myself,* Kipling follows his recollection of happy Decembers at the Burne-Jones villa with an account of the physical abuses to which he was subjected the rest of the year, he invokes "Fra Lippo Lippi" to suggest that boyhood deprivations helped shape his mature art:

Nor was my life an unsuitable preparation for my future, in that it demanded constant wariness, the habit of observation, and attendance on moods and tempers; the noting of discrepancies between speech and actions; a certain reserve of manner; and automatic suspicion of sudden favours. Brother Lippi, in his own harder case, as a boy discovered:—
Why, soul and sense of him grown sharp alike,
He learns the look of things, and none the less
For admonition. (*SoM* 11)[2]

Although Kipling's memoir repeatedly casts Fra Lippo Lippi as "a not too remote—I dare think—ancestor of mine" (*SoM* 22),[3] his narrative conceals the indirect role that Browning had played in bringing together his

---

2. Kipling is quoting "Fra Lippo Lippi" 124–26.
3. See also the epigraph for chapter 3 of *SoM* ("I'm poor Brother Lippo by your leave / You need not clap your torches to my face") and Kipling's account of his father's citation of lines 217–18 ("If you get simple beauty and naught else, / You get the best thing God invents") (25, 83–84).

parents, Alice MacDonald and John Lockwood Kipling.[4] Reading Browning was also encouraged at the school Rudyard attended, for Westward Ho was directed by a friend of the Burne-Jones circle. Kipling stuck to the twice-told tale about his classroom encounter with the "wondrous Men and Women" hurled at the bespectacled student nicknamed "Giglamps," "Giggers," or "Gigs" to let him "see whence the name Gigadibs came." Invited to see his reflection in the journalist Gigadibs of "Bishop Blougram's Apology," the boy editor of the school's paper began to devour all major poems in that "brown-backed volume." The "quietly annexed" and "quarter-comprehended verses" absorbed by Beetle in *Stalky* "lived and ate with him, as the dew-dropped pages showed" (*The Complete Stalky*: "Slaves of the Lamp Part I" 59). The young Kipling's ability to assume the voices of others with such ease led his classmate G. C. Beresford ("M'Turk" in *Stalky*) to wonder whether lines he remembered had originated with "Giggers" or with Browning himself (Beresford 87).

Alice and Lockwood Kipling privately published their son's *Schoolboy Lyrics* in 1881, a year before his return to India. Although Kipling later destroyed the manuscript, he preserved a drawing his artist-father had created as a friendly spoof of the young author's literary ambitions. The "scandalous sepia-sketch," mentioned in the memoir's last chapter (*SoM* 120), places a bespectacled British schoolboy (looking remarkably like today's Harry Potter) at the tail of a procession of great poets. Homer, Chaucer, and Shakespeare come first, followed by a trio of nineteenth-century successors, Byron, Tennyson, and Browning. Jauntily in step with the latter, imitating his very posture by carrying the same top hat in his right hand and by clutching a manuscript book instead of Browning's folded umbrella, the cocky schoolboy even replicates the older gentleman's optimistic smile.

Lockwood Kipling knew that his son had enlisted Browning to hone his poetic skills. Although two early poems the teenager published in the school magazine were printed with the subheading "By R*****t B******g," neither bears much of a relation to their presumed originals.[5] Yet the inter-

---

4. Taking a stroll after the picnic at which they had first met, the pair stumbled upon a badly undernourished nag. Recalling Browning's description of the "stiff blind horse" in "'Childe Roland,'" Lockwood quoted line 78 of the poem to which Alice promptly retorted with line 84 of the same stanza. As Andrew Lycett notes, the affinities proved to be irresistible: when a smitten Lockwood said, "You read Browning," Alice knew that their union "was done in that moment" (Lycett 52).

5. "A Mistake," published in the school's magazine on 1 November 1881, is hardly a mock counterpart of "Soliloquy of the Spanish Cloister." "The Worst of It" (later called "The Jam Pot (In the Manner of Robert Browning)") appeared on 3 June 1882. Both are reprinted in Kipling,

textual relation between Kipling's "An Echo," a four-stanza poem in *Schoolboy Lyrics,* and Browning's "A Woman's Last Word" (moved from the 1855 *Men and Women* to the 1863 *Dramatic Lyrics*), is far more palpable.

Eschewing the rhyme scheme of "A Woman's Last Word," Kipling's "An Echo" relies on a female speaker who is the obverse of Browning's self-renouncing wife. To preserve the harmony of a hardly Edenic marriage, Browning's superior speaker submits to an unworthy husband who wants to be deified into a "god": "Where the apple reddens / Never pry— / Lest we lose our Edens, / Eve and I" ("A Woman's Last Word" 31–32).

The young woman in "An Echo," however, is indifferent to masculine insecurities. A submissive Victorian spouse has become a *fin de siècle* temptress whose careless disposal of "bruised" pieces of fruit suggests a similar discarding of her lovers:

> Let the fruit ripen one by one
>   On the sunny wall;
>   If it fall
> Who is it suffers? What harm is done?
>   None at all.
>
> An Eve in the garden am I;
>   Behold, this one
>   In the sun
> Falls with a touch, and I let it lie,
>   My first one.
>
> One fresh from the bough; I break it;
>   The red juice flies
>   Into my eyes.
> Shall I swallow, leave, or take it,
>   Or despise?
>
> Sweet to my taste was that second
>   And I hold it meet
>   That I eat;
> But ah me! Are the bruised ones reckoned
>   At my feet? (*EV* 88, "An Echo" 1–20)

Early Verse by Rudyard Kipling, 1879–1889, 77–79; 151–52. Future references to *EV* will be given in the text.

Kipling's empowering of a young femme fatale's voice in this 1881 poem may well tap the bruised feelings of schoolboys thwarted in puppy love. Less accountable, however, is the misogyny of a blank-verse narrative he described in 1884 as "a psychological poem on Jack and Jill, in Browning's vein" (11 July 1884, *Letters* I: 71).

Back in India by now, the nineteen-year-old apprentice-journalist and his recently returned sister Trix gathered their old and new parodies in a collection called *Echoes: by Two Writers*. In elongating the eight-line nursery rhyme of "Jack and Jill" into 86 lines of the blank-verse pseudo-epic he called "The Flight of the Bucket," Kipling was unaware that "The Flight of the Duchess," the poem he was ostensibly parodying, had also undergone a considerable expansion, for as Browning later explained, a single line from a ballad he had heard as a boy, "Following the Queen of Gypsies, O," eventually became a 915-line narrative in seventeen verse-paragraphs (DeVane 172–73).[6]

Targeting the older poet's long-windedness, Kipling repeatedly halts the verse's flow with digressive dashes and parentheses that retard the appearance of a "rotten bucket" and Jack's "broken head." Thirteen lines are required before the subjects, "Jack and Jill," can even be yoked to a predicate: "must climb the hill." Only Jill's laughter at Jack's injury, an "unmeaning girl's tee-hee / That womankind delight in," and the wounded boy's "brimstone-flavored" curses, allow the poem's narrator to catch his breath (*EV* 226–27, "The Flight of the Bucket" 16, 28, 41–42, 35).

Kipling overtly identifies this garrulous narrator with Browning himself by calling him "*THE WRITER*" and by giving him the role Browning had assigned to the speaker of "The Heretic's Tragedy: A Middle-Age Interlude" in *Men and Women*. The grisly tortures that this inquisitor so "gaily" recounted had jarred with his pious "pre-admonishing" opening and "subjoining" conclusion. Yet they are now transferred to the poet who had tortured early readers of his endless *Sordello*:

> *Pre-admonishes* THE WRITER:
> H'm, for a subject it is well enough!
> Who wrote 'Sordello' finds no subject tough.

Faced with a text left bare by some previous "poet," this narrator feels free to improvise and elaborate. The nursery rhyme that featured a boy's

---

6. Kipling probably knew that "The Flight of the Duchess" was also a collaboration of sorts, since Elizabeth Barrett had made major editorial changes in the long dramatic lyric that anticipated her and Robert's own flight.

broken crown can be converted into a narrative that delights in breaking the reader's patience:

> Well, Jack and Jill—God knows the life they led
> (The poet never told us, more's the pity)
> Pent in some dark kennel of their own,
> Beneath the hillside; but it once befell
> That Jack or Jill, niece, cousin, uncle, or aunt
> (Some one of all the brood) would wash or scour—
> Rinse out a cess-pit, swab the kennel floor,
> And water (*liquor vitae,* Lawson calls,
> But I—I hold by whisky. Never mind;
> I didn't mean to hurt your feelings, sir,
> And missed the scrap o' blue at buttonhole—)
> Spring water was the needful at the time,
> So they must climb the hill for't. (1–16)

It is Kipling, of course, and not THE WRITER, who has decided to turn "Jack and Jill" into a narrative as sadistic as "The Heretic's Tragedy." When a "shrieking" Jill tumbles down the hill, she is spared from being hurt (48). But an unexpected "Nemesis" soon punishes this "graceless giggler" for laughing at Jack's wounds with the alacrity "Roman ladies" once displayed when beholding broken male bodies (79, 78, 72).

Both the original "Jack and Jill" nursery rhyme and Browning's "The Flight of the Duchess" had given prominence to a caring maternal figure. Just as kindly "Old Dame Dob" mends Jack's broken head in the child-text, so does an old "Gipsy mother" liberate the "little duchess" from male domination. But the matriarch who appears at the end of "The Flight of the Bucket" is a masculinized avenger whose severe drubbing of Jill "THE WRITER" endorses with the same fierce growl that opens and ends Browning's "Soliloquy of the Spanish Cloister": "I like that horny-handed mother o'Jill, / The world's best woman died, sir, long ago. / Well, Jack's avenged; as for the other, *gr-r-r!*" (84–86).

How are we to read this clever stitchwork of Browning *topoi*? Is Kipling using a Browning mask to conceal scars left from the childhood beatings he received from Mrs. Holloway after he and his sister had been left in England by his parents? The narrator's professed affection for a "horny-handed mother" seems suspect. The final tribute to this paragon who "died, sir, long ago" is as dubious as the Duke of Ferrara's account (to yet another "sir") of his dead wife in "My Last Duchess." In "Baa, Baa, Black Sheep," the 1888 autobiographical tale that used another nursery rhyme as a framing device, Kipling would find a better means to transform, Brother-Lippo-like, childhood abuses into art.

Kipling was ready to transfer Browning's art of concealment from poetry to prose fiction. The forty short stories the young writer collected in his 1888 *Plain Tales from the Hills* were, according to the biographer C. E. Carrington, "constructed on the same plan as 'My Last Duchess' or 'The Bishop Orders his Tomb'" (16). The flight of Browning's little duchess could be recast in "Lispeth," the story Kipling placed first in *Plain Tales*. The betrayed convert who flees back to her native hills rightly rebukes the smug missionaries who have exploited her naiveté. Unlike the boy Punch in "Baa, Baa Black Sheep," she has not been physically violated. It is her faith in adult caretakers that has been broken. Kipling retained Browning's sympathy for the innocent Pippas and Pompilias of this world. But he also questioned his predecessor's faith in a providential justice.

II

As editor/writer for the *Civil and Military Gazette* and the *Pioneer* from 1882 to 1889, Kipling "echoed" Browning's lyrical and satirical tonalities for an audience of Anglo-Indian readers far more diverse and demanding than that which had welcomed a schoolboy's *jeux d'ésprit*. Kipling likened the creative challenge of filling blank newspaper pages to that faced when "young Lippo Lippi, whose child I was" had "to decorate" the blank "walls of his monastery" (*SoM* 43). By 1889, when he left India as a well-established author, he had relocated Browning in a variety of fresh settings and forms.

"In Springtime," an early poem, deftly transplants the lyric nostalgia of Browning's 1845 "Home Thoughts, from Abroad" into a lush Indian garden, while "A Lost Leader" (1885) offers a colonial counterpoint to the older poet's 1845 excoriation of English Toryism. The speaker of "In Springtime" vainly tries to recall "the sights and sounds" of his vernal home country (*CV* 12). The "brightly" (1) blazing tropical vegetation and the screams of the Indian blue jays, Asian babblers, and cuckoo birds perched on perfumed acacia bushes block this exile's memory of all those English wildflowers and birds on whose names and shapes Browning had so lovingly lingered. The exotic *köil* proves to be as unresponsive to homesickness as a Keatsian nightingale when vainly asked, "Can *you* tell me of England and of Spring in England now?" (16, *CV* 77–78).

Instead of excoriating Wordsworth's Tory politics as Browning had done in "A Lost Leader," Kipling's similarly titled poem faults Bengali intellectuals for believing the worthless words of a Liberal viceroy: "George Samuel, Marquis of Ripon, is sadly in need of a *chit*. / Chatterjees, Bannerjees, Mookerjees, rise ye and fashion it! / What did his Lordship do for the land that you live in? Write, / *This* was his 'policy,'—turmoil and babble and causeless strife" (1–4, *EV* 278–79).

Few readers of "The Strange Ride of Morrowbie Jukes," in *Quartette,* an 1884 Christmas annual written by all four Kiplings and published by the *Civil and Military Gazette,* would have detected that this phantasmagoric Indian tale was grounded in "'Childe Roland to the Dark Tower Came [hereafter "CR"].'" Kipling's disoriented protagonist, a delirious horseman who brandishes a spear as he gallops away from camp, soon reprises the plight of the young knight who left a "safe road" to enter a disturbingly grotesque realm ("CR" XI: 52). The "horrid mews" that "penned" stragglers in the poem ("CR" XXIII: 135, 134) now imprisons an Anglo-Indian *sahib* who has tumbled into a hallucinatory world that threatens his very identity. Just as Browning's knight relies for directions on the "hoary cripple, with malicious eye" who misleads him ("CR" I: 2), so does Jukes vainly seek his bearings from the lying Gunga Dass, "a withered skeleton, turbanless, and almost naked," who takes "a malicious pleasure" in watching his plight. (*The Man Who Would be King and Other Stories* 12).

A few years later, upon recording an Englishman's real-life immersion into another nightmarish underworld, Kipling became more overt in invoking the same Browning analogue. Chapter XI of his "Letters of Marque," which describes a horrid descent into the putrid Gau-Mukh, a subterranean reservoir under one of the towers at Chitor, is titled *"Proves conclusively the Existence of the Dark Tower visited by Childe Roland [sic], and of 'Bogey' who frightens Children."*

Terror also infects the delirious speaker of Kipling's "After the Fever or Natural Theology in a Doolie," a dramatic monologue in which Kipling tackles Browning's philosophico-religious concerns by invoking three of his predecessor's poems. Carried to safety by native bearers on a stretcher, a fever-racked civil servant called "Browne" but later renamed "Jones" has barely escaped death. Yet, unlike the stolid, literal-minded Morrowbie Jukes, this speaker shares Kipling's command of Browning's work. Jones not only quotes "A Grammarian's Funeral" at the outset of his reverie but also remembers "An Epistle Containing the Strange Medical Experience of Karshish" as well the poem from which Kipling borrows his own subtitle, "Caliban Upon Setebos; or Natural Theology on an Island."

After mumbling the opening lines of "A Grammarian's Funeral"—"'Let us begin and carry up this corpse, / Singing together,'" Jones adds his own coda: "So their song to me / Sounds all the day-long, racking, restless climb / Past cactus hedge and scrub-oak of the down, / And here at noon the wind-swept mountain path, / And rock and pine below" (1–6, *EV* 266). Kipling enlists Browning's "mock-encomium" (Bohm 165) to create a jarring counterpoint. The Grammarian's disciples had removed their master's corpse, "famous calm and dead," to a secluded mountain-top "sepulture." But Kipling's agitated speaker is being carried back to life. Having nearly perished only "two days ago," he feels himself dubiously resurrected:

Now Lazarus
Uncertain 'mid his fellow ghosts, who hears
The 'Rise! Come forth!' And wonders:—'Am I called?'
Aye. *Am* I called? The call is faint at least.
The wind across the snows comes to my cheek
And murmurs some half fragment of it—'Rise!
Stand up! Be healed!' Who knows I hear aright?
Another fancy of the fever left
To mock me. It may be so. (9–17, *EV* 266–67)

As an expert diagnostician of fevers and diseases, Browning's Karshish was perplexed by the bodily resurrection of the seemingly deranged Lazarus. Kipling transfers this puzzlement to the patient stretched out on a stretcher. Neither dead like the Grammarian nor someone resurrected by the mysterious Jewish healer Karshish fails to meet, Jones muses about his inexplicable return to life. As he wonders how to interpret his salvation, he stumbles upon something that resembles the "natural theology" of the befuddled Caliban, an underground squatter like Jukes and Gunga Dass.

Although he is no Darwinian ape-man cowering before his own self-projection as a vengeful god, Kipling's speaker is plagued, like Caliban, by the mental demons he has unleashed. He fears that his "Face to face" mountain encounter, not with Sinai's God, but with "Death," has left him unprepared for a "new life" (66, 61). Is he, Jones wonders, still the solid "Materialist" he once professed to be (58)? He cannot ascribe his survival to any singular creed: "That isn't Darwin's notion." And "Buddhism, / Mixed up with half-a-dozen old beliefs," is a lesser prop than his love for "Edith," a woman whose memory he evokes to fend off Setebos-like phantasms (63–65, *EV* 268).

"After the Fever" demonstrates Kipling's ability to cull phrases and ideas from a poet noted for reanimating the voices of long-dead men and women. By mastering Browning's art of resurrection, he could dramatize his own wrangling with uncertainty and disbelief. The poem that Kipling next refashioned, "Bishop Blougram's Apology [hereafter "BBA"]," which Beetle's schoolmaster had held up as a model for the "inky boy" he called "Master Gigadibs" (*Complete Stalky* 56) dramatized the clash between materialism and faith. But the blank-verse monologue first called "One Word More: In the Manner of Robert Browning" and then retitled "One Viceroy Resigns: Lord Dufferin to Lord Landsowne" no longer addresses questions of belief. The Bishop's voice now serves a political apologia that, at first, seems to lack the subtleties of the original a schoolboy had once been told to study.

Although Kipling perfectly catches Blougram's inflections, his weary speaker lacks the Bishop's polemical skills. Blougram had steadily dismantled the self-confidence of his interlocutor, young Gigadibs, the "literary man." But the retiring Viceroy, who, like Kipling, is about to leave India, hardly regards his successor as an antagonist. By having Dufferin sadly acknowledge the failure of his Liberal policies, Kipling merely seems to retread the earlier attack of "A Lost Leader."

It is hardly surprising that critics who have rightly stressed Kipling's so-called Blougramism have not commented on his reduction of Browning's clever ironist into a defeated Indian Viceroy.[7] His identification with Blougram's emphasis on the veiled identity of a creative "I" certainly seems undeniable. Indeed, the epigraph for "One Word More: In the Manner of R. Browning" approvingly cites the Bishop's words before his confident counterattack: "Don't you protest now! It's fair give and take. / You've had your turn and spoken your home truths. / The hand's mine now and here you follow suit" ("BBA" 46–48).

These lines can hardly apply to Kipling's self-belittling Dufferin. Like Blougram, Kipling's speaker repeatedly stresses his interlocutor's youth: "you're so young"; "You're younger"; "You're young, you're young" (6, 99, 117, *CV* 68, 71). Yet whereas Blougram exploited Gigadib's inexperience, Kipling's Viceroy seems envious of a successor who still is in the bloom of life. Youth seems to be as much of an asset for this newcomer as, one assumes, for a precocious Anglo-Indian writer about to resettle in Eng-

---

7. Philip Mason finds the "gospel of Blougram" embedded in the 1919 poem "The Sons of Martha" and "at the heart" of the 1926 story of "The Eye of Allah" (175); Nora Crook shows, just as persuasively, that Blougram's belief in a self-veiling Creator helped shape Kipling's Browningesque "concept of the artist as a concealer" (16).

land). When Dufferin tells Landsowne, "I can teach you naught" (188), his lament distinguishes him from the pugnacious Bishop who drove young Gigadibs into exile.

Kipling's parents abjectly apologized for this irreverent treatment of a viceroy who had been kind to the family. Yet their son's poem involves more than a repudiation of the real-life Dufferin. It also offers, I think, a covert manifesto. Browning had turned Gigadibs into a sadder and wiser "Outward-bound" colonist. But the twenty-three-year-old reporter, who left his post soon after impersonating an ejected viceroy, was returning to England with a Blougram-like confidence. It was *his* turn now. He was no longer the schoolboy nicknamed Gigadibs. Attuned to contradiction and multëity, he could blend youthful insouciance with Blougram's mature sophistry. Kipling had privately derided Dufferin's adeptness at being "sincerely insincere" (28 June 1888, *Letters* I: 222). Yet a colonial overlord's liability was an asset for a writer capable of colonizing Robert Browning's art of sincere insincerity.

By conflating speaker and interlocutor, Kipling flattens the opposition dramatized in "Bishop Blougram's Apology." Although he removes the original poem's tension, he injects dramatic possibilities that lurk outside the text. There is an extratextual alliance between the young author who masks himself as old Dufferin and an implied reader who knows "Bishop Blougram's Apology" well enough to identify both Browning and his clever Bishop as foils for a speaker who admits his ineffectuality. These powerful polemicists provide a counterweight to Dufferin's rhetorical impotence.

Recasting Browning's poem also allowed Kipling to convert it into a veiled dialogue between his own past and present selves. By exposing Dufferin's tenuous grasp of the subcontinent's realities, a former reporter could bid farewell to his Gigadibs baggage. The Browning epigraph in which an "I" addresses a "you" thus can serve as a marker for the turn in the career of a writer no longer tied to quotidian "home truths."

Lastly, this nondialogic conversation between equals separated by age may well involve a covert reassessment of Kipling's literary relation to Browning. A valediction to India's colonial rulers may mark a distancing by a disciple who merely adopts the surface "*manner* of R. Browning" rather than his master's actual substance. If so, the discarded title, "One Word More," had fitted Kipling's objective far better than "One Viceroy Resigns." For the original title echoed that of the epilogue for Browning's 1855 *Men and Women*. Dropping his multiple masks, the poet had addressed Elizabeth Barrett there "in my true person, / Not as Lippo, Roland, or Andrea"

(137–38). A masked Kipling, however, prefers to enlist two real-life figures, Dufferin and "R. Browning," in order to conceal the personal import of his own Indian epilogue.

"The Last of the Stories," a prose farewell published in the previous year, also suggests that the young writer felt that he had reached a parity with Browning. An "I" who is the author of *Plain Tales from the Hills* is conducted to a netherworld to meet, not fifty men and women, but fifty-one of his very own characters. Before he can face these creations, however, the writer stumbles into Browning's cowering Caliban and "the great Bishop Blougram." The latter, "calm and smiling," insists that "Mr. Gigadibs despised him no longer" (Kipling, *Kipling's Lost World* 5).

As Kipling knew, Gigadibs had been preceded in Browning's canon by a worthier émigré in the poem "Waring."[8] As disenchanted with English politics in 1842 as Kipling would become with the Anglo-Indian scene of 1889, Browning's friend Alfred Domett had left England for more congenial climes. Idealizing Domett as a "star" who, though "lost here," would surely rise "afar," Browning tried to console his bereaved associates: "Look east, where whole new thousands are! In Vishnu-land what Avatar?" (259–62). When, thirty years later, Domett returned to England from New Zealand rather than the Vishnu-land of India, he was hardly the incarnated godling or "Avatar" whose triumphal return Browning had predicted.

But in early October of 1889, a much younger avatar from Vishnu-land had come back to the mother country. Though warmly welcomed by London's intelligentsia, Kipling missed Robert Browning, who had just left for Italy and was to die there on 12 December 1889. Soon, however, the newly transplanted author wrote a pendant to "In Springtime." Recalling "Sylvester Blougram, styled in *partibus / episcopus, nec non*" ("BBA" 972–73) and feeling himself similarly stranded "*in partibus infidelium,*" he produced "the wail of a fog-bound exile howling for sunlight" in a fourteen-stanza poem called "In Partibus" for his old outlets, the *Pioneer* and the *Civil and Military Gazette* (*EV* 470):

    I cannot tell when dawn is near
        Or when the day is done,

---

8. As Judith Plotz has pointed out in an unpublished conference paper, although "Waring" is cited "at random" by Beetle in "Slaves of the Lamp, Part I," where it is accompanied by excerpts from "Soliloquy of the Spanish Cloister' and "Caliban upon Setebos," the poem acquires a more distinct meaning in "Slaves of the Lamp, Part II," when Beetle and M'Turk exalt the absent Stalky as an "invulnerable" Guru whose regal manner as an Anglo-Indian officer has made him godlike. (In what is surely a pun, we are told that "Stalky was "brownin'" the natives—that is, firing at random—in one of the battles he fought.) *The Complete Stalky* 63, 289.

>   Because I always see the gas
>   And never see the sun,
>   And now, methinks, I do not care
>   A cuss for either one.
>   . . . .
>   It's Oh to see the morn ablaze
>   Above the mango-tope,
>   When homeward through the dewy cane
>   The little jackals lope,
>   And half Bengal heaves into view,
>   New-washed—with sunlight soap. (31–36, 42–48)

On publishing "this amusing doggerel," the Indian newspapers alerted "sympathetic readers" that "Mr. Rudyard Kipling," who had not always been too "satisfied with India," was now "apparently" as "dissatisfied with England" (*EV* 470). The truncated Blougram allusion in the poem's title may have gone as unnoticed by those Anglo-Indian readers as the fact that Kipling was creating a comic pendant for "In Spring Time," his earlier metamorphosis of Browning's nostalgic "Home Thoughts."

III

For the remainder of his long literary career, Kipling took a great delight in transporting Robert Browning's work into highly unlikely sites. He continued to relocate some of the older poet's most memorable characters, situations, and phrases in startling new settings. Yet these relocations also signaled a growing separation from Browning's larger-than-life historical or semihistorical figures. In her careful study of Kipling's reading, Anne Weygandt long ago noted the intense "interest in people" and in historical reconstructions both writers shared (106). Like his father, however, Kipling identified his craft with the productions of artisans such as Fra Lippo Lippi and was receptive to a greater "diversity of creatures" than those represented by Browning's men and women.

Browning may have tried to distance himself from aspiring poet-kings such as Paracelsus or flawed idealists such as Chiappino in *A Soul's Tragedy*, the 1846 two-act, mixed-form play that Kipling knew well. But there was something disingenuous about the protestations Browning has Shakespeare utter in "At the Mermaid" (1876), when he has the Bard assure an ambitious Ben Jonson that he does not want to be exalted above his peers.

Browning had fully expected to succeed Tennyson as Poet Laureate. But Kipling, who repeatedly rejected the Laureateship, was suspicious of an aggrandizing elitism. His demotic art was closer to the self-effacing "negative capability" that Keats and Hazlitt had identified with Shakespeare. The learned Victorian poet who had strutted behind Elizabethan masks needed to be culturally updated in the twentieth century.

The later Kipling resituates Browning's creations in everyday, material settings. To see the organ player of "Abt Vogler" parodically turned into a driver who has misused his car's clutch in "The Beginner: After He Has Been Extemporizing on an Instrument Not of His Own Invention" is deliciously funny. Equally amusing is the 1903 poem "Files: the Sub-Editor Speaks," in which Kipling toys with a refrain about "leaders" mouthed by a cynical sixteenth-century manipulator in Browning's *A Soul's Tragedy*. This crafty Papal Legate boasts about having "known Four-and-twenty leaders of revolt" in sixteenth-century Faenza. But for the lowly subeditor of a modern newspaper, "leaders" merely are lead articles that must be filed for future reference: "Files— / The Files— / Office Files! / Oblige me by referring to the Files / . . . / Ere we discovered Mammon and his wiles— / Faenza, gentle reader, spent her—five-and-twentieth leader— / (You will find him, and some others, in the Files). / Warn all coming Robert Brownings and Carlyles, / It will interest them to hunt among the Files" (1–4, 11–15, *CV* 350).

Kipling also modernizes the more serious preoccupations that Browning had removed to distant Renaissance or medieval pasts. Like many of Browning's complementary monologues, Kipling's "The 'Mary Gloster'" and "McAndrew's Hymn" are blank-verse pendants. Spoken by a wealthy capitalist and by the Scot machinist who works on one of this magnate's ships, the pairing not only links the two men to each other but also yokes Browning's "The Bishop Orders His Tomb" to his "Rabbi Ben Ezra."

In "The 'Mary Gloster,'" Browning's dying Bishop has become a Carlylean captain of industry. Instead of addressing his many "nephews," the dying Sir Anthony Gloster, a self-made man, harangues his spoiled and overeducated only son "Dickie." Abjuring wealth, mistresses, and knighthood, this modern worldling is haunted by the memory of the dead wife who made "a man of me." He informs Dickie that "your mother" was buried "in the "Macassar Straits" after she perished onboard the *Mary Gloster*. The widower orders his son to place the widower's own coffin on the ship named after his wife. By scuttling the vessel at a location he has marked, Anthony's old friend, McAndrew, will allow the couple to be reunited (5, 24, 32, *CV* 128–29).

If the magnate who orders a nautical tomb is a dying Bishop's fellow materialist, his counterpart, McAndrew, a "dour" Presbyterian bachelor, is a latter-day Rabbi Ben Ezra who yearns to be united with his God. Unseen by the wealthy passengers he safely ferries across the seas, this ship's engineer cannot readily commune with an invisible *Deus absconditus*. The divinity he celebrates in his "Hymn" oddly manifests itself in the hydraulic power that propels a modern steamship. McAndrew regards the "clangin' chorus" of the ship's engines as the equivalent of those heavenly choirs that once celebrated a Hebrew God. By lauding human invention, "Man—the Arrtifex," rather than Ben Ezra's potterlike divinity, McAndrew tries to bring an alienated Maker closer to modern maker-men (115, 158, 159, 177, *CV,* 123, 125).

Like Browning, Kipling was a master of mixed forms. The triple point of view that operates in Browning's "Holy Cross Day" is expressed through three radically different modes of diction (J. Hillis Miller 87–88; Melchiori 20–42). The prose "diary" of the secretary who reports the "awakening" of Jews harangued by his master is subverted by droll rhymes that render what "they really said"; yet this comic grumbling is superseded by the stately cadences of "Ben Ezra's Song of Death" in verses that draw on the New Testament rather than on the actual Abraham Ben Meir Ibn Ezra, whose commentaries on the Book of Isaiah both Brownings knew.

Kipling, too, produces a generic friction when he places a poem called "The Rabbi's Song" after the ghost story of "The House Surgeon" in his 1909 *Actions and Reactions*. The contrast between this grim "Song" and a story that had seemingly ended on a happy note signified by a song that affirms a young woman's belief in a benign providential order sharpens the effect he had produced much earlier in a grim 1890 story he had headed with an epigraph taken from Browning's *Pippa Passes*.[9]

"The Rabbi's Song" reactivates the note of alienation on which "The House Surgeon" began when an amiable merchant is shunned by fellow passengers who have detected his Jewishness. When the ghost of a Calvinist woman who haunts this merchant's house is successfully exorcised, his Christian daughter, Thea, celebrates the purification with "an old English song" that proclaims, like Pippa's, her absolute trust in God. Yet the complacency of this closure is immediately offset by "The Rabbi's Song." Our thoughts, a new speaker now suggests, turn heavenward only to help us flee

---

9. The eight-line epigraph from *Pippa Passes* that heads "The Record of Badalia Herodsfoot" (in the 1890 *Many Inventions*) jars with the murder of the story's marginalized Cockney protagonist in a grisly scene that matches Nancy's brutal murder in *Oliver Twist*.

a "Hell" built on the residues of "hate" and "pain." If ineradicable memories of universal "anguish" are needed for any relation with God, the benign bond that Browning had Rabbi Ben Ezra articulate has been utterly erased:

> Our lives, our tears, as water,
>   Are spilled upon the ground;
> God giveth no man quarter,
>   Yet God a means hath found;
> Though faith and hope have vanished,
>   And even love grows dim;
> A means whereby his banished
>   Be not expelled from Him! (25–32, *CV* 596)

Kipling here adapts the speech of the "wise woman" of Tekoah in 2 Samuel 14.14.[10] But why does he invent a "rabbi" to utter words likelier to be spoken by the female ghost whom a "house surgeon" may have failed to silence? Like the embittered specter of a twelfth-century Sephardic Jew transported to modern England in *Puck of Pook's Hill* (1906), the speaker of this poem acts as a foil to Rabbi Ben Ezra as well as to Robert Browning. Known for his serene parleyings with the dead, Browning has been pressed into a narrative that houses spirits who refuse to be quieted.

Kipling's previous venture into the uncanny had redeployed Browning's own ghost poem, "'Childe Roland.'" Like Morrowbie Jukes, the nameless narrator of "They" (1904) is on a quest that turns hallucinatory as soon as he reaches a goal neither he nor the reader could have foreseen. Riding a motorcar through lush Sussex downs rather than a horse through a wasteland, this narrator signifies his kinship with the speaker of "'Childe Roland'" early in the story: "I had run myself out of my known marks," he notes, as his car grinds to a halt on "a great still lawn from which sprang horsemen with leveled lances." When the "green spear" of one of these clipped-yew-figures touches his breast, the narrator feels transported in time: "'if this knight does not ride a wallop at me,' thought I, 'Shakespeare and Queen Elizabeth at least must come out of that half-open garden.'" Yet his final encounter in the "weather-worn" mansion he enters will be as startling as the sight of the ghosts that line the Dark Tower at the close of Browning's poem.

---

10. Around this time, Kipling planned a set of "old Biblical" poems that would have included "David eating his showbread" [1 Samuel 21], "Jonah cursing beneath the withered gourd" [Jonah 4.8–9], and "a few other matters" (8 November 1908, *Letters* III: 344).

Browning had called attention to his poem's intertextuality by placing the title of "'Childe Roland'" in quotation marks and by directing readers to "See Edgar's song in *Lear*." Not only "At the Mermaid" but also "House" (the poem in which he disparaged Wordsworth's notion that Shakespeare had "unlocked" his "heart" in the sonnets) tried to counter Alfred Austin's disparagement of Browning as a chatty self-promoter. Yet the mask of Shakespeare did not quite fit. It was Ben Jonson, after all, who provided the epigraph for "At the Mermaid." Hardly averse to fame, Browning would have accepted the offer of a Laureateship.

Kipling, who emphatically rejected the honors and titles that three prime ministers and one king wanted to bestow on him, recalled Browning's verses in his own Mermaid poem, "The Craftsman" (1910), as well as in "Proofs of Holy Writ" (1934). In "The Craftsman," Kipling's Shakespeare reminds an "overbearing" Jonson that he created his Cleopatras and Ophelias by observing ordinary figures in everyday life. In the later short story, however, the two writers become collaborators of sorts after one of the "fifty" clergymen King James has commissioned to produce a new Bible asks Shakespeare to help him "trick out" the "first three verses of the Sixtieth of Isaiah, and the nineteenth and twentieth of that same" ("Proofs of Holy Writ," *Kipling's Lost World* 130).

Kipling makes much of Shakespeare's willingness to rely on his vain and overly wordy associate's mastery of Latin. Initially jealous, Ben Jonson proves to be helpful even though he cannot quite curb his Browningesque pedantry by letting loose "an avalanche of instances from Ovid, Quintilian, Terence, Columella, Seneca, and others" to a Will whose aroused imagination requires no such displays of erudition:

> 'Quiet, man'! said he. 'I wait on my Demon!' He fell into the stage-stride of his art that time, speaking to the air.
> 'How shall this open? "Arise" No! "Rise!" Yes. And we'll have no weak coupling. 'Tis a call to a City! "Rise—shine" . . . Nor yet any schoolmaster's "because"—because Isaiah is not Holofernes. "*Rise—shine, for thy light is come, and—*!"' He refreshed himself from the apple and the proofs as he strode. '"And—the glory of God!"—No! "God's" over-short. We need the long roll here. "*And the glory of God is risen on thee.*" (Isaiah speaks the part. We'll have it from his own lips.)' ("Proofs of Holy Writ" 131–32)

In this historical extravaganza about the revision of a printer's "proofs," Kipling's Shakespeare has no need to leave a tangible "proof" of his "Englishing" of words that seem to emanate from a prophet's "own lips." England's greatest dramatist gladly acts as a humble ghostwriter for a small sliver of the King James Bible. The words he dictates to Ben will not correspond exactly to those of the final version. Although he knows little Latin, less Greek, and no Hebrew, a writer who lacks the erudition of a Jonson or a Milton can capture the sublimity of the prophet studied by Ben Ezra as well as by the two Brownings. Kipling's gentle Will is content with his subservient role. He knows that no text, however holy, is wholly permanent, immune to further modification.

Kipling's identification with Shakespeare's ventriloquist art here is as pronounced as that of his Romantic and Victorian forebears, Hazlitt, Keats, and Browning. But he aligns his own fitful "Demon" with Shakespeare's inimitable imagination only to stress a master craftsman's exemplary self-effacement. Kipling adopts Browning's investment in Shakespeare yet uses it to signify a more modest acceptance of the fragmentary nature and ephemerality of all "writ."

Thirty-five years earlier Kipling had written a letter to John St. Loe Strachey to repudiate the notion that the "power of interpretation" demonstrated in his "sea-poems" entitled him to become the Empire's next laureate ("The Poet's Function" 15). Far from being a jingoistic "rhymester," Kipling pleads, he is merely a "story-teller" whose verses and prose became less popular when "people found out I was putting two meanings into my work" (*Letters* II: 357). As a poet, Kipling adds, "I am only getting ready for the real poet who will appear in the first quarter of the next century. He will appropriate everything he wants—perhaps six lines and half an idea—out of all that I and scores of others have done: he will add his own poems to it and then we shall have Browning's successor—not Browning but another" (II: 357–58).

Kipling never left "a private letter of suggestions" for a new Browning (II: 358). Yet he correctly predicted that future Browning acolytes might not be the true-blooded Britons John St. Loe Strachey had privileged. Ezra Pound taught T. S. Eliot (who would later edit Kipling) how to master the dramatic monologue. W. H. Auden and Randall Jarrell (another Kipling editor) would create new Browning echoes in their own dramatic lyrics.[11]

11. See, for instance, Randall Jarrell's "The Truth," a dramatic lyric spoken by a severely traumatized boy who has lost both his sister as well as his dog "Stalky" during a London blitz and who repudiates the white lies told by his mother. Set in a clinic, this modern "Madhouse Cell" not only calls attention to a profound identification with Kipling's narratives about the vulnerability of childhood imaginings but also relies on the mixture of lyricism and irony Jarrell valued in Browning, whose "My Last Duchess" he extolled in a letter written to Adrienne Rich a mere seven days before his death.

But, ultimately, Kipling himself was the best translator of a poet who had converted old yellow texts into sparkling new constructs. He cast the Man-Who-Would-Be-Shakespeare as his valued collaborator and his most steady foil.

CHAPTER 10

THE VICTORIANISM OF STRACHEY'S *EMINENT VICTORIANS*

Despite his professed hostility to the age of Victoria, the modernist Lytton Strachey employed a rhetoric of likeness-in-difference for his 1918 collective biography *Eminent Victorians*. Claiming that the book is far more complicated than the diatribe for which it has so often been taken, Knoepflmacher shows how Strachey's empathetic treatment of Florence Nightingale, General George Gordon, and John Henry Newman differs markedly from his sardonic handling of Cardinal Manning, Dr. Thomas Arnold, and Matthew Arnold. Although Strachey seeks to distance himself from all of his Victorian Others, he creates his own set of marginalized Carlylean "heroes" whose points of view he can partially embrace. By way of contrast, the confident certitude of Dr. Thomas Arnold and Cardinal Manning grates on a Strachey who views truth as fragmentary, artistic value as relative, and aesthetic abstractions as meaningless.

The Victorians were obsessed with self-translations. In order to come to grips with their own historical identity, they planted surrogate selves into earlier eras of transition. Indeed, it might be argued that a key feature of what Michael Timko has called the "Victorianism of Victorian Literature" lies precisely in the compulsion to assume the shape of an Other removed in time and space. Even grotesque figures—Carlyle's Teufelsdroeckh, Tennyson's St. Simeon Stylites, Emily Brontë's Lockwood—hide authorial selves barely masked by a shift in ideology or gender. The "poor," brown "Mahomet" whom Carlyle treats with seeming condescension possesses physical features that decidedly resemble Carlyle's very own. The audience who attended Carlyle's second lecture on Heroes in May of 1840—"the bonniest and brawest of people" (MacMechan, "Introduction," *Carlyle: On Heroes* xxxviii)—thus could detect affinities between the speaker and his subject: the "fine sagacious honest face, brown florid complexion, beaming black eyes" (60); the "rude" but sincere speech; the "vein on the brow which swelled-up black when he was in anger" (60–61).

Yet there is a different kind of Victorian Other seldom considered by specialists: writers who, like Strachey, Woolf, Beerbohm, and Nicolson, outgrow the Victorian age, who may even profess to be inimical to that age, but who acknowledge their ties by appropriating the Victorian mode of self-inspection and self-definition: personation through Otherness. Ironically, then, this other-than-Victorian is compelled to assume the shape of a Victorian Other. If the Victorians burrowed into their own cultural pasts to seek likeness-in-difference, the early modernists adopted the same methods of association to establish a difference-in-likeness.

In 1914, just as cannons volleyed and thundered to mark an end to the optimistic era that Lytton Strachey claimed to have already ended in 1898 when "Major Kitchener and his Maxim-Nordenfeldt guns" had triumphed at Khartoum (Strachey, *Eminent Victorians* [hereafter *EV*] 349), he proposed creating an association dedicated to the preservation of Victorianism. Though his proposal was made tongue-in-cheek, Strachey here anticipated not only our own latter-day Victorians Institutes and Associations but also the goal of his *Eminent Victorians,* published four years later, at the end of the Great War:

> Surely, before it is too late, a club should be started—an old Victorian Club—the business of whose members would be to protect the reputation of their Age and give it a fair chance with the public. Perhaps such a club exists already—in some quiet corner of Pimlico; but if so, it has sadly neglected one of its most pressing duties—the hushing-up of Matthew Arnold. ("Victorian Critic" 175)

Too long misread as a purely destructive assault on Victorianism, *Eminent Victorians* could well have been written by a member of that old Victorian Club of Pimlico. The portraits of "the lives of an ecclesiastic, an educational authority, a woman of action, and a man of adventure," as Strachey calls his Eminent Four in his Preface, are, for all their irony, sketched with considerable empathy, even affection. Of these four portraits, two—those of Florence Nightingale and General Gordon—carry highly personal self-inscriptions. Although Strachey casts Cardinal Manning as a Trollopian Mr. Slope, and John Henry Newman as a Mr. Harding (thus paying an indirect tribute to his favorite Victorian novelist), the two clerical figures, though antithetical, also carry a sufficient investment to make them into his personal Others. Only the fourth portrait (also the shortest and least complicated) remains totally negative. Still, Strachey's unmitigated hostility toward Dr. Arnold, who, as a historian, is a rival of the writer who calls himself an "explorer of the past" (*EV* vii), allows him to be true at least to his claim that any friend of things Victorian must hush up the author of "Rugby Chapel."

Thus it is that Matthew Arnold should be allowed just one brief appearance in *Eminent Victorians* and, moreover, that he should appear as a small chorister still in knee breeches. The writer who regarded *Eminent Victorians* as a sort of musical composition in four parts—with "Cardinal Manning" as an *allegro vivace*, "Florence Nightingale" an *andante*, "Dr. Arnold" a *scherzo*, and "The End of General Gordon" a *rondo*—delights in the image of a tone-deaf father who listens to the chirpings of one soon to become a Strayed Reveller:

> Music he did not appreciate, though he occasionally desired his eldest boy, Matthew, to sing to him the Confirmation Hymn of Dr. Hinds, to which he had become endeared, owing to its use in Rugby chapel. But his lack of ear was, he considered, amply recompensed by his love of flowers; "they are my music," he declared. Yet, in such a matter, he was careful to refrain from an excess of feeling, such as, in his opinion, marked the famous lines of Wordsworth:
> > To me the meanest flower that blows can give
> > thoughts that do often lie too deep for tears.
> He found the sentiment morbid. "Life," he said, "is not long enough to take such intense interest in objects themselves so little." (*EV* 231)

Strachey's animosity toward the Arnolds, father and son, seems the only truly vindictive note unrelentingly struck in *Eminent Victorians*. Why did he need to hush up the boy Matthew and portray him as the dutiful son of an unmusical (and unpoetic) father?[1] Let me defer a possible answer to

---

1. Strachey does allow some phrases from Arnold's prose to filter into his own writing, yet such appropriations always strip away a sentimental veneer through which Arnold tries to soften his own detachment and often turn on Arnold himself. Arnold's guarded identification with Ox-

that question and consider, first, the nature of Strachey's involvement with the other figures in his book.

In a letter Strachey received shortly before his death at the age of fifty-two, Sir Max Beerbohm wrote: "Much older though I am than you, my admiration for your prose, since first I knew it, has had the fresh wild hot quality that belongs rather to a very young man's feeling for the work of a great congenial veteran" (21 March 1931, 180). The sixty-year-old Beerbohm's willingness to confer on Strachey the authority of an elder is noteworthy, considering the prominence accorded to old age, endurance, and survival in *Eminent Victorians*. Like Virginia Woolf, another "congenial" admirer, Strachey tends to see himself as a late-born Victorian. Even more than Leslie Stephen's daughter, he was the child of a very old man, Sir Richard Strachey, who lived from 1817 to 1908 and had already attained the age of sixty-three when Lytton was born.[2] Like Woolf, then, Strachey wandered between two worlds: he is, as he calls his narrator in *Eminent Victorians*, both a "modern inquirer" as well as "the explorer of the past" (3, vii). Though more than half a century younger than Matthew Arnold, he is as connected to the early Victorians as Dr. Arnold's "eldest boy." Both Lytton's grandfather as well as his uncle, Sir Edward Strachey (who lived to be a mere eighty-nine), were the benefactors and supporters of Thomas

---

ford and with the Oxford movement is one of Strachey's favorite targets. Thus Arnold's famous phrases about the moon-bathed "she" who whispers "from her towers the last enchantments of the Middle Age" (*Lectures and Essays in Criticism,* Preface 290) are tersely condensed by Strachey to render Newman's inevitable seduction in this home of lost causes: "At Oxford, he was doomed. He could not withstand the last enchantment of the Middle Age. It was in vain that he plunged into the pages of Gibbon or communed for long hours with Beethoven over his beloved violin" (*EV* 17). Similarly, Arnold's characterization in *Culture and Anarchy* of "Dr. Newman's movement" as a subterranean current of feeling that carries his own desire for a "beauty and sweetness" to overflow and bathe the "ground" of liberalism in the 1860s (107) is exposed as a lesser bit of wishfulness than Newman's own metaphoric irrigations of history: "No, the waters of the true Faith had dived underground at the Reformation, and they were waiting for the wand of Newman to strike the rock before they should burst forth once more" (*EV* 20). For Strachey, Newman is at least a genuine poet, as much a Romantic as Wordsworth. It is Newman, therefore, not Arnold, who can be cast as a Moses, one doomed to "die in the wilderness" ("The Function of Criticism at the Present Time" 285). Strachey delights in turning against Arnold and Arnold's biological father those phrases by which Arnold tried to signify his distance from poetic fathers such as Wordsworth and Newman. Arnold may fault Wordsworth for not reading enough books, "among them, no doubt, those of that Goethe whom he disparaged without reading" ("The Function of Criticism" 262), but Strachey wrests the phrase away and applies it to Thomas Arnold—"Dr. Arnold, who had held up to scorn and execration Strauss's 'Leben Jesu' without reading it" (*EV* 229).

2. Sir Richard was, moreover, seventy when Lytton's brother James was born—a fact that undoubtedly has something to do with the youngest Strachey's devotion to the oedipal theories of Sigmund Freud.

Carlyle; for her part, Lytton's mother had befriended and been encouraged by George Eliot.

This heritage is very much in evidence in *Eminent Victorians.* Unlike Pater and Arnold, who distanced themselves, as refined Oxford men of letters, from Carlyle's notions about heroism and action, Strachey, like George Eliot, feminizes the Carlylean hero,[3] whom he recognizes as a fellow outsider, into a "woman of action." "She was heroic," he writes of Florence Nightingale. "Certainly, she was heroic. Yet her heroism was not of that simple sort so dear to the readers of novels and compilers of hagiologies— the romantic sentimental heroism with which mankind loves to invest its chosen darlings: it was made of sterner stuff" (*EV* 155). If Carlyle shocked the expectations of his audience by the unorthodox choice of the Others he cast as heroes (the hero as divinity, a pagan Odin rather than Jesus; the hero as prophet, an alien "Mahomet" rather than Isaiah), so does Strachey demolish his own readership's anticipation of a "gracious angel of mercy." Kindly Prince Albert, ever the gentleman, sees only the demure surface of Miss Nightingale: "'Sie gefällt uns sehr,' noted the Prince, 'ist sehr bescheiden'" [We like her very much; she is very modest (my translation)] (*EV* 166). But Queen Victoria is not taken in by the appearances of feminine modesty. Her assessment is shrewder by far. "Her Majesty's comment was different—'Such a *head*! I wish we had her at the War Office'" (166).

In Carlyle's *On Heroes,* the Valkyrs, gatherers of slain warrior-heroes, are the only female presences in a mythical male world of action ruled by Odin or Wotan or "the God *Wünsch,* or Wish . . . who could give us all that we *wished*!" (18). In Strachey's *Eminent Victorians,* however, even the wishes of modern Europe's most powerful monarch cannot be realized. To Queen Victoria's correct surmise that Miss Nightingale would make a far better War Minister than any one of the male bureaucrats slumbering in her Cabinet, the narrator adds his caustic confirmation that such a wish, though eminently proper, cannot yet be realized: "But Miss Nightingale was not at the War Office, and for a very simple reason: she was a woman. Lord Panmure, however, *was*" (*EV* 166–67). In his Trollopian deflation of all the ineffectual men strutting in their ministries, hospitals, and armies, Strachey suggests again and again that the jobs they bungled would have been far better handled by a "woman of action" as unorthodox as Florence the Valkyr, the Mrs. Proudie of Crimea. Proscribed by the cowing males who both fear and serve her, this outsider is the *true* Victorian as

---

3. For connections between *On Heroes* and *The Mill on the Floss,* see my "Genre and the Integration of Gender" (chapter 2) in this volume.

Other Victorian. If the monarch who gave the era her name recognizes the impressiveness of the "head" she is prevented from making the head of a ministry, Lytton Strachey delights in rendering both the appearance and angry intelligence of the "capacious brow" that can triumph "not by gentle sweetness and womanly self-abnegation" but by a Swiftian sarcasm that searches "the ranks of the officials with the deadly and unsparing precision of a machine-gun" (156, 157–58).[4] Himself shaped by female wit, his lively mother's as well as that of *"cette grande femme,"* his iron-willed teacher, Marie Souvestre (Holroyd 1: 214), Strachey understands and endorses the power that marginalized figures can hold.

Strachey, then, amends Carlyle's masculine ideology by the central role he accords to a she-hero. Nonetheless, his belief that history can best be glimpsed through the biographies of famous personages remains thoroughly Carlylean. And his idea to look at the Victorians through a composite portrait gallery chimes with the admiration he professes for the "stylistic imagination" that shaped Carlyle's sketches of his contemporaries in both *The Life of Sterling* and the posthumous *Reminiscences* ("Carlyle" 181).[5] Pater had tried to separate himself from Carlyle's precedent in his first work, "Diaphaneitè"; Arnold had preferred "cultivated inaction" to Carlylean activism.[6] It is apparently Strachey's own affiliation with Carlyle, in a 1908 essay called "The Prose Style of Men of Action," that makes him turn on Pater: "Some writers—Walter Pater was one of them—seek through a lifetime, with all the laborious refinement of scholarship and taste, to achieve style, and in the end achieve only the imitation of it" (Sanders 289). The attack seems surprising, coming from one who described the effects of Villon's poetry in his first book, *Landmarks in French Literature* (1912), in phrases that seem straight out of Pater's *Renaissance*. What is more, Strachey insists as strongly as Pater does that ventures into biohistory must above all be aesthetic, crafted by a designer's impressions and temperament rather than by an ideologue's search for some predetermined truth. Sounding for a moment even like the Matthew Arnold

---

4. As Strachey suggests, Nightingale hardly sees herself as a melodious songbird: "I am lying without my head, without my claws, and you all peck at me" (*EV* 179).

5. Hugh Kingsmill, Strachey's enemy, probably understood the extent of Strachey's identification with Carlyle when he chose to adopt a Carlylean voice to fulminate against the "Wart-School of Modern Portraiture" of "Biographer Strachey and his apes" (25–26) in the January 1933 diatribe, "Parodies No. 7: Some Modern Light-Bringers as They Might Have Been Extinguished by Thomas Carlyle," 25–26.

6. For discussions of Arnold's attitudes toward Carlyle, see Kathleen Tillotson; David J. DeLaura.

who proclaimed himself to be an unsystematic thinker in an age of system builders, Strachey protests in his Preface to *Eminent Victorians*:

> My choice of subjects has been determined by no desire to construct a system or to prove a theory, but by simple motives of convenience and of art. It has been my purpose to illuminate rather than to explain. (viii)

Art is indeed a crucial word in *Eminent Victorians*, as important to Strachey as to Beerbohm and Woolf, each of whom praised the book's artistry, singling out "The End of General Gordon" as their favorite (Holroyd 2: 251). Like Nightingale (herself likened to Samuel Butler and to Ibsen), Gordon possesses a writer's sensibility, a "sardonic humour," a mastery over words. Both figures are less fragile and more immersed in a world of action than John Henry Newman, Strachey's third hero. The female satirist who could have run the War Office and the warrior who preferred to write disquisitions on Plutarch are, like the lonely Cardinal, respected as displaced artist figures. Even the opportunistic Manning is allowed to win "by art" rather than sheer "force" (*EV* 4). But Newman remains the preeminent artist figure. More poetic than Gordon, more feminine than Nightingale, he is described as "a child of the Romantic Revival, a creature of emotion and of memory, a dreamer whose secret spirit dwelt apart in delectable mountains, an artist" (*EV* 16). Displaced by history in ways that Rimbaud, presented at the end of the book, is not, he must suppress what that "amazing poet" and lover of Verlaine can fully act out (*EV* 339). As a victim of the Zeitgeist, unable to indulge appetites that Hopkins might sublimate in his poetry, Newman becomes for Strachey, paradoxically enough, superior to Rimbaud, who is introduced as an overly impatient and overly irritated anti-Victorian. This ineffectual Romantic child can triumph only as a prose stylist, a late-blossoming craftsman whose *Apologia* appears when he is already sixty-three. Newman thus offers a model for a similarly displaced Victorian child, a Lytton Strachey who, until his death at fifty-two, remained convinced that he would not produce a major book until after he had attained the age of sixty.

Longevity is a leitmotif in *Eminent Victorians*. Manning becomes most accessible as an "old man" reviewing "for the thousandth time, the long adventure of his life" (*EV* 126). Dying at the age of eighty-five, Manning exceeded the life span of the eighty-three-year-old Tennyson but fell short of Carlyle who died at eighty-six, Newman who reached eighty-nine, Nightingale who attained the age of ninety, and, of course, Lt. General Sir Richard Strachey, the indestructible Tithonus who lived to be ninety-one. General Charles George Gordon, whose hardiness and military rank resemble those of Strachey's father, his fellow engineer, fellow administrator, fellow naturalist, and fellow fighter in exotic places, might easily have become a nonagenarian were it not for his Tennysonian death wish. Thus when Strachey claims that Newman's longevity was responsible for his immortality as a writer, the statement carries a decidedly personal resonance. Newman's "future course" was aided, Strachey holds, by a "singular chance": "If Newman had died at the age of sixty, to-day he would have been already forgotten, save by a few ecclesiastical historians; but he lived to write his *Apologia,* and to reach immortality, neither as a thinker nor as a theologian, but as an artist" (17–18).

Strachey's intense identification with his subjects as artists allows him to appropriate their point of view. At the end of the book, a decapitated General Gordon still hovers like a grinning Cheshire Cat over the battlefield site on which an earnest service is conducted in his honor. Strachey playfully adopts the ironic omniscience of Gordon's translated spirit:

> Everyone agreed that General Gordon had been avenged at last. Who could doubt it? General Gordon himself, possibly, fluttering, in some remote Nirvana, the pages of a phantasmal Bible, might have ventured on a satirical remark. But General Gordon had always been a contradictious person—even a little off his head, perhaps, though a hero; and besides he was no longer there to contradict. . . . At any rate, it had all ended very happily—in a glorious slaughter of twenty thousand Arabs, a vast addition to the British Empire, and a step in the peerage for Sir Evelyn Baring. (350)

Gordon's "sardonic humour" (312) so chimes with Strachey's own that this final impersonation of his satirical ghost seems natural and fitting. Like Newman and Nightingale, Gordon is the outsider as insider; his enemies are precisely those who deny Otherness, alterity, alienation, and the subversiveness of play.

In his lectures on the odd men he had anointed as his heroes, Thomas Carlyle repeatedly projected his own brown face and rude and "earnest" speech on a brown and rude and earnest "Mahomet" or Knox or Cromwell or Dr. Johnson. Strachey, too, always looked for self-reflections in his subjects. Yet these reflections also yielded what Carlyle's did not: a transposition in gender. Newman is cast as a decidedly female figure, with his obsessive concern about virginity, his identification of saints with women, and his final "impregnation" (18) by Froude. Even more pointedly, Florence

Nightingale begins to resemble her male biographer when the aquiline face of a Victorian lady aristocrat becomes as sexually blurred as that of Woolf's Orlando. Casual observers, we are told, might only glimpse the "pattern of a perfect lady,"

> but the keener eye perceived something more than that—the serenity of high deliberation in the scope of the capacious brow, the sign of power in the dominating curve of the thin nose, and the traces of a harsh and dangerous temper—something peevish, something mocking, and yet something precise—in the small delicate mouth. There was humour in the face; but the curious watcher might wonder if it was humour of a very pleasant kind. (156)

The portraiture of an Other yields a self-portrait. Only a long beard needs to be added to convert Miss Nightingale into Mr. Strachey. Detachment becomes possible only through an "alteration in her physical mould," as the "thin, angular woman, with her haughty eye and her acrid mouth" vanishes in the senility of old age, "and in her place was the rounded bulky form of a fat old lady, smiling all day long" (201).

Strachey's self-inscriptions into his Victorian Others are not necessarily as overtly physical. In one of the narrator's many speculations on fortune's quirks, he wonders whether the Oxford Movement might not easily have "flickered out its little flame unobserved in the Common Room of Oriel" if Newman's father, "when the gig came round on the fatal morning, still undecided between the two universities, had chanced to turn the horse's head in the direction of Cambridge" (16). Had Newman gone to Cambridge, Strachey speculates, he might well have become a major poet, but he was doomed at Oxford, where he "could not withstand the last enchantment of the Middle Age" (17). The passage carries a double resonance. It allows Strachey one further stab at the earnest Oxonians whom he mocks throughout his book, as I have already suggested:[7] Clough, who winds up tying Florence Nightingale's parcels; Dr. Arnold, whose Oxford connections take him to Rugby; and Clough's friend and Arnold's son, the boy Matthew, whose phrase about the last enchantment of the Middle Age is here so ironically deployed. But the passage also carries a more personal subtext. Lytton Strachey went to Cambridge only after having been turned down by Balliol. What might have happened to him had he become a son of Oxford? Might he have followed the path of the star of Balliol, Pater's

---

7. See note 1.

student, who chose to be received by Newman as the future Father Hopkins? Or, horror of horrors, might he not have turned into someone like Matthew Arnold?

I can now at last return to some speculations about Strachey's relentless hostility toward the Arnolds in *Eminent Victorians*. I have already seeded some of the elements that account for that enmity in my attempts to document the nature of his identifications with the figures he treats so much more empathetically. Unlike the questioning, artful, marginal, ambivalent figures of Gordon, Nightingale, Newman, and even Manning, Dr. Arnold is persistently depicted as smug and reductive in his certitudes. His need to pare things down—an attribute inherited by his son—is even reflected in Strachey's description: "His legs, perhaps, were shorter than they should have been" (210). Unlike the lean and long-legged Stracheys, this stocky figure is made uneasy by all those who resist his notion that an English gentleman should be "Christian, manly, and enlightened" (210).

Dr. Arnold wants to screen his students from a too "close and friendly contact with civilised men, and even, perhaps, with civilised women" (213). Though he sees himself as an Old Testamental lawgiver who must expound on the possible impact of "the incidents of Jewish history in the sixth century B.C. upon the conduct of English schoolboys in 1830" (221), he is disturbed to find that, despite his protests, "not only were Jews admitted to Parliament, but a Jew was actually appointed a governor of Christ's hospital" (225). According to Strachey, Dr. Arnold assumes that, as a thinker/educator, he is obliged "to decide precisely which classes of people were to be excluded" (225). Thus he not only bars women, Jews, Unitarians, the lower classes, satirists, scientists, and poets (since boys "do not like poetry"!) from the insular community over which he presides but also fears his young wards. He is disturbed by their lack of a "true, *manly* sense of the degradation of guilt or faults"; he notes their "essential inferiority" when "compared with a *man*," their tendency to betray the "best promise of a noble *man*hood" (217, 216, italics added).

It is this insistence on a limited (and homophobic) masculinity that leads Strachey to depict Dr. Arnold as a noxious patriarch. If the childless Gordon or Newman or Nightingale can be cast as parental surrogates in whom Strachey invests an "almost filial tenderness" (Holroyd 2: 307), Dr. Arnold is the father *in malo*. In a pointed contrast to the childless ancients, this father of ten dies as a young man, at the age of forty-seven. He has left little behind that Strachey considers to be lasting. Wordsworth's lines about the meanest flower may have struck Dr. Arnold as excessively morbid, but his guarded appreciation of the surrounding flora was far more exuberantly embraced by the flock of boys allowed, after school hours, "to ramble for long afternoon in the country, collecting eggs or gathering flowers" (*EV* 241). When Strachey notes that, despite Arnold's stern "prefectorial system," the boys still played games for sheer "pleasure," and when he quotes an old Rugbian who remembers that "at this period" one of their intensest delights was furnished by the gathered wildflowers, he deliberately underscores their headmaster's inability to exult in a Wordsworthian splendor in the grass or glory in the flower. One is reminded that Strachey's own father, a botanist who donated numerous specimens to the Herbarium at Kew Gardens and had thirty-two plants named after him, was hampered by no such impediments.

But why does *Eminent Victorians* hush up the Master of Rugby's son? What is Strachey's quarrel with Matthew Arnold? The fellow ironist of *Lectures and Essays in Criticism* is not merely a literary competitor in the genre of collective biography: the writer to whom Strachey elsewhere likes to refer as "Dr. Arnold's son" ("Pope" 266) is the proclaimer of a lineage that his rival seeks to replace. There is too much of the father in the son who could not bear the dissidence of dissent. Strachey questions Matthew Arnold's ability to obtain a vision of the "mysterious Goddess" of truth (*Lectures and Essays in Criticism,* Preface 286) through his tactics of paring, excluding and refining.[8] Arnold's superior intelligence, Strachey caustically suggests in "A Victorian Critic," might have resulted in "some excellent and lasting work upon the movement of glaciers or fertilization of plants. . . . But no; he *would* be a critic" (180).

Deliberately opposing Arnold's contention that his *Essays in Criticism* might furnish an "outline" of truth, Strachey insists in his own Preface that it "would have been futile to hope to tell even a *précis* of the truth about the Victorian age." Hence, unlike the Victorian who feared becoming all fragments, this other-than-Victorian is content merely to "elucidate certain fragments of truth which took my fancy and lay to my hand" (*EV* viii). Arnold's need to confirm certitude through his magisterial assertions goes back, as far as Strachey is concerned, to the little boy asked to sing the Confirmation Hymn for his tone-deaf father. Remembering Arnold's dictum that Pope's poetry lacked "high seriousness" as well as "poetic largeness, freedom, insight, benignity" ("Study of Poetry" 180), Strachey quotes the words only to overturn them. Such abstractions are as meaningless, he insists, as if one were to "point out that Wordsworth had no sense of

---

8. For an analysis of Arnold's rhetoric of exclusion see chapter 6 in this volume, "Arnold's Fancy and Pater's Imagination."

humour, that Shelley did not understand human beings, that Keats could not read Greek, and that Matthew Arnold did not wear a wig" ("Pope" 274). Writers and writing, Strachey holds, ought to be assessed on the merits of what they have to offer. His insight is worth remembering by those willing to look at his sympathy with Victorian Otherness. The result may well be a belated acceptance of both *Eminent Victorians* and *Queen Victoria* (1921)[9] as texts perfectly congruous with the deconstructive/reconstructive efforts of today's Old Victorian Clubs, whether located in some quiet corner of Pimlico or in some hidden hamlet of our North American Continent.

---

9. Even Strachey's *Queen Victoria* deserves to be seen in the same light, as Beerbohm long ago pointed out in his Rede lecture on Strachey: "And by the way, literature apart, aren't there in the Elysian Fields two other worthies who have reason to be grateful to the supposed iconoclast?— Queen Victoria and the Prince Consort? The Prince in his life-time had never been popular; and after Sir Theodore Martin's saccharine biography he had become a veritable mock. I never heard a kind word for him. The Queen, who in my childhood and youth had not only been revered but worshipped, was, soon after her death, no longer in public favour. Her faults had become known, and her virtues were unheeded. This is not so now; and it is not so by reason of Lytton Strachey's fully judicial presentment of her with all the faults over which her virtues so very much preponderated. And it is, by the same token, through him that we know the Prince not as just dreadfully admirable, but as someone to be loved and to be sorry for" (351).

CHAPTER 11

ENDINGS AS BEGINNINGS
Woolf and Nineteenth-Century Women Novelists

Virginia Woolf and George Eliot, novelists linked via Wordsworth in chapter 2, are joined by Mary Shelley and the Brontë sisters in this last chapter in which Knoepflmacher looks at nineteenth- and twentieth-century fictional endings. Closures, he insists, became increasingly problematic for the post-Romantic writers of longer narratives. The fragmentation that propelled so many nineteenth-century poets and essayists back to the presumed "wholeness" of the early Wordsworth also affected women novelists who devised endings that evoke, but refuse to resolve, the wishful anticipations seemingly promised by the beginnings of their texts.

𝒱erse-narratives and novels fuel desire. Even the harshest of antiromances inevitably teases a reader with the promise of an ending that will validate the windings and counterwindings of the plot lines we have followed. As Peter Brooks has noted, the form of the novel endows a succession of moments with meaning because we read those moments "in anticipation of endings that will retrospectively give them the order and significance of plot" (Brooks 94). Yet the closures of most major nineteenth- and twentieth-century fictions all too often reopen the conflicts and fissures that fueled the energies of the plot.

The precedent of the Romantic verse-narrative was of little help to Victorian poets like Alfred Tennyson, Elizabeth Barrett, and Robert Browning. *The Excursion,* begun in 1798 and published in 1814, was but a fragment of the larger philosophic poem "Nature, Man, and Society" that Wordsworth never completed; the artistry of his *Prelude,* published posthumously in 1850, went unrecognized by most mid-Victorians, having been displaced by the linked lyrics of Tennyson's *In Memoriam* earlier in that same year. Nor could psychological narratives such as Byron's *Don Juan* and Keats's *Hyperion* be brought to completion. Barrett's *Aurora Leigh,* Browning's *Ring and the Book,* and even Tennyson's "serial" *Idylls of the King* are still read as verse-novels that seem much closer to Victorian prose fiction than to the long poems the major Romantics had left unfinished.

As suggested in chapter 2, a lyrical novelist such as Virginia Woolf is as conscious of Wordsworth's and Tennyson's precedent as she is of the nineteenth-century novelists who came before her. She is aware of the difficulties a linear progression poses for narratives that often had to rely on double or even alternative endings or on prefaces that were, in effect, epilogues born out of hindsight, hence furnishing what George Eliot called the mere "make-believe of a beginning" (*Daniel Deronda* 36). Ironically implanted at the very start of the epigraph that opens Eliot's last complete novel, this statement is elaborated in that epigraph's last sentence: "no retrospect can take us to a true beginning" (36). The warning suggests that George Eliot was renouncing the very feature that had marked most of her previous fictions. Except for "The Lifted Veil," her narratives had always been set in the past.[1] She had retreated to simpler periods of history and earlier phases of human development in order to gain the control of hindsight. By regarding her fictions as successive "phases" in her own development as a thinker and an artist, George Eliot acknowledged their revisionary nature. The Worsdsworthian ending of *Silas Marner* thus revises the ending of *The Mill on the Floss,* as I have had occasion to show, while the ending of *Romola,* as Alison Booth has suggested, greatly complicates the pastoral and paternalistic closure of *Silas* (see Knoepflmacher, *George Eliot's Early Novels* 229–230; Booth, "The Silence," *Famous Last Words* 112, 129n).

Like George Eliot, Virginia Woolf steadily revised her previous fictions in each succeeding novel. But in *To the Lighthouse,* a novel in which she dramatized her family's Victorian roots, she also reinspected a literary heri-

---

1. It seems significant that the male narrator's prophetic ability to predict the exact *ending* of his life should convert George Eliot's narrative into a Shelleyan horror story.

tage she could no more bypass than her friend Lytton Strachey. As we shall see, Woolf now recognized her kinship with the Romantic and Victorian women writers whose narratives confronted divisions within a cultural order that the Great War would eventually raze. Not only George Eliot but also Mary Shelley and the Brontë sisters had to be indirectly acknowledged as progenitors. The idealistic Mrs. Ramsay thus became more than a fictionalized version of Julia Duckworth Stephen, Virginia Woolf's mother. Like Dorothea Brooke, she is a "foundress of nothing" whose "unattained goodness" can at best inspire a literary daughter who faces even greater "hindrances" than those that had obstructed and "dispersed" her well-meant efforts (Eliot, *Middlemarch* 4).

I

"He has landed," says Lily Briscoe at the end of *To the Lighthouse*; "It is finished." She is referring to the linear voyage undertaken by the patriarch who has sprung, "lightly like a young man," onto the rocky promontory Lily cannot see (*Lighthouse* 309, 308). Lily's "*it*," however, involves more than a concluded spatial movement. We also retreat in time to the very start of a narrative that began with Mrs. Ramsay's conditional opening sentence: "Yes, of course, if it's fine tomorrow" (9). But the "extraordinary joy" and "wonder" to which a six-year-old had "looked forward" (9) can no longer be realized. The long years that have intervened between Mrs. Ramsay's promise and its realization have destroyed the childish notion of a voyage "fringed with joy" (9). James and his sister Cam are grown-ups now, and their father is a widower. The dead Mrs. Ramsay has become a ghostly memory.

Despite the seeming finality of Lily Briscoe's utterance, *it* remains unfinished. The artist standing on the shore turns to her blurred canvas: "There it was—her picture" (9). She must still, "with a sudden intensity," see "it clear for a second" before she can finally draw "a line there, in the centre" (310). Only now can this "fatigued" painter lay down her brush and, relying on a past rather than a present tense, think: "It was done; it was finished" (310). Unlike Mr. Ramsay's last words in the book's previous section, Lily's "line" provides a closure that visually reincorporates the Victorian matriarch she wants to preserve.

But Woolf has slipped another male figure into her novel's last pages. Lily's first "It is finished" was addressed "aloud" to Augustus Carmichael, who suddenly materializes besides her, "puffing slightly" and "looking like an old pagan god" (309). Shading his eyes, this elderly poet confirms the painter's assumption when he says, "'They will have landed,' and she felt that she had been right. They had not needed to speak. They had been thinking the same things and he had answered her without her asking him anything" (309). There is a delicious ambiguity in these last two sentences. Has there or has there not been an actual dialogue? And why does Woolf deflect from Lily's "*He* has landed" to Carmichael's "*They* will have landed"?

Mr. Carmichael frees Lily from her investment in Mr. Ramsay's single-minded rush to a finish. Unlike the egotistic widower, this old poet man handles loss, Lily thinks, by "surveying, tolerantly and compassionately," the universal condition of a humanity beset by "weakness and suffering" (309). Mr. Carmichael thus emerges as Mr. Ramsay's ultimate foil. The poet who dreams about the shredded body of Andrew Ramsay, the boy he had loved, shares Lily's unwillingness to forgo desire. Freed from a linear bondage represented by the man who could not go beyond the letter *R,* she feels enabled to go back to beginnings. Mr. Carmichael's empathetic and compendious vision now allows Lily to complete the painting that restores a lost symbiosis between a late-Victorian mother and her youngest child.

Although depicted as a Victorian relic who, like Thomas Hardy, finds himself unexpectedly honored by a disillusioned twentieth-century public, Mr. Carmichael also functions as a replacement for the omniscient narrators whom Woolf and Joyce had eliminated from the modern novel. This surveyor of human weakness curiously resembles the narrator who took over the Finale of *Middlemarch* by assuring us that as long as quiet, "unhistoric acts" of fellow-feeling can propel us onward, "things are not so ill with you and me as they might have been" (*Middlemarch* 613). Eliot's Finale deliberately circles back to the phrasing and transhistoric allusions of her Prelude. Similarly, Lily's alliance with Mr. Carmichael allows Woolf to create a circular motion for a narrative that resists a single closure. Mr. Ramsay "might" well be thinking, "I have reached it. I have found it" (*Lighthouse* 308). But Lily's and Carmichael's collaboration frees both artists from such a limiting teleological sequence.

In *To the Lighthouse,* not only does Woolf evoke the great novel she had upheld as a fiction for adults, but she also toys with the Gothic trappings of romances such as *Frankenstein* and *Jane Eyre* when she adopts the spatial voyage undertaken by a debilitated male. Victor Frankenstein cannot be reanimated by the penitent creature who hovers over his corpse in a ship's cabin near the North Pole. But Jane Eyre, whose odyssey began when she surveyed the polar icescapes in Bewick's *Book of Birds,* is allowed to reanimate the frozen Rochester, her crippled "master." When Woolf freed Lily from a crippling pity for another older patriarch (whose last name also begins with *R*), she engaged in a revision that is more indirect and yet just as deliberate as that undertaken by Jean Rhys in *Wide Sargasso Sea.*

Rhys altered the closure of *Jane Eyre* by reinstating in her last pages the rebel figure whom Charlotte Brontë had subdued when she transformed the fiery Jane into a conventional Mrs. Rochester. As Antoinette holds the flickering candle that will burn down her prison house, she remembers the Coulibri estate, where her young mother allowed her to roam free. Lily's action is far less subversive. Yet, like Antoinette's candle, her brush also acts as an instrument that allows her to regain antecedents in need of redefinition. Lily senses the incompleteness of her earlier representation of Mrs. Ramsay. The composition somehow was askew: "It was a question, she remembered, how to connect this mass on the right hand with that on the left. She might do it by bringing the line of the branch across so; or break the vacancy in the foreground by an object (James perhaps) so. But the danger was that by doing that the unity of the whole might be broken" (*Lighthouse* 82–83).

Lily's (and Woolf's) need to refract what might otherwise offer too simple or too reductive a "unity" is in direct opposition to the rushed closure of *Jane Eyre* that disturbed others besides Woolf and Rhys.[2] Woolf's strictures on Brontë's romance in "*Jane Eyre* and *Wuthering Heights*" were reissued in *The Common Reader: First Series* in 1925, only two years before the publication of *To the Lighthouse*. Drawn to "the genius, the vehemence, the indignation" of Charlotte Brontë, Woolf is also repelled by the egotism of a "self-centered and self-limited" art that lacks the Keatsian negative capability of a Lily Briscoe. That egotism strikes her as excessively masculine and self-indulgent not unlike that of Wordsworthian Mr. Ramsay. If, among the survivors of the Victorian age, she finds that Thomas Hardy most resembles Charlotte Brontë "in the power of his personality and the narrowness of his vision," she also rates his *Jude the Obscure* above *Jane Eyre* because, in it, "we are not rushed to a finish" but "allowed to brood and ponder and drift away from the text in plethoric trains of thought" ("*Jane Eyre* and *Wuthering Heights*" 127, 129, 128).

---

2. Among the Victorian revisions of *Jane Eyre,* George Eliot's "Janet's Repentance" and Barrett's *Aurora Leigh* spring to mind. But it is Anne Brontë's sororal revision in *The Tenant of Wildfell Hall* that seems most relevant to Woolf: Helen Huntingdon, Anne's anti-Jane, is not only a young mother, as devoted to her male child as Mrs. Ramsay is to James, but also an accomplished painter who ekes out a living by selling her canvases.

Lily's completion of her unfinished artwork, I shall argue, reinstates materials that Brontë had half-suppressed in her novel's rush toward closure. In the next sections, I will connect Jane's voyage to self-completion to the endings of *Villette,* the narrative in which Charlotte Brontë rearranged elements that had vied with each other in her earlier novel. But I shall also allude to other works—*Wuthering Heights* and *Frankenstein,* for example—to widen the frame of reference. A yearned return to primal origins inevitably gets released whenever nineteenth-century narratives collapse the binaries of sex or try to resolve clashes between generations and between opposing spheres of interest. Finally, with Mr. Carmichael in mind, I shall also look at the role repeatedly played in such closures by androgynous male figures who are either feminized or desexualized in order to serve as agents of resolution.

II

Nineteenth-century novelists tried to control the narrative excess of their plots through double endings that encouraged the simultaneity of double meanings. By yoking marriage to death, they could signify two separate kinds of fulfillment. The fusion of the unquiet spirits who haunt the moors at the close of Emily Brontë's *Wuthering Heights* thus vies with the culmination of the marriage plot supervised by Nelly Dean. When Nelly's nurslings wed, Hareton and the second Catherine can also regain the estates their Earnshaw and Linton forebears had lost. Material possessions no longer concern Heathcliff. To repossess his lost double, he starves himself to death and "cedes all rights" to a Hareton "who looks more like Catherine than Catherine's daughter" (Knoepflmacher, "*Wuthering Heights:* A Study" 69). The newlyweds may settle at the Grange, but the mobile spirits seen by a shepherd boy are back in the primal wilderness that had sheltered them as children. They have recovered a lost beginning. Like the ghostly waif glimpsed "on a wide moor" at "the break of day" in "Lucy Gray" (6, 3), these liminal lovers acquire a mythical permanence.

In realistic fictions, however, such triumphal returns are harder to effect. The death embrace that reunites a brother and a sister at the end of *The Mill on the Floss* is not enough to bring that novel to a halt. The childhood symbiosis supposedly regained by Tom and Maggie Tulliver hardly resembles that recovered by Cathy and Heathcliff. An epilogue in which their tombs are revisited by newlyweds and by a lonely outsider must serve as a supplement. And, what is more, George Eliot's narrator must also circle back in the book's last sentence to the biblical phrase already cited on its title page: "In death they were not divided."[3]

Romanticism, with its Werthers and Manfreds, had not only lent a new intensity to the longing for fusion but also magnified a new century's increasing anxieties about death and separation. Before vanishing into "darkness and distance," the remorseful avenger who hovers over the corpse of Victor Frankenstein vows to commit suicide by consuming "to ashes this miserable frame" (*Frankenstein* 221). Yet that projected ending may not occur, given the novel's emphasis on broken promises. The creature who witnessed the destruction of the mate Frankenstein had agreed to animate may prefer to renew his search for origins. After his mother's death, Victor had probed into the sources of life. Similarly deprived, Mary Shelley used her "monster" to devise a narrative that might fill vacancies for an orphan who cannot "remember the original aera [*sic*]" of its "being" (97). In a Preface added in 1831, Mary Wollstonecraft's daughter claimed that an encounter with "dark, shapeless substances" had prompted her to seek a "beginning" that could, in turn, be meaningfully "linked to something that went before" (226).

As a reader-turned-novelist, Frankenstein's creature is capable of bringing the plot to a close. Having identified himself with Adam (and the curious Eve), Lucifer, and Cain, this revisionist reader of *Paradise Lost* acquires the plot-making capacities of that archnovelist, Milton's God. As reader/author of a narrative of unfulfilled desire, he may prefer to keep that desire in permanent suspension. By continuing to seek a sexual mate or a child playmate "as my companion and friend" (138), the "monster" might well keep alive his obsessive need to replace the parent it had lost—as had Mary Shelley—upon its birth.

Still, the impossibility of recovering a prelinguistic oneness deprives the self-conscious creature of a true beginning. By sailing back to the maternal older sister he had introduced at the start of *Frankenstein*, Captain Walton can resume his own control over a linear narrative. He can bring the plot to a close by simply declaring its warring protagonists to be dead and by reembracing, like Nelly Dean, the comforting safety of civilization. Like Heathcliff and Cathy, however, the expelled creature is still free to roam as

---

3. The inscription on the tomb that contains "two bodies" is taken from 2 Samuel 23 and refers, significantly enough, not to a brother and sister, but to a father and a son, Saul and Jonathan. Susan Stewart's contention that unmarked closures instill universal fears seems to the point here: "Our terror of the unmarked grave is a terror of the insignificance of a world without writing. The metaphor of the unmarked grave is one which joins the mute and the ambivalent; without the mark there is no boundary, no point at which to begin [or end]" (*On Longing* 31).

an embodiment of a perpetual yearning. The countless sequels to Shelley's novel attest that the shape who vanished in the dark is recoverable, easily brought back to life.

As a romance indebted to *Frankenstein* and similarly subject to revisions, Charlotte Brontë's *Jane Eyre* also closes with a male character's expression of a death wish. Although St. John Rivers is less verbose than the loquacious creature, his dramatic last words unexpectedly challenge the control Jane has maintained over her autobiography. Indeed, by endorsing St. John's eager anticipation of death, the new Mrs. Rochester undermines the domesticity she had presented as a happy reward for her and her Edward's travails. No longer inaccessible and no longer her tormentor, Jane's Byronic "master" has submitted to her control. But the chapter that began with the promised closure implied by Jane's "Reader, I married him" now privileges St. John's decision to consume his union with a divine bridegroom (*Jane Eyre* 395).[4] Mesmerized by this ecstatic surrender, the second Mrs. Rochester now defers to a new "master-spirit" (398).

St. John eroticizes his impending demise in the exultant fashion of a Heathcliff sure to be reunited with his ghostly mate. His ardent yearning for an otherworldly "Master" almost parodies Jane's earlier infatuation with her unattainable master. Instead of closing a story we expected to culminate in the merger of elective affinities, Jane deflects from her professions of marital happiness. She lingers on the "boy" who has inherited his father's eyes and finds her female cousins to be as "happy" as she is in their choice of mates. But she is far more excited by the fate of a traveler who has reached regions as exotic as those arctic zones penetrated in *Frankenstein* and visited by Jane herself as an escapist child reader.[5] Her imagination now joins this "undaunted" and still "unmarried" cousin to a tropical India full

---

4. If the Frankenstein creature's final death wish replicates that of an earlier female martyr, Justine Moritz, so does St. John's death wish reenact that of Jane's schoolmate Helen Burns. Motherless—like Jane, Justine, and the Frankenstein creature—Helen tries to evade the pains and excesses of adult desire that Jane has yet to face. But Helen's evasion of adult conflict, though alluring, is firmly repudiated by Jane. By the end of the novel, however, an adult woman, secure in her identity as the author of a retrospective narrative, mutes her own voice and gives primacy to the speech of her self-suppressing cousin.

5. Milton's rendition of a frozen "universe of death" where "all life dies, death lives, and nature breeds, / Perverse, all monstrous, all prodigious things" (*Paradise Lost* II: 623, 625–26) was extended by Coleridge in *The Rime of the Ancient Mariner* before novelists like Shelley and Brontë adopted the setting for their own purposes. Jane's account of the "reservoir of frost and snow" (6) and the scenes she will depict in her watercolors show her attraction to the same turbulent oceanic imagery relied upon, in *Villette*, by the protagonist first called Lucy Frost and then renamed Lucy Snowe.

of "rocks and dangers" (398). She repeats that he "will never marry now" (398) and "eagerly" supports his repudiation of all fleshly ties.

Earlier in the novel, St. John had echoed Helen Burns's charge that Jane overvalued "the love of human beings" (60). But when he insisted that "this world is not the scene of fruition" and asked her to "look a little higher than domestic endearments and household joys" (344), Jane strongly rejected his derogation of sexual passion and procreative bliss. In the novel's last paragraphs, however, the matron who exalts a death seeker's "zeal and energy" (398) seems as discontented with domesticity as the imaginative little girl who had fled Mrs. Reed's home by transporting herself into remote "death-white realms" (6). By moving from an account of her presumed fruition as wife and mother to a martyr's hope for a hierogamous union, she replaces autobiography with hagiography.

Although this final shift does not weaken the hold of Jane's forceful voice on readers of her narrative, it also compels us to see gaps that undermine the attempt to bring the plot to a tidy end. Not only does St. John Rivers's longing now reactivate the heroine's intense desire for consummation with an elusive other, but little Adèle must also reenact Jane's even earlier yearning for maternal warmth. In her Conclusion, Jane assures us that she has "not quite forgotten" the motherless child she sent away to a "severe" and "strict" institution that clearly resembles Lowood (396). When the girl returns "pale and thin," she is still denied a permanent "home" by her former governess. Under "a more indulgent system" at an alternate school, Adèle can obtain the "sound English education" that may "in great measure" correct her "French defects" (396).

Saddled with Jane's earlier marginality, an adolescent Adèle can at best expect to become a "docile" subordinate, a "pleasing and obliging companion" to her social superiors—in a repetition of the role that the Lowood graduate had found so repulsive (396). Still, though destined to remain an alien in Jane's narrative, Adèle might fare better in a sequel. There may even be a value in those "French defects" deemed to be as offensive as the alien traits Mrs. Reed had once derided in Jane. In *Villette,* a novel that demands a mastery of French dialogue, Lucy Snowe learns that Gallic defects can turn out to be far more profitable an investment than the job of serving as a pleasing and obliging lady's companion to the demanding Miss Marchmont.

What is more, *Villette* also refashions St. John Rivers. The taskmaster who drilled Jane in German and "Hindoostani" (290) can now be transformed into Lucy's Snowe's French instructor. Though given the physical characteristics of Rochester, M. Paul Emmanuel combines the traits of both of Jane's suitors. Like St. John, he is devoted to a patriarchal faith once again signified by the resonance of sacred names. As a latter-day apostle, however, Paul Emmanuel effects no conversion in the woman he wants to claim as a disciple, and, as a Messiah, he must be prevented from ever returning. His extinction makes it possible for a new Jane to obtain a fuller independence than that allowed to the wife of Edward Rochester. St. John had invited his divine Master to "come" quickly, but Lucy depends on her knowledge that her earthly master cannot come back at all. In *Villette,* M. Paul's death at sea restores to a female protagonist the intensity of desire that *Jane Eyre* had shifted from Jane to a male martyr's final words.

While still a child, the orphaned Jane learned that maternal surrogates need not be female. With Mrs. Reed as her prime model of a "mamma" and Miss Abbot and Bessie (not yet softened by maternity) as equally unsatisfying exemplars, the deprived girl gratefully received from the apothecary Mr. Lloyd the nurturance denied by these women. Victor Frankenstein's misguided assumption of a mother's life-giving role was followed by more benign fictional transformations in the age of Victoria. Characters such as William Dobbin, Silas Marner, and Paul Emmanuel are cast as nurturing male mothers. Yet these fictional figures acted as wishful counters to the realities of an actual patriarchal order. The daughters of characters such as Silas and Dobbin could derive benefits not available to the literary daughters of William Godwin, Edward Moulton-Barrett, Patrick Brontë, Robert Evans, or Leslie Stephen.

In *Villette,* Charlotte Brontë found a new way to handle Jane's yearning for female nurturance in a male order. Jane had to rely on her maternal and paternal uncles to recover the social identity denied by her Aunt Reed. The dispossessed Lucy Snowe may also be an orphan. But, unlike Jane's aunt, Lucy's godmother Mrs. Bretton is hospitable to children not her own. The sudden arrival of Paulina, a "little girl" who "had recently lost her mother," merely disrupts whatever exclusive claims Lucy might have had on the "notice" of the kind widow whose surname is an anagram of "Brontë" (*Villette* 62).

Lucy is doubly displaced at her godmother's home by the arrival of young Graham, the son whom Mrs. Bretton privileges as much as Mrs. Reed had favored the unsavory John Reed. Whereas a fiery Jane had chafed at her subsidiary position, the cool Miss Snowe actually welcomes a deflection from her own emotional wants when the intensity of Graham's and Paulina's interactions allows her to adopt the role of observer. Without ever revealing any information about her parentage, status, or the identity of the "kinsfolk" (62) from which Mrs. Bretton has wrested her, Brontë's reclusive narrator masters the art of detachment. She seems surprised that the needy Paulina expects her father to supply her with maternal nurture. And she clinically observes the little girl's subsequent need to find a maternal substitute in Graham. Her distancing from Pauline's emotional hunger is even frostier than St. John's icy self-repressions in *Jane Eyre*. Lucy professes to see no "use" in attaching to a male love object a yearning that boys "full of faults" are unlikely to satisfy (92).

Thus, at the very outset of *Villette*, Charlotte Brontë revises the conclusion of *Jane Eyre*. In this new beginning, she has Lucy dismiss the transferences that had only half-satisfied the wife of a suddenly dependent Rochester and the mother of his infant boy.[6] At the end of this revisionary novel, it is Paulina who acts as a vessel for male fulfillment when she allows her husband to see "himself live again in a son who inherited his looks and disposition" as well as in "stately daughters, too like himself" (533).[7] By placing this domestic conclusion in a chapter called "Sunshine" five chapters before she brings Lucy's story to an end in "Finis," Brontë breaks up the double ending of *Jane Eyre* and screens Lucy from Jane's half-hearted domestication. She even inserts a sly cross-reference to her earlier novel when she has M. Paul protest that Lucy might find him acceptable only if he were to become "quite blind and helpless" (413). But the disempowerment of another Rochester can no longer suffice as a palliative.

Desire, as Brontë now knows, must feed on absence. "I thought I loved him when he went away," Lucy confides, but after M. Paul's disappearance in one of those storms she has metaphorized throughout her narrative, his survivor can love him "in another degree; he is more my own" (595).[8] A closure desired by "sunny imaginations" has become unacceptable: "Let them picture union and a happy succeeding life" (596). There is to be no succession, no biological heirs, no indebtedness to male patrons such as Jane's Uncle Eyre. The delayed inheritance Lucy finally receives comes from Miss Marchmont, another lover whose passion remained unconsummated.

---

6. In *Aurora Leigh*, Elizabeth Barrett Browning follows yet also modifies the closure of *Jane Eyre*: when Aurora marries her blind cousin Romney Leigh, she finds that he had loved her while still "a boy" (*Aurora* IX: 414–15). Yet it is Marian Earle, the woman who refused to become Romney's wife, who will raise a boy who, like Adèle, is illegitimate but requires no earthly father: "never call him fatherless / Who has God and his mother" (IX: 765). Whereas St. John yearned to be possessed by a male "Master," Marian becomes her own mistress by assuming the role of a living Madonna.

7. Given Brontë's reliance on her own family configurations, is it possible to speculate whether there are three of those "Bretton" surviving daughters as well as that single son?

8. The echo of Cathy's Earnshaw's contention that Heathcliff is more herself than she is can hardly be coincidental in this sororal reformulation.

And yet, paradoxically, Lucy owes M. Paul Emmanuel her ability to enact the role of a maternal surrogate. By helping her become a teacher like himself and by bequeathing her the building in which she will tutor a succession of Adèles, the groom who failed to consummate their union has provided Lucy with a "succeeding life" that demands neither marriage nor procreation. Only near the end of her narrative does Lucy discover that her benefactor has secretly discharged the role of a parental surrogate. Whereas Rochester may have fathered Adèle and hence felt morally responsible for her upbringing, M. Paul is far more disinterested when he looked after Justine Marie Sauveur, his "god-daughter and ward," with "the affection proper to a daughter" (590, 592).

By becoming an independent caretaker, Lucy Snowe can emulate Mrs. Bretton more effectively than if she had become this matriarch's daughter-in-law. Her prime model, however, is not her godmother but another mother, Mme. Beck, M. Paul's cousin, whose daughters were Lucy's first pupils. Although her "French defects" are as inimical to Lucy as Adèle's were to Jane Eyre, Mme. Beck is not repudiated as a potential double or alter ego. The novel's concluding paragraph assures us that this cool and efficient manager "prospered all the days of her life" (596). Although she vied with Lucy over the affections of both Graham Bretton and M. Paul and now presumably competes with her over prospective female pupils, this rival also is Lucy's mentoria. Despite her deviousness, she has been more instrumental than her male cousin in shaping Lucy's new self. Indeed, Lucy's final identity is, in effect, Mme. Beck's very own.

As someone worthy of emulation and yet one from whom the younger woman must also distance herself, Mme. Beck enacts the role mothers discharge in the formation of a daughter's selfhood. Jane Eyre had found no such model in a narrative that relied on marriage and death as compensations for mother-want. Jane had identified herself with the headmistress of Lowood Institution, "who stood me in the stead of mother, governess, and latterly, companion." Yet when Miss Temple became the wife of the Reverend Nasmyth, Jane promptly left Lowood in search of a "new servitude" (*Jane Eyre* 72, 73).

If the ending of *Villette* acts as a corrective for the closure of *Jane Eyre*, it also retreats to the point at which Jane became a successful mistress of a village school for "poor girls—cottagers' children" (312). Unlike Jane, however, Lucy does not have to live in a modest rural cottage; her wealthy students are hardly impoverished rustics. Even though her name may evoke that of the mysterious Lucy whom Wordsworth had celebrated as Nature's short-lived "darling" ("Three Years She Grew" 7), this urban headmistress is decidedly a survivor. Lucy begins her narrative as a much older child than little Jane; she ends it as an older and wiser woman.

By having Lucy adopt a vocation rejected by Jane Eyre, the last of three Brontë sisters chastens the expectations that readers of her earlier romance might have harbored. As her Victorian contemporaries and her Edwardian successors would increasingly find, a "return" to Romantic origins could not bring desire to "fruition." The recovery of lost and half-remembered fusions became a wishful invention that writers born later in the nineteenth century could no longer validate.

As a "sleepless watcher" of water-tossed male seafarers (*Villette*), Lucy Snowe anticipates the mixture of detachment and longing that Virginia Woolf dramatizes as she has Lily Briscoe turn to her painting after having observed Mr. Ramsay's voyage out. Lily had to explain that her painting was not an "attempt at likeness" (*Lighthouse* 81). Instead, she tells Mr. Banks, this "tribute" is a modern equivalent of the "universal veneration" once expressed by religious paintings of a Madonna and her child. But the "reverence" Lily wants to convey, she insists, is "something profoundly private" (83).

However indirect, Lily's yearning for the dead Mrs. Ramsay is more openly expressed in *To the Lighthouse* than Jane's or Lucy's unsatisfied desire to be united with a female Other. Just as Lucy knows that her small schoolhouse cannot enshrine that desire, so does Lily acknowledge that its pictorial representation, her "attempt at something" (309), is bound to remain obscure. The painting, she anticipates, will be flung into some "attic," where it will lie concealed, forgotten, until eventually "destroyed," incinerated like that other attic discard, Bertha Mason, the embodiment of unsatisfied female desire.

"But what did that matter?" Lily asks (310). She draws the connecting line that brings her and the reader back. And, having had her vision, she lays down her brush "in extreme fatigue" (310). Lucy Snowe, Lily's predecessor, is similarly fatigued when she asks her readers not to long for what her narrative refuses to provide: "Here pause: pause at once. There is enough said" (*Villette* 596).

I can do no better than to adopt Lucy's and Lily's final words as my own. There is enough said. It is finished.

WORKS CITED

Adler, Alfred. *Cooperation between the Sexes: Writings on Women and Men, Love and Marriage, and Sexuality.* Ed. and trans. Heinz L. Ansbacher and Rowena R. Ansbacher. New York: Norton, 1978. Print.

Althusser, Louis, and Etienne Balibar. *Reading Capital.* Trans. Ben Brewster. London: NLB, 1970. Print.

Armstrong, Paul B. "Form and History: Reading as an Aesthetic Experience and Historical Act." *MLQ* 69.2 (2008): 195–219. Print.

Arnold, Matthew. *Culture and Anarchy with Friendship's Garland and Some Literary Essays.* Ann Arbor: U of Michigan P, 1965. Vol. 5 of *Complete Prose Works of Matthew Arnold.* Ed. R. H. Super. 11 vols. 1960–77. Print.

———. *Lectures and Essays in Criticism.* Ann Arbor: U of Michigan P, 1962. Vol. 3 of *Complete Prose Work of Matthew Arnold.* Ed. R. H. Super. 11 vols. 1960–77. Print.

———. *On The Classical Tradition.* Ann Arbor: U of Michigan P, 1962. Vol. 1 of *Complete Prose Works of Matthew Arnold.* Ed. R. H. Super. 11 vols. 1960–77. Print.

———. "Preface." *Poems of Wordsworth.* Chosen and Edited by Matthew Arnold. London: Macmillan, 1882. Print.

———. *The Poems of Matthew Arnold.* Ed. Kenneth Allott. London: Longman, 1965. Print.

———. "The Study of Poetry." *English Literature and Irish Politics.* Ann Arbor: U of Michigan P, 1973. Vol. 9 of *Complete Prose Works.* Print.

Auerbach, Nina. "Robert Browning's Last Word." *Victorian Poetry* 22.2 (1984): 161–73. Print.

———. *Woman and the Demon: The Life of a Victorian Myth.* Cambridge: Harvard UP, 1982. Print.

Auerbach, Nina, and U. C. Knoepflmacher, eds. *Forbidden Journeys: Fairy Tales and Fantasies by Victorian Woman Writers.* Chicago: U Chicago P, 1993. Print.

Bailey, J. O. *The Poetry of Thomas Hardy: A Handbook and Commentary.* Chapel Hill: U of North Carolina P, 1970. Print.

Barthes, Roland. *Camera Lucida: Reflections on Photography.* Trans. Richard Howard. New York: Hill and Wang, 1982. Print.

Baum, Paull F. *Ten Studies in the Poetry of Matthew Arnold.* Durham: Duke UP, 1958. Print.

Beer, Gillian. "Myth and the Single Consciousness." *This Particular Web: Essays on Middlemarch.* Ed. Ian Adam. Toronto: U Toronto P, 1975. 91–115. Print.

Beerbohm, Sir Max. *Letters of Max Beerbohm: 1892–1956.* Ed. Rupert Hart-Davis. London: Murray, 1988. Print.

———. "Lytton Strachey." The Rede Lecture, 1943. *The Incomparable Max.* New York: Dodd, 1962. Print.

Bennett, Andrew. "Wordsworth's Survival." *Romantic Poets and the Culture of Prosperity.* Cambridge: Cambridge UP 1999. 95–115. Print.

Beresford, G. C. *Schooldays with Kipling.* New York: Putnam's Sons, 1936. Print.

Best, Stephen, and Sharon Marcus. "Surface Reading: An Introduction." *Representations* 108.1 (Fall 2009): 1–21. Print.

Bewes, Timothy. "Reading with the Grain: A New World in Literary Criticism." *differences* 21.3 (2010): 1–33. Print.

Billone, Amy. *Little Songs: Women, Silence and the Nineteenth-Century Sonnet.* Columbus: The Ohio State UP, 2006. Print.

Blank, G. Kim. *Wordsworth's Influence on Shelley: A Study of Poetic Authority.* London: Macmillan, 1988. Print.

Blank, G. Kim, and Margot K. Louis, eds. *Influence and Resistance in Nineteenth-Century Poetry.* New York: St. Martin's, 1993. Print.

Blazhenkova, Olesya, and Maria Kozhevnikov. "The New Object-Spatial-Verbal Cognitive Style Model: Theory and Measurement." *Applied Cognitive Psychology* 23 (2009): 638–63. Wiley Interscience. 5 November 2013. Web.

Bloom, Harold. "Browning: Good Moments and Ruined Quests." *Poetry and Repression: Revisionism from Blake to Stevens.* New Haven: Yale UP, 1976. Print.

Bohm, Arnd. "Increasing Suspicion about Browning's Grammarian." *Victorian Poetry* 44.2 (Summer 2006): 165–82. Print.

Booth, Alison, ed. *Famous Last Words: Changes in Gender and Narrative Closure.* Charlottesville: U of Virginia P, 1993. Print.

———. "The Silence of Great Men: Statuesque Femininity and the Ending of *Romola*." *Famous Last Words: Changes in Gender and Narrative Closure.* Charlottesville: U of Virginia P, 1993. 110–34. Print.

Brontë, Anne. *The Tenant of Wildfell Hall.* Ed. G. D. Hargreaves. New York: Penguin, 1979. Print.

Brontë, Charlotte. *Jane Eyre.* Ed. Richard J. Dunn. New York: Norton, 1971. Print.

———. *Villette.* Harmondsworth: Penguin, 1979. Print.

Brontë, Emily. *Wuthering Heights.* Eds. William M. Sale and Richard J. Dunn. New York: Norton, 1990. Print.

Brooks, Peter. *Reading for the Plot: Design and Intention in Narrative*. New York: A. A. Knopf, 1984. Print.

Browning, Elizabeth Barrett. *Complete Works*. Eds. Charlotte Porter and Helen A. Clarke. 6 vols. New York: George D. Sproul, 1901. Print.

Browning, Robert. *Dearest Isa: Robert Browning's Letters to Isabella Blagden*. Ed. Edward C. McAleer. Austin: U of Texas P, 1951. Print.

———. *Robert Browning: The Poems*. Eds. John Pettigrew and Thomas J. Collins. 2 vols. New Haven: Yale UP, 1981. Print.

Browning, Robert, and Elizabeth Barrett. *The Letters of Robert Browning and Elizabeth Barrett: 1845–1846*. Ed. Elvan Kintner. 2 vols. Cambridge: Harvard UP, 1969. Print.

Browning, Robert, and Julia Wedgwood. *Robert Browning and Julia Wedgewood: A Broken Friendship as Revealed in Their Letters*. Ed. Richard Curle. New York: Frederick A. Stokes, 1937. Print.

Bush, Douglas. "Wordsworth and the Classics." *University of Toronto Quarterly* II (April 1933): 359–79. Print.

Bygrave, Stephen. *Coleridge and the Self*. New York: St. Martin's P, 1986. Print.

Byron, Lord George Gordon. *Byron's 'Don Juan': A Variorum Edition*. Austin and London: U of Texas P, 1971. Vol. 2 (Cantos I–V). Eds. Truman Guy Steffan and Willis W. Pratt. 4 vols. Print.

Calverley, Charles Stuart. *The Complete Works of C. S. Calverley*. Ed. Walter J. Sendall. London: G. Bell, 1902. Print.

Carlyle, Thomas. *On Heroes, Hero-Worship, and the Heroic in History*. Ed. Carl Niemeyer. Lincoln: U of Nebraska P, 1966. Print.

Carrington, C. E. *The Life of Rudyard Kipling*. Garden City: Doubleday, 1955. Print.

Carroll, David R. "*Middlemarch* and the Externality of Fact." *This Particular Web: Essays on Middlemarch*. Ed. Ian Adam. Toronto: U of Toronto P, 1975. 73–90. Print.

Carroll, Lewis. *Alice's Adventures in Wonderland and Through the Looking-Glass: and What Alice Found There*. London: Macmillan, 1911. Print.

———. *Alice in Wonderland: Authoritative Texts*. Ed. Donald H. Gray. New York: Norton, 1971. Print.

———. *The Complete Works of Lewis Carroll*. Ed. Alexander Woollcott. New York: Random House, 1939. Print.

———. *The Humorous Verse of Lewis Carroll*. New York: Dover, 1960. Print.

———. *Lewis Carroll's Library*. Ed. Jeffrey Stern. Charlottesville: U of Virginia P and the Lewis Carroll Society of North America, 1981. Print.

Catalogue of the Library of Charles Dickens from Gadshill. Ed. John Harrison Stonehouse. Reprinted from Sotheran's 'Price Current of Literature,' nos. CLXXIV and CLXXV. London: Piccadilly Fountain P, 1935. Print.

Cohen, Morton, ed. *Rudyard Kipling to Rider Haggard: The Record of a Friendship*. Rutherford: Fairleigh Dickinson UP, 1965. Print.

Colebrook, Claire. "The Context of Humanism." *New Literary History* 42.4 (Autumn 2011): 701–18, 757. Print.

Coleridge, Samuel Taylor. *Biographia Literaria*. London and New York: Everyman Library, 1962. Print.

———. *Collected Letters of Samuel Taylor Coleridge*. Vol. 4 (1815–19). Ed. Earl Leslie Griggs. 4 vols. Oxford: Clarendon P, 1959. Print.

———. *Complete Poetical Works*. Vol. 1. Ed. Ernest Hartley Coleridge. 2 vols. Oxford: Clarendon P, 1957. Print.

Collingwood, Stuart Dodgson. *The Life and Letters of Lewis Carroll*. London: Unwin, 1898. Print.

Collins, Philip. *Dickens and Education*. London: Macmillan, 1965. Print.

Colombat, André-Pierre. "Three Powers of Literature and Philosophy." *A Deleuzian Century*. Ed. Ian Buchanan. Durham: Duke UP, 1999. 199–217. Print.

Compact Edition of the Oxford English Dictionary. 2 vols. Oxford: Oxford UP, 1971. Print.

Cooke, George Willis. *A Guide-Book to the Poetic and Dramatic Works of Robert Browning*. New York: Houghton Mifflin, 1896. Print.

Cooper, Helen. "Mrs. Browning and Miss Evans." *Nineteenth-Century Fiction* 35 (December 1980): 257–59. Print.

Crook, Nora. *Kipling's Myths of Love and Death*. London: Macmillan, 1989. Print.

Cross, J. W. *George Eliot's Life as Related in Her Letters and Journals*. Vol. I. 3 vols. London: Blackwood, 1885. Print.

DeLaura, David. "Arnold and Carlyle." *PMLA* 79 (1964): 104–29. Print.

———. *Hebrew and Hellene in Victorian England: Arnold, Newman, and Pater*. Austin: U of Texas P, 1969. Print.

———. "The 'Wordsworth' of Pater and Arnold: 'The Supreme, Artistic View of Life.'" *Studies in English Literature* 6 (1966): 651–67. Print.

DeVane, William Clyde. *A Browning Handbook*. New York: Appleton-Century-Crofts, 1995. Print.

Dickens, Charles. "Associations of Childhood." *All the Year Round* (30 June 1860): 274–78. Print.

———. *Barnaby Rudge, and the Mystery of Edwin Drood*. New York: D. Appleton, 1872. Print.

———. *Bleak House*. Ed. Morton Dauwen Zaubel. Riverside Edition. Boston: Houghton Mifflin, 1956. Print.

———. *Great Expectations*. Ed. Earle Davis. New York: Rinehart, 1959. Print.

———. *Little Dorrit*. Ed. John Holloway. Harmondsworth: Penguin, 1971. Print.

———. *The Speeches of Charles Dickens*. Ed. K. J. Fielding. Oxford: Clarendon P, 1960. Print.

Duerkson, Roland A. "Shelley in *Middlemarch*." *Keats-Shelley Journal* 14 (Winter 1965): 23–31. Print.

Elfenbein, Andrew. *Byron and the Victorians*. Cambridge: Cambridge UP, 1995. Print.

Eliot, George. "Brother and Sister." *The Legend of Jubal and Other Poems*. Cabinet Edition. Ed. John Cross. Edinburgh: Blackwood and Sons, 1879. Print.

———. *Daniel Deronda*. Ed. Barbara Hardy. Harmondsworth: Penguin, 1967. Print.

———. *The George Eliot Letters*. Ed. Gordon S. Haight. 9 vols. New Haven: Yale UP, 1954–55. Print.

———. *The Lifted Veil*. New York: Viking Penguin, 1985. Print.

———. *Middlemarch*. Ed. Gordon S. Haight. Boston: Houghton Mifflin, 1956. Print.

———. *The Mill on the Floss*. Ed. Gordon S. Haight. Boston: Houghton Mifflin, 1961. Print.

———. "The Natural History of German Life." *Westminster Review* LXVI (July 1856): 51–79. Reprinted in *Essays of George Eliot*. Ed. Thomas Pinney. London: Routledge & Kegan Paul, 1963. 270–72. Print.

———. "Self and Life." *The Legend of Jubal and Other Poems*. Cabinet Edition. Ed. John Cross. Edinburgh: William Blackwood and Sons, 1879. Print.

———. *Silas Marner, The Weaver of Raveloe*. Ed. Jerome Thale. New York: Holt Rinehart and Winston, 1962. Print.

Eliot, T. S. "Arnold and Pater." *The Bookman* LXXII.1 (September 1930): 1–7. Print.

Faflak, Joel, and Julia M. Wright, eds. *Nervous Reactions: Victorian Recollections of Romanticism*. Albany: SUNY P, 2004. Print.

Farrell, John P. "'What I Want the Reader to See': Action and Performance in Arnold's Prose." *Matthew Arnold in His Time and Ours: Centenary Essays*. Ed. Clinton Machann and Forrest D. Burt. Charlottesville: U of Virginia P, 1988. 123–34. Print.

Felski, Rita. "Critique and the Hermeneutics of Suspicion." *M/C Journal* 15.1 (2012). 25 November 2013. Web.

———. "Suspicious Minds." *Poetics Today* 32.2 (Summer 2011): 215–34. Print.

Ferguson, Frances. "Recent Studies in the Restoration and Eighteenth Century." *SEL* 54.3 (2014): 717–68. Print.

Fineman, Joel. *Shakespeare's Perjured Eye*. Berkeley: U of California P, 1986. Print.

Finn, Mary E. "The House (of Cards) that Rome Built: Shelley's *The Cenci* and Browning's *The Ring and the Book*." *Influence and Resistance in Nineteenth-Century Poetry*. Eds. G. Kim Blank and Margot K. Louis. New York: St. Martin's, 1993. Print.

Frank, Ellen E. "The Domestication of Nature: Five Houses in the Lake District." *Nature and the Victorian Imagination*. Ed. U. C. Knoepflmacher and G. B. Tennyson. Berkeley: U of California P, 1977. 68–92. Print.

Gelpi, Barbara Charlesworth. "'Verses with a Good Deal about Sucking': Percy Bysshe Shelley and Christina Rossetti." *Influence and Resistance in Nineteenth-Century Poetry*. Eds. G. Kim Blank and Margot K. Louis. New York: St. Martin's, 1993. Print.

Gilbert, Sandra, and Susan Gubar. *The Madwoman in the Attic: The Woman Writer and the Nineteenth-Century Literary Imagination*. New Haven: Yale UP, 1979. Print.

Gill, Stephen. *Wordworth and the Victorians*. Gloucestershire: Clarendon P, 1998. Print.

Gravil, Richard. *Romantic Dialogues: Anglo-American Continuities*. College Park: U of Maryland P, 2000. Print.

Griffin, W. H., and C. H. Minchin. *The Life of Browning*. London: Methuen, 1910. Print.

Haight, Gordon S. *George Eliot: A Biography*. New York: Oxford UP, 1968. Print.

Hanley, Keith, "In Wordsworth's Shadow: Ruskin and Neo-Romantic Ecologies." *Influence and Resistance in Nineteenth-Century Poetry*. Eds. G. Kim Blank and Margot K. Louis. New York: St. Martin's, 1993. Print.

Hardy, Barbara. "*The Mill on the Floss*." *Critical Essays on George Eliot*. Ed. Barbara Hardy. New York: Routledge & Kegan Paul, 1970. 46–49. Print.

Hardy, Florence Emily. *The Early Life of Thomas Hardy: 1840–1891*. London: Macmillan, 1928. Print.

Hardy, Thomas. *Complete Poetical Works*. 5 vols. Ed. Samuel Hynes. Oxford: Clarendon P, 1982–85. Print.

———. *Jude the Obscure*. Ed. F. R. Southerington. Indianapolis: Bobbs Merrill, 1972. Print.

Harris, Wendell V. "The Road to and from Eliot's 'Place of Pater.'" *Texas Studies in Language and Literature* 23 (1981): 183–96. Print.

———. "Where Late the Sweet Birds Sang: Looking Back at the Victorians Looking Back at the Romantics Looking Back . . ." *Victorian Poetry* 16.1–2 (1978): 167–75. Print.

Harrison, Antony H. "Christina Rossetti and the Romantics: Influence and Ideology." *Influence and Resistance in Nineteenth-Century Poetry*. Eds. G. Kim Blank and Margot K. Louis. New York: St. Martin's, 1993. Print.

———. *Victorian Poets and Romantic Poems: Intertextuality and Ideology*. Charlottesville: U. Virginia P, 1992.

Hazlitt, William. "Lectures on the English Poets." *Selected Writings of Hazlitt*. Vol. 2. Ed. Duncan Wu. London: Pickering and Chatto, 1998. Print.

Hickey, Alison, "'The Body of My Father's Writings.'" *Literary Couplings: Writing, Couples, Collaboration, and the Construction of Authorship*. Eds. Marjorie Stone and Judith Thompson. Madison: Wisconsin UP, 2006. Print.

Hirshberg, Edgar W. *George Henry Lewes*. New York: Twayne, 1970. Print.

Holroyd, Michael. Lytton Strachey. Vol. 1: *The Unknown Years, 1880–1910*; Vol. 2: *The Years of Achievement, 1910–32*. New York: Holt, 1967, 1968. Print.

Homans, Margaret. "Eliot, Wordsworth, and the Scenes of the Sisters' Instruction." *Critical Inquiry* 8.2 (Winter 1981): 223–41. Print.

Hopkins, Gerard Manley. *The Correspondence of Gerard Manley Hopkins and Richard Watson Dixon*. Ed. Claude Colleer Abbott. London: Oxford UP, 1955. Print.

———. *The Letters of Gerard Manley Hopkins to Robert Bridges*. London: Oxford UP, 1955. Print.

———. *The Poems of Gerard Manley Hopkins*. Eds. W. H. Gardner and N. H. Mackenzie. 4th ed. London: Oxford UP, 1967. Print.

Hudson, W. H. *Nature in Downland*. London: Longman, Green, 1900. Print.

Jaffe, Audrey. "Face Value: Victorianism and the Status of Surface Reading." NAVSA, Pasadena, October 2013. Lecture.

James, D. G. Matthew. *Arnold and the Decline of English Romanticism*. New York: Oxford UP, 1961. Print.

Jameson, Anna. *Legends of the Madonna as Represented in the Fine Arts*. London: Longman, Green, 1885. Print.

Jameson, Fredric. *The Political Unconscious: Narrative as a Socially Symbolic Act*. Ithaca: Cornell UP, 1981. Print.

Jamison, William A. *Arnold and the Romantics*. Copenhagen: Rosenkilde and Bagger, 1958. Print.

Jarrell, Randall. *Randall Jarrell's Letters*. Ed. Mary Jarrell. Boston: Houghton Mifflin, 1985. Print.

Jauss, Hans Robert. *Aesthetic Experience and Literary Hermeneutics.* Trans. Michael Shaw. Minneapolis: U of Minnesota P, 1982. Print.

The John Keats Memorial Volume. Issued by the Keats House Committee. Hampstead/London: John Lane, 1921. Print.

Johnson, E. D. H. *The Alien Vision of Victorian Poetry.* Princeton: Princeton UP, 1952. Print.

Johnson, W. Stacy. *The Voices of Matthew Arnold: An Essay in Criticism.* New Haven: Yale UP, 1961. Print.

Johnston, Kenneth R. *Wordsworth and 'The Recluse.'* New Haven and London: Yale UP, 1984. Print.

Jung, C. G., and Karl Kerényi. *Essays on a Science of Mythology: The Myth of the Divine Child and the Mysteries of Eleusis.* New York: Princeton UP, 1969. Print.

Jurecic, Ann. "Empathy and the Critic." *College English* 74.1 (September 2011): 10–27. Print.

Keats, John. *The Letters of John Keats.* Vol. 1 (1814–21). Ed. Hyder Edward Rollins. 2 vols. Cambridge: Harvard UP, 1972. Print.

———. "Letter to J. H. Reynolds 3 May 1818." *Letters of John Keats to His Family and Friends.* Ed. Sir Sidney Colvin. London: Macmillan, 1891. Print.

———. *The Poems of John Keats.* Ed. Miriam Allott. London and New York: Longman/Norton, 1972. Print.

Keen, Suzanne. *Empathy and the Novel.* Oxford UP, 2007. Print.

Kelley, Theresa M. "Robert Browning and Romantic Allegory." *Influence and Resistance in Nineteenth-Century Poetry.* Eds. G. Kim Blank and Margot K. Louis. New York: St. Martin's, 1993. Print.

Kincaid, James R. *Child-Loving: The Erotic Child in Victorian Culture.* New York: Routledge, 1992. Print.

Kingsmill, Hugh. "Parodies No. 7: Some Modern Light-Bringers as They Might Have Been Extinguished by Thomas Carlyle." *English Review* 56 (January 1933): 23–27. Print.

Kipling, Rudyard. *Actions and Reactions.* London: Macmillan, 1909. Print.

———. *The Complete Stalky & Co.* Ed. Elizabeth Quigley. Oxford: Oxford UP, 1999. Print.

———. *Complete Verse.* New York: Doubleday, 1984. Print.

———. *The Early Verse by Rudyard Kipling, 1879–1889.* Ed. Andrew Rutherford. Oxford: Clarendon P. Print.

———. *The Jungle Book.* Ed. Daniel Karlin. New York: Penguin, 1987. Print.

———. *Kipling: Interviews and Recollections.* Ed. Harold Orel. 2 vols. Totowa, NJ: Barnes & Noble, 1984. Print.

———. *Kipling's Lost World.* Ed. Harry Ricketts. Padstow, Cornwall: Tabb House, 1989. Print.

———. *Letters.* Ed. Thomas Pinney. 6 vols. Iowa City: Iowa UP, 1990–2004. Print.

———. "Letters of Marque." *From Sea to Sea and Other Stories.* Vol. I. 2 vols. London: Macmillan, 1900. Print.

———. *The Man Who Would Be King and Other Stories.* Ed. Louis L. Cornell. Oxford: Oxford UP, 1987. Print.

———. *Plain Tales from the Hills.* London: Macmillan and Co., 1888. Print.

———. *Something of Myself and Other Autobiographical Writings*. Ed. Thomas Pinney. New York: Cambridge UP, 1990. Print.

———. *Traffic and Discoveries*. London: Macmillan, 1904. Print.

Knoepflmacher, U. C. "Arnold's Fancy and Pater's Imagination: Exclusion and Incorporation." *VP* 26.1–2 (1988): 103–15. Reprinted in this volume. Print.

———. "The Balancing of Child and Adult: An Approach to Victorian Fantasies for Children." *Nineteenth-Century Fiction* XXXVII (March 1983). Print.

———. "Fusing Fact and Fiction, the New Reality of *Middlemarch*." *This Particular Web: Essays on Middlemarch*. Ed. Ian Adam. Toronto: U of Toronto P, 1975. 43–72. Print.

———. "Genre and the Integration of Gender: From Wordsworth to George Eliot to Virginia Woolf." *Victorian Literature and Society*. Eds. James R. Kincaid and Albert J. Kuhn. Columbus: The Ohio State UP, 1984. Reprinted in this volume. Print.

———. *George Eliot's Early Novels: The Limits of Realism*. Berkeley: U of California P, 1968. Print.

———. "A Nineteenth-Century Touchstone: Chapter XV of *Biographia Literaria*." *Nineteenth-Century Literary Perspectives in Honor of Lionel Stevenson*. Ed. Clyde de L. Ryals. Durham: U of North Carolina P, 1974. 3–16. Print.

———. "On Carlyle, Carlylism, and the Carlylean in Fiction." *NCF* 22 (1977): 73–80. Print.

———. "Thoughts on the Aggression of Daughters." *The Endurance of 'Frankenstein.'* Eds. George Levine and U. C. Knoepflmacher. Berkeley: U of California P, 1979. 88–119. Print.

———. "Unveiling Men: Power and Masculinity in George Eliot's Fiction." *Men by Women*. Ed. Janet M. Todd. New York: Holmes and Meier, 1981. 130–45. Print.

———. *'Wuthering Heights': A Study*. Athens: Ohio UP, 1994. Reprint of *Emily Brontë: 'Wuthering Heights.'* Cambridge: Cambridge UP, 1989. Print.

Landow, George P. *The Aesthetic and Critical Theories of John Ruskin*. Princeton: Princeton UP, 1971. Print.

Langbaum, Robert. *The Poetry of Experience*. New York: Random House, 1957. Print.

Levine, Caroline. Guest Post. *The Valve, a Literary Organ*. 16 April 2007. 2 December 2003. Web.

Levine, George. "The Ambiguous Heritage of Frankenstein." *The Endurance of 'Frankenstein.'* Eds. George Levine and U. C. Knoepflmacher. Berkeley: U of California P, 1979. Print.

———. "George Eliot's Hypothesis of Reality." *Nineteenth-Century Fiction* 35 (June 1980): 1–28. Print.

———. "The Mill on the Floss." *Critical Essays on George Eliot*. Ed. Barbara Hardy. New York: Routledge & Kegan Paul, 1970. 50–58. Print.

Lewes, George Henry. "The Novels of Jane Austen." *Blackwood's Edinburgh Magazine* 86 (1859): 99–113. Print.

———. "Percy Bysshe Shelley." *Westminster Review* LXIX (April 1841): 303–44. Print.

———. *Ranthorpe*. London: Chapman and Hall, 1847. Print.

Leys, Ruth. *From Guilt to Shame: Auschwitz and After*. Princeton: Princeton UP, 2007. Print.

Littau, Karen. *Theories of Reading: Books, Bodies, and Bibliomania*. Malden: Polity, 2008. Print.

Lycett, Andrew. *Rudyard Kipling*. London: Weidenfeld & Nicolson, 1978. Print.

MacDonald, George. *The Complete Fairy Tales*. Ed. U. C. Knoepflmacher. New York: Penguin, 1999. Print.

MacMechan, Archibald. Introduction. *Carlyle: On Heroes, Hero-Worship, and the Heroic in History*. Boston: Athenaeum, 1901. Print.

Martineau, Harriet. *Autobiography*. 2 vols. Ed. Maria Weston Chapman. Boston: James R. Osgood and Co., 1877. Print.

Mason, Philip. *Kipling: The Glass, the Shadow, and the Fire*. London: Jonathan Cape, 1975. Print.

May, Charles E. "Hardy's 'Darkling Thrush': The 'Nightingale' Grown Old." *Victorian Poetry* 11.1 (Spring 1973): 62–65. Print.

McGavran, James Holt Jr., ed. *Literature and the Child: Romantic Continuations, Postmodern Contestations*. Iowa City: U Iowa P, 1999. Print.

———. *Romanticism and Children's Literature in Nineteenth-Century England*. Athens: U Georgia P, 1991. Print.

McGillis, Roderick. "Childhood and Growth: George MacDonald and William Wordsworth." *Romanticism and Children's Literature in Nineteenth-Century England*. Ed. James Holt McGavran. Athens: U Georgia P, 1991. Print.

McGowan, John P. "The Turn of George Eliot's Realism." *Nineteenth-Century Fiction* 35 (September 1980): 171–92. Print.

McKenzie, K. A. *Edith Simcox and George Eliot*. London: Oxford UP, 1961. Print.

McSweeney, Kerry. "Hardy's Poetic Antecedents." *Influence and Resistance in Nineteenth-Century English Poetry*. Eds. G. Kim Blank and Margot K. Louis. New York: St. Martin's P, 1993. Print.

McWilliams, John P. "'*Great Expectations*': The Beacon, the Gibbet, and the Ship." *Dickens Studies Annual* 2. Ed. Robert B. Partlow, Jr. Carbondale and Edwardsville: Southern Illinois UP, 1972. 255–66. Print.

Melchiori, Barbara. "Browning and the Bible: An Examination of 'Holy Cross Day.'" *Review of English Studies* 7.2 (April 1966): 20–42. Print.

Mellor, Anne K. *English Romantic Irony*. Cambridge: Harvard UP, 1980. Print.

Mermin, Dorothy. "The Domestic Economy of Art: Elizabeth Barrett and Robert Browning." *Mothering the Mind: Twelve Studies of Writers and Their Silent Partners*. Eds. Ruth Perry and Martine Watson Brownley. New York: Holmes & Meier, 1984. 82–101. Print.

Miller, Betty. *Robert Browning: A Portrait*. New York: Scribner's, 1952. Print.

Miller, J. Hillis. *The Disappearance of God*. Cambridge: Harvard UP, 1963. Print.

———. "Narrative and History." *ELH* 42 (1974): 455–73. Print.

———. "Optic and Semiotic in *Middlemarch*." *The Worlds of Victorian Fiction*. Ed. Jerome Buckley. Cambridge: Harvard UP, 1975. 125–45. Print.

———. *Reading for Our Time: 'Adam Bede' and 'Middlemarch' Revisited*. Edinburgh: Edinburgh UP, 2012. Print.

Millgate, Michael. *Thomas Hardy: A Biography*. New York: Random House, 1982. Print.

Mitchell, Rebecca N. *Victorian Lessons in Empathy and Difference*. Columbus: The Ohio State UP, 2011. Print.

Myers, Mitzi. "Reading Children and Homeopathic Romanticism, or 'Plus ça change, plus c'est la même chose?'" *Literature and the Child: Romantic Continuations, Postmodern Contestations.* Ed. James Holt McGavran Jr. Iowa City: U of Iowa P, 1999. Print.

Nehamas, Alexander. "The Postulated Author: Critical Monism as a Regulative Ideal." *Critical Inquiry* 8.1 (Autumn 1981): 133–49. Print.

O'Neill, Michael. *The All-Sustaining Air: Romantic Legacies and Renewals in British, American, and Irish Poetry.* Oxford: Oxford UP, 2007. Print.

Otter, Samuel. "An Aesthetics in All Things." *Representations* 104 (Fall 2008): 116–25. Print.

Pace, Joel, and Matthew Scott, eds. *Wordsworth in American Literary Culture.* New York: Palgrave Macmillan, 2005. Print.

Pater, Walter. "The Child in the House." *Miscellaneous Studies; a Series of Essays.* London: Macmillan, 1920. Print.

———. *Marius the Epicurean: His Sensations and Ideas.* Library Edition of *The Works of Walter Pater.* Vol. 1. London: Macmillan, 1920. Print.

———. *The Renaissance: Studies in Art and Poetry: The 1893 Text.* Ed. Donald. L. Hill. Berkeley: U of California P, 1980. Print.

———. "Wordsworth." *Appreciations, with an Essay on Style.* London: Macmillan, 1920. Print.

Perkins, David, ed. *English Romantic Writers.* New York: Harcourt, 1967. Print.

Plotz, Judith. "Happy Masters, Slaves, and Schoolboys: The Psychology of Empire in Kipling's 'Slaves of the Lamp.'" Children's Literature Association Conference. Wilkes-Barre, PA. June 2002. Lecture.

———. *Romanticism and the Vocation of Childhood.* New York: Palgrave, 2001. Print.

Prickett, Stephen. *Romanticism and Religion: The Tradition of Coleridge and Wordsworth in the Victorian Church.* Cambridge: Cambridge UP, 2008. Print.

Rader, Ralph. *Fact, Fiction, and Form: Selected Essays of Ralph W. Rader.* Eds. James Phelan and David H. Richter. Columbus: The Ohio State UP, 2011. Print.

Redinger, Ruby. *George Eliot: The Emergent Self.* New York: Knopf, 1975. Print.

Rev. of Charles Dickens, *The Cricket on the Hearth. Chambers's Edinburgh Journal* (17 January 1846): 44. Reprinted in *Dickens: The Critical Heritage,* ed. Philip A. W. Collins. London: Routledge & Kegan Paul, 1971. Print.

Richardson, Alan. "Wordsworth, Fairy Tales, and the Politics of Children's Reading." *Romanticism and Children's Literature in Nineteenth-Century England.* Ed. James Holt McGavran Jr. Athens: U of Georgia P, 1991. Print.

Richardson, James. *Thomas Hardy: The Poetry of Necessity.* Chicago: U of Chicago P, 1977. Print.

Robinson, Henry Crabb. *The Diary of Henry Crabb Robinson: An Abridgement.* Ed. Derek Hudson. New York: Oxford UP, 1967. Print.

———. *Henry Crabb Robinson on Books and Their Writers.* Ed. Edith J. Morley. Vol. II. London: J. M. Dent and Sons, 1938. Print.

Rooney, Ellen. "Live Free or Describe: The Reading Effect and the Persistence of Form." *differences* 21.3 (2010): 112–39. Print.

Rosenberg, John D. *The Darkening Glass: A Portrait of Ruskin's Genius.* New York: Columbia UP, 1961. Print.

Ross, Anne Marie. "Seeing Through a Glass Darkly: Perspective in Romantic and Victorian Landscapes." *Influence and Resistance in Nineteenth-Century Poetry.* Eds. Kim G. Blank G. Kim and Margot K. Louis. New York: St. Martin's, 1993. Print.

Ross, Marlon B. *The Contours of Masculine Desire: Romanticism and the Rise of Women's Poetry.* Oxford: Oxford UP, 1989. Print.

Ruskin, John. *The Poems of John Ruskin.* Volume II. Ed. W. G. Collingwood. London: George Allen, 1891. Print.

———. *Modern Painters.* 5 vols. London: Smith, Elder, 1843–1860. Print.

———. *The Winnington Letters: John Ruskin's Correspondence with Margaret Alexis Bell and the Children at Winnington Hall.* Ed. Van Akin Burd. Cambridge: Belknap P, 1969. Print.

———. *The Works of John Ruskin.* Eds. E. T. Cook and Alexander Wedderburn. 39 vols. London: George Allen, 1903–12. Print.

Ruskin, John James. *The Ruskin Family Letters: The Correspondence of John James Ruskin, His Wife, and Their Son, John, 1801–1843.* Vol. I. Ithaca: Cornell UP, 1973. Print.

Sanders, Charles Richard. *Lytton Strachey: His Mind and Art.* New Haven: Yale UP, 1957. Print.

Scarry, Elaine. *Dreaming by the Book.* Princeton: Princeton UP 2001. Print.

Schelly, Judith May. "A Like Unlike: Brother and Sister in the Works of Wordsworth, Byron, George Eliot, Emily Brontë, and Dickens." Diss. Univ. of California, Berkeley, 1980. Ann Arbor: University Microfilms International, 1980.

Scott, Peter Dale. "Vital Artifice: Mary, Percy, and the Psychopolitical Integrity of *Frankenstein*." *The Endurance of 'Frankenstein.'* Eds. George Levine and U. C. Knoepflmacher. Berkeley: U of California P, 1979. 172–202. Print.

Scott, William Bell. *Autobiographical Notes.* Ed. W. Minto. 2 vols. London: Osgood, McIlvain, 1892. Print.

Sedgwick, Eve Kosofsky. "Paranoid Reading and Reparative Reading; or, You're So Paranoid, You Probably Think This Introduction Is About You." *Novel-Gazing: Queer Readings in Fiction.* Ed. Eve Kosofsky Sedgwick. Durham: Duke UP 1997. 1–37. Print.

Shaw, W. David. "Shelley's 'Adonais' and Arnold's 'Thyrsis': Words of Power in Pastoral Elegy." *Influence and Resistance in Nineteenth-Century Poetry.* Eds. G. Kim Blank and Margot K. Louis. New York: St. Martin's, 1993. Print.

Shelley, Mary Wollstonecraft. *Frankenstein, or, The Modern Prometheus.* Ed James Rieger. New York: Bobbs-Merrill, 1974. Print.

———. *The Journals of Mary Shelley, 1814–1844.* Eds. Paula R. Feldman and Dina Scott-Kilvert. Vol. 1 (1814–22). 2 vols. Oxford: Clarendon P, 1987. Print.

Shelley, Percy. *The Letters of Percy Bysshe Shelley.* Ed. Frederick C. Jones. Vol. II. 2 vols. New York: Oxford UP, 1964. 434. Print.

———. *Shelley's Poetry and Prose.* Eds. Donald H. Reiman and Neil Fraistat. New York and London: Norton, 2002. Print.

Showalter, Elaine. "The Greening of Sister George." *Nineteenth-Century Fiction* 35.3 (1980) 292–311. Print.

Siskin, Clifford. "Textual Culture and the History of the Real." *Textual Culture* 2.2 (Autumn 2007): 118–30. Print.

Slinn, E. Warwick. "Poetry." *A Companion to Victorian Literature and Culture.* Ed. Herbert F. Tucker. Oxford: Blackwell, 1999. Print.

Sontag, Susan. "Against Interpretation." *Against Interpretation and Other Essays.* New York: 1966. Print.

Stein, Edwin. *Wordsworth's Art of Allusion.* University Park: Penn State UP, 1988. Print.

Stewart, Susan. *On Longing: Narratives of the Miniature, the Gigantic, the Souvenir, the Collection.* Baltimore: Johns Hopkins UP, 1990. Print.

Stimpson, Catharine. "Gertrice/Altrude: Stein, Toklas, and the Paradox of the Happy Marriage." *Mothering the Mind: Twelve Studies of Writers and Their Silent Partners.* Eds. Ruth Perry and Martine Watson Brownley. New York: Holmes & Meier, 1984. 122–139. Print.

Stoler, Ann. *Along the Archival Grain: Epistemic Anxieties and Colonial Common Sense.* Princeton: Princeton UP, 2009. Print.

Stone, Marjorie, and Judith Thompson. *Literary Couplings: Writing, Couples, Collaboration, and the Construction of Authorship.* Madison: Wisconsin UP, 2006. Print.

Strachey, John St. Loe. *From Grave to Gay: Being Essays and Studies Concerned with Certain Subjects of Serious Interest, with the Puritans, with Literature, and with the Humours of Life Now for the First Time Collected and Arranged.* London: Smith Elder, 1897. Print.

Strachey, Lytton. "Carlyle." *Portraits in Miniature and Other Essays.* New York: Harcourt, 1931. Print.

———. *Eminent Victorians.* New York: Harcourt, 1974. Print.

———. "Pope." *Characters and Commentaries.* New York: Harcourt, 1933. Print.

———. *Queen Victoria.* New York: Harcourt Brace, 1921. Print.

———. "A Victorian Critic." *Characters and Commentaries.* Ed. James Strachey. New York: Harcourt, 1933. Print.

Swinburne, Algernon Charles. *The Complete Works of Algernon Charles Swinburne.* Eds. Edmund Gosse and T. J. Wise. 20 vols. Bonchurch Edition. London: William Heinemann; New York: Gabriel Wells, 1925–27. Print.

———. *New Writings by Swinburne.* Ed. Cecil Y. Lang. Syracuse: Syracuse UP, 1964. Print.

———. *The Swinburne Letters.* 2 vols. Ed. Cecil Y. Lang. New Haven: Yale UP, 1959. Print.

Tennyson, Alfred Lord. *The Poems of Tennyson.* Ed. Christopher Ricks. London: Longman, 1969. Print.

Thackeray, William Makepeace. *Vanity Fair.* Ed. John Sutherland. Oxford: Oxford UP, 1983. Print.

Thompson, Francis. "Daisy." *Merry England* 14.83 (1890): 331–33. *ProQuest.* 26 Feb. 2016. Web.

———. *Literary Criticisms by Francis Thompson. Newly Discovered and Collected by Rev. Terence L. Connolly. [With a Bibliography and a Portrait.].* Ed. Terence Leo Connolly. New York: Dutton, 1948. Print.

———. *The Poems of Francis Thompson.* London: Hollis and Carter, 1946. Print.

———. "The Poppy." *Merry England* 17.99 (1891): 167–69. *ProQuest.* 26 Feb. 2016. Web.

Tillotson, Geoffrey. *Criticism and the Nineteenth Century.* London: Athlone P, 1951. Print.

Tillotson, Kathleen. "Matthew Arnold and Carlyle." Warton Lecture on English Poetry. *Proceedings of the British Academy* xlii, 1956. 133–53. Print.

Timko, Michael. "The Victorianism of Victorian Literature." *New Literary History* 6.3 (Spring 1975): 607–27. Print.

Tinker, C. B., and H. F. Lowry. *The Poetry of Matthew Arnold: A Commentary.* London: Oxford UP, 1940. Print.

Townsend, Francis G. *Ruskin and the Landscape Feeling: A Critical Analysis of His Thought during the Crucial Years of His Life, 1843–56. Illinois Studies in Literature and Language* XXXV.3. Urbana-Champaign: U of Illinois P, 1951. Print.

Tracy, C. R. "Browning's Heresies." *Studies in Philology* 33.4 (1936): 610–25. Print.

Trilling, Lionel. *Matthew Arnold.* New York: Meridian Books, 1955. Print.

Vincent, J. Keith. "Shame Now: Ruth Leys Diagnoses the New Queer Shame Culture." *Criticism* 54.4 (2012): 623–32. Project MUSE. 3 December 2013. Web.

Ward, Mrs. Humphry. *Milly and Olly, or, A Holiday among the Mountains. A Story for Children.* London: T. Fischer Unwin, 1907. Print.

———. *A Writer's Recollections.* Vol. I. New York and London: Harper & Bros., 1918. Print.

Warner, Michael. "Uncritical Reading." *Polemic: Critical or Uncritical.* Ed. Jane Gallop. New York: Routledge, 2004. 13–38. Print.

Watson, Jeannie. "'The Raven: A Christmas Poem': Colderidge and the Fairy Tale Controversy." *Romanticism and Children's Literature in Nineteenth-Century England.* Ed. James Holt McGavran Jr. Athens: U of Georgia P, 1991. Print.

Weygandt, Ann. M. *Kipling's Reading and Its Influence on His Poetry.* Philadelphia: U of Pennsylvania P, 1939. Print.

Wolfson, Susan J. *Borderlines: The Shifting of Genders in British Romanticism.* Stanford: Stanford UP, 2006. Print.

———. *The Questioning Presence: Wordsworth, Keats, and the Interrogative Mode in Romantic Poetry.* Ithaca and London: Cornell UP, 1986. Print.

———. "Reading for Form." *MLQ* 61.1 (2000): 1–16. Print.

Woolf, Virginia. "George Eliot." *Women and Writing.* Ed. Michèle Barrett. New York: Harcourt Brace Jovanovich, 1979. Print.

———. "Jane Eyre" and "Wuthering Heights." *Women and Writing.* Ed. Michèle Barrett. New York: Harcourt Brace Jovanovich, 1979. Print.

———. *To the Lighthouse.* New York: Harcourt, 1955. Print.

Wordsworth, Dorothy. *Journals of Dorothy Wordsworth.* Ed. Mary Moorman. London: Oxford UP, 1971. Print.

Wordsworth, William. *The Little Maid and the Gentleman; or, We Are Seven.* York: J. Kendrew, n.d. Print.

———. *Poems of William Wordsworth.* Ed. Matthew Arnold. London: Macmillan, 1882. Print.

———. *Wordsworth: Poetical Works.* Eds. Thomas Hutchinson and Ernest DeSelincourt. London: Oxford UP, 1966. Print.

———. *Wordsworth: Poetical Works.* Vol. 2. Ed. William Knight. London: Macmillan, 1896. Project Gutenberg. 26 Feb. 2016. Web.

Wordsworth, William, and Samuel Taylor Coleridge. *Lyrical Ballads with a Few Other Poems.* London: J. & A. Arch, 1798. Print.

Yonge, Charlotte. *History of Christian Names.* London: Macmillan, 1884. Print.

Zimmerman, Bonnie. "'The Mother's History' in George Eliot's Life, Literature and Political Ideology." *The Lost Tradition: Mothers and Daughters in Literature*. Eds. Cathy N. Davidson and E. M. Broner. New York: Ungar, 1980. 81–94. Print.

INDEX

Adam Bede (George Eliot), ixn1, 8n4, 46, 58, 61, 63, 67, 68, 70, 71, 84, 86, 89, 90, 92

Adler, Alfred, 57, 57n1

adult and child: in conflict, 24, 32, 35, 40–41, 44, 45, 147; interacting: 33, 35–36, 44

Albert, Prince, 205, 212n9

alchemists, 96

Allott, Kenneth, 26n1

Althusser, Louis, xivn8

androgyny: x, 4, 58, 218. *See also* gender-fusions

Anglicanism, 15, 17

Arabian Nights, 18

Armstrong, Paul B., xiv, xv

Arnold, Augusta. *See* Ward, Mary Augusta

Arnold, Matthew, 2, 3, 4, 15, 17, 18, 25–30, 32, 33, 34, 36, 37, 42, 46, 47, 118–34, 151, 173; and Pater, 3, 130–34; and Wordsworth, 3, 25–30, 118–29. *See also* "Dover Beach"; "To a Gipsy Child"; "Resignation"; "Wordsworth"

Arnold, Thomas (the elder): Strachey satirizes, 4, 22, 201, 203, 204n1, 209–10; and Wordsworth, 22, 203, 210

Arnold, Thomas (the younger), 25, 26n1

"At Lulworth Cove" (Hardy), 163, 173, 177–79

Auden, W. H., 128

Auerbach, Nina, 18, 113

Aurora Leigh (Barrett), 86, 86n5, 87, 98, 113, 214, 217n2, 223n6

Austen, Jane, 47, 73, 77, 79, 84

Austin, Alfred, 114, 116n7, 198

Bailey, J. O., 164n2, 174n6, 175n7, 178, 178n8

Barrett, Elizabeth, 3, 14, 16, 76, 77, 86, 86n5, 87, 88, 95, 98, 105, 113, 116, 186n6, 192, 214, 217n2, 217n6, 223. *See also* *Aurora Leigh*

Barthes, Roland, 96, 100

Baum, Paull F., 119, 119n1

Beer, Gillian, 58

Beerbohm, Sir Max, 17, 28, 29, 202, 204, 207, 212n

Beethoven, Ludwig van, 204n1

Bennett, Andrew, 15n10

Beresford, G. C., 184

· 241 ·

Best, Stephen, and Sharon Marcus, xiii, xiiin4, xiv, xivn6, xivn8

Bewes, Timothy, xii, xiiin4

Bewick, Thomas, *Book of Birds,* 216

Bible, the, 7, 41, 62, 86, 140, 196, 198, 199, 208; *Isaiah,* 196, 198–99, 205; *Jonah,* 197n9; *Psalms,* 143; 1 *Samuel,* 196, 219n3

Billone, Amy, 16

binary thinking: limits of, ix, xii–xiv, xivn7; vs. "mixiness," x–xi, 59, 135, 137, 138

Biographia Literaria (Coleridge), 8–10, 27, 51, 74, 146

"Bishop Blougram's Apology" (Browning), 184, 189–93, 194

Blagden, Isabella, 114, 115

Blake, William, 17, 18, 100

Blank, G. Kim, and Margot K. Louis, *Influence and Resistance in Nineteenth-Century Poetry,* 17, 166n3

Blazhenkova, Olesya, and Maria Kozhevnikov, xvn11

Bloom, Harold, 5, 14, 100, 101, 102, 103, 104n2

Bodichon, Barbara Leigh Smith, 81, 83

Bohm, Arnd, 190

Booth, Alison, 214

Brontë, Anne, 217n2

Brontë, Branwell, 57

Brontë, Charlotte, 1, 4, 17, 22, 66, 71, 77, 79, 213, 215, 216–17, 217n2, 218, 220, 220n5, 222, 223, 223n7. See also *Jane Eyre*; *Villette*

Brontë, Emily, 2, 4, 17, 213, 215, 218, 222. See also *Wuthering Heights*

Brontë, Patrick, 222

Brooks, Peter, 213

Browning, Elizabeth. *See* Barrett, Elizabeth

Browning, Robert, 2, 3, 4, 14, 17, 34, 34n4, 35, 36, 77, 85, 86, 87, 88, 91, 93, 95, 96–117, 144, 180, 181, 182–200, 214; and Coleridge, 109n5–110n5; and Keats, 3, 98, 99, 103–4, 105, 106–10, 117; and Kipling, 4, 180, 182–200; and Shelley, 17, 86–88, 100, 102, 104n2; and Wordsworth, 34–35, 104, 104n2, 189, 198. *See also* "Bishop Blougram's Apology"; "'Childe Roland to the Dark Tower Came'"; "Fra Lippo Lippi"; "My Last Duchess"; "Porphyria's Lover"

Buddhism, 190

Bulwer-Lytton, Edward Lord, 17, 47

Burke, Edmund, 143

Burne-Jones, Edward and Georgina, 182, 183, 184

Burney, Fanny, 71

Bush, Douglas, 127

Butler, Samuel, 207

Bygrave, Douglas, 13n9

Byron, George Gordon Lord, 2, 6n2, 17, 39, 41–42, 42n7, 57, 91, 92, 95, 102, 128, 137, 140, 145, 146, 147, 152, 184, 214, 219, 220

Calverley, Charles Stuart, 30–32, 33, 36

Carlyle, Thomas, 4, 14, 17, 18, 65, 131–32, 141, 145, 195, 201–2, 205, 205n3, 206, 206n5, 206n6, 207, 208

Carrington, C. E., 188

Carroll, Lewis, 3, 18, 24, 31, 144, 145–61, 208; and Wordsworth, 145–60. *See also* "The White Knight's Song"

Chapman, John, 81, 83n4

Chatterton, Thomas, 149

Chaucer, Geoffrey, 66n5, 184

"'Childe Roland to the Dark Tower Came'" (Browning), 101, 104, 184n4, 189, 192, 193, 194, 197

childhood: deified, 25, 38, 124; as Edenic, 6, 14, 18, 33, 38, 42, 50, 60, 66, 74, 141, 149

Clairmont, Claire, 92, 105

Clough, Arthur Hugh, 17, 209

Cohen, Morton, 181

Colebrook, Claire, xi

Coleridge, Hartley, 17

Index

Coleridge, Samuel Taylor, 2, 4, 5, 6–9, 10, 11, 12, 13, 13n9, 14, 17, 27, 28, 29, 47, 51, 74, 77, 101, 109, 110n5, 137, 146, 167, 220n5; and Wordsworth, 5, 6, 7n3, 7–10, 27, 28, 29, 77. See also *Biographia Literaria*

Coleridge, Sara, 16

Coleridge, Sara Fricker, 101

collaborations. See "partnerships, creative"

Collingwood, Stuart Dodgson, 150

Collins, Philip, 19, 51, 52

Cooper, Helen, 86

Crook, Nora, 191n7

Cross, John W., 77, 78, 80, 81, 93

Cudworth, Ralph, 111, 111n6

Darwin, Charles, 15, 35, 190

DaVinci, Leonardo, 106, 113, 132, 142

Defoe, Daniel, 4

de Guérin, Maurice, 141, 142

DeLaura, David, 133, 133n1, 135–36, 206n6

Deleuze, Gilles, xi–xii, xvii

den Hartog, P. D., 52

De Quincey, Thomas, 2, 17

DeVane, William, 259

Dickens, Charles, 2, 17, 36, 41, 43–46, 46n8, 51–54, 79, 80, 147, 196n9; and Wordworth, 46n8, 51–54. See also *Great Expectations*

Disraeli, Benjamin, 17

Domett, Alfred, 193

"Dover Beach" (Arnold), 3, 119, 123, 124–27

Du Bellay, 132, 142

Dufferin and Ava, Marquis Frederick Temple, 191–93

Edgeworth, Maria, 71

Eliot, George (Mary Anne Evans), xiv, 2, 3, 8n4, 15, 36, 41, 43, 44–51, 56–61, 62–75, 76–88, 93–94, 140, 147, 148, 205, 205n3, 213, 214, 214n1; and the Shelleys, 82, 88–92, 93, 94; and Woolf, 72, 72n9, 73, 75, 213, 215; and Wordsworth, 3, 8n4, 46–51, 57–59, 61–63, 64–66, 70, 213. See also *Adam Bede*; "The Lifted Veil"; *Middlemarch*; *The Mill on the Floss*; *Silas Marner*

Eliot, T. S., 133n1, 135, 136, 199

Elizabeth I, Queen, 197

Eminent Victorians (Strachey), 4, 201–12

Evans, Christiana ("Chrissey"), 82, 83

Evans, Christiana Pearson, 81–82

Evans, Isaac, 46, 81–83

Evans, Robert, 61, 81, 222

"Eve of St. Agnes, The" (Keats), 103, 106–10, 140, 181

Excursion, The (Wordsworth), 5–6, 6n2, 7, 8, 8n4, 9, 11, 11n8, 13, 14, 37, 40, 46, 48, 58, 59, 61, 63, 64, 65, 75, 102, 140, 214

Faflak, Joel, and Julia M. Wright, 16

Farrell, John P., 133

Felski, Rita, xiiin5, xiv

Ferguson, Frances, 4

Finn, Mary E., 17

Fleming, Alice ("Trix") Kipling, 186

Fliess, Wilhelm, 57

Foucault, Michel, xii

"Fra Lippo Lippi" (Browning), 99, 113, 182, 183, 183n3, 188, 192, 194

Frank, Ellen, 39n5

Frankenstein (Mary Shelley), 4, 77, 88, 89, 90, 93, 105n, 149, 216, 218, 219–20, 220n4

Fuller, Margaret, 91

Freud, Sigmund, 57, 204n2

Froude, Richard Hurrell, 208

Gelpi, Barbara Charlesworth, 17

gender-divisions, 3, 4, 49, 56, 69; dramatized through: lost Edens, 60, 149–50; ironized masculinities, 75, 97, 105n3,

108, 111–13; silenced female voices, 57, 95, 99

gender-fusions, 57, 58, 60–62, 68, 95, 102; dramatized through: feminized masculinities: 17, 48, 60, 61, 80, 114, 218, 222, 224; childhood symbiosis: 2, 3, 50, 60, 70, 218

genre, and gender, 2–3, 95; shifts in: 5, 6–9, 15, 18, 18n13, 58, 65, 69, 71, 97–99, 113, 128, 147, 153, 188, 196. *See also* parody

Goethe, Johann Wolfgang von, 91, 92, 119, 119n1, 120, 128, 131, 132, 142, 204n1, 209n7

ghosts, 2, 7n3, 22; in the writings of: Emily Brontë, 23, 218; George Eliot, 63, 65, 218; Hardy, 164, 176, 177, 179; Kipling, 190, 197; Strachey, 208; Woolf, 62, 75, 215; Wordsworth: 218. Wordsworth's supposedly seen by: Hardy, 55; Dorothy Ward, 23, 24

Gibbon, Edward, 204n1

Gilbert, Sandra, and Susan Gubar, 58, 71, 77n2

Gill, Stephen, 15

Giorgione, 39, 43, 135n2

God / godheads, 13, 18, 25, 38, 42, 74, 101, 103, 111, 125, 126, 185, 190, 191n7, 193n8, 196–97, 205, 219, 223n6

Godwin, Mary. *See* Shelley, Mary

Godwin, William, 80, 222

Gordon, General Charles George, 4, 201, 203, 207, 208, 210

Gravil, Richard, 15

Great Expectations (Dickens), 44–45, 51–54, 147

Greenwell, Dora, 16

Griffen, Hall, and C. H. Minchin, 89n6

Grimm, Jakob and Wilhelm, 18

Haggard, H. Rider, 180

Haight, Gordon S., 77, 81n3, 84

Hanley, Keith, 17

Hardy, Barbara, 58, 69

Hardy, Emma, 164, 176

Hardy, Florence, 164n2

Hardy, Thomas, 2, 3–4, 15, 27, 54–55, 117, 140, 162–66, 169–179, 216, 217; and Keats, 4, 162, 163–65, 164n2, 165, 172–79; and Shelley: 4, 163, 164, 164n2, 165, 169–72; Woolf on, 217; and Wordsworth, 4, 55, 162, 164–66, 169, 171. *See also* "The Darkling Thrush"; "At Lulworth Cove"; "The Selfsame Song"; "Shelley's Skylark"

Harris, Wendell V., 133, 163, 163n1

Harrison, Anthony H., *Victorian Poets and Romantic Poems,* 17

Hazlitt, William, 4, 141, 181–82, 181–82n1, 191, 195, 199

Heine, Heinrich, 131–32, 133, 142

Hemans, Felicia, 16

Hickey, Alison, 16

Hill, Donald L., 131

Hogg, T. J., 91

Holloway, Sarah Slatter, 188

Holroyd, Michael, 207, 210

Homans, Margaret, 57–58, 101

Homer, 137, 184

Hopkins, Gerard Manley, 2, 33–34, 34n3, 36, 207, 210

Hudson, W. H., 174n6

Hunt, Thornton, 79, 92

Huxley, T. H., 24

Ibn Ezra, Rabbi Abraham Ben Meir, 196, 197

Ibsen, Henrik, 207

Ingelow, Jean, 16

Jaffe, Audrey, xivn7

James, D. G., 118

James, Henry, 8n4

"James Lee's Wife" (Browning), 3, 96–97, 98, 100, 102, 104–6, 114, 116

Jameson, Anna, *Legends of the Madonna*, 66–67

Jameson, Frederic, xiii

Jamison, William A., 118

Jane Eyre (Charlotte Brontë), 4, 66, 71, 216, 217, 220, 220n4; revised in *Villette*, 221–25

Jarrell, Randall, 199, 199n11

Jauss, Hans Robert, xv, xvi

Jesus, 84, 190–99, 204n1, 205, 220, 222

Jewishness, ix, xi, 19, 90, 114, 131, 190, 196, 197, 210

Jewsbury, Maria Jane, 16

Johnson, E. D. H., viii, 19, 119

Johnson, Samuel Dr., 208

Johnson, W. Stacy, 119, 127

Johnston, Kenneth R., 9n6

Jonson, Ben, 183, 194, 198, 199

Joyce, James, 216

Jung, Carl, and Karl Kerényi, 24

Jurecic, Ann, xiiin3, xiv

Keats, John, 3, 4, 9, 11–14, 16, 17, 66, 95, 98, 99, 102, 103, 104, 104n1, 105, 106, 107, 108, 109, 110, 116–17, 140, 145, 146, 162–65, 167–79, 180, 181, 199; and Browning, 3, 98, 99, 103–4, 105, 106–110, 117; and Hardy, 4, 162, 163–65, 164n2, 172–79; and Kipling, 180, 181, 188, and Wordsworth, 4, 11–14, 140, 162, 164–66, 168, 168n5, 170, 171. *See also* "Eve of St. Agnes"; "To One Who Has Been Long in City Pent"

Keen, Suzanne, xiiin3

Kelley, Theresa M., 17

Kincaid, James, 17

Kingsmill, Hugh, 206n5

Kipling, Alice MacDonald, 184, 184n4, 192

Kipling, John Lockwood, 183n3, 184, 184n4, 192, 194

Kipling, Rudyard, 2, 4, 54, 180–200; and Browning, 4, 180, 182–200; and Keats, 180, 181, 188; and Wordsworth, 180, 189. *See also* "Proofs of Holy Writ"; *Something of Myself*

Knoepflmacher, U. C., biographical details, vii–ix; as critic, ix–xii, xiv–xvi, 39fn5, 58, 69, 77, 82, 89, 90, 214, 218

Lamb, Charles, 2, 7, 17

Landon, Laetitia, 16

Landow, George P., 36, 39

Landsowne, Henry Charles, Marquis of, 191, 192

Langbaum, Robert, 100, 101

Laureateships, xii, 14, 98, 128, 169, 195, 198, 199

Leigh, Augusta, 57

Levine, Caroline, xiii, xiiin4

Levine, George, 58, 69, 77n2

Lewes, Agnes Jarvis, 79, 87, 91

Lewes, George Henry, 3, 70, 73, 76, 77–81, 81n3, 82, 83, 84, 86, 87, 91–93; on Shelley, 79, 91–92

Leys, Ruth, xiiin3

Liddell, Alice, 158

"Lifted Veil, The" (George Eliot), 71, 82, 89–92, 93, 214, 214n2

Littau, Karen, xvn10

longevity, 207–8

"Lucy Gray" (Wordsworth), 7n3, 22, 23, 24, 34, 36, 41, 49, 61, 80, 101, 147, 218

Lukács, Georg, xiv

Lycett, Andrew, 184n4

Macaulay, Thomas Babington Lord, 137

MacDonald, George, 2, 18, 66n5

MacMechan, Archibald, 202

Madonnas, 66, 67, 72, 75, 112, 113, 223n6, 225

Manning, Cardinal Henry Edward, 201, 203, 207, 210

Marcus Aurelius, 142, 143

Martineau, Harriet, 82, 82n4, 87

Masefield, John, 163

Mason, Philip, 191n7

May, Charles E., 163

McGavran, James Holt, *Romanticism and Children's Literature*, 18

McGillis, Roderick, 18

McGowan, John, 58, 68–69

McKenzie, K. A., 93

McSweeney, Kerry, 164, 169

McWilliams, John P., 53

Melchiori, Barbara, 196

Mellor, Anne K., 145–48

Mermin, Dorothy, 87

Meredith, George, 54

metaphor, as governing nineteenth-century trope, xi

"Michael" (Wordsworth), 47–50, 127, 147

Middlemarch (George Eliot), 61, 63, 68, 69, 70, 72–73, 93, 94, 215

Mill on the Floss, The (George Eliot), 3, 44, 45, 47–50, 57, 59, 60–71, 74, 75, 85, 86, 89, 93, 94, 145, 147, 148, 214

Miller, Betty, 88–89

Miller, J. Hillis, ixn1, 69, 69n7, 196

Millgate, Michael, 162, 163

Milton, John, 4, 5, 6–9, 11, 12, 13, 14, 74, 101, 157, 162, 164, 166n4, 167, 199, 219, 220n5. See also *Paradise Lost*

Mitchell, Rebecca, xiiin3

Mohammed: Carlyle identifies with, 202, 205, 208

Morris, William, 98, 104, 114, 115

Moses, 142, 204n1

Moulton-Barrett, Edward, 87, 222

"My Last Duchess" (Browning), 96, 97, 98, 99, 100, 103, 105, 111, 112, 115, 187, 188, 199n11

Myers, Mitzi, xvi, 18, 19

"negative capability," defined by Hazlitt and Keats, 4, 108, 162, 172, 174, 180, 181–82, 195, 217; retained by later writers, 4, 172, 180–82, 212

Nehamas, Alexander, xn2

Newman, Cardinal John Henry, 4, 201, 203, 204n1, 207, 208, 209, 210

Nicolson, Sir Harold, 202

Nightingale, Florence, 4, 201, 203, 205–6, 206n4, 207, 208–9, 210

nostalgia, 25, 42; distortions by adult, 144, 148, 157, 160, 188

Novalis (Friedrich von Hartenberg), 18, 131

"Ode: Intimations of Immortality" (Wordsworth), 11, 21, 26, 27, 29, 34, 34n3, 41, 74, 127, 139, 141, 147, 203

O'Neill, Michael, 16

Orel, Harold, 182n1

Pace, Joel, and Matthew Scott, 15

Paradise Lost (Milton), 6, 12, 84, 166n4, 219, 220n5

parodies, 31–32, 101, 109, 144, 145–46, 159, 206; of Browning: by Kipling, 183, 186–87, by Swinburne, 115–16; of Wordsworth: by Calverley, 30–31, by Carroll, 148, 152–54, 156, 157, 159–61; Coleridge on, 146

partnerships, creative, 3, 16; of the Brownings, 76, 77, 87–88, 186n6; of Coleridge and Wordsworth, 9n5, 77; of Eliot and Lewes, 76–88, 93; of Jonson and Shakespeare, 198–200, of the Shelleys, 76, 77, 88–92

Pater, Walter, xi, 2, 3, 4, 42–44, 130–43, 205, 206, 209, 211n8; contrasted to Arnold, 130–43. See also "Wordsworth"

Perkins, David, 163

Phelan, James, ixn1

photography, 96, 100, 152, 154

pleasure: as aesthetic criterion, xi, 38; for Wordsworth: xii, 130, 134; for Pater, 131, 132, 134

Plotz, Judith, *Romanticism and the Vocation of Childhood*, 17; 193n8

Plutarch, 207

Pope, Alexander, 211

Porphyrianism, 111, 111n6

"Porphyria's Lover" (Browning), 96–115

Pound, Ezra, 199

Prelude, The (Wordsworth), 3, 6, 7, 8, 9, 14, 16, 21, 22, 34, 35, 37, 39, 44, 46, 52–54, 58, 63, 80, 102, 127, 140, 144, 146–7, 148, 149, 153, 214

Prickett, Stephen, 15

projection: adult's on child, 157, 158; dramatized in Romantic lyric, 11, 96, 97, 101–3, 117, 157, 179; ironized in Victorian dramatic monologue, 99–100, 106–12

"Proofs of Holy Writ" (Kipling), 4, 180, 182, 198–99

Quiller-Couch, Sir Arthur, 127

Rader, Ralph, ixn1, 4, 19

reader: as author's textual ally, ix–xii, 5–6, 100, 113; Pater on function of, 130, 131, 138

reading: current critical debates, xii–xiv, xvi

Redinger, Ruby, 77, 81, 82, 83, 84

Renan, Ernest, 137

"Resignation" (Arnold), 3, 119, 119n1, 120–28

revisitations: in Romantic/Victorian constructs, 40, 44–45, 144, 145, 149, 153

Rhys, Jean: 217

Richardson, Alan, 18

Richardson, James, 164

Richter, David H., ixn1

Rimbaud, Arthur, 207

Ripon, George Frederick, Marquis of, 189

rivers: metaphorized by, Arnold, 133; Carroll, 147, 148; Dickens, 44; George Eliot: 44–45, 49, 63n4, 64, 67, 74, 145; Ruskin, 40; Wordsworth, 14, 44, 63n4, 66, 120, 125, 126, 145

Robinson, Henry Crabb, 46, 47

Romantic/Victorian intertextual affiliations. See listings under individual authors (*e.g.*, "Arnold, and . . ." or "Wordsworth, and . . .")

Rooney, Ellen, xiv, xivn1

Rosenberg, John, 36, 39

Ross, Anne Marie, 17

Ross, Marlon B., 16

Rossetti, Christina, 2, 16, 17, 115

Rossetti, Dante Gabriel, 3, 98, 114, 115

Ruskin, John, 2, 17, 36–41, 41n6, 42, 43, 45, 46

Ruskin, John James, 42n7

Sand, George, 140

Schelly, Judith M., 63n4

Scott, Peter Dale, 89

Scott, Sir Walter, 14, 38, 41, 137

"Selfsame Song, The" (Hardy), 163, 173, 175, 176, 178–79

Severn, Joseph, 177, 178, 178n8

Shakespeare, William, 4, 7, 10n7, 149, 162, 164, 184, 197; Browning and Kipling impersonate, 180, 181, 183, 194, 198–99, 200; Coleridge on, 8–9; Hazlitt and Keats on, 162, 164, 181–82, 195; Wordsworth on, 7, 198

Shaw, W. David, 17

Shelley, Harriet Westbrook, 88, 89, 105

Shelley, Mary Wollstonecraft, 3, 4, 11, 71, 76, 77, 80, 82, 87, 88, 89–90, 91, 92, 93, 98, 105, 105n3, 114, 213, 214n1, 215, 219; and the Brownings, 3, 88–89, 98, 105; and George Eliot and Lewes, 82, 89–92. See also *Frankenstein*

Shelley, Percy, 2, 3, 4, 9–11, 14, 15, 17, 76, 77, 79, 80, 88, 91–92, 92n7, 95–97, 100,

101, 102, 104, 104n2, 105, 106, 110, 140, 162, 163, 163n1, 164–66, 166n3, 166n4, 167–72, 212; and Browning, 17, 86–88, 103–4, 104n2, 105, 106; and Hardy, 4, 163, 164, 169–72, 174, 175, 179; and Lewes, 79, 91–92, 98; and Wordsworth, 9–11, 164–69. *See also* "To a Skylark"; "To Wordsworth"

"Shelley's Skylark" (Hardy), 4, 163, 164, 165, 168, 169–72, 173, 175

Showalter, Elaine, 72n8

Silas Marner (George Eliot), 8n4, 45, 47, 48, 50, 67, 68, 69–70, 71, 80, 85, 214, 222

Slinn, E. Warwick, 16n11

Smith, Charlotte, 16

Something of Myself (Kipling), 182, 183, 183n3, 188

Sophocles, 124, 126, 142

Souvestre, Marie, 206

Spinoza, Baruch, 142

Stein, Edwin, 15n10

Stein, Gertrude, 93

Stephen, Julia Duckworth, 72, 73, 215

Stephen, Leslie, 2n1, 72, 72n8, 73, 204

Stevens, Wallace, 100

Stewart, Susan, *On Longing*, 219n3

Stimpson, Catherine, 93

Stone, Marjorie, and Judith Thompson, *Literary Couplings*, 16

Strachey, James, 204n2

Strachey, John St. Loe, 199

Strachey, Lytton, sides with the marginalized in *Eminent Victorians*, 4, 201–12, 215

Strachey, Sir Edward, 204

Strachey, Sir Richard, 204, 204n2, 207

Strauss, David Friedrich, 84, 204n2

Swinburne, Charles Algernon, 98, 114, 115–16, 116n7, 117; Hopkins derides his "bathos" about "babies," 34

Tenniel, John, 159

Tennyson, Alfred Lord, 2, 9, 14–15, 17, 35–36, 57, 95, 102, 104, 114, 115, 137, 184, 185, 195, 201, 207, 208, 214

Teresa of Avila, Saint, 61, 81

Thackeray, William Makepeace, 147, 148, 161, 222

Thompson, Francis, 31–32, 32n2, 33, 34, 34n4, 36

Thoreau, Henry David, 15

Thorwaldsen, Albert, 84

Tillotson, Geoffrey, 26n1

Tillotson, Kathleen, 206n6

Timko, Michael, 201

Tinker, C. B., and H. F. Lowry, 119n1

"Tintern Abbey, Lines Written Above" (Wordsworth), xvn9, 11, 16, 38, 58, 59, 66, 96, 119, 119n1, 120–23, 124, 125, 127

"To a Gipsy Child" (Arnold), 26, 27–29, 37, 121, 121n2, 127

"To a Skylark" (Shelley 1820), 164, 166–68

"To a Skylark" (Wordsworth 1807), 165–68

"To a Skylark" (Wordsworth 1825), 165, 168–69. *See also* "Shelley's Skylark"

"To One Who Has Been Long in City Pent" (Keats), 9, 11–14

To the Lighthouse (Woolf), 2n1, 3, 4, 59, 62, 72, 73–75, 214, 215–18, 225

"To Wordsworth" (Shelley), 7, 9–11, 15

Townsend, Francis G., 37

Tracy, C. R., 111n6

Trilling, Lionel, 119, 127

Trollope, Anthony, 203, 205

Turner, J. M. W., 39, 40, 42, 43

Verlaine, Paul, 207

Victoria, Queen, 4, 14, 72, 84, 169, 201, 205, 212n9

Villette (Charlotte Brontë), 4, 71, 169, 201, 218, 220n; as revision of *Jane Eyre*, 221–25

Vincent, J. Keith, xiiin3

Ward, Dorothy, 23, 24
Ward, Mary Augusta Arnold: revisits Wordsworthian settings in *Milly and Olly*, 22–25
Warner, Michael, xiii
Watson, Jeanie, 18
Webster, Augusta, 16
Wellington, Arthur Wellesley, Duke of, 61
Wesley, John, 68, 91
Weygandt, Anne, 194
"White Knight's Song, The" (Carroll), 31, 144, 145, 152, 154, 158, 159–61
Whitman, Walt, 15
Winckelmann, Johann Joachim, 133n1, 141, 142
Wise, John Richards de Capel: attacks Shelley, 92n7
Wolfson, Susan, xiv, 14, 16–17
Wollstonecraft, Mary, 11n8, 16, 80, 91, 114
Woolf, Virginia, 1, 2n1, 3, 4, 56, 58, 59, 61, 71, 72–75, 77, 135, 202, 204, 207, 209, 213, 214–18, 225; and George Eliot, 72, 72n9, 73, 75, 214; and Wordsworth, 73, 75, 214. See also *To the Lighthouse*
"Wordsworth" (Arnold), 3, 136–41
"Wordsworth" (Pater), 42, 134–38, 140–41
Wordsworth, Catherine, 2
Wordsworth, Dorothy, 57, 60, 60n2, 62, 63, 63n4, 66, 96, 97, 101, 120, 121, 124, 154n2

Wordsworth, Mary, 63
Wordsworth, William, xi, xii, xv, xvn9, xvi, 2, 3, 4–9, 9n5, 10–16, 17, 18, 21, 22–25, 26–30, 33–55 *passim*, 56–75 *passim*, 96, 97, 101–2, 104n2, 118–29, 130, 134–43, 144, 145–60, 162, 163, 163n1, 164, 165, 166, 166n3, 167–69, 171, 179, 180, 181, 189, 203, 204n1, 210, 211, 213, 214, 217, 224; and Arnold, 3, 25–30, 118–29, 136–41; and Browning, 34–35, 104, 104n2, 180, 189, 198; and Carroll, 145–60; and Coleridge, 5, 6, 7n3, 7–10, 27, 28, 29, 77; and Dickens, 46n8, 51–54; and George Eliot, 3, 8n4, 46–51, 57–59, 61–63, 64–66, 70, 213; and Hardy, 4, 55, 162, 164–66, 168, 169, 171; and Keats, 11–14, 140, 162, 164–66, 168, 168n5, 169, 171; and Pater, 134–38, 140–1; and Ruskin, 17, 36–42; and Shelley, 9–11, 164–69; and Woolf, 73, 75, 214. See also *The Excursion*; "Lucy Gray"; "Michael"; "Ode: Intimations of Immortality"; *The Prelude*; "To a Sky-Lark"; "Tintern Abbey, Lines Written Above"
World War One, 202, 215
Wuthering Heights (Emily Brontë), 4, 23, 24, 65, 217, 218, 223n8

Yeats, William Butler, 36, 128, 135
Yonge, Charlotte, *History of Christian Names*, 67n6

Zimmerman, Bonnie, 82

www.ingramcontent.com/pod-product-compliance
Lightning Source LLC
Chambersburg PA
CBHW030040240426
43667CB00035B/180